EMPLOYABILITY SKILLS
for Law Students

EMPLOYABILITY SKILLS
for Law Students

EMILY FINCH • STEFAN FAFINSKI

OXFORD
UNIVERSITY PRESS

OXFORD
UNIVERSITY PRESS

Great Clarendon Street, Oxford, OX2 6DP,
United Kingdom

Oxford University Press is a department of the University of Oxford.
It furthers the University's objective of excellence in research, scholarship,
and education by publishing worldwide. Oxford is a registered trade mark of
Oxford University Press in the UK and in certain other countries

Published in the United States of America by Oxford University Press
198 Madison Avenue, New York, NY 10016, United States of America

British Library Cataloguing in Publication Data

Data available

Library of Congress Control Number: 2013950110

ISBN 978–0–19–966323–1

Printed in Great Britain by
Ashford Colour Press Ltd, Gosport, Hampshire

For STG

This book is enriched with a range of practical features. This guided tour shows you how to get the most out of *Employability Skills for Law Students*.

Practical exercise: doing a skills audit

You will find a downloadable template to help you Centre. The skills that are listed on the template are add others if you wish. Then, as before, rate yourself which used a very broad rating system with three p

Practical exercises
These handy exercises will help you to consider the issues discussed in more depth, try out new techniques, and apply the knowledge you have learnt throughout the text.

Practical example: finding voluntary wo

One of the categories of voluntary work available th always be worth investigating as it might turn up so had not previously considered. For example, if you w Reading area, you would have the following options:

Practical examples
Examples give you more details about real placements and careers, allowing you to hear from those who are more experienced and giving you a fuller, more rounded understanding.

Practical advice: organising a negotiati

If you want to start a negotiation competition from so

• **At least one negotiation scenario.** The ne
  instructions, one from each fictitious client, ar

Practical advice
You can refer to the 'practical advice' feature when you would like to know how to put an idea into practice or would like further guidance.

All work experience has value and all work expe away from mentioning work that they think is in should think about what they gained from the e looking for. Leaving things out can leave tell-tale brought up suddenly at interview—if they get t

Quotes from recruiters, practitioners, lecturers, and graduates
Insights from a range of people in the field to give you a taste of both individuals' and companies' experiences.

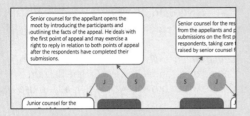

Diagrams and tables
Useful information is distilled into easy-to-follow diagrams and tables so that you can visualise concepts.

Tell us

If you are trying to organise your own moot feel fi
offer to run a mooting skills workshop for you or
might feature a film of your moot on our website: a
Or simply tell us how you got on. Get in contac
FinchFafinski on Twitter.

'Tell us'
Get in touch with the authors and tell them about your experiences or let them know what you think!

WHERE NEXT?

This chapter has set out an overvi
Where you go next in the book rea
your plan. As you will have seen fr

'Where next?'
These sections help to guide you through the book, giving a useful review of the chapter and signposting what comes next.

APPENDIX A – VACATION SCHEMES

Information in this table is correct at the time o
where the information was not available online
to our request for information. Help us to keep
changes that you might come across. Tell us vi

Appendices
Invaluable information on vacation schemes and training contracts all in one place; the perfect starting point for your work experience and careers research.

 www.oxfordtextbooks.co.uk/orc/finch_employability/

Employability Skills for Law Students is accompanied by a comprehensive Online Resource Centre which provides you with ready-to-use learning resources. These resources are free of charge, and are designed to maximise your learning experience.

Worksheets and templates

Downloadable activity templates and worksheets as well as annotated resources are provided as follow up to practical exercises within the book to help you put your plans into action.

Suggested answers

The authors provide suggested answers to questions in the book to compare with your own answers to questions. Commentary is also provided where appropriate to help you understand the issues involved and how the answers were reached.

Sample material

Example letters and applications give you a range of material to look at as you write your own letters and applications.

Listings

Useful listings of deadlines for scholarships, competitions, and applications will be included as appropriate.

Web links

Annotated web links provide a gateway to further internet research.

Video clips

Video clips of students participating in a range of practical activities bring these skills to life, providing examples of good practice to emulate and bad practice to avoid. Clips featuring different individuals demonstrating their skills and talking about their experiences will help you to overcome nerves, avoid common errors, and develop your own style.

Podcasts

Podcasts of interviews with a range of people in the field help you to gain insights into various practical activities, careers, and industries.

Audio commentary

Audio commentary on a range of documents such as CVs and covering letters to give you pointers on what works well and how to write and refine your own material.

By one of those strange coincidences, we had been thinking about the challenges that law students face in getting a job at the same time that Helen Swann from OUP had been thinking about exactly the same thing. The topic came up in discussion over lunch at a meeting that was supposed to be about a new edition of one of our other OUP books—*Legal Skills*—in which we had planned to put in a *whole chapter* on employability. As we talked about it more, it rapidly dawned on us that a single chapter could never do the subject justice, and so we worked up a plan for a new book. First thanks of the Preface, then, must go to Helen Swann for her vision and boldness in developing the idea and commissioning us to write the book you are now holding.

Although this isn't our first book by any means, it's probably fair to say that it's been the most difficult to write by a considerable margin. First of all, there was a huge amount of research that needed to be done, particularly as we wanted the book to be about far more than becoming a solicitor or barrister. This meant that we had to research many other careers of which we had no direct experience ourselves. So we've learnt a lot in putting it together and hope that you'll find that we've been able to impart that knowledge to you. Second, we've had to find, and encourage, a whole variety of different contributors to provide comments and little case studies throughout the book. To each and every one of them, we are extremely grateful. That's not to say that we never want any more, so if you want to feature in the next edition (they said, slightly presumptuously) then get in touch with us and offer a contribution. More on how to do that later. Third, there was an unscheduled sojourn in hospital for Stef to have two discs in his neck replaced with titanium ones. Thanks, therefore, to everyone at CircleReading for a surprisingly pleasant stay, all things considered (especially the food), and particularly to Mr Patrick McKenna, consultant spinal surgeon, who dismantled and reassembled half of the author team with considerable aplomb, and enabled pain-free typing to resume after a year of compressed spinal cord agony. If Stef ever tells you that the scar across his throat was a result of a duel, or saving babies from the mouths of hungry lions, it is just a lie.

This book has seen two (soon to be three) departures from the team and two new arrivals. First to go was our longest-standing OUP contact, Sarah Viner, with whom we have worked since she commissioned *Legal Skills* in 2005 and remains, still, the only person we know who can navigate the entire OUP building without having to leave a trail of crumbs behind her. We'll miss her. Next was our editor, Helen Davis, who announced that she was going to work in Costa Rica. We've worked with Helen on two editions of *Legal Skills* as well as *Criminology Skills*, so we're not entirely surprised that she decided to flee half way round the world. We hope all is well with her, and are really grateful for 'that Helen thing' she did on the first part of the book's development. The imminent final departure is Helen Swann, for whom motherhood is approaching as we write this Preface. We hope to see her back again soon.

During the writing process, our editor becomes one of the most important people in our world so we were worried about the loss of Helen (Davis) part way through the project. We thought that she would be a tough act to follow, but, enter stage right (like all the good people), Joanna Williams. Jo has been amazing, and, to be honest, we really don't think we could have finished the book without her. She's diligently read everything we've written (more than once), collated a huge amount of reviewer feedback, and come up with some close-to-last-minute structural changes that have made the whole book (we think) tons better. It's been great to have her keeping a watch on the book as a whole as well as on each of the constituent chapters. Thanks, Jo.

Speaking of reviewers, we've already mentioned that there were several. Thanks to all of the following for their helpful and constructive comments; we've done our best to incorporate them: Gwilym Owen, University of Bangor; Alison Turnbull, Birmingham City University; Michael Doherty, University of Central Lancashire; Dr Lars Mosesson, Buckinghamshire New University; David Hodgkinson, University of Derby; Prof Owen Warnock, University of East Anglia; Jacqui Longman, University of East Anglia; Robert Collinson, Edge Hill University; Julia Paci, University of Exeter; Prof Charles Wild, University of Hertfordshire; Risham Chohan, London South Bank University; Sallie Spilsbury, Manchester Metropolitan University; Susan Clarke, Nottingham Trent University; Juliet Tomlinson, University of Oxford; Caroline Strevens, University of Portsmouth; Christopher Newdick, University of Reading; Stephen Gurman, a Careers Consultant from The Careers Group, currently allocated at UCL.

The second new arrival is a small apricot-coloured puppy called Fraggle. She eats drafts of chapters and requires a lot of walking, having refused to take notice of the book that said that 'eight-week-old puppies need 20 minutes of exercise a day'. Fraggle has a bed in the office where she watches writing with occasional interest, and will continue to be part of Team Finch & Fafinski.

As ever, with the exception of a few tweaks, our work really stops when we hand over the manuscript, but there is a lot of production work that will have gone on between then and publication: so thanks to Hannah Marsden for sorting it all out, Nick Wehmeier for the ORC, Fiona Tatham our copy editor, Catherine Abbott our proofreader, and John Martin, our indexer, who really knows his alphabet.

We'd really like to hear what you think of the book, which you can do by visiting www.finchandfafinski.com, Twitter at @FinchFafinski or via email to hello@finchandfafinski.com.

To everyone who is here with us on the island, our love and thanks. If you don't know what this means, we don't mean you!

And finally, thanks to you, our readers, without whom this whole exercise would have been a tremendous waste of time and effort. We hope you enjoy the book, find it supportive, useful and inspiring, and that it takes you closer to achieving your dream career.

Emily & Stef
September 2013

ACKNOWLEDGEMENTS

Grateful acknowledgement is made to all authors and publishers of copyrighted material which appears in this book, and in particular to the following: 5 Essex Court, ADR group, BCL Graduates, Chambers and Partners, do-it.org.uk, Field Fisher Waterhouse, jobs.ac.uk, © Law Society, Law Society Gazette, Law Staff Legal Recruitment Ltd, Legal Hub © Thomson Reuters, Pupillage Gateway, Taylor Root, and The Pupillage Pages.

Qualification routes for licensed conveyancers provided by the Council for Licensed Conveyancers. Please check their website—**www.clc-uk.org**—for updates to the qualification routes after the first quarter of 2014.

Every effort has been made to trace and contact copyright holders prior to publication. If notified, the publisher will undertake to rectify any errors or omissions at the earliest opportunity.

OUTLINE CONTENTS

DETAILED CONTENTS

Everybody needs a job. Presumably, as a law student, you embarked upon your studies with the hope and expectation that you would ultimately gain employment. You may already know that you want to be a solicitor, or a barrister, you may not be decided, or you might want to keep your options open. This book is for you, regardless of the stage of your academic life, or your career aspirations.

We find that lecturers talk about skills a lot and you will hear about skills all the way through your time at university: personal skills, academic skills, legal skills, practical skills, and transferable skills. Acquiring and developing skills, though, should not be an aim in itself. The ultimate aim in acquiring and developing skills is to gain employment, and, very simply, *skills enhance employability*. So, in this book, we talk about employability skills; that is, skills that are valued by employers as essential for success in the workplace.

It is undeniable that competition for jobs is fierce: there are considerably more law graduates each year than there are jobs in the traditional legal professions of barrister or solicitor. It should be obvious then that you need to do as much as you can to stand out from the competition. Excellent academic results are a start, but they are not everything. The very fact that you are reading this book means that you have already taken an active step towards building up your employability skills and thus ultimately to being able to differentiate yourself as the most employable individual in the competitive world of recruitment.

There were a number of reasons that we decided to write this book. First and foremost, we wanted to give law students a useful and practical resource to maximise their chances of getting the job that they want. We both remember how daunting it can be to be part way through a degree with no clear idea of how to get from that to the career you want at the end of it so the aim is to help you bridge the gap from study to the workplace: we like to think of this book as making the link from *learning* to *earning*. It supplements the guidance available from university careers advisers and academic tutors who will naturally be able to give more personalised advice than we are able to do in a single textbook. We also wanted to write something that was specifically aimed at law students: so we take an approach that is narrower than general employability books (recognising that the needs of law students are quite specific), but broader than that taken in books written for would-be solicitors or barristers (recognising the reality that there are more law graduates than there are training contracts or pupillages each year). Finally, we wanted to maintain a specific focus on *employability* skills, not just 'ordinary' legal skills. In our *Legal Skills* book we give you the skills for success *in* legal studies: in *Employability Skills for Law Students* we give you the skills for success *beyond* your legal studies.

Throughout this book, we aim to help you recognise the value of skills in terms of your future career, regardless of whether this is within law or within a non-law profession. You will come to identify the skills you have or will develop by virtue of your academic studies (many of which you may not even realise that you had!), but to appreciate that you will most likely still find gaps in your overall employability skills portfolio. We will explain how you can equip yourself to fill those gaps by participating in a wide variety of different activities and to present your skills effectively to potential employers.

The book is structured around the journey to employment, leading you from the basics of understanding what employability skills actually are (and why they are important) and putting together a plan, through *identifying* your academic and practical legal skills, *building* upon them, *focusing* them and then *demonstrating* them.

You will find that we have included practical exercises and advice, along with comments from students, lecturers, careers advisors, legal practitioners, and other employers which should add the voice of real-world experience. In addition, you will also find a 'Tell us' feature which invites you to contact us about your own experiences on the quest for employment. We will use the best responses in subsequent editions of the book and also build them up on our website. You can contact us via email at **hello@finchandfafinski.com**, through our website **www.finchandfafinski.com** or, somewhat more succinctly, on Twitter **@FinchFafinski**. We would very much like to hear from you.

We both wish you every success in your legal studies and in your future career.

Emily Finch
Stefan Fafinski

Part I

Understanding employability skills

This first part of the book is designed to get you starting to think systematically about employability, skills, and employment. In Chapter 1, we introduce what is meant by employability skills and explain why they are important before getting you to think about your own level of proficiency. Chapter 2 builds on this by introducing some of the possible career paths open to law graduates and building a plan to develop your skills and take practical steps towards your chosen career.

Understanding employability skills

INTRODUCTION

In an uncertain job market, skills are your best security.[1]

The title of this book is *Employability Skills for Law Students*; but what do we actually mean by this? As a law student you will undoubtedly gain many practical, personal, interpersonal, and professional skills throughout your degree. The purpose of this book is to help you to:

- Understand the different type of skills employers are looking for when recruiting graduates

- Identify the skills which you will build by studying throughout your law degree, and participating in extra-curricular activities

- Take positive action to develop and add to your personal skills portfolio during your time at university

- Demonstrate effectively to employers the skills and attributes you possess, which will make you stand out from other graduates.

This chapter will begin by setting out our approach to the subject and then looking at the term 'employability skills' both in general and in the context of legal studies. After this, it will move on to explain just why these employability skills are so important and why you should take every opportunity to develop them throughout your time at university. Having set the scene, it will next give you a brief overview of some of the possible career pathways that can be pursued with a law degree before getting you to start thinking about the skills that you already have and spotting any gaps that might need to be addressed.

This chapter will be a valuable foundation for the rest of the book in helping you to understand what is meant by employability skills so that you can begin to understand why they are important and how you can develop them throughout your study of law. Remember that you are not just studying law to get a degree but to get a job and you need to be aware of what you should do to maximise your chances of getting the one you want. Overall, this chapter explains how this book will help you to emerge from your three or four years of study with the best chance of entering your chosen field of employment in an increasingly competitive market.

....

1. Donna Dunning, 'Top nine transferable skills' (2010) <**http://www.dunning.ca/blog/top-9-transferable-skills/**> accessed 19 July 2012.

Our approach

We have constructed this book around three key themes:

- **Maximising opportunities to develop skills.** Throughout this book you will find a variety of ways in which you will be able to develop your 'transferable skills'. These are generic skills that are equally applicable in a whole range of careers, such as problem solving skills and IT skills. Throughout your law degree you will grow these skills which will be useful across a range of different jobs and industries, not just those which are directly related to law. In essence, these are the skills that make you attractive to employers, and you should take every opportunity to develop them during your time at university.

- **Demonstrating skills to obtain employment.** As well as developing your skills to enable you to seek out job opportunities and successfully negotiate the appointment process, you will also need to demonstrate those skills to potential employers. This book will cover the process from the initial application form or CV, through to the face-to-face assessment at interview or assessment centre, so that you come to the attention of suitable employers and maximise your chances of getting the job you want.

- **Applying skills in the workplace.** Finally this book will cover the development and application of the particular skills that will ensure you are able to carry out the requirements of your desired job in a proficient and professional way; such as advocacy skills for working at the Bar or legal research skills for employment in academia.

The book is designed for *all* law students, regardless of their chosen career path or the stage of their university life. It is never too late to start developing your employability skills. Indeed, you should be developing them continually throughout your working life as it is virtually certain that you will change jobs at some stage between graduation and retirement and the skills you demonstrate to get your first job will be supplemented by those that you acquire throughout your career. So, you should not panic if you are not in your first or second year— there are still practical steps that you can take in order to enhance your skills and thus your prospects of success in the world of work. Your skills development will be more effective if it is done in a systematic way which this book is here to support.

Defining 'employability skills'

The term 'employability skills' means different things to different people. For some, it means everything that is involved in getting a job, for others, it is little more than interview technique or writing a good CV. For us, employability skills are those that make the link from learning to earning.

There are two formal definitions of employability skills that are widely adopted in higher education. The first is found in a report published jointly by the National Union of Students (NUS) and the Confederation of British Industry (CBI):

> A set of attributes, skills and knowledge that all labour market participants should possess to ensure they have the capability of being effective in the workplace – to the benefit of themselves, their employer and the wider economy.[2]

2. Confederation of British Industry and National Union of Students, 'Working towards your future: Making the most of your time in higher education' (May 2011) 14 <http://www.nus.org.uk/Global/CBI_NUS_Employability%20report_May%202011.pdf> accessed 19 July 2012.

This definition focuses on applying employability skills in the workplace. However, as previously explained, we think that employability skills go further than that, since they are also needed to obtain employment in the first place: you cannot be effective in a workplace without a job! Moreover, it does not focus specifically on graduate jobseekers. This second definition, from the Enhancing Student Employability Co-ordination Team funded by the Higher Education Funding Council for England includes these two missing aspects and is more in line with our view of employability skills:

A set of achievements—skills, understandings and personal attributes —that makes graduates more likely to gain employment and be successful in their chosen occupations, which benefits themselves, the workforce, the community and the economy.[3]

Therefore, employability skills can be considered to be a range of skills and capabilities that virtually every employer is looking for in potential graduate recruits and an essential pre-condition for the effective development and use of other, more specialist or technical skills required for particular jobs. They are also a key underpin to your effectiveness at work.[4] However, since every employer is seeking such skills, you need to take every opportunity to develop your employability skills so that you can maximise your prospects of success in an increasingly competitive job market by demonstrating those skills to employers. Exploring these themes of development and demonstration of skills is the primary purpose of this book.

Types of employability skills

Just as there is no set definition of employability skills, there is no definitive list of what types of skills are included within the term. However, there are several skills that are commonly listed as key to overall employability. These include:

- Self-management
- Team working
- Problem solving
- Application of information technology
- Communication
- Application of numeracy
- Business and customer awareness.

You will see from this list the general nature of these skills. They are good examples of *transferable skills* which can be equally well applied to non-law as well as legal careers. For example, a barrister and a human resources manager will both be required to understand the needs of their clients and a solicitor and a management consultant will both benefit from a methodical approach to problem solving.

3. M Yorke, 'Employability in higher education: what it is – what it is not.' (Learning and Employability Series One, ESECT and HEA, 2006) 8 <http://www.heacademy.ac.uk/assets/documents/tla/employability/id116_employability_in_higher_education_336.pdf> accessed 19 July 2012.
4. Confederation of British Industry and National Union of Students, 'Working towards your future: Making the most of your time in higher education' (May 2011) 8, 11.

These transferable skills can be categorised under a number of broader headings:

- **Practical skills:** such as literacy and numeracy, problem solving and use of IT
- **Personal skills:** such as self-management, professional, and ethical behaviour and organisational skills
- **Interpersonal skills:** such as team working, written and verbal communication, customer service, and networking.

Although you may not yet realise it, not only will you have some of these skills already but you will also have the opportunity to develop them further during your studies as well as being able to add new skills to your portfolio.

Practical exercise: transferable skills

Think about the transferable skills listed in this section and how they might apply to a 'traditional' career in law as a barrister or solicitor.

By way of example to get you started, literacy and numeracy will be important to a barrister as they will need to draft accurate skeleton arguments and legal opinions that are precise and grammatically correct (literacy) and they will also need to submit invoices and deal with their accountant or the Inland Revenue (numeracy)!

☟ Compare your answers with those provided on the Online Resource Centre.

Practical legal skills

As well at these transferable skills, you will appreciate that there are, of course, specific practical legal skills that you will need in your portfolio, particularly if you are pursuing a career in one of the traditional legal professions. Therefore, we can add a fourth category to the list from the previous section:

- **Professional skills:** such as legal research, legal analysis, drafting, negotiation, and advocacy.

If you are planning a career in a part of the legal profession—or even considering it as a possibility—then it is obvious that you will need to develop the skills that will enable you to find, understand, and use the law in a work environment. However, if you do not intend to enter the legal profession but are studying law out of general interest as a good starting point for any number of non-law careers, these legal skills will still be useful to you in impressing potential employers. This is because these legal skills are simply more general skills that you will learn in a subject-specific context. To put it another way, you will learn how to conduct legal research as part of your law degree but if you take away the law focus then you have learned how to organise and carry out an effective research plan that enables you to identify and locate relevant information. This research proficiency can be deployed in any number of non-law settings. Similarly, advocacy and negotiation skills may seem to have a particular relevance to law but are really just different methods of oral communication that will be valuable to you irrespective of your career path. So whatever your career plans or your ultimate destination, legal skills will be an important part of your skills portfolio.

Skills acquired from legal study

The Higher Education Academy has produced a list of the skills that a graduate with an honours bachelor's degree in law will have. This is based on the benchmark for law produced by the Quality Assurance Agency (QAA) which describes the nature and characteristics of the law programme together with the attributes and capabilities that those with a law degree should have demonstrated.[5] The QAA stipulates that, by the end of a law degree, students should be able to:

- Demonstrate an understanding of the principal features of the legal system(s) studied
- Apply knowledge to a situation of limited complexity so as to provide arguable conclusions for concrete actual or hypothetical problems
- Identify accurately issues that require researching
- Identify and retrieve up-to-date legal information using paper and electronic sources
- Use relevant primary and secondary legal sources
- Recognise and rank items and issues in terms of relevance and importance
- Bring together information and materials from a variety of different sources
- Synthesise doctrinal and policy issues in relation to a topic
- Judge critically the merits of particular arguments
- Present and make a reasoned choice between alternative solutions
- Act independently in planning and undertaking tasks
- Research independently in areas of law not previously studied starting from standard legal information sources
- Reflect on own learning and proactively seek and make use of feedback
- Use English (or, where appropriate, Welsh) proficiently in relation to legal matters
- Present knowledge or an argument in a way that is comprehensible to others and which is directed at their concerns
- Read and discuss legal materials, which are written in technical and complex language
- Use, present and evaluate information provided in numerical or statistical form
- Produce word-processed essays and text and present such work in an appropriate form
- Use the World Wide Web and email
- Work in groups as a participant who contributes effectively to the group's task.

This list might seem quite daunting but try not to worry: it is likely that you have some of these skills already and you should remember that this is the list of skills that the QAA requires that your university cultivates in its law students so you can guarantee that there will be opportunities to develop these skills in the course of your studies. However, just because the law degree is designed to give you these skills, it is your responsibility to take the opportunities which arise to cultivate and develop them. It is not enough simply to sit back and assume that you will be sufficiently skilled to make yourself stand out in the job market. Remember that the QAA says that each law student should be equipped with these skills. You will have to take action in order to demonstrate your enhanced skills capability and really differentiate yourself as positively as possible:

....

5. Higher Education Academy, 'Student employability profiles: law' (September 2006) <http://www. heacademy.ac.uk/assets/documents/employability/studentemployability/student_employability_ profiles_law.pdf> accessed 19 July 2012.

I have done a number of things to make myself stand out from any other candidates who are applying for the same job. I have looked online at larger law firms to see what they are looking for in future employees and applicants for work experience. These law firms are all looking for the same qualities in an employee such as research, problem solving, team work and communication skills. In my second year module 'Legal Research and Reasoning' I enhanced and developed these skills by participating in presentations and various workshops.

To stand out more I have worked hard to make my CV look more appealing to the interviewer by doing some voluntary work and gaining some work experience. I have organised a charity football event for Overgate Hospice and I was also a marshal for their charity Midnight Walk. Last summer I worked for an insolvency company, Spencer Hayes, gaining experience in insolvency law and made valuable contacts. These contacts have enabled me to form relationships with higher management in a top law firm with offices based in the UK and overseas. I am now hoping to be accepted onto one of their graduate schemes once I have completed my law degree. By being involved in multiple football and rugby teams as well as being a student ambassador, I can demonstrate team working and communication skills to prospective employers and also show my willingness to get involved and to work.

Matthew, University of Central Lancashire

Practical exercise: building a reflective employability skills portfolio—self-assessment against QAA benchmark

As you work through this book you will find various practical exercises that invite you to reflect, review, and plan your skills development and to gather evidence that you have done so. You might find it helpful at this stage to get somewhere to keep all your employability materials together. This might be as simple as a ring binder with a set of dividers or, if you prefer to keep things electronically, a folder on your computer with various subfolders within it.

The first activity is to review your own current proficiency against the QAA benchmark skills in law. You will find a downloadable template to help you with this on the Online Resource Centre. Think about each of the skills in turn and then rate yourself as follows:

- I am confident that I can do this to a high standard
- I can do this to some degree but am aware that I could do it better
- I cannot do this at all.

This exercise will give you an initial self-evaluation snapshot of your capability in each of the QAA skills. You should repeat this exercise periodically so that you can chart your progress and skills development over time.

So far, you have discovered many of the skills which go towards making up the overall employability skills portfolio, which is shown graphically in Figure 1.1.

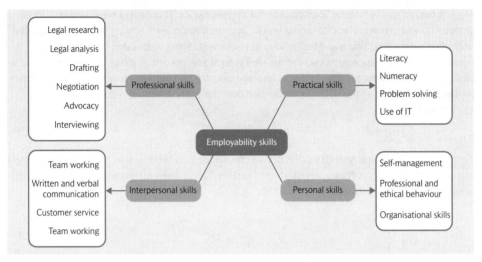

Figure 1.1 The employability skills portfolio

The importance of employability skills

While the importance of employability skills should be self-evident—they maximise your chances of getting the job you need to set you on your chosen career path desire—they are not always recognised as such by students as the following comment illustrates:

I've always been told to work hard and get good qualifications. Everyone has said that education opens doors, so the key to getting the job you want is to get as good a degree result as is humanly possible.

Sam, University of Northampton

However, as well the seemingly obvious benefit, there are broader reasons as to why employability skills are so valuable. First, as the CBI and NUS jointly recognise, they 'underpin success in working life'.[6] As you have already seen, employability skills are not just useful for getting a foot on the career ladder. They are valuable, and should be developed, throughout your working life so that you are able to seek out new job opportunities as your career develops. They also enable you to 'adapt to an unknown future'.[7] This is key. Not only should you be able to seek out new positions within your career, you should also be capable of taking your transferable skills and applying them equally well to a related as well as a non-related alternative:

6. Confederation of British Industry and National Union of Students, 'Working towards your future: Making the most of your time in higher education' (May 2011) 11 <**http://www.nus.org.uk/Global/CBI_NUS_ Employability%20report_May%202011.pdf**> accessed 19 July 2012.
7. <**http://www.nus.org.uk/Global/CBI_NUS_Employability%20report_May%202011.pdf**> accessed 19 July 2012.

My first degree was in Natural Sciences, specialising in physics. That taught me – amongst other things – how to take a methodical and scientific approach to problem solving which I then applied in my first career in software and technology development. Some years later, I studied law and found that the same approaches served me well in legal analysis and drafting. The management skills I picked up during my time in the technology industry also help when dealing with publishers and writing plans. So all the skills I've developed over the years in various settings are still useful today.

Dr Stefan Fafinski (author)

Development of employability skills is also crucial for two further reasons. First, employers consistently state that they are not always satisfied with the employability skills of graduates as Figure 1.2 illustrates.

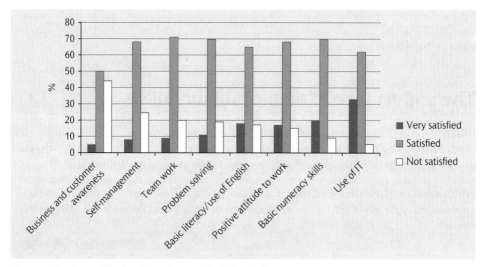

Figure 1.2 Employer satisfaction with graduate employability skills[8]

Similarly, 70% of employers said that they would like to see 'more effective development' of graduates' employability skills although they emphasise that it is up to students themselves to 'seize the opportunities available to strengthen their employability'.[9]

We need students who have more to offer than just academic brilliance. They need to be well-rounded individuals who will work well with others in our firm and, perhaps more importantly, with our clients. They should also be capable of understanding the world in which we work. So it's a package of skills that we're looking for.

Training partner, London

8. Confederation of British Industry and Education Development International, 'Building for growth: business priorities for education and skills—Education and skills survey 2011' (May 2011) 22 <**http://www.cbi.org.uk/ media/1051530/cbi__edi_education___skills_survey_2011.pdf**> accessed 19 July 2012.
9. <**http://www.cbi.org.uk/media/1051530/cbi__edi_education___skills_survey_2011.pdf**> accessed 19 July 2012.

So, in summary, employability skills are important because:

• They help you to get the position you want
• They are highly desired by employers who want them to be developed further.

Doing a skills audit

The next chapter will help you to begin putting together a plan for developing the employability skills that you need for success. Before that, though, you should spend some time thinking about the skills that you currently have as well as identifying the 'attainment gaps'[10] that you need to address: that is, parts of your skills portfolio that are either missing or need further development.

Think about the activities that you currently do or have done in the past. These do not have to be academic. They could equally be sporting or musical, or some particular favourite hobby or pastime, or to do with paid or voluntary work that you have undertaken. Then think about what skill or skills you use to carry out each of these activities. For instance, if you have done voluntary work in a charity shop, you might think of the associated skills of timekeeping and customer service. If you have been captain of your netball team, you could consider your leadership as a skill. You could also ask other students, friends, or family what they see as your skills: these are more likely to be the transferable skills rather than specific professional skills. It can be quite illuminating to see yourself as others see you. Be honest with yourself: there is nothing to be gained if you rate yourself as expert at everything. By being realistic about your current skills capabilities, you will give yourself the best opportunity to engage actively with your skills development and take personal responsibility for your future employment prospects.

Practical exercise: doing a skills audit

You will find a downloadable template to help you begin your skills audit on the Online Resource Centre. The skills that are listed on the template are just a starting point and you should feel free to add others if you wish. Then, as before, rate yourself against each of the skills. Unlike the last exercise, which used a very broad rating system with three possible options against each of the QAA benchmark competencies, you should this time use a five point scale:

1—No current knowledge of the skill (no current competency)

2—Some awareness but not sufficiently competent to use the skill with confidence (partially competent)

3—Familiar with and able to use the skill (competent)

4—Proficient with the skill and able to demonstrate this to others (highly competent)

5—Expert in the skill (fully competent)

So that you get used to demonstrating evidence-based skills, you should also use the space in the template to describe the evidence that you have to support your self-assessment of each of the skills.

....

10. Confederation of British Industry and Education Development International, 'Building for growth: business priorities for education and skills—Education and skills survey 2011' (May 2011) 11 <http://www.cbi.org.uk/media/1051530/cbi__edi_education___skills_survey_2011.pdf> accessed 23 July 2012.

If you do not have evidence at this stage, then you should just write a brief note or comment: you will be adding evidence as you build your portfolio of skills over time. You will find an example of a completed audit in Table 1.1.

You may also wish to complete these with a friend from your course, or with someone that you trust and who knows you well. Alternatively, you could compare your answers with a friend's responses and discuss them together. Sometimes others may offer a more constructive insight into you own skills than you are honestly able to do for yourself.

As you work through the remaining chapters in this book, you will find suggestions on how you could develop these skills. Note the actions that you are going to take in the 'Action plan' column. Remember to set a target date against each item if you can.

You will be revisiting this audit as part of your future personal development planning, so make sure that you put the date on your audit and keep your answers in the 'Reviews' section of your portfolio.

You will find information on personal development planning (PDP) in Chapter 2.

Table 1.1 Example skills audit

Skill	Self-assessment rating (1–5)	Evidence	Action plan
Practical skills			
Written communication skills	4	I normally get good feedback on clarity, grammar, etc in my assessed pieces of work.	
Numeracy	3	I hated maths at A-level and I'm pleased my phone has a calculator on it: but I can do mental arithmetic pretty well. I had to when the till broke at the Oxfam shop.	
Problem solving	4	When I did my Duke of Edinburgh expedition we had loads of practical problems along the way that we needed to solve.	
Use of IT	2	I'm ok with Word but still struggle with what to do if it doesn't quite do what I want it to. I can never format footnotes correctly.	
Personal skills			
Time management skills	3	I usually get my assignments in time but I do tend to leave things to the last minute.	

Skill	Self-assessment rating (1–5)	Evidence	Action plan
Professional and ethical behaviour	2	I have a basic understanding about things like client confidentiality but have never had to put them into practice.	
Organisational skills	3	I suppose I've got my own system for filing and finding things, but I'm not sure anyone else would be able to follow it easily.	
Flexibility	2	I often get really flustered if things don't go according to plan.	
Planning	3	I make lots of lists of things, but could probably be more effective to be honest.	
Decision-making	3	I guess I have to make decisions all the time, but I'm not convinced that I'm skilled at it.	
Interpersonal skills			
Team working	4	I love working with other people.	
Verbal communication	3	I don't mind speaking up in tutorials, but sometimes struggle to make myself clear.	
Customer service	4	I worked in the Oxfam shop in the holidays and much preferred being out at the front, rather than sifting through all the stuff out the back.	
Leadership	4	Again, my DofE helped me with leadership. It went along with team working.	
Professional skills			
Legal research	4	I think I am a good legal researcher. I can find and use case law, Acts and journal articles, but prefer the databases to using the law library.	
Legal problem solving	2	I am a bit unsure when I have to identify legal issues in a problem question—I worry that I go off on tangents…	

(Continued)

Table 1.1 *Continued*

Skill	Self-assessment rating (1–5)	Evidence	Action plan
Drafting	1	Don't even know what this means in practice!	
Negotiation	3	I had a go at the internal negotiation competition and found it really enjoyable. Would like to do it again next year.	
Advocacy	2	I had to do an assessed moot, but it didn't go very well.	
Knowledge of legal practice and procedure	1	I have never worked in any form of legal practice.	
Interviewing	1	We don't have the option of doing any client interviewing.	
Presentation skills	3	I don't mind doing presentations, so long as I'm prepared.	
Commercial awareness	1	I know that law students are supposed to know about this, but couldn't really explain what it means at the moment.	

Remember that this initial audit is the baseline for continued improvement: your skills will only improve from here. No-one is perfect! If you have been realistic in your assessment of your own competencies then you will undoubtedly have identified areas that would benefit from some development. You should return to complete this exercise again periodically as part of your personal development planning. This will show you that you have developed your employability skills which will, in turn, build the confidence that you will need to demonstrate those skills effectively and to realise your potential in the competitive job market.

The chapters that follow will help you build your employability skills and then use them to pursue your chosen career. As you work through the book, you will learn how to understand, identify, build, focus, and demonstrate your employability skills. The chapters are grouped around these themes, as shown in Figure 1.3.

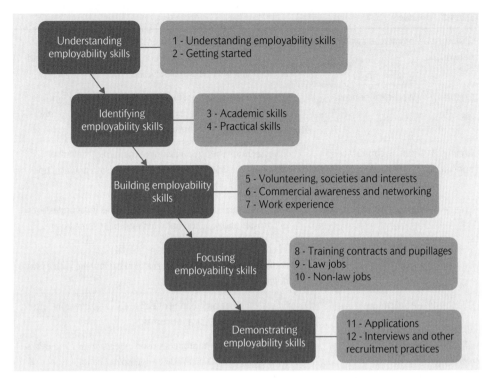

Figure 1.3 Structure of the book

A more detailed synopsis of each chapter is set out in Table 1.2.

Table 1.2 List of chapters

Chapter 2—Getting started	Helps you to build a plan for your skills development activities.
Chapter 3—Academic skills	Highlights the relationship between academic skills and employability skills so that you can maximise the value of the skills acquired through legal study for gaining employment.
Chapter 4—Practical legal skills	Reviews various practical legal activities that are available to you and demonstrates how you can develop both legal and transferable skills.
Chapter 5—Volunteering, societies, and interests	Considers the contribution that voluntary work, involvement in University societies, and your general spare time activities can make to your employability skills development.

(Continued)

Table 1.2 *Continued*

Chapter 6—Commercial awareness and networking	Focuses on two key development areas that you can use to make yourself stand out: awareness of the commercial world and building your personal network.
Chapter 7—Work experience	Covers all facets of work experience with particular emphasis on identifying placement opportunities and subsequently developing your skills through work experience.
Chapter 8—Training contracts and pupillages	Gives a comprehensive account of the steps involved in obtaining a training contract or pupillage with practical tips from former students and employers.
Chapter 9—Law jobs after graduation	Considers careers other than the traditional legal professions of barrister and solicitor, but which still offer some legal content.
Chapter 10—Non-law jobs	Looks at other career options that you can pursue with a law degree.
Chapter 11—Applications	Offers guidance on creating effective CVs and covering letters and completing application forms.
Chapter 12—Interviews and other recruitment practices	Outlines common approaches used in recruitment and offers a wide range of practical advice, including the importance of commercial awareness, that will help you perform to the best of your ability and highlight your employability skills.

WHERE NEXT?

You should by now have a clearer idea of what we mean by employability skills and why they are significant. Perhaps most importantly you should have an honest assessment of where you currently stand in terms of your own personal employability skills portfolio. The next step is to start planning not only for skills development but also for the practicalities of seeking employment including taking time to reflect on the sorts of career pathways you could explore with a law degree. This will be covered in Chapter 2.

Getting started

2

INTRODUCTION

Having explained what we mean by employability skills and why they are important, this chapter moves you on to start the planning stage: how do you get from where you are now to working in the career that you want to pursue? The chapter begins by considering one of the key questions that all law students must answer: to practise or not to practise? It then moves on to give an overview of the two traditional branches of the legal profession—solicitors and barristers—before explaining the stages in qualification, the employability skills that are essential in each and some insight into the likely competition and costs involved. After this, it introduces some of the alternative possible career pathways that can be pursued with a law degree on the strength of the transferable employability skills you will develop. The chapter then explains the idea of personal development planning (PDP) which gives you a framework within which to build an action plan of activities that will enhance your employability skills portfolio. Finally, the chapter will give you an initial timetable of actions to reflect on and consider and orientate you to the chapters later in the book, which will support you in achieving each step in the journey to employment.

You will develop two key plans in this chapter. The first will give you a structured means of developing (and documenting the development of) your employability skills while the second will serve as a useful reminder of the key stages and activities that you will need to do throughout your undergraduate studies. As there is much to do in addition to your academic legal studies, careful planning allows you to prioritise, focus on what is important and make informed decisions. In addition, this chapter should help you to realise that there are many different careers that can be pursued with a law degree, and that it is essential that you think carefully and objectively about the pathway that is right for you.

To practise or not to practise?

Having worked through the first chapter, you should now have an understanding of the nature and importance of employability skills and should be ready to start planning to develop them in pursuit of your chosen career. One of the most important decisions that you will need to make is whether or not you want a career in legal practice. If you complete your law degree with the intention to practise law, your only further decision—in terms of career path—is whether to qualify as a solicitor or a barrister. If, on completion of your studies, you have decided not to enter into legal practice then your choices are much wider as you have a choice of almost any career. Before we address the issues of the various career paths that are available, the very first question for you to consider is whether or not you do want to practise law. Remember that the world of legal practice is very different to the academic study of law so it really is advisable to ensure that you have opportunities to see the law in action to help you make a decision about your future career path.

The best way to work out whether or not you want to practise law is to get as much first-hand experience of the legal profession in operation as possible. This means finding opportunities for work experience and trying to ensure that this is as varied as possible: different size firms, different areas of practice, and gaining insight into the work of both solicitors and barristers. You will also find that court visits provide a useful basis to observe much of the daily life in legal practice.

You will find more detail on work experience in Chapter 7.

You may also want to give some thought to the following points that may influence your decision as they are often overlooked aspects of legal practice:

- **You need to be able to work with people who do not understand the law.** It should be obvious that people come to solicitors and barristers for legal advice because they lack legal knowledge but one of the facets of practice that is often a struggle for newly qualified lawyers arises from the need to talk to non-lawyers about the law in a way that they can understand. Remember that people often have entrenched preconceptions about the law that you will need to overcome and that many people are simply not able to grasp the complexities of the law and the way that it applies to their problem. Moreover, people who need legal advice do not appreciate what aspects of their problem are relevant to its legal resolution so you will need to listen to a mass of detail and be able to pick out the parts that have legal relevance in order to address their problems. And do not fall into the trap of thinking 'ah yes but I want to practise commercial law' as if this means that you will not have to deal with people—commercial entities are comprised of people so you will never conduct an interview with a company but with a person who represents that company and this, of course, raises a whole new set of problems.

- **You need to be both passionate and dispassionate.** It is hard work being a lawyer. You need to be passionate about the law because you will have to know your area of practice in a degree of depth that makes the work that you do as a student seem trivial and you will need to read about that area of law constantly to ensure that you are up-to-date with all new developments. You will also need a passion for the practical aspects of practice—an eye for detail, a determination to win, and a commitment to all clients irrespective of how pleasant or otherwise they are and their behaviour has been—combined with an ability to remain dispassionate as it is inevitable that you will lose cases, some of which you will have been convinced you could and should have won. You need to care about your clients whilst remaining at an objective distance from their problems: just as a nurse needs to treat a patient's injuries rather than weep for the pain they suffer, a lawyer needs to try to resolve a client's problems rather than agonise over the circumstances of the case.

- **You need to be robust.** As well as being passionate about the law, you should also remember that a law career is a lifestyle choice: you will also need to be competitive, driven, and determined as well as being capable of taking criticism and complaints. There is a lot of hard work: early starts and late finishes are commonplace.

- **Can you deliver bad news?** Imagine telling an injured client that their claim for compensation has been rejected, a prisoner who has protested his innocence that his appeal against conviction was not successful, or a parent that they have lost a custody battle and can no longer live with their children. As a lawyer, you will often be the bearer of bad tidings and need to be able to deal with the upset, disappointment, and frustration that this causes for a client. You will also need to be prepared for the client to blame you for the consequences of a lost case and to be able to carry on your own working life with confidence as you represent other clients.

Despite these considerations, law remains a rewarding and exciting career path that offers the opportunity to have a real and positive impact on the life of others. It offers an ongoing intellectual challenge in a setting where your skills, knowledge, and ability can be used to protect others and to resolve problems for people that they are not able to solve themselves. However, be aware that it is not a career that suits everyone and even if you are knowledgeable and passionate about the law, you may nonetheless lack some of the professional skills and personal qualities that are necessary to practise the law successfully.

The roles of solicitor and barristers have several employability skills in common: interpersonal skills, intellectual ability, written and oral communications skills, commercial awareness, and initiative. However, the differing nature of the roles means that solicitors need to have well-developed team working skills, since they may work with other members of a legal team on a case. They also engage in more direct client contact, and so must be able to develop and sustain long-term client relationships. Barristers are usually self-employed and therefore need to be more confident in working independently as well as part of a team. The nature of advocacy requires barristers to develop their oral presentation skills and the ability to think quickly in response to challenges in court. If you are considering a career as a practising lawyer, you should think about the types of activity you enjoy and how those fit with the basic requirements of the professions. For example, if you are not comfortable with public speaking, then you can either decide that you are not suited to advocacy and therefore that a career at the Bar is not really for you, or you can decide to take active steps to plan to develop your advocacy skills.

If you are still unsure, it is worth remembering that this is not necessarily a decision for life. Indeed some people find out that they are better suited to an alternative career once they are in legal practice:

I was in medical practice—not the 'injured in a trip or fall' kind—but dealing with cases where individuals had sustained life-altering injuries that required long-term specialist care and treatment. This involved working with all sorts of other professions to work out what each client needed and to predict how their capability would change in the future. I became fascinated by the work of occupational therapists—now that was a job that made a real difference to people's lives—and eventually gave up my career as a solicitor to retrain in occupational therapy. That was four years ago and I don't regret it for a single minute—the financial rewards may be less than legal practice but the personal and professional satisfaction of helping people on a hands-on basis is immense.

Huw, University of Reading (graduated 2004)

As you will have seen, there are many factors to consider when making the decision whether or not to pursue a career in practice, and it may even be that you change your mind over time. The next two sections in this chapter move on to look in more detail at the practising and non-practising options open to law graduates, starting with solicitors and barristers.

Solicitors and barristers

This section deals with the two 'traditional' branches of the legal profession— barristers and solicitors. Although many law students embark on their studies with a clear idea of what they want to do, it is useful to clarify the differences between the two options as there are sometimes misconceptions, particularly as some of the distinctions between the professions are beginning to become more blurred.

Solicitors have direct contact with their clients and provide expert legal advice on a huge range of legal matters. They can represent clients in the lower courts (magistrates' courts, county court, and tribunals). Once qualified, solicitors generally work in private practice in a firm although other options, such as working as an in-house legal advisor to a large non-law organisation, are possible.

Barristers are specialist legal advisers and courtroom advocates with rights of audience in all courts. The usual route to a barrister is through a solicitor. Solicitors are likely to be able to identify the most suitable barrister to deal with a particular case. However, members of the public may now, in certain circumstances, access a barrister directly (without first going through a solicitor) should they have an enquiry. In addition, organisations or individuals that have an identifiable area of expertise or experience can apply to the Bar Standards Board to be licensed to instruct barristers directly. Most qualified barristers are self-employed, working in a set or chambers, being a group of barristers in a building sharing office facilities, clerks and administrators (and paying a contribution towards their costs). There are also opportunities for employment in the government and private sectors. Barristers must also be members of one of the four Inns of Court: Lincoln's Inn, Gray's Inn, Middle Temple, and Inner Temple. These are the only institutions with the authority to call a person to the Bar, and students must join one of the four Inns before starting their professional training.

Solicitor-advocates are solicitors who have undertaken further specialist training post-qualification to enable them to represent clients in the higher courts (Crown Court, High Court, and Court of Appeal).

Routes to qualification

Having introduced the two branches of the legal profession, this section will outline the routes to qualifying as a solicitor or barrister. Although the professions are different, they both have a similar three-stage process to qualification, depicted in Figure 2.1 for the Bar and Figure 2.2 for solicitors:

- **Academic.** The academic stage requires a qualifying law degree or a non-law degree plus a conversion course known as the Graduate Diploma in Law (GDL).
- **Vocational.** The vocational stage requires successful completion of the Bar Professional Training Course (BPTC) for barristers or the Legal Practice Course (LPC) for solicitors.
- **Professional.** The final stage of training is a two-year training contract for solicitors, or a one year pupillage for barristers.

The GDL

The GDL is a mandatory qualification for students without a qualifying law degree to progress to the vocational (LPC) stage of training. The GDL covers the seven core foundations of legal knowledge that are required in a qualifying law degree along with the English legal system and legal research skills. The GDL is a very intensive and expensive course. You may also encounter the term 'CPE'. The CPE (standing for Common Professional Examination)

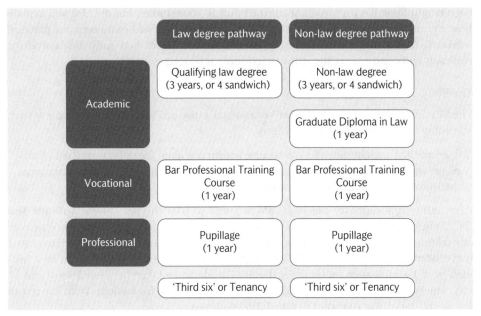

Figure 2.1 Routes to the Bar

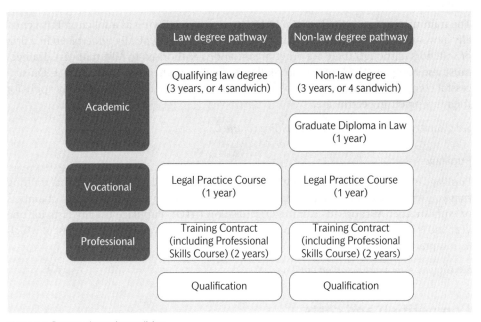

Figure 2.2 Routes to becoming a solicitor

was the forerunner of the GDL and was, for all practical purposes, the same qualification. The Solicitors Regulation Authority continues to use the term CPE.

The LPC

The LPC builds on the academic stage of training. In essence, it teaches how the core legal principles learned in the academic stage are used in practice. For instance, you will have been taught remedies for breach of contract during your studies, but the LPC will explain how to bring a contractual dispute to course. In addition it will build on your practical legal skills such as client interviewing and negotiation and teach new ones, such as drafting contracts and court papers and using practitioner research resources.

The BPTC

The BPTC (formerly known as the Bar Vocational Course or BVC) is a practical course that, according to the Bar Standard Board aims:

> to ensure that students intending to become barristers acquire the skills, knowledge of procedure and evidence, attitudes and competence to prepare them, in particular, for the more specialised training in the twelve months of pupillage.

From 2013, applicants for the BPTC are required to pass the Bar Course Aptitude Test (BCAT) before an offer of a place on the course can be confirmed. The BCAT tests the core critical thinking and reasoning skills required for the BPTC. The aim of the test is to ensure that students undertaking the BPTC stand the best chance of success. Tests can be scheduled from 1 March after applying for the BPTC and can be taken between 3 April and 31 July. The BCAT costs £150 for UK and EU students and £170 for students from the rest of the world. You pay at the point of scheduling your test.

Training contracts

The training contract is the last step in the process of qualifying as a solicitor. It is generally a two-year full-time period of paid practical experience, typically undertaken in a firm of solicitors (although there are other organisations authorised to take trainees). Trainees must also complete the Professional Skills Course during their training contract. On successful completion, a solicitor can be admitted to the Roll of Solicitors and may apply for their first practising certificate.

See Chapter 8 for more detail on the training contract.

Pupillage

Pupillage is the final stage of training to be a barrister and combines the vocational training that you will have acquired with practical work experience in a set of barristers' chambers or with another Authorised Training Organisation (ATO). Pupillage usually lasts for one year and is formally divided into two six month periods, known as 'sixes', the first of which is non-practising.

See Chapter 8 for more detail on pupillage.

Competition and costs

In order to be as well-equipped as possible to make an informed decision regarding your future career aspirations, you need to appreciate two very important considerations from the outset: first that there is great competition for places in the traditional legal professions and second that the process of qualifying involves considerable cost.

Although it remains true that most students who embark upon a law degree intend to pursue one of the traditional legal professions of solicitor or barrister, not all graduate law students end up in such legal practice. In the year ending 31 July 2011, there were 8,402 new solicitors admitted to the Law Society Roll; of these, 5,441 started a training contract—around 65%.[1] Similarly, in the legal year 2009/10,[2] 1,432 students successfully completed the BPTC, of which 460 began pupillage—around 32%.[3] Therefore, one-third of students who completed the LPC and two-thirds of students who completed the BPTC did not manage to secure a place in legal practice. The attrition at each stage of the process is shown in Figures 2.3 and 2.4.

Entry to the traditional legal professions, then, is hugely competitive. To maximise your prospects of success, you will need to look carefully at the skills needed for your chosen branch of the profession and take every opportunity to develop them and gather evidence of that development to demonstrate to potential employers. The chapters in the rest of this book will support you in doing that.

As well as the prospect of stiff competition, you should also be aware of the costs of qualification over and above the costs associated with your first undergraduate degree. For non-law graduates, the cost of the full-time GDL varies, depending upon location, from around £3,500 to £9,500. The BPTC costs from around £12,000 to £16,500 and the LPC from around £8,000 to £14,000.

There are financial awards and scholarships available from a range of sources. In addition, some (larger) firms of solicitors will pay LPC fees and some chambers may allow pupils to take some of their pupillage award (payment) in advance.

See Chapter 8 for more detail on finding funding.

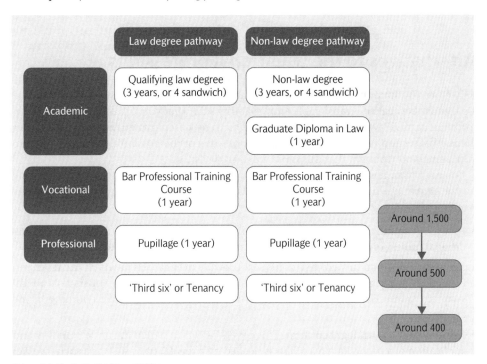

Figure 2.3 Routes to the Bar—attrition

1. Nina Fletcher, 'Trends in the solicitors' profession: Annual statistical report 2011' (May 2012, Research Unit, The Law Society) <**http://www.lawsociety.org.uk/representation/research-trends/ annual-statistical-report/documents/annual-statistical-report-2011---executive-summary-(pdf-1mb)/**>.
2. The legal year runs from 1 October —30 September.
3. Bar Council Statistics <**http://www.barcouncil.org.uk/about-the-bar/facts-and-figures/statistics/**> accessed 23 July 2012.

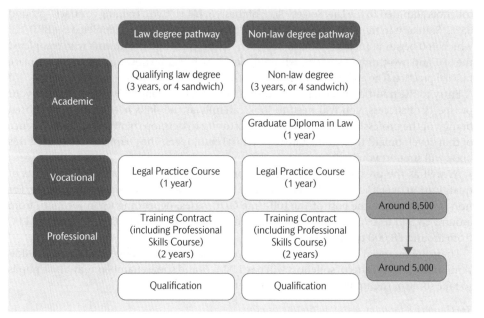

Figure 2.4 Routes to becoming a solicitor—attrition

Alternatives to the traditional professions

As well as the traditional legal professions already covered in this chapter, you should also remember that the transferable employability skills that you will acquire and develop throughout your law degree will also enable you to seek employment in many alternative fields. This section will give you an overview of some of the possibilities that are open to you. Remember, though, that this is not a definitive list!

Careers with a law degree can be broken down into four broad categories, depending on the extent to which the professional skills covered in Chapter 1 are used in everyday working life:

- **Law jobs.** This includes careers which involve working with the law, but not in the traditional professions, such as paralegal, licensed conveyancer, or law teacher.

- **Non-law work in a law context.** This section will cover careers in which the tasks performed are not legal in nature but are performed in a law environment such as a legal secretary (administrative work in a law firm) or a witness care officer (working in the criminal courts).

- **Non-law work with legal content.** This covers careers in which the understanding and application of a particular area of law is needed on a regular basis such as a social worker (who applies social welfare law) or a career in human resource management (using employment law).

- **Non-law work with no legal context or content.** This includes careers where there may be a legal framework that regulates how the job must be done, for instance the regulatory framework of professions such as dentistry and accountancy, but where this is very much a peripheral part of the role as well as careers with no legal basis whatsoever.

See Chapter 9 for more detail on law jobs, and Chapter 10 for the three different categories of non-law work.

These categories, and some example careers within each of them, are depicted in Figure 2.5.

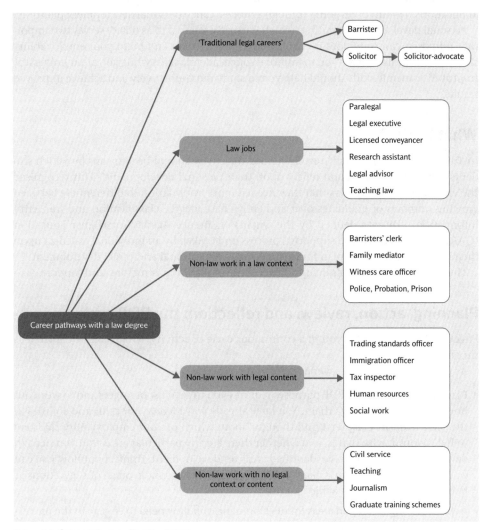

Figure 2.5 Career pathways with a law degree

Planning to develop your employability skills

Having introduced some of the career destinations possible with a law degree, the next step in getting started is to plan to develop your employability skills. The skills audit that you undertook in Chapter 1 should have helped you to highlight the areas in which you need to develop your skills. Chapters 3 to 7 will cover a wide variety of means in which you can develop your employability skills through your studies, undertaking practical legal skills activities, extra-curricular activities, and work experience. You should get into the habit of documenting and recording your skills development activities and building up a set of documentary evidence that you can use later on when you come to start completing applications. This involves going through a process called personal development planning.

Personal development planning (which is usually referred to as 'PDP') serves two important purposes. Not only does it enable you to reflect upon and build your employability skills, but it will also enable you to improve your academic skills while you are at university. Improved academic skills should help you to study more effectively and achieve improved results.

What is PDP?

In 1997, the Dearing Report[4] recommended that there should be 'a means by which students can monitor, build and reflect upon their personal development'. This recognised the views of some employers that they needed more information to differentiate between growing numbers of graduates over and above basic degree classification and transcript information. PDP was defined by the Quality Assurance Agency for Higher Education (QAA)[5] as: 'a structured and supported process undertaken by an individual to reflect upon their own learning and to plan for their personal, educational and career development'.[6]

The key points within this definition are those of planning, structure, and support.

Planning, action, review, and reflection: the PDP cycle

Effective PDP will involve you in a continuous cycle of activity, which can be depicted as shown in Figure 2.6.

As you can see, there are several stages in the process:

- **Planning.** Planning for PDP purposes requires you to set a list of targets and to work out how you can best achieve them. You have already considered your skills and abilities in the skills audit in Chapter 1 and thought about which of your employability skills are well developed, why that is, and whether there are any particular areas that you need to develop. Now that you have identified areas for development, think about how you can go about improving them. Chapters 3 to 7 will give you a whole range of suggestions as to how you can go about achieving this.

- **Action.** Having identified areas for development, you now need to engage in the process necessary to reach the planned targets. Start taking the steps that you considered useful after completing the planning stage.

- **Recording.** You should start compiling a set of evidence of the achievements that you have made while putting your plans into action and the activities that you have

4. The Dearing Report is actually a series of reports commissioned by the UK government into Higher Education in the UK. It is available online at **<https://bei.leeds.ac.uk/Partners/NCIHE/>**.
5. The body which checks standards in UK higher education institutions.
6. QAA, *Guidelines for Higher Education Progress Files* (2001) **<http://www.qaa.ac.uk/Publications/informationAndGuidance/Pages/Guidelines-for-HE-Progress-Files.aspx>**.

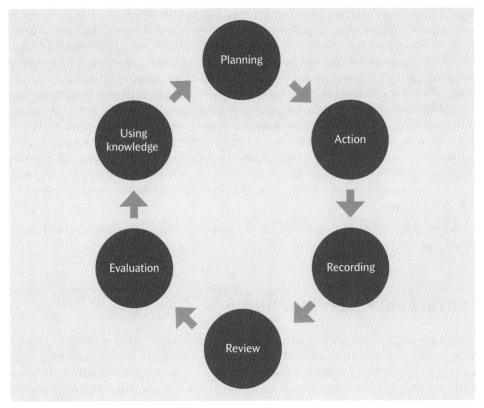

Figure 2.6 The PDP cycle

undertaken in doing so. In other words, you should compile a set of information that will not only help you to document the steps you have taken to grow your employability skills, but also help you in the next stage of the process.

- **Review.** So far you have come up with a plan, put it into action, and recorded evidence of how it is progressing. You should now review your plan in the light of the recorded evidence. Is the plan making the difference you wanted? Are you making progress towards the targets you identified for yourself in the light of your own evaluation of your strengths and weaknesses?

- **Evaluation.** This is an important stage in the process that requires you to pass critical judgement upon yourself and to reflect on your review of your plan to evaluate its overall success or otherwise.

- **Using knowledge.** By the time you get to this stage, you will have been through a whole cycle of PDP. You will now be in a position to plan future actions, and to identify if there are new areas for development, or whether you need to enhance existing areas further. This will inform the next stage of your planning process and the start of a brand new cycle of PDP.

Structure and support

The extent to which an institution provides structure and support for PDP will vary. You may be required to provide evidence of PDP by an academic or personal tutor throughout your studies. There may be a formal means of recording PDP either online, or in some sort of handbook. Alternatively, the arrangements may be more *ad hoc*, with less formal structure. You should see if your university has a member of staff responsible for PDP within law, and make contact with them. There may also be information provided in your student handbook, or PDP may be covered as part of a Legal Skills course or employability workshop. Whatever structure your university provides (and even if there is very little), you should take the time to go through the PDP process yourself, or with a group of friends, or suggesting that a more formal arrangement might be of benefit to students. All that is required is a desire to improve, self-reliance to take action for your own learning and career development, and the maturity to reflect critically on your own abilities. Practically speaking, evidence of PDP and the ability to describe your own PDP experience is something that will be of use to you in moving on to the next stage of your career, whichever route you choose to take.

⬤ On the Online Resource Centre, you will find a template that you can download and use to record your PDP activities and progress.

Putting your plan together

As well as your personal development planning which will enable you to identify areas for skills enhancement and to document your activities, you should also start to put together a checklist of activities to undertake so that you do not miss any key deadlines, or leave skills development activities too late for them to have any meaningful impact on your applications.

There are no absolutely hard and fast rules about when you should plan to do things—of course, every student is different and individual circumstances might dictate that certain activities may be easier to do at certain times. The two most important things are to put together a plan that works for you and to start now, regardless of what stage you are at in your studies. This should help you to avoid coming to the end of your degree and being lost as to what to do next:

I'm in my final year and I don't want to practise law. When I say this out loud, it is usually met with gasps of horror. 'What will you do?' I get asked as if there is no other career but law for me to follow. The truth is that I don't know what I'm going to do but I do know that I don't want to be a lawyer. I've enjoyed my degree but I just don't fancy working in the law so I'm looking around at other graduate opportunities. At the end of the day, this is far more sensible than doing the LPC just because I don't know what else to do, which is what some of my friends are doing. Am I making the right decision? It feels like the right decision for me but I guess you'll have to come back in a few years' time and find out whether things have worked out for me or not!

Mollie, Southampton University (2013)

The checklists that follow (see tables 2.1, 2.2, and 2.3) are also not exhaustive, but should give you a starting point as to the things that you should consider doing. You may wish to add to or amend your own personal plan as you work through the chapters in the rest of the book, but your initial checklist should sit alongside your PDP plan as a list of 'practical things to do'.

You will find downloadable versions of the tables that follow on the Online Resource Centre, which you can then edit and use in the way that suits you.

Finally, we cannot put together a checklist of practical steps towards every potential career that we discuss throughout the book. We have, therefore, concentrated on the two traditional branches of the legal profession, although there are many steps that will be transferable to other careers (such as 'put together a draft CV'). Where there is more information in this book, there is a cross reference to the relevant chapter. There are some important activities for you to consider that are outside the scope of this book, but they are still included in the checklists.

The advice for first year undergraduates is geared to building up a solid foundation in skills (see Table 2.1), before diverging in the second and third years (see Tables 2.2 and 2.3).

Table 2.1 First year checklist

When	What	Look at
First year undergraduate	Start to build your contacts within the legal profession	Chapter 6 on networking
	Join the university law society	Chapter 5 on building skills through social activities
	Get some legal work experience/volunteer work	Chapter 7 on work experience
	Get involved with practical legal skills activities (client interviewing, negotiation, mooting) at your institution	Chapter 4 on practical legal skills and Chapter 6 on finding opportunities
	Focus on your academic studies	Chapter 3 on academic legal skills
	Investigate pro bono opportunities through your institution	Chapter 6 on finding opportunities
	Think about doing some charity work or organising events	Chapter 5 on building skills through social activities
	Plan for/apply for holiday work	Chapter 10 on applications

Solicitor route

Table 2.2 Second and final year checklist

When	What	Look at
Second year—autumn term	Consider whether the solicitor route to practice is right for you	Chapter 2 for an overview and Chapter 8 for the realities of the training contract
	Think about your preferred area of practice	Chapter 8 for overview of the major practice areas

(Continued)

Table 2.2 (*Continued*)

When	What	Look at
	Look out for and attend law fairs and other career events	Chapter 8 on law fairs
	Draft your CV and have it checked	Chapter 10 on CVs
	Research possible LPC providers	
	Investigate funding options for the LPC	
Second year—Christmas holidays and spring term	Apply for vacation schemes	Chapter 7 on work experience
	Draw up a shortlist of firms of interest	Chapter 8 on training contracts
Second year—summer holidays	Apply for work experience	Chapter 7 on work experience and Chapter 10 on applications
	Compile a list of deadlines for your training contract applications	
	Apply for training contracts in good time	Chapter 8 on training contracts and Chapter 10 on applications
Final year—autumn term	Training contract interviews	Chapter 11 on interviews and other assessment methods
	Apply for the LPC	
Final year—spring and summer	Enrol with the Solicitors Regulation Authority as a student member	
	Focus on your final exams and getting the best degree classification you can	Chapter 3 on academic legal skills
	Continue training contract applications	Chapter 8 on training contracts and chapter 10 on applications
	Continue work experience	Chapter 7 on work experience and Chapter 10 on applications

Barrister route

Table 2.3 Second and final year checklist

When	What	Look at
Second year—autumn term	Consider whether the barrister route to practice is right for you	Chapter 2 for an overview and Chapter 8 for the realities of pupillage
	Think about your preferred area of practice	Chapter 8 for overview of the major practice areas

When	What	Look at
	Take part in mooting	Chapter 4 on practical legal skills and Chapter 6 on finding opportunities
	Draft your CV and have it checked	Chapter 10 on CVs
	Research possible BPTC providers	
	Investigate funding options for the BPTC	
Second year—Christmas holidays and spring term	Apply for mini pupillages	Chapter 10 on applications
	Undertake legal work experience	Chapter 7 on work experience
Second year—summer	Continue legal work experience	Chapter 7 on work experience
Final year—autumn	Join an Inn of Court	
	Apply for the BPTC	
	Make arrangements for the BCAT	
	Submit scholarship applications	
Final year—spring and summer	Submit pupillage applications	Chapter 8 on pupillage and Chapter 10 on applications
	Attend pupillage interviews	Chapter 11 on interviews
During the BPTC	Continue gathering as much work experience as possible; non-legal work experience can still be valuable and help fund studies	Chapter 7 on work experience
	Reapply for pupillage	Chapter 8 on pupillage and Chapter 10 on applications

WHERE NEXT?

This chapter has set out an overview of the possibilities that a law degree can open up for you. Where you go next in the book really depends on what stage you are at in your studies and in your plan. As you will have seen from the outline plans in the last section of this chapter, there are many different routes through the book. The important thing is to have a plan for what you need to do next and to stick to it.

Part II

Identifying employability skills

This part of the book concentrates on identifying the academic and practical legal skills that you will be able to develop throughout your time at university. Chapter 3 takes a look at the contribution that legal study makes to your employability and then moves on to Chapter 4 covering the more practical skills-rich activities of mooting, negotiation, and client interviewing.

Academic skills

3

INTRODUCTION

This chapter considers the contribution that academic activities make to your acquisition of the key employability skills. These skills have been explained in Chapter 1 where you were encouraged to undertake a skills audit to identify which skills you have and to what degree of proficiency and to note any gaps in your skills portfolio. In this chapter, you will be encouraged to think about the employability skills that you have developed as a result of your academic studies. It explains how each of the activities that you do as part and parcel of being a law student can be unpicked to discover important employability skills that can be expanded and developed to enhance your attractiveness to employers.

Think for a moment about the academic activities that you undertake on your degree: you write essays, answer problem questions, revise for and sit examinations, carry out research, learn how to reference, attend lectures and make notes, participate in tutorial discussion, and perhaps give a presentation or take part in an assessed moot. You may think that the link between these activities and your future employment lies solely in their contribution to your degree classification but this is not so: all of these activities have the potential to allow you to develop and strengthen the employability skills that you need to be able to demonstrate to prospective employers, irrespective of whether or not you are seeking work within the legal profession. This chapter shows you how to use your studies to showcase your skills and, crucially, highlights skills that are not triggered by your academic activities so that you are aware of the need to look elsewhere for opportunities to develop them.

Academic skills and employability skills

It can be difficult to see an immediate link between the academic skills that you develop through your study of the law and the employability skills that are valued by employers. Of course, it is obvious that you demonstrate your written communication skills by writing an essay but it may be less obvious how this can be used to impress a potential employer when you will not be required to write essays as a solicitor or barrister (or in most other careers if you are not destined for legal practice) and, in any case, all other law graduates will have the same experience of essay writing. Moreover, there are other employability skills that may seem to have no bearing on academic study. Sometimes it is the case that the employability skills are just quite well hidden within the academic activity and have to be teased out but it is true to say that not all employability skills are demonstrated by your studies. In any case, it is not suggested that you should rely on your studies to demonstrate any of the employability skills: rather, that you should start out by considering what skills you have developed during your studies and how you can build on this foundation and strengthen the skills by demonstrating them in action in some other setting. This will become clear as the chapter progresses.

Practical exercise: identifying skills

Make a list of all the study-related activities that you routinely do: this will include things like 'going to lectures', 'preparing for tutorials', 'answering problem questions', and 'revision'.

◡ Visit the Online Resource Centre where you will find a downloadable template containing the skills categories you have already encountered in doing the skills audit activity at the end of Chapter 1.

Think about the skills listed in turn. For each skill, review your list of study-related activities and decide if the activity does anything to help you build that particular skill. Some of these might be quite obvious; for instance, 'answering problem questions' clearly develops the professional skill of 'legal problem solving'. Others may be less immediately apparent.

You will probably find that by the time you have finished there is more of an overlap between academic skills and employability skills than you first anticipated.

The other reason that it is important to focus on your academic skills is that they are at the heart of one factor that will be influential to a prospective employer in any profession: your overall degree classification. Employers tend to be looking for students with a 'good' degree; that is, a 2.1 or a first. This means that it is essential that you think about your studies in order to identify areas of weakness and address these to maximise your prospects of obtaining a degree classification that will be most attractive to potential employers. Do not let this deter you if your academic performance is not as strong as it could be as it is still possible to get a training contract or pupillage with a 2.2 provided you can supplement your degree with a really strong collection of work experience that demonstrates your aptitude for legal practice, particularly if you do well on the LPC or BPTC.

In the sections that follow, you will find a discussion of each of the academic activities undertaken by law students and an explanation of how these develop key employability skills. The skills themselves will not be explained in any great detail so you may want to read this chapter in conjunction with Chapter 1.

Essay writing

As it is a popular method of assessment in law, it is inevitable that you will have had quite a bit of experience of writing essays during the course of your degree, both as formative and summative coursework and in examinations. It would be easy to assume that essay writing demonstrates written communication skills and nothing else but that would be to overlook the other processes that contribute to the finished essay. In order to extract the full range of skills from the activity, let's think for a moment about the things that you do in order to produce an essay:

• Identify the subject matter of the essay and conduct preliminary reading to get a feel for the topic

- Make a set of notes that captures the relevant points from your reading and eliminates irrelevant or peripheral points
- Conduct more detailed research to identify a range of relevant primary and secondary sources
- Extract information from the source material including useful quotations to incorporate into the essay
- Make a plan of the essay that establishes a working structure
- Start to write ensuring that the essay flows and makes sufficient links back to the question
- Refine and polish the essay until you have a finished version that is written in clear and eloquent language and is fully referenced.

Obviously the process is a little different for everyone but these are the basic stages that most people would incorporate into the essay writing process at some point. So what employability skills are involved in this process?

Written communication skills

Language is the primary tool of the trade for a lawyer. The ability to communicate information about the law—to clients, other lawyers, professionals in other fields, judges, jurors, and so on—is a central component of the daily work of solicitors and barristers. It should go without saying, then, that all prospective lawyers should have outstanding written (and verbal) communication skills.

This means that you should be able to do the following things:

- Write at a level of formality that is appropriate to the nature of the document and that is pitched at a suitable level for the recipient
- Construct documents and correspondence that uses words and punctuation in an accurate way so that your precise meaning is captured and no ambiguity arises
- Follow legal convention in the way that you refer to cases, statutes, and judges and in your use of legal terminology.

These skills are developed through your essay writing as you will need to adhere to the formalities of written language that are required within academic law and use terminology correctly. You will be expected to understand terms such as *inter alia*, *per incuriam* and *res ipsa loquitur* and to be able to reference a case, statute, statutory instrument, and the law of the European Union correctly.

Why is this important?

No law firm or chambers (or employer in any other profession) will rush to recruit an applicant who lacks written communication skills.

Within the legal profession, an employer would be concerned that you would not be able to draft legal documents with the required degree of precision. For example, a Canadian contract dispute about the placement of lampposts focused on the meaning of one sentence in a 14-page document and the misplacement of a single comma in that sentence ultimately cost Rogers Communications over one million dollars. As this example demonstrates, a lawyer who does not understand the nuances of language, the shades of meaning between different words and the impact on the meaning of a sentence created by punctuation would be a dangerous (and costly) liability in practice. So try not to be exasperated when your lecturers pick up on your misuse of punctuation in your essays: they are not being pernickety, they are trying to help you to reach the standard of written communication that will be expected of you in practice.

Employers in every profession will be unimpressed by poor use of language in communications with clients and other people outside of the organisation. It reflects very badly on the firm if correspondence is ungrammatical, inappropriate in style, or badly punctuated. Many people associate poor written language skills with incompetence or laxity, neither of which are characteristics that any professional organisation will want to convey to its clients or business partners.

Do you have good written communication skills?

Look for evidence in the feedback that accompanies essays that have been marked by your lecturers that will enable you to understand whether or not you have sufficient proficiency in written language. If you have been told that your meaning was not always clear, that your writing style was not appropriate, or that you are too long-winded then there is work to be done on your written communication skills.

- If your written communications skills are strong then find a way to demonstrate this to prospective employers over and above pointing to your prowess at essay writing. Perhaps you could make regular contributions to the student newspaper or to a blog about life as a law student. Alternatively, you could enter one of the essay writing competitions that are aimed at law students such as the Times Law Award or the UK Supreme Court Blog Essay Competition.

- If your written communication skills are not strong then find a way to improve them. Ask your lecturers for help when you receive your essay marks, visit the study skills advisor in the library, or attend a course aimed at helping students to improve their writing. There should be plenty of resources available at your university.

- Demonstrate your written communication skills in your application. There should be no need to say 'I have excellent written communication skills'; your use of language and command of grammar and punctuation should speak for itself in your application. A surprising (and alarming) number of applications are marred by poor spelling, grammar, and punctuation and are doomed to failure as a result as the employer will either think that you cannot do these things properly or that you cannot be bothered to check that you have done them properly. Neither of these situations will make an employer want to invite you for interview or take your application further.

Use of information technology

Given the prominence of information technology in all facets of professional life, potential employers will require you to possess a high degree of competency in the use of various forms of information technology. In legal practice, for example, you will be expected to file court papers electronically, to create legal documents that comply with particular formatting requirements, and to use databases to locate cases and legislation.

You should be able to see parallels between these tasks and things that you do as part of the process of essay writing. For example, many universities have presentation requirements for formative and summative coursework that specify that you must use a particular font and formatting style or that the pages of the document are numbered as well as requiring that your essay is accompanied by a bibliography or table of references. Although the presentation requirements for legal documents may differ to those of an essay, the processes for creating a document in a particular style will be familiar to you. The process of saving and uploading legal documents will not be dissimilar to the electronic submission of coursework to the university virtual learning environment and the same legal databases that you use to locate primary and secondary resources for your essays will be used in practice.

Time management skills

Every employer will be looking for employees with good time management skills. Employees who are able to manage their time stay in control of the work and are more productive in achieving work targets and objectives. This is particularly important in professions where you are expected to work unsupervised and organise your own working day in the way that best enables you to achieve your objectives. The legal profession is particularly demanding in terms of the pressures of time: you must arrive at court on time, file court papers within a time limit and be punctual and prepared for client meetings.

How long does it take you to write an essay?

Writing a coursework essay is a good test of your time management skills. You have a regular pattern of commitments upon your time with the structure of lectures and tutorials and coursework interrupts this by requiring additional work over and above the ordinary flow of academic life. This has to be fitted in with your other work commitments and extra-curricular activities that you take part in on a regular basis.

But do you know how long it takes you to write an essay? The answer, unfortunately, for many students is that they start writing when everyone else does and continue until its finished, staying up later and later at night if the essay is not going well and the deadline is looming. If you work out how long it takes you to carry out the various tasks involved in essay writing, you will be able to make a realistic estimate of the time that it will take you and select a start date that will avoid the last-minute panic that leaves you with the sense that your essay could have been much better if only you had more time.

In legal practice, people will often give you a task and ask you how long it will take you to finish it. They will need to know when they can expect the task to be complete so that they can plan their own work around it so you will not be popular if you either under- or over-estimate how long you will take to complete your work. You need to have an idea of how long it takes you to do things so practise this with your essay writing and not only will you improve your time management skills but it should help you to work more efficiently towards the essay submission deadline.

Practical exercise: honing time management skills

Look at each of the activities that could be involved with writing an essay and estimate how long (in hours) you would spend on each. Ignore any activities that you would not do and add any others that are not listed. This will give you an approximate idea of how many hours you need to devote to your essay.

- Reading around the topic
- Searching for cases and articles in legal databases

- Reading cases and articles and making notes
- Discussing the essay with your friends
- Looking for inspiration on the Internet
- Planning the structure of the essay
- Writing a first draft
- Redrafting, polishing, and reflecting
- Creating a bibliography.

So you now have an estimate of how long it will take you to write an essay. Does it seem realistic? How does it compare to the time that you usually take? The next time that you write an essay, time each of the stages and compare how long you actually take with how long you thought you would take. This will help you to plan your time more effectively in the future.

By using strategies such as this to estimate how long you will need to complete tasks, you will be honing your time management skills and gaining a greater insight into your own productivity. You will understand what tasks you can undertake quicker and which ones take you longer to complete. Remember that time management is a personal skill so an awareness of your own working habits is essential to utilising this skill effectively. You will be managing your time at both high and low levels. High level time management will involve 'big' tasks, such as 'complete essay' and 'prepare for contract law tutorial'. Within each of the big tasks, you will have series of sub-tasks, like those listed in the practical exercise on essay writing. You should plan and allocate time for each of these individually.

You will need to be able to manage your time effectively once you start to make applications for work experience, training contracts, and pupillages as the application forms ask challenging questions so can be quite time-consuming to complete. Employers will not even read a late application so there is no leeway on the deadline, however good the reason.

Legal research

When you enter legal practice, you will not be expected to know the law but you will be expected to be able to find the law. In other words, the purpose of your law degree is to provide a foundation of understanding of key concepts in law and of the operation of the legal system and to equip you with the skills to find, understand, and use the law. The ability to conduct research that will enable you to identify and locate primary and secondary sources of law—statutes, statutory instruments, bye laws, regulations, case law, official reports, and articles published in academic journals— is crucial. You will have gained experience of finding these sources as you conducted research for an essay although you may find that other activities, such as writing a dissertation or taking part in a moot, provide a better example of your legal research skills (discussed later in the chapter).

Other skills involved in essay writing

The previous sections have covered the main skills involved in essay writing but there are others that merit at least a mention even though you should be able to find a better way to demonstrate them than by reference to your essay-based coursework:

- **Problem solving.** It is possible that you will have encountered a problem when writing at least one of your coursework essays which you will have had to have solved in order to complete and submit it. For example, Jade from Bournemouth University tells of her two-hour drive to another university library to get hold of a particular book that she felt was essential for her coursework.

- **Planning, organisation, and flexibility.** To complete the essay in time, you will need to work out what source materials you need and ensure that you get hold of them. You will need to plan your work and plan the structure of the essay. You will need to be adaptable if your plans do not work and make changes that improve your chances of success.

- **Team working.** Have you been required to produce a group essay? These are quite a common approach to assessment as universities are conscious of the need to ensure that undergraduates get opportunities to develop this important employability skill. Working on a group essay would be a good example of your ability to collaborate with others to achieve a shared goal and may also demonstrate leadership and decision-making if you took control of the group to coordinate the different contributions and to ensure that the group produced the finished essay within the timeframe allowed.

Practical example: group essays

We were allocated to groups of five for our assessed Legal Skills essay and it was clear after our first attempt at a meeting that my group was not going to work well. One girl never turned up and another didn't speak. One of the guys was really argumentative and wanted it all done his way and so we all went along with it. Our next meeting was a shambles as only myself and the silent girl had done the work that we were supposed to do and the third meeting never happened at all. It was clear that we were going to fail if something did not change so I took charge of the group. I worked out what still needed to be done and divided it into five tasks, which I allocated to group members with a dead-line for completion. I emailed this to them and printed copies which I gave to them in person and sent chasing emails every couple of days which I copied to my contract lecturer so that he could see that I was trying to make sure that the essay was completed. I think that these four people now hate me with a passion but they all did their work, after a fashion, and I spent a lot of time turning it into the finished product. It was submitted in time and we got a reasonable mark but, more than any-thing, I realised that I did have leadership skills in me which I would never have believed before the group essay.

Saira, University of Surrey

Answering problem questions

Problem questions are a popular method of assessment in legal education and it is likely that you will encounter them in most subjects that you study as coursework and examination questions. They provide the opportunity to develop a number of key employability skills.

Legal problem solving

Have you ever wondered why problem questions are used to assess law students? It is because they offer an approximation of a key part of legal practice—offering legal advice to a client. It is a simulation of the situation that occurs when a client comes into a solicitor's office and sets out details of their problem as the solicitor sifts through the facts to isolate those that are legally relevant and gives advice based upon them. In the same way, you analyse the facts of a problem question, filter out the facts that have no relevance, and apply the law to those that remain in order to reach a conclusion as to the strength, or otherwise, of the fictitious client's case.

It is because legal problem solving is such an important lawyering skill that prospective employers will be interested to see evidence of your proficiency in this area. Of course, you could point to your prowess in answering problem questions in coursework and examinations but remember that this will not help you to stand out from other applicants (unless your marks are truly exceptional) because all law students will have experience of answering problem questions. As such, you should seek to build upon the foundation of legal problem solving skills that you have acquired in your coursework and examinations by finding other opportunities to demonstrate your ability to sift through facts and give legal advice:

- Client interviewing is an extra-curricular practical skills activity that simulates a first interview between a solicitor and client that requires the students taking the role of solicitor to elicit facts from the client with a view to offering some preliminary legal advice. You will find more details of this activity in Chapter 4.

- You may be able to find voluntary work that includes opportunities to use the law to resolve problems for other people such as working at the Citizens Advice Bureau, training as an appropriate adult or undertaking pro bono work. You will find information about those and other forms of law-related voluntary work in Chapter 6.

- The best way to see legal problem solving in action is to obtain work experience with a solicitor or barrister and observe their client conferences as this will give you insight into the use of questioning to elicit facts and the way in which legal advice is given in practice. There is guidance on all aspects of legal work experience in Chapter 6.

The other skills involved in answering problem questions have much in common with those outlined in the section on essay writing so, in order to avoid repetition, they will not be revisited here.

Dissertation

There is sometimes a temptation for students to view a dissertation as a long essay but the two pieces of work differ in a number of ways, with the dissertation posing a far greater challenge in terms of the skills required. Not only is a dissertation a longer piece of work—anything between 10,000 to 15,000 words—that requires far greater planning and organisation than a 2000 word essay, it also places far greater responsibility in the hands of the student to make the decisions that determine the success, or otherwise, of the piece of work. For example, the student decides on the research question, what to include and what to omit, how the work is to be divided into chapters, the extent of the research—everything in fact, albeit under the supervision of a lecturer. It is for this reason that a dissertation is often regarded to be the truest reflection of a student's ability and it is certainly a good way to develop and showcase key employability skills.

Legal research

Legal research is probably the skill with which the dissertation is most closely associated. Certainly, it provides a greater challenge to your research skills than almost any other activity that you will undertake during your time as an undergraduate and, as such, provides a perfect means of evidencing your proficiency as a researcher to prospective employers.

I am always interested to see a student's marks for their dissertation as our area of practice involves a great deal of research so it is essential that our trainees have excellent library skills and can get on with a piece of research under their own steam without asking for help every two minutes. A good dissertation mark says to me firstly 'this person can think for themselves' and secondly 'this person can research' and these qualities are so important that their application invariably finds its way onto my shortlist.

Training partner, Manchester

These quotations show that the two qualities most associated with a good dissertation performance is proficiency in research and an ability to work under your own initiative. There may be aspects of the subject matter of your dissertation that enable you to really emphasise these qualities:

- Did it involve the law of any other jurisdiction that required you to use unfamiliar databases or take into account the differences between two (or more) legal systems?

- Was it inter-disciplinary in any way?

- Was the subject something that was wholly unrelated to any law that you had covered on the syllabus of your degree?

Anything that takes you into unfamiliar territory will highlight your ability to conduct independent research. You may also want to consider whether you can make links between your dissertation and your future employment: perhaps the subject matter links to an area of specialism within the firm or it may be that you covered a topic that is of general relevance to legal practice.

Flexibility

A dissertation can require a great deal of flexibility as it gives you so much more choice about structure, content, and focus so it is likely that you will need to change your plans in light of feedback from your supervisor or due to the discovery of new articles that you find once you have started writing or the law itself may change. If you have already committed a great many words to paper, it can require a great deal of courage to make the change but it can be worth it if you realise that a different structure or approach would work better.

My dissertation was about youth offender panels and I always felt that there was something not quite right with it but I couldn't put my finger on what it was. Three days before I had to submit, I suddenly saw a way that it could be restructured so that it would work much better. My supervisor was rather wary but told me it was my decision but to make sure I kept a copy of the first version to fall back on if the restructuring didn't work or couldn't be done in time. It was hard work but I did manage to get it done and it eventually was awarded a mark of 67%.

Jordan, Birmingham City University

Employers will value employees who are flexible in their approach to work as they are more ready to adapt to changes that are made to the time, place, or method of working and can therefore fit in with the employer's requirements. Flexibility will enable you to respond to last-minute changes or emergency situations in a calm and unruffled way and to be happy to switch to an alternate course of action if the need arises rather than sticking with rigid determination to the original plan.

Time management

A dissertation is a long piece of work with a long deadline. Students often find it difficult to work out how to divide up the tasks involved in the dissertation so that they are spread out across the time available so it can prove to be a very good way of strengthening your time management skills. Some universities provide a timetable that students writing a dissertation are expected to follow but, in the absence of this, you will need to work out your own timetable. Your supervisor will be there to help you with this but do not expect them to manage the project for you.

Practical example: planning your time

It can be very difficult to create a timetable for your whole dissertation particularly if this is the first project with a high level of complexity that you have had to organise for yourself. Build up your time management skills gradually by setting yourself a goal—completing a first draft of the first chapter within two months is not unreasonable—and make a list of the things that you need to do in order to achieve this goal. Work out what order the tasks need to be done in and then set a deadline for each task. This will give you a timeline to follow that will take you towards your first goal.

Problem solving

Remember that this sort of problem solving refers to the more general ability to overcome setbacks and resolve difficulties rather than law-focused meaning of problem solving in the sense of answering a problem solving question. A dissertation is a complex project that requires you to do far more work under your own steam than is usually the case so it would be surprising if you did not encounter problems. It may be possible to use these to demonstrate your ability to work your way through difficulties that you encounter.

Practical example: identify and resolve problems

If you write 'I opted to write a dissertation in my final year which gave me an opportunity to develop my problem solving skills' on an application form, the prospective employer does not have sufficient information to make an assessment of the standard of your skills. You should be specific about the nature of the problem and give an indication how you went about solving it. For example:

• My supervisor told me to read three articles by a particular author but they are published in sociology journals and I don't understand the terminology. I borrowed a sociology dictionary from the library but still felt that I needed to do more to get to grips with the subject matter so asked if I could attend a lecture on social theory that was being given in the School of Sociology. This really helped me to get to grips with the unfamiliar material and I was able to incorporate different social theories into my dissertation.

As you can see, this provides far greater evidence of the student's ability to resolve problems than an unsupported assertion that the writing of a dissertation developed problem solving skills. Think about the following three problems, all of which are real problems encountered by recent students writing a dissertation. What would you do to resolve them and how would you use this to demonstrate your problem solving abilities to a prospective employer?

- There is an old Law Commission Report that I have to read for my dissertation as the extracts that are in the books don't provide enough detail but it isn't available online and the library copy is missing.

- One of the articles that I read for my dissertation made it clear that Australian law had taken a very different approach to the problem so I wanted to look at this in more detail and maybe have a comparative chapter but I don't know how to find Australian law.

- I've done a lot of reading and I know what I want to write but I don't know how to break it down into chapters.

🌐 You will find some suggested answers on the Online Resource Centre.

Professional and ethical behaviour

This category of skills relates to your ability to regulate your own conduct in a way that is appropriate to the circumstances and act in accordance with a moral code even when your behaviour is not under scrutiny and when there is little or no risk that contravention would be detected. It is essentially concerned with self-discipline and self-regulation. It is something that is of great importance within the legal profession but is a skill that few students are able to evidence.

You may be able to use your dissertation as evidence of your appreciation of the importance of professional and ethical behaviour if you collected data for your dissertation. Unlike other disciplines, law students tend not to collect data—by interviews or questionnaires, for example—for their dissertations, preferring to stick to library-based methods of research—that is, reading books, articles, cases, and materials. However, it may be possible to conduct interviews or administer a questionnaire or even conduct focus group discussions to collect data which can then be amalgamated with the literature in your dissertation. This sort of research has to comply with strict ethical guidelines and you would need to make an application for permission to go ahead with your research from the university Ethics Committee.

I wanted to carry out interviews with members of the child protection team in the social services department where I had worked before I started to study law as a mature student. As this involved conducting interviews with professionals working in a sensitive area, I had to obtain ethical approval. The application procedure was complex and I had to make several amendments to my proposal before ethical approval was granted. I was able to speak about this during my pupillage interview when asked about the resolution of ethical dilemmas and this led to an interesting discussion with a member of the interview panel about whether a system of regulation was any substitute for a strong personal sense of what is ethical.

Samia, University of East London

The other ethical issue that has some bearing on a dissertation is plagiarism. You will notice that you will be expected to complete a declaration that is submitted with your dissertation that declares that it is all your own work and that all sources have been fully acknowledged and referenced. This is because the dissertation offers more scope for inadvertent plagiarism than other types of coursework; when a piece of work is created over a period of six months or more, it can be difficult to keep track of your references and to remember whether the scribbled words in your notes were your own inspiration or a quotation from some long-forgotten source. It is very important to keep track of all your source material and to take particular care in noting the provenance of any quotations that you use in your dissertation as unattributed material could give rise to a suspicion of plagiarism. Of course, this applies equally to all other coursework that you produce as a student.

Practical example: academic integrity

You may be struggling to see the link between plagiarism and professional and ethical behaviour in legal practice. If so, then you are probably not aware that your university has an obligation to report all 'unfair academic practice' (as plagiarism is often known) to the Bar Standards Board or the Solicitors Regulatory Authority (depending upon your career path) where your lack of academic integrity is likely to be regarded as evidence that you are not suited to entry into the legal profession. It would also be very likely to feature in any reference regardless of the job opening and may even be indicated on your final academic transcript.

Other forms of assessment

This section completes the discussion of the skills involved in the different forms of assessment used during an undergraduate law degree by considering some of the less common methods of assessment that you may encounter.

Case note

It is often the case that students in their first year of legal study are asked to produce case note or case commentary, often as part of their assessment in a Legal Skills, Legal Methods, or English Legal Systems module. The objective of this activity is to make sure that students are able to read case law and extract relevant information from it. A case note is usually broken down into sections:

- **Facts.** This section tests your ability to distinguish the material facts, i.e. those which are legally relevant, from the background detail that sets the scene of the case.
- **Law.** The second section requires that you set out the legal provisions—from statute, case law, or a combination of the two—that governs the case.
- **Held.** Here you will be expected to state the outcome of the case. This usually includes a note of whether the decision upholds or reverses the ruling of the lower court.
- **Analysis.** This should be the longest section of your case note and it is where you move beyond picking details out of the case into a discussion of the implications of the judgment. It may be further divided into sections such as *ratio decidendi, obiter dicta* and academic commentary.

The ability to pick essential information out of a case and extract the legal principle is an important one for incipient lawyers to acquire. So your mastery of case noting will be useful in practice but does not offer a great deal of opportunity to demonstrate employability skills over and above those demonstrated by other methods of assessment.

Presentation

There has been an increasing move towards the use of presentation as part of the assessment strategy in recent years in acknowledgement that prospective employers in many professions are interested in applicants who can demonstrate strong verbal communication skills. Alternatively, it may be a requirement that students deliver a presentation in a tutorial but without it forming part of the formal assessment for the module. This may be made optional in recognition that some students would find the idea of speaking in front of their peer group awkward.

If you do get the opportunity to give a presentation, be sure to take it. Many employers within the legal profession have introduced presentations as a part of the recruitment process so it would be beneficial if you were to have some experience of presenting in less demanding circumstances. You will be able to demonstrate skills over and above verbal communication:

- **Use of IT.** Most presentations are accompanied by slides that capture key points. Take time to learn how to use presentation software and ensure that you produce slides that are professional but also visually attractive. You could try to master one of the mainstream packages such as PowerPoint or Keynote but there is also a lot of free software that will give your presentation an individual and polished feel such as Haiku. Remember not to get too carried away with images and animation though; your presentation has to be suitable for a professional audience.

- **Time management.** There is a different type of time management at issue in a presentation as you have to ensure that you cover all the material that is relevant to your topic within a set time. This has to be done without rushing—speaking too fast makes your presentation very hard for the audience to follow—or running out of time: it is very unprofessional to say 'that's it for now but you can catch up on the remaining slides in your own time'. So do not try to cram too much material into the time and practise to ensure that you can cover the points in the time available.

- **Legal Research.** If you are given an unfamiliar topic as the focus for your presentation, you will be able to demonstrate the strength of your research skills by finding relevant and complete information on the topic.

You will find information on delivering a presentation in Chapter 12.

Mooting

Some universities have incorporated mooting into their structure of assessment. This ensures that all students have the opportunity to take part in one of the greatest skills-building activities rather than leaving it as an optional extra-curricular activity. Mooting is an immensely skills-rich activity and it is one that is valued by prospective employers within the legal profession.

You will find a detailed discussion of mooting including a breakdown of the skills that it develops in Chapter 4.

Revision and examinations

The primary purpose of your revision is to ensure that you perform well in the exams and the primary purpose of the exams is for you to obtain the best mark possible to ensure that you achieve a good degree classification. However, the process of revising and the exam itself also provide opportunities for you to develop key employability skills:

- **Planning and organisation.** The revision period spans several weeks and so you will need to plan your revision carefully to ensure that you cover sufficient topics in all of the examined subjects. You will need to be organised to ensure that you have all the materials that you need in order to revise successfully. In the exam, you will need to plan your answers.

- **Written communication skills.** There are two separate processes involved here: you will need to have an effective approach to note-taking during the revision period and a clear and concise written style to capture your answers within the time available during the exam.

- **Time management.** This can be challenging during the revision period: many students report that they spend far more time on topics that they revise at the start of the revision period and then have to cram several topics into a single day as the exam date approaches. Make sure that you have a more balanced approach by creating your own timetable that spreads your work across the revision period and sets goals which are realistic and achievable. During the exam, the ability to manage your time is crucial to your success as you need to be able to complete the required number of questions within the time available.

- **Decision-making.** You will have to make decisions about which topics to revise and how many topics to cover as well as deciding which questions to answer from the exam paper.

- **Team working.** Working with other students can be a great way of sharing the workload and, for many students, discussing the law in a group can help to clarify areas of uncertainty and make the material more memorable. If you set up a revision group, this would be a good example of your ability to work in a small team.

Lectures and tutorials

The final academic activity to consider is the day-to-day business of student life of attending lectures and tutorials. The function of the lecture is to communicate a framework of knowledge about a subject to the students whilst tutorials give you the opportunity to explore particular aspects of a topic in greater depth by means of group discussion. As such, it may seem that their focus is on providing you with knowledge but do not overlook the skills that you are developing by attending lectures and tutorials:

- **Written communication skills.** Whether it is taking notes in a lecture or writing answers to tutorial questions, you will be developing your written communication skills. You may well use a word processing package so will also be using your IT skills.

- **Time Management, organisation, and planning.** You need to work out how long it takes you to prepare for each lecture and organise your time accordingly so that you can work around your timetable and other commitments. This may be a particular challenge if all of your tutorials are timetabled for the same day, for example, or if you have to divide your time between study and work or social activities.

- **Flexibility.** Even though tutorial questions tend to be set in advance, it is sometimes the case that you will have to adapt your preparation to suit an activity that the lecturer announces in the tutorial.

- **Team working.** You may work with other students to prepare for tutorials and it is often the case that lecturers allocate students to small groups with different tasks within the tutorial.

- **Verbal communication.** Tutorials require you to join in with discussion and to answer the lecturers questions so are an opportunity for you to develop your verbal communication skills.

- **Legal research and legal problem solving.** Most tutorials require preparation so you will be conducting legal research if you are finding cases, statutes, and articles and it is common for students to be given problem questions as tutorial preparation.

- **Presentation skills.** You may be asked to give a presentation in a tutorial (see the earlier discussion and Chapter 11).

Skills gap

This chapter has pointed out the employability skills that are involved in various aspects of your academic work so it should be clear to you that some skills are very well demonstrated by certain academic activities whereas others are demonstrated less well and others are not demonstrated at all.

You might find it useful at this stage to create a list or a table that divides the employability skills outlined in Table 3.1 into three categories so that you can see at a glance which ones are:

- **Demonstrated to a high degree.** These are the skills that you have developed to a high standard and where the evidence from your academic studies provides a good example of the skills in action that will be suitable to use to impress prospective employers.

- **Demonstrated to some degree.** These are skills that are either only demonstrated in a peripheral way and where you would like to expand the skill further and gain a better example of your ability or where the skill is highly developed but in a way that is common to many other students so you would like a more compelling example.

- **Not demonstrated at all.** These are skills that have not been developed to any meaningful extent by your studies.

By categorising your skills in this way, you have an idea of your skills gap: that is, the areas where you have not yet had the opportunity to develop a particular skill or where you would like an example of the skill in action other than your academic studies. You can then build upon this as you start to think about your other activities—extra-curricular skills activities, sports, voluntary work, and work experience. The aim is to develop all your employability skills to a high degree.

You will find more about personal development planning and addressing your skills gap in Chapter 2.

Table 3.1 Skills categorisation

High degree	Some degree	Not at all
Legal research and the assessed moot in contract (dissertation)	Written communication skills are good but want a better example than essay writing.	Numeracy
Team work (study group for final year revision and the group essay in ELS)	Problem solving skills have been developed but I'd like to have something that stands out more than problems finding materials for the moot.	Professional and ethical behaviour.
Verbal communication skills and presentation skills (tutorial presentation in public law and land law)	IT skills are good but I don't feel that I can do anything that other students won't be able to do.	Customer service
Knowledge of legal practice and procedure (writing a dissertation about the impact on legal practice of ABS was a stroke of genius!)	Time management skills are fine but need to make reference to all my other activities too.	Leadership
	I'd like better examples than my studies for things like organisation, planning, decision-making, and flexibility.	Drafting
		Advocacy
		Negotiation
		Interviewing

WHERE NEXT?

By thinking about the employability skills involved in academic activities, you will have a clearer idea of the skills that you already possess and your level of proficiency in them (see Table 3.2). You will also be aware of the skills that you will not get an opportunity to develop or demonstrate through your participation in academic activities. Armed with this knowledge, you can start to build your skills portfolio through your participation in other activities outlined in later chapters of this book. It is important to do this because your academic studies alone will not be sufficient to impress prospective employers, irrespective of whether you intend to work within the legal profession or in some other industry. So make a decision as to which employability skills you can demonstrate by reference to academic activities—you could use your dissertation to demonstrate legal research skills, for example, and a study group that you have set up as evidence of your team working skills—and which skills that you have developed through your studies need to be demonstrated in action in some other activity. For example, you might want to find some example of your written communication skills in action other than by reference to your coursework grades. Similarly, you will need to be conscious of the gaps in your skills portfolio where your academic skills do not give you the opportunity to demonstrate things like customer service or advocacy and look for other activities that will enable you to develop these important employability skills. You will find some good suggestions in Chapter 4 which covers practical legal activities such as mooting, Chapter 5 where the focus is on building skills through activities undertaken in your spare time, and Chapter 7 which looks at all aspects of work experience.

Table 3.2 Employability skills and academic activities

Skill	Lectures	Tutorials	Note-taking	Writing	Referencing	Essays	Dissertation	Problems	Revision and exams
Practical skills									
Written communication skills			x	x	x	xxx	xxx	x	x
Numeracy							x		
Problem solving						x	x	x	
Use of IT		x				xx	x	x	
Personal skills									
Time management skills	x	x				x	x	x	x
Professional and ethical behaviour							x		
Organisational skills	x	x				x	x	x	x
Flexibility		x	x				x		x
Planning	x	x				x	x	x	x
Decision-making							x		x
Interpersonal skills									
Team working		x				x	x		
Verbal communication		x							
Customer service									
Leadership									

(Continued)

Skill	Lectures	Tutorials	Note-taking	Writing	Referencing	Essays	Dissertation	Problems	Revision and exams
Professional skills									
Legal research	x	x			x	x	x	x	
Legal problem solving		x						x	x
Drafting									
Negotiation									
Advocacy		x							
Knowledge of legal practice and procedure					x				
Interviewing									
Presentation skills		x							

Practical legal skills (4)

4

INTRODUCTION

This chapter looks at the three main practical legal activities that students most commonly encounter during their time at university: mooting, negotiation, and client interviewing. It is divided into three parts, dealing with each activity in turn: what it is, what it involves, and how to take part successfully. This is followed by an outline of the employability skills that are developed by each activity. Each section concludes with guidance on finding opportunities to take part in the activities, both within your own university and by taking part in national and international competitions.

Practical skills activities such as mooting, negotiation, and client interviewing are simulations of aspects of legal practice and so offer an unparalleled opportunity to move your experience beyond the academic study of the law and gain some insight into how the law is used in practice. Not only do they give you the chance to understand interactions between lawyers and clients (interviewing), other lawyers (negotiation), and judges (mooting) but they also give you an opportunity to develop skills that are valued by employers, both within law and in other professions. Moreover, participation in these extra-curricular activities demonstrates a commitment to the acquisition of skills that are relevant to a career in legal practice as well as your ability to balance your time between your studies and other activities. Finally, success in internal and, in particular, external competitions will really help you to stand out from other applicants.

Mooting

A moot is a simulation of the appeal stage of a court case in which students take on the roles of barristers presenting legal arguments in the appellate courts, usually the Court of Appeal or Supreme Court. It is an immensely skills-rich activity. Mooting will improve your ability to conduct research, to understand fine points of law, and to use case law in a persuasive and flexible manner to support your line of argument. It is also an excellent activity in terms of the development of verbal communication and advocacy skills and is a wonderful way to improve your confidence at public speaking. It is important that you take the opportunity to moot at some point during your undergraduate career: law employers will expect this and non-law employers will be impressed by the skills that you will develop as a result of participation.

I expect students applying for work experience and training contract places to have mooted. Why wouldn't they? It is the closest replication of legal practice on offer to undergraduates and so I would expect anyone who was keen to practise in any area of law to have been equally keen to get involved with mooting.

Training partner

What is mooting?

In ordinary conversation, a 'moot point' is one that can be argued either way: it is a way of indicating that a point is open to debate and can be argued from more than one perspective. For example, one person might say 'the *Hostel* films revitalised the horror genre' and another would disagree, saying 'that's a moot point: they really only replicated the torture horror theme introduced by the *Saw* films'. In other words, when someone responds 'that's a moot point' to a statement, they are saying 'that's not the only way of looking at this issue. It can be argued from another perspective'.

If you think about it, the essential characteristic of a legal dispute is that it is an argument from (usually) two opposing perspectives. Sometimes this will be about a matter of fact, such as a dispute over who owes how much money to whom, but a great many cases, especially at appellate level, involve a dispute over the interpretation of a point of law and/or its application to a particular set of facts. In other words, these cases involve a moot point of law.

For this reason, mooting developed as a method of introducing law students to the sorts of legal issues that they were likely to encounter in practice with a view to fostering the skills that they would need in the professional realm. A moot is a fictitious appeal case involving an unresolved legal argument that could be decided in favour of either of the two parties depending upon the way that the law is used and the skilfulness and persuasiveness of the oral arguments presented by the mooters.

You will see an example of a typical moot problem in Figure 4.1. This will be used in the sections that follow to explain how mooting works.

Before moving on, it would be useful to ensure that you understand the distinction between a moot and a mock trial. A moot is a simulation of an appeal case based upon arguments about the interpretation of a point of law whereas a mock trial is a re-enactment of a first instance hearing, usually involving the presentation of evidence and the examination of witnesses. Both activities are excellent vehicles for the development of advocacy skills but the latter is little used, largely owing to the complexities of its organisation. Mooting, by contrast, is far easier to organise and can go ahead with just five people—four mooters and a judge (although it is often the case that the judge will be assisted by a clerk).

How does mooting work?

A moot involves two opposing teams—the appellants and the respondents—each of whom represent one of the parties to the legal dispute outlined in the moot problem. If you look at the moot in Figure 4.1, you will see that the two parties are the Crown (represented by the letter R for Regina) and PC McGarry so you will need to work out which of these parties you are representing. This is very important as it is always unfortunate when two sides turn up to moot against each other only to find that they have both prepared the same side of the argument. Not only will the moot not go ahead but the team who were in error will often be disqualified.

IN THE Court of Appeal (Criminal Division)

R v McGarry

On 7 April, PC McGarry (a serving police officer with Camberwick Constabulary) was off duty, drinking in the Ship public house. He was approached by a friend, Jonathan Bell, the local farmer. Bell told McGarry that the barn at his farm had been broken into on the evening of 2 April and that three of his prize pigs had been stolen. Bell also told McGarry that he suspected Michael Murphy, the local baker, who had recently fallen out with Bell over the cost of his wheat which, in turn, had driven up the cost of the flour he bought from Mr Miller, who owned the nearby mill. Murphy had also started advertising fresh hot bacon rolls in his shop which had proven to be very popular with the local villagers. Bell was very angry and said that if he knew for sure that Murphy was the culprit then 'he'd make him pay for what he did'. McGarry knew that Bell had previous police cautions for violent, threatening, and abusive behaviour. Bell's temper was also well known in the local community.

The following morning, when back on duty on the beat, McGarry used his iPhone to access the police station database to see if he could find any information on the alleged burglary at Bell's farm. He discovered that Murphy had been questioned and subsequently released. However, new information had come to light since Murphy's questioning and it appeared from the information on the police database that Murphy was likely to be arrested.

McGarry sent Bell a text message saying 'It's who u think it is. U need to get him quick'. Bell immediately went to Murphy's shop and stabbed him with a pitchfork, causing a serious but non-fatal wound to Murphy's chest. PC McGarry was convicted at Trumptonshire Crown Court of *inter alia* gaining unauthorised access to computer material with intent to commit or facilitate commission of further offences contrary to section 2 of the Computer Misuse Act 1990. In the Crown Court, Mopp J stated that:

> This could not have been a clearer instance of the perils associated with the misuse of mobile technology. McGarry abused his position to access the data and, as a result, Murphy could have died.

PC McGarry appeals to the Court of Appeal on the following grounds:

1. That his access to the police database was not unauthorised within the meaning of the Computer Misuse Act 1990 since, as a police constable on duty, he was impliedly authorised to access police computer systems; and, in any event

2. An iPhone is not a computer within the meaning of the Computer Misuse Act 1990.

Figure 4.1 A typical moot problem

- **Appellants.** As the name suggests, the appellant is the party who is bringing the case before the appeal court. It follows that this must be the party who lost the case at an earlier hearing (because you would not appeal against a decision that went in your favour) so the appellant will always want the decision of the previous court to be overturned. So in the example moot, the counsel for the appellants are representing PC McGarry. It is the job of the appellants to establish the basis for the appeal by setting out the grounds upon which the decision of the previous court can be challenged so it is the appellants that set the agenda for the moot with their submissions.

- **Respondents.** Again, there is a clue in the terminology used to describe the two sides to the moot as the role of the respondents is to respond to the points raised by the appellants. In other words, the respondents have to tailor their submissions to match those put forward by the appellant and to persuade the judge to favour a different interpretation of the law. Failure to address a submission advanced by the appellants is taken as conceding that point: in other words, accepting that the appellants are correct. Therefore, the respondents must negate the arguments of the appellants before advancing their own submissions. The respondents represent the party who was successful at an earlier hearing so they want the decision of the previous court to be upheld. In this moot, the respondents represent the Crown.

So a moot involves a team of two students who represent the appellant and a team of two students who represent the respondent. Within each team, one mooter takes on the role of senior counsel and the other becomes the junior counsel with each of these roles involving a slightly different task and with each having responsibility for a separate point of law. The roles of the various participants are set out in Figure 4.2.

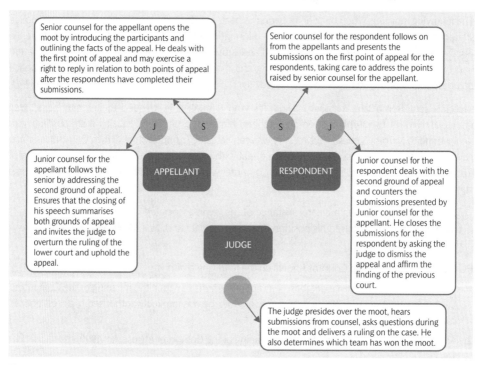

Figure 4.2 Mooting roles

You will notice from the sample moot in Figure 4.1 that the appellant is making two challenges to the ruling of the trial judge—the first about the lawfulness of his access to the computer data and the second concerning the definition of a computer. These are called grounds of appeal. It is usual for senior counsel to take responsibility for the first ground of appeal and for junior counsel to deal with the second ground of appeal. This means that your line of argument in the moot would depend upon whether you are representing the appellant or the respondent and whether you take the role of senior or junior counsel. In *R v McGarry*, this breaks down as follows:

• Senior counsel for the appellant will submit that PC McGarry was authorised to access the data on the police computer

- Junior counsel for the appellant will submit that an iPhone is not a computer for the purposes of the Computer Misuse Act 1990
- Senior counsel for the respondent will submit that PC McGarry was not authorised to use the police computer to obtain information for his friend
- Junior counsel for the respondent will submit that an iPhone does fall within the legal definition of a computer for the purposes of the Computer Misuse Act 1990.

Irrespective of your role in the moot, the central task of all four mooters is the same which is to conduct research into your point of law and formulate submissions which address your ground of appeal that are presented in oral form to the judge. In the sections that follow, there will be a more detailed breakdown of the core activities involved in mooting followed by an evaluation of how these activities will help you to develop skills that will enhance your employability.

The stages of mooting

Mooting has given me a great insight into the legal profession and its operation and I have gained skills from advocacy, teamwork, research, legal writing, and drafting.

Rhian, University of Central Lancashire

As students who have taken part in moots appreciate, mooting is an immensely skills-rich activity. It is not, as many students initially think, only an opportunity to develop verbal communication skills. The best way to understand the full range of skills involved in mooting is to consider the steps that need to be taken in order to prepare for and participate in a moot. These can be broken down into three stages as Figure 4.3 illustrates.

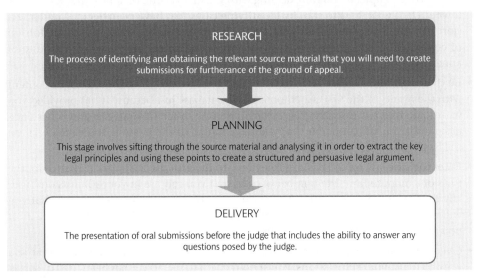

Figure 4.3 The stages of mooting

Each of these stages will be explained in a little more detail in the sections that follow in order to enable you to understand the skills involved in mooting and how these relate to employability.

The research stage

The first stage of preparation for a moot is to undertake research into the relevant point of law in order to find the source material that you need to create a moot speech. The starting point for this research will depend upon the information in the moot problem and the way that your ground of appeal is framed but it should be possible to identify a general area of law. In the sample moot problem, there is a reference to the Computer Misuse Act 1990 that would give you a place to start your research whereas some moots will specify particular cases or use terminology that enables you to identify the law that is central to each ground of appeal.

Many students will start the research process by reading about the relevant area of law in a textbook in order to get an overview of the topic and to identify relevant statutory provisions and case law. This can be a useful starting point but remember that you cannot write your moot argument from a textbook. It is essential that a moot is based upon your reading, interpretation, and application of primary sources of law—that is, statute and case law—as this ability to use the law is at the heart of mooting. So even if your starting point is a textbook, the bulk of your research should be focused on finding and reading case law using one of the databases such as Westlaw provided by your university.

The ability to conduct an effective database search that enables you to identify a range of relevant source material is essential to the overall success of your moot. After all, however competent and compelling your oral delivery, your submissions will not be a success if they are based upon out-of-date law or if you have failed to identify the leading case law on the issue at hand. As such, it is important that your research skills include the ability to do the following things:

- **Conduct a search that identifies relevant case law.** This may be a search which uses a particular case or statutory provision as a starting point or which is based upon keywords. For example, if you were dealing with the first ground of appeal in *R* v. *McGarry*, it would be a good idea to start by identifying cases that have been decided under section 2 of the Computer Misuse Act 1990 whereas you might want to use 'definition of computer' as a keyword search if you were responsible for the second ground of appeal.

- **Be thorough and flexible in your approach to searching.** You should not be content with the results of the first search on a single database just because it has provided you with some relevant case law. Keep searching using different strategies and other databases until you are confident that you have found all the possible source material on the issue.

- **Filter the case law on the basis of relevance to the ground of appeal.** It is usual for the rules of a moot to limit the number of cases that you can use in your submissions, usually to three or four authorities. This means that you have to be selective and that you will need to read the cases carefully to ensure that you select those that offer the most potential for you to create a forceful line of argument.

- **Check the status of your authorities.** When you find a case that you think that you want to use in your submissions, you should check to see how it has been used in subsequent cases. It may have been overruled or criticised, in which case you may need to find a different authority, or you may find that it leads you to a more recent case that actually works more effectively as part of your legal argument. You will also want to bear in mind the hierarchy of the courts and ensure that you do not use a lower court case when a higher court has made the same point and will carry more weight.

In order to conduct research for a moot, you must be able to locate authorities that you know exist (perhaps because you have read about them in the relevant section of a textbook) and to find new authorities relevant to the ground of appeal by keyword searching. To do this effectively, you must have a good level of proficiency in using law databases to identify relevant source material using flexible and creative search strategy and this includes the ability to check that you have selected the most authoritative and up-to-date cases.

There are a number of skills involved in legal research that will be of value in an employment context irrespective of whether or not you are working within the legal profession. Within the legal profession, the ability to carry out research that identifies relevant sources of law is essential and it will be important for you to convince potential employers that you are a confident and thorough researcher who can be relied upon to produce a comprehensive account of the law on any given topic irrespective of your prior knowledge of it. It is important to remember that your law degree does not equip you with complete knowledge of the law so you are likely to encounter a vast range of cases in practice where you have no prior knowledge of the law. It is for this reason that proficiency in finding out what the law is on a new topic is so important.

....

Preparing for my first moot was so hard that I nearly gave up because I didn't know how to find cases and work out what ones to use—I was so worried that I was picking the wrong cases and that I was going to have missed a really important point of law. But I survived and found my preparation for each moot was easier and easier as I got better at being creative in searching. Now that I'm in the first year of my training contract, I can see the benefits of this as I often need to find cases on areas of law that are totally new to me but I'm good at picking out good search terms and confident in my ability to find everything that there is to find about the point of law.

James, University of Surrey

....

Any number of non-law careers may require the ability to trawl through databases or other electronic or paper-based records systems to locate particular material so employers in a wide range of professions will value an employee who can conduct research with minimal supervision and guidance. Your experience in researching for a moot can be used to demonstrate your resourcefulness at finding relevant material and your doggedness in formulating creative search strategies that ensure that your findings are comprehensive and complete. Finding case law on Westlaw is a specific instance of your more general ability to carry out a search to locate relevant data.

The planning stage

Once you have conducted some preliminary research and identified a range of possible authorities, your next task is to create a structured legal argument from these sources that addresses your point of appeal. This involves engaging in careful analysis of the case law to ensure that you can recognise the important legal principles in each case and extract these to use as the basis of your submissions. There is also a need to identify useful quotations from each case as it is usual in a moot to quote directly from the case. This process of sifting through the case to extract the really important points and to build these together into a coherent argument is one of the most valuable skills that you will develop by taking part in mooting. In essence, you are breaking down a large amount of information found in different sources and bringing it together as a series of submissions that combine together to create a persuasive legal argument.

I can remember struggling as a student to work out which three of the many cases that I'd found I would use in my moot. You look out for killer quotations and cases that provide the strongest support for your arguments. It teaches to you to be selective and to identify the most effective authorities so that you build the strongest case possible in the most concise way. This is very important in practice.

Neshan Minassian, barrister

As this stage of the preparations, you will also need to create a written skeleton argument and plan your oral submissions. Both of these activities utilise core communication skills: the skeleton argument needs to be a concise and precise encapsulation of the essence of your submissions whilst your oral presentation must be clear and easy-to-follow for the listener. It is important to give careful thought to the way in which your skeleton is worded and to the planning of your oral submissions as good written and spoken language differs and it is essential in particular that you do not sound as if you are reading submissions to the judge.

Mooting has helped develop key skills such as communication (listening and responding effectively to the opposition's remarks) and also team building through working together to get the end result.

Laura, Leeds Metropolitan University

It is important to think about the content of your oral submissions during the preparation stage. Many students write down every word that they intend to say and then read this to the judge. This is never a good idea. Reading a script always sounds very stilted and it gives the judge the impression that you do not have a good enough knowledge of the law to depart from your planned speech.

I found that mooting was the best possible way of gaining confidence in public speaking. This was invaluable in helping me get my training contract as there was a moot and a group presentation at the selection centre. I wasn't nervous, unlike some of the other participants, and I received a lot of praise for my advocacy skills.

Mark, University of the West of England

The best moot speeches are those that sound natural and the best way to achieve a natural delivery is to avoid the temptation to write a speech—if you write a script you will probably want to read it so it is better not to write one in the first place. Instead, make a list of bullet points that capture the essential nature of each separate point that you want to make. You can then express these in ordinary spoken language to the judge.

The important skill involved in this stage of moot preparation is the ability to process a large volume of information and extract the key points from it. These points, taken from a number of sources, are then woven together to create a legal argument relevant to the point of appeal. In the context of legal practice, this replicates the process of putting together a legal argument for court but there is also a more general skill that would be useful in a wider range of employment settings. Think, for example, of a social worker writing a report on a child that incorporates key points from interviews with family members, medical reports, and witness statements or a teacher putting together a presentation from a range of sources for a class of students. There are any number of professions in which the ability to filter sources for relevant data, extract key points, and create a new document, report or presentation would be an essential skill.

The delivery stage

This is the stage that most students focus on when they think about mooting: the oral delivery of your submissions to the judge. The delivery of oral submissions also tends to be the aspect of mooting that causes the greatest anxiety as many students do not feel comfortable with public speaking. Of course, it is this opportunity to gain competence and confidence in public speaking that makes mooting such a truly valuable activity for skills development. Even if the thought of delivering a moot speech makes you feel nervous, do try to get involved in mooting and make sure that you take a step further each time in developing your oral presentation skills. Despite the limitations of delivering a speech from a written script, if this is the only way that you feel that you can take part in mooting then go ahead on this basis but with the plan in mind that you will moot a second time and take a less scripted approach. Nobody expects you to be an outstanding public speaker on the first occasion that you moot so the important thing is to have a go and treat each moot as a step on the ladder towards becoming a more polished and professional presenter.

Mooting has significantly enhanced my social skills, public speaking skills, and confidence.

Sarah, University of Southampton

In addition to the inculcation of oral presentation skills, the delivery stage of mooting also provides an opportunity to further develop your oral communication skills as it is usual for the moot judge to intervene during your speech to ask you questions about your submissions. Again, this is an aspect of mooting that gives many students qualms but it is really no different to answering a question in a tutorial: in fact, it should be easier as you will probably have a far greater depth of understanding of the law relevant to your ground of appeal than you do in relation to many tutorial topics. The questioning aspect of mooting is valuable in terms of skills development as it forces you to depart from your planned submissions and this should help to increase your confidence when speaking in public.

Responding to questions from the judge in a moot forces you to dredge up answers and really develops your ability to think on your feet.

Jennie, University of Westminster

There is a great myth attached to mooting which is that it is only really useful for prospective barristers who will have to stand up and give speeches in court. Whilst it is true that the main business of a moot is presenting oral arguments on the interpretation of a point of law much as a barrister would do in an appeal case, the core skill involved in the delivery of a moot speech is oral communication. The ability to present ideas and arguments to a listening audience in a clear and confident manner is a most valuable skill in any range of professions. Public speaking is daunting for so many people so if you have experience in speaking in front of others (either from mooting or other types of presentation) then this is likely to impress potential employers. Furthermore, even if you find employment that does not involve public speaking, there are other situations at work where you will have to speak out in front of others so the confidence gained from mooting will be valuable in preparing you to do this, particularly if you find yourself needing to persuade others about the value of your ideas or to defend your views in the face of opposition.

What employability skills does mooting develop?

Mooting is essentially a simulation of the presentation of oral arguments by barristers in an appeal case. However, the skills that are involved in researching for a moot and in composing and delivering oral submissions are ones that are of a far wider application. The application of these skills in a professional context can be highlighted by considering the categories of employability skills that was outlined in Chapter 1. You may also like to refer to the table at the end of the chapter (Table 4.1) that provides a summary of the skills involved in all three practical activities covered in this chapter. Remember too that mooting, along with negotiation and client interviewing, often provides excellent networking opportunities as the judge is usually a solicitor or barrister so an impressive performance might result in the offer of work experience as well as being the means by which you win the competition.

Practical skills

This category of skills covers your ability to do basic things that are required in the majority of workplace situations. These are core transferable skills that every employer will look for in a prospective employee.

- **Written communication skills.** Although the main emphasis in mooting is on oral communication, there is still a need for proficiency in written communication skills due to the requirement to produce a skeleton argument for the judge. This one-sided document is a concise outline of the submissions that will be made in your oral presentation thus it involves skills in précis and must be expressed in good written English and in line with the conventions that govern the use of legal language.

- **Problem solving.** There are a number of problems that might be encountered in the course of mooting. Can you be sure that you have found all the relevant case law? Is your law up-to-date? How do you find a copy of a very old case or an authority from another jurisdiction? It is always interesting from the perspective of a moot judge to find out which students were determined enough to track down a copy of a Canadian case from the 1920s and which ones gave up and referred to the two sentence summary that they found in a textbook!

- **Use of IT.** There are some quite specific requirements for the formatting of a skeleton argument so proficiency in the presentation of documents is necessary.

Personal skills

This is a cluster of skills that refer to an individual's ability to regulate their own behaviour in the workplace and covers skills such as time management, organisation, and flexibility.

- **Time management.** There are two facets to time management that are relevant to mooting. Firstly, as an extra-curricular activity, it has to be fitted in with your other study (and personal) commitments so it requires an ability to prioritise tasks and manage deadlines. Secondly, the time allowed for preparation is often short: it is not unusual for students to receive only a few days to prepare for a moot so it is a good demonstration of your ability to work under pressure within tight time constraints.

- **Professional and ethical behaviour.** Mooting is a great activity for developing awareness of expected behaviour within the legal profession as mooters are expected to adhere to courtroom etiquette in the way that they address the judge and refer to cases. There are also ethical considerations at play in relation to the expectation that your skeleton argument will be sent to your opponent prior to the moot and will provide a transparent account of the nature of your oral submissions.

- **Organisation.** Mooting involves management of a great deal of material. You have to create a bundle of cases for the judge and ensure that this is organised in a way that is easier for him to navigate plus you need to make sure that your own papers are arranged so that you are able to find the points that you need when you need them. Nothing annoys a judge more than the sound of rustling papers as a mooter rummages around looking for a case that should have been to hand.

- **Flexibility.** Although you will have planned your oral submissions in advance of their delivery, mooting does require an ability to 'think on your feet' because the judge will inevitably ask questions during the moot. It is good practice to answer the question when it is asked rather than to dismiss the judge by saying 'I will be addressing this point later in my submissions' as this displays a woeful lack of flexibility.

- **Planning.** The structure of moot submissions requires careful planning. Your moot speech must develop a logical line of argument in which each point builds incrementally on those that precede it.

Interpersonal skills

This category of skills refers to a person's ability to get along with other people so, in a work-place context, this involves factors such as team working, leadership, and communication that will help to get the job done efficiently.

- **Team working.** A moot team is comprised of two students so the ability to work together is useful. Of course, it is possible to prepare your own ground of appeal and turn up and deliver your submissions without any contact with your moot partner but mooting tends to work much better when both students in the team work together. It is beneficial to be able to share ideas with your moot partner and to practise your oral submissions with them. Moreover, you do have the ability to 'consult with your learned colleague' in response to judicial questioning and this can give the judge a very good impression of your team work (which is often part of the judging criteria in a moot). So mooting is a good opportunity for collaboration and to build on your team working skills.

- **Verbal communication.** The oral delivery of moot submissions and the requirement to answer questions posed by the judge will strengthen your verbal communication skills and build your confidence in speaking out in front of others.

Professional skills

These skills are those that have particular relevance to the legal profession but, remember, that many of these will nonetheless be a specific example of a broader skill that will be of interest to other employers. For example, a student who is proficient in legal research should be able to take the general skills of formulating a search strategy and filtering out irrelevant data and apply it in a non-law setting.

- **Legal research.** Thorough research is one of *the* skills at the heart of mooting. It offers a real opportunity to conduct wide-ranging research in an attempt to find an authority that gives unequivocal support to your submissions.

- **Legal problem solving.** A moot could be said to be the oral equivalent of a written prob-lem question as it involves the application of the law to a set of facts in order to resolve a legal dispute. As such, it is a great opportunity to strengthen your problem solving skills. In fact, students who moot usually find that their coursework marks for problem questions improve as a result.

- **Drafting.** The ability to encapsulate your submissions in a concise and precise way is central to the success of your skeleton argument thus provides some insight into the intricacies of legal drafting.

- **Advocacy.** As a simulated courtroom situation, a moot provides a unique opportunity to experience advocacy skills during the undergraduate stage of your legal education.

In conclusion, participation in mooting provides an unparalleled opportunity to develop a number of skills that are attractive to potential employers both within the legal profession and more generally. In particular, it strengthens independent research skills and oral communication. Moreover, for students hoping to enter into the legal profession, mooting should be an essential activity not just for the skills that it develops but because there is an expectation that prospective solicitors and barristers will have taken part in mooting because it involves skills so closely allied to the legal profession.

Finding opportunities to moot

You should be aware that students wishing to enter the legal profession will generally be expected to have found an opportunity (and time) to moot. It is a myth that mooting is only relevant to students who are prospective barristers: both avenues of legal practice, irrespective of the area of specialism, require students who are skilled in legal research and at formulating legal arguments in both written and oral form. Indeed, it is possible that you will find yourself disadvantaged in the highly competitive race for training contracts and pupillage if you do not have any mooting experience:

I ask all students at interview one of two questions about mooting depending upon whether or not they have mooted. If they have mooted, I ask them what they gained from it that would benefit them in practice but otherwise I ask 'why didn't you moot?'. I have never had a satisfactory answer to the latter question.

Training partner

It should not be difficult to get involved in mooting as it is likely that opportunities to do so already exist at your university. The vast majority of law schools run at least one internal moot competition and this may be supplemented by workshops and demonstrations that will introduce you to mooting and help you to understand what is expected. In addition to this, some universities use mooting as a method of assessment or as a tutorial activity. Finally, you may get the opportunity to compete against students from other universities if you enter one of the external moot competitions. If mooting is a compulsory part of one of your modules at university, you will not have to find an opportunity to moot as the opportunity will have been created for you as part of your studies but you may nonetheless want to think about building on that experience by taking part in internal and external competitions.

Internal mooting

An internal moot is one that is organised within your university and so it involves competing against your fellow students. It is usual for internal moots to start quite early in the academic year so look out for details within a few weeks of the start of term. The competitions are usually run on a knock-out basis and so you will get the opportunity to moot more than once if you win in the first and subsequent rounds.

Mooting is often organised by the student law society and there is usually a member of the committee with specific responsibility for mooting either known as the mooting officer or the master of moot. In this case, the obvious source of information about mooting and opportunities to get involved is the student law society website and/or notice board. Alternatively, you could contact a member of the committee and enquire whether there are any moots being organised. It is sometimes the case that mooting is organised not by the students themselves but by a member of the academic staff in which case you would need to identify the lecturer concerned and alert them to your interest in taking part and ask for details of the internal competition.

Practical advice: getting involved in internal mooting

If it is your first or second year and you have not taken part in an internal moot, you can resolve to do so in your final year. Find out now when the internal competition usually takes place and what you need to do to take part and make sure that you remember to enter.

If it is your final year, find out if there is still time for you to get involved with the internal competition. If it is too late for you to enter, see if there is anything that you can do to assist with the running of the competition such as help with organising judges or acting as a clerk. At least this way, you will have seen moots take place and gained some mooting-related experience as a result. You can then make your own arrangements to moot outside of the competition. You will find some advice on this in the section on organising your own moot further on in this chapter.

External mooting

Many universities enter teams in external mooting competitions that are organised on a regional, national, or international basis. These are more challenging competitions, generally requiring longer speeches and competing against the best mooters from other universities. As such, they can be a more impressive addition to your CV than an internal moot, particularly if you manage to progress through the knock-out rounds.

Entry into external moots varies from university to university. In some law departments, selection for participation in an external moot is based upon success in the internal competition; in essence, entry into the competition is part of the prize awarded to the winners. Alternatively, external moot teams may be selected from amongst any interested students who have previous experience in the internal moot. In both cases, participation in the internal moot is a prerequisite to entry into an external competition. There is sound reasoning behind this: the university wants to field its best and most able mooters to maximise its chances of success in the competition and, on the flip side, does not want to give a bad impression of the university by sending out inexperienced, ill-prepared, or unskilful mooters to represent the law school.

An alternative method of selection is based upon some sort of public speaking trial and it is also the case that sometimes students are selected from a pool of those who have attended a course about mooting skills. Finally, it may be that students who seem as if they would be competent and confident mooters are approached by the lecturer in charge of coordinating external moots to see if they would like to take part. Do not presume that you will be approached though as it may be that the lecturer responsible for selecting teams does not teach you or has never considered you as a potential mooter.

Practical advice: getting involved in external mooting

Find out who is responsible for selecting teams for the external moots and what method of selection is used. If there is a condition for entry, such as participation in the internal competition or attendance on a mooting skills course, make sure that you satisfy it and ensure that the person responsible for team selection is aware of your interest. If nobody seems to be organising entry into external competitions, find out for yourself how to enter and seek permission from an appropriate person within your law school (the Head of School if nobody else seems to be in charge of mooting) to get involved in the competition. Be aware, though, that agreement may not be forthcoming if you lack prior experience in mooting because the university's reputation is at stake if you put up a very poor performance. For this reason, it is advisable to develop your skills and establish your proficiency through internal competitions before seeking to represent the university in external moots.

There are a number of well-established external moots that you could consider entering. Some of these are general law moots, which means that the moot problem could involve any area of law, whereas others are specialist law moots such as the European law moot. Make sure that you find out what is required from each competition before committing to take part—they vary enormously in terms of the timing of the rounds and whether they involve written as well as oral submissions. If you are not sure what is involved, check the competition website or contact the organiser of the competition.

⚫ You will find an up-to-date list of these moots with the deadlines for entry on the Online Resource Centre.

- **ESU-Essex Court Chambers Moot.** This is a national moot open to undergraduate and GDL students at universities in the United Kingdom. The moot problems are set on the core subjects (the first four rounds in 2012–13 involved problems dealing with tort, crime, contract, and property law). Entry opens in mid-October and requires payment of an entry fee plus submission of an original moot problem. There are 64 teams in the first round and the competition proceeds on a knock-out basis through three heats, quarter-finals, semi-finals, and the final. The final is held in the Royal Courts of Justice and is judged by a senior member of the judiciary. The winners receive £1000 each and a mini pupillage at Essex Court Chambers. For more details, visit the competition website: **www.nationalmooting.org**.

- **ICLR Annual Mooting Competition.** The Incorporated Council of Law Reporting (ICLR) moot is a national competition open to undergraduate and CPE students in England and Wales. Entries open in September and close in mid-October and must be accompanied by a £15 fee plus an original moot problem. The first round of the competition is open to 32 teams and proceeds on a knock-out basis to the final which is held in April. The winning team receives a one-year full subscription to ICLR Online Full Suite. Further details can be found online: **www.iclr.co.uk/learning-zone/mooting**.

- **OUP and BPP National Mooting Competition.** This national competition is open to undergraduate law students, CPE students, and LLM students whose first degree was not law. There are 32 teams in the first round and it operates on a knock-out basis. The first round is held between October and December and the competition picks up pace after Christmas with the final being held towards the end of June at BPP Law School. The problems are based upon core subjects and you can find examples of problems used in the competition plus further information and advice on mooting on the OUP website: **www. oup.co.uk/academic/highereducation/law/mooting/**.

- **UK Law Students Association Moot.** This national moot takes place over five or six rounds (depending upon the number of teams entered) with the semi-finals held at the Old Bailey and the final at the Supreme Courts of Justice. Entries close towards the end of October and the competition is open to students at any stage of their legal education. Further details are available on the UKLSA website: **www.uklsa.co.uk/mooting_2.htm**.

- **UniLawStudents** in association with StretLaw Ltd, run a moot competition in which the winners have received mini pupillages and work experience. Forthcoming competitions will be found at **www.unilawstudents.com**.

- **UK Environmental Law Student Moot Competition.** This competition is open to undergraduate and postgraduate law students who have not commenced or completed a vocational training course. Students compete in teams of two but you do not have to work with someone from the same university and you can enter as an individual in which case the UKELA will try to find you a partner. Teams enter a skeleton argument for the appellant and the respondent and the best four are selected for the semi-finals which are based upon oral submissions. The final is held at UCL and is heard by Lord Carnwath, Justice of the Supreme Court. The prizes for the winning team include a mini pupillage at No 5 Chambers. Training is available prior to the competition at venues in London, Birmingham, Bristol, and Glasgow: it is free and takes place in the evening. Further details are available on the website: **www.ukela.org/rte.asp?id=22**.

- **Philip C. Jessup International Law Moot Court Competition.** This international competition attracts entrants from 550 teams from 80 different countries. The focus of the competition is public international law and is based upon a combination of written and oral submissions to address a dispute between nations heard in the International Court of Justice. The competition is open to teams of two to five students studying law or another degree with an international law component. The qualifying rounds take place between January and March with those teams that are successful proceeding to the preliminary oral rounds. There is a wealth of information including a detailed guide for competitors on the competition website: **www.ilsa.org/jessuphome**.

- **Tedlers International Law Moot Court Competition.** This international competition is also based upon written submissions (memorials) and oral pleadings in respect of a fictitious dispute between two states. It is open to all undergraduate and postgraduate European university students. Teams from over 40 universities compete in the national rounds with the successful teams going on to represent their countries in the international rounds held at the Peace Palace in The Hague. Detailed guidance on the different stages of the competition can be found on the competition website: **www.grotiuscentre. org/TeldersMootCourt.aspx**.

- **ELSA Moot Court Competition.** This competition is a simulated hearing of the World Trade Organisation dispute settlement system which is open to teams of four students from universities around the world. The final is held over one week at the WTO headquarters in Geneva and is attended by teams who have progressed from the selection rounds which, for teams from the UK, involves taking part in the European regional rounds. The competition website provides information and tips for successful participation: **www.elsamootcourt.org**.

- **International Intellectual Property Law Moot.** The focus of this moot is intellectual property. The competition is open to undergraduate and taught postgraduate students from universities around the world. Twenty teams are selected on the basis of two written memorials (each of approximately 3000 words) to attend the oral proceedings which take place over three days in Oxford during March. The final is judged by senior members of the judiciary: in 2012, the judges were Lord Justice Mummery, Lord Justice Kitchin, and Mr Justice Floyd. The instructions for the moot and the details of the problem used in 2013 can be found on the website: **www.oiprc.ox.ac.uk/moot.php**.

- **IASLA Space Law Moot Court Competition.** This moot was introduced to promote awareness amongst lawyers of the principles of space law and is based upon a combination of written memorials and oral submissions. It is open to teams of two to four students at undergraduate or taught postgraduate level who take part in regional rounds to determine which teams progress to the international finals held in July or August. Students do not need prior knowledge of space law in order to enter this competition and very detailed and helpful information is provided for entrants on the competition website: **www.spacemoot.org**.

- **The London Universities Mooting Shield (LUMS).** This moot is open to teams of four students attending one of the London universities and is organised on a league basis rather than operating a knock-out system. This means that all teams will be able to moot a number of times thus affording greater opportunities for skills development. Moreover, there are rounds based upon different advocacy skills in addition to traditional moot such as criminal law pleas in mitigation, civil applications, and commercial issues. There is also a junior moot for first-year students and first-time mooters and a training scheme for students taking part. For further details, visit the competition website: **www. lumshield.co.uk**.

- **DAC Beachcroft Mooting Shield.** This competition is open to students attending universities based in Yorkshire, Manchester, and the North-East and involves 16 teams of two students from LLB, LLM, CPE, GDL, LPC, and BPVC courses. It is organised on a knock-out basis with three initial rounds followed by semi-finals and a final, all of which are judged by lawyers from DAC Beechcroft and regional barristers' chambers. Moot topics are based upon the firm's areas of practice and the winning team receive a shield and a one week work placement. Further details are available in the careers section of the DAC Beachcroft website: **www.dacbeachcroft.com/careers/mooting**.

Practical advice: benefits of external mooting

Taking part in an external moot is an additional demand upon your time, particularly the international competitions involving written and oral rounds. However, it is well worth thinking about taking part as this is something that can make your application stand out to potential employers. Think about it like this: every law student at every university can take part in an internal competition but only a few students from each university can take part in each external competition. If you compete in, say, the OUP and BPP National Moot, you will be one of only 64 students who do so that year. Even if you are one of the 32 students who does not proceed beyond the first round, you still have something on your CV that is limited to a very small number of students. More than that, many of the external moots are judged by legal professionals, including senior members of the judiciary, or carry mini pupillages as a prize so offer useful networking and work experience opportunities.

Start your own moot

If there is no internal moot at your university or you have missed the opportunity to get involved in the current academic year or would simply like more opportunities to expand your mooting experience, the answer is to make your own arrangements to moot. Moots do take quite a lot of organisation but it would be worthwhile from your point of view as not only will you benefit from the opportunity to develop key employability skills as a result of taking part in a moot, you will also show the entrepreneurial spirit in creating your own opportunities that is likely to impress prospective employers. There are a number of ways that you could do this, depending on the circumstances at your university and the level of time and enthusiasm you are prepared to devote to the endeavour:

- **A single moot.** All you need to moot is three other students, a judge, and a moot problem. You might find that a lecturer is prepared to organise this for you, perhaps in one of your modules as a means of exploring a particular issue in more detail, and to act as a judge. Alternatively, you could ask a student with mooting experience to act as a judge for you and perhaps also to provide you with some hints and tips on preparation and presentation if you have no prior mooting experience. This could be a mutually beneficial exercise as the other student then gets to strengthen their own skills portfolio by taking the opportunity to mentor students with less mooting experience.

- **An internal competition.** If no internal competition exists, you can offer to start one. If there is a competition and you have missed it, then you could try to arrange another one. In this case, it would need to be different to the existing moot so you could suggest a separate competition for students who have never taken part in a moot before or propose a moot that is on specific subject matter: perhaps an intellectual property moot or a computer law moot. You might be able to persuade a local law firm to sponsor the moot by providing judges and/or prizes (a work placement for the winning team would be an excellent prize) in which case you could tailor the subject matter of the moot to suit the firm's area of legal expertise.

- **An inter-varsity moot.** Why not challenge another university to a moot? You can offer to make all the arrangements if they will travel to moot against you. You will then gain some useful organisational skills in finding a venue, a judge, and refreshments (budget permitting—ask the Head of School). You will need to contact local solicitors and barristers to find a judge which is, in itself, a useful networking opportunity. You could find a law firm that is half way between the two universities and ask to hold the moot at their offices or contact the local court to see if you could hold the moot there one evening or weekend.

- **Take on the professionals.** If you were feeling particularly ambitious and confident of your mooting ability, you could contact a local law firm or barristers' chambers and challenge them to a moot. Alternatively, you could throw down the gauntlet to the law lecturers by asking them to put forward a team to moot against you. Staff against student moots can be really entertaining, particularly if you recruit a panel of student judges as it gives them the opportunity to put their lecturers on the spot by asking tricky questions.

In essence, the opportunity to organise a moot is one that is too good to miss if you are trying to strengthen your skills portfolio. You could take this even further and make arrangements for the moot to be filmed to create a resource that can be used in future years by other students or you could edit it to create a short demonstration of mooting that could be used on the university website or shown at open days.

Practical advice: organising a moot

If you are going to organise a moot, you will need a problem, a set of rules and some judging criteria.

🌐 You will find some suggestions and examples on the Online Resource Centre.

Tell us

If you are trying to organise your own moot feel free to ask us for help. Who knows, we might offer to run a mooting skills workshop for you or to judge your competition. Alternatively, we might feature a film of your moot on our website: a great advertisement for your mooting skills! Or simply tell us how you got on. Get in contact at finchandfafinski.com/get-in-touch or @ FinchFafinski on Twitter.

Negotiation

All legal disputes that are resolved in court have a winner and a loser. One party gets everything that they want and the other party gets nothing. Negotiation is a method of alternative dispute resolution in which the parties, or their representatives, engage in a process of bargaining in order to reach an agreement that gives each of the parties something of what they want thus avoiding the need to litigate. Negotiation is based upon cooperation between seemingly opposed parties: although both sides want different things, agreement is only possible if they are prepared to compromise. Negotiation competitions offer an excellent opportunity to strengthen communication skills and to develop a flexible approach to fact management and problem resolution. These skills are central to legal practice but will be valued by employers in a wide range of professions as they enhance your ability to create consensus out of conflict and demonstrate a flexible approach to problem solving as well as showcasing excellent verbal communication skills. Participation in negotiation competitions will also help you to appreciate the way in which the law works in the real world which will help you to prepare for legal practice.

What is negotiation?

Everyone can negotiate. We negotiate all the time as we strike bargains with other people and make concessions that will ultimately gain us something that we want. For example, if you want to borrow your mother's car to go to the shops, you might promise to drive carefully and to pick up her dry cleaning for her. By giving another person something they want, we can persuade them to give us what we want. That is the essence of negotiation. Negotiation as a legal activity is not so very different. It is about mastering a set of facts that encapsulate your client's circumstances and managing these facts to obtain their desired outcome by ensuring that the other party also received something that is important to them. It is an excellent activity that encourages quick thinking and a flexible approach to problem solving as well as providing a valuable opportunity to develop communication skills in a professional setting.

In legal practice, negotiation is a method of alternative dispute resolution that seeks to resolve the dispute without the need for litigation. The role of alternative dispute resolution has increased dramatically in recent years with over 90% of civil and family disputes settled by negotiation or mediation rather than in the courtroom. It plays a role in the lives of most legal professionals and the ability to conduct an effective negotiation that reaches a settlement which is acceptable to both parties is an important legal skill. In recognition of the importance of negotiation as a skill in legal practice, it has become increasingly common for negotiation to be encountered by undergraduate law students, either as an extra-curricular activity or as part of a skills programme embedded within the curriculum. There is a national negotiation competition each year which is open to teams of undergraduate and postgraduate students and is organised by the Centre for Effective Dispute Resolution.

A typical negotiation scenario involves a set of common facts that are shared with both teams. Each side will also receive a set of confidential instructions that lays out the details of the problem from the perspective of their client and explains what it is that the client wants to achieve from the settlement. An extract from a negotiation scenario is given in Figure 4.4.

◎ You will find a more detailed scenario on the Online Resource Centre.

COMMON FACTS

Alice was injured when she was struck by a car driven by Jemima as she was crossing the road by the train station in Swindon. The police attended the accident and administered a breathalyser test to Jemima which was negative. There were no witnesses to the accident and the police do not intend to charge Jemima with any driving offence. Alice is seeking compensation for her injuries and both parties have instructed solicitors to reach an agreement on their behalf.

CONFIDENTIAL FACTS: ALICE

Alice knows that she had not checked for oncoming traffic when she stepped into the road as the only thing on her mind was getting across as quickly as possible as she was afraid she was going to miss her train to Leeds. However, Alice believes that the driver of the car was speeding and may have been using a mobile phone as she certainly had one in her hand when she got out of the car following the accident. Presumably the police would be able to check the driver's phone for recent calls if the matter progressed further. However, Alice does not really want the police to become involved as they would check her medical records and discover that a great many of her injuries had been sustained in the fight with her boyfriend the following day. She does, however, feel that she is entitled to compensation as she was hurt in the accident, albeit not as badly as she claimed at the outset, and instructs you to obtain as much money as possible from the driver of the car. At the very least, she would like £150 because this will enable her to repay the money she owes her boyfriend and she thinks that the driver of the car should pay for her train ticket as she was in too much pain to make the journey. When Alice was receiving medical treatment at the side of the road, her bag was stolen and she would like Jemima to cover the cost of replacing the bag and its contents which she values at £500.

CONFIDENTIAL FACTS: JEMIMA

Jemima absolutely refutes the allegation that she was using her mobile telephone at the time of the accident: she simply grabbed it as she jumped out of the car in case she needed to call an ambulance for the injured pedestrian. However, she does not want to take the risk that the police will become involved with the accident investigation as she had been taken prescription medication on the day in question and had been advised that she should not drive as it might make her drowsy or affect her judgement. Although she feels that she is not in any way to blame for the accident as Alice walked out in front of her car without looking, she is prepared to pay a sufficient sum of money to Alice simply to stop the matter from progressing any further but would prefer not to pay more than £2000 (this is half of the money in her savings account).

Figure 4.4 Extract from a negotiation scenario

◎ You may also want to look at the video clip of a negotiation competition on the Online Resource Centre to give you an idea of what is involved and how negotiation works in practice.

How does negotiation work?

Simulated negotiations usually involve two teams of two students with each team representing one party to a legal dispute. The four participants will sit around a table together and try to find a resolution to the dispute that suits both clients. It is usual for the negotiation to start with each side identifying the issues that they want to discuss during the course of the negotiation. This may take the form of a written agenda or the participants may simply list the points for discussion. There will usually be a fair degree of correspondence between the two sides about the issues to be discussed even though they will be coming at it from different angles: for example, the team representing Alice in the negotiation scenario in Figure 4.4 will want to discuss how much compensation she will receive whilst the team representing Jemima in that scenario will want to cover how much compensation she will have to pay. So there is a single issue here—the level of compensation payable—viewed from two different perspectives. Of course, there may be an issue that is raised by one side which will come as a surprise to the other side as it is not contained in their facts but this should not prove too much of a problem provided that it is revealed at this early stage of the negotiation. As part of this initial stage of the negotiation, the two sides will agree not only what points will be addressed but what order these will be taken in and this creates a structure for the negotiation.

Once discussion of the first issue has commenced, the negotiation will involve a combination of questioning and bargaining. Questioning is an important part of negotiation as both sides have only a partial knowledge of the facts having heard the story from the perspective of their client only. The more facts that you have, the easier it will be to bargain effectively so you should never be afraid to ask questions: if you are wondering why the other side want something, ask them. When you know why somebody wants something, you can exercise more flexibility and creativity in finding a way for them to have it that does not damage the interests of your own client.

As the negotiation progresses, the teams work through each of the issues and try to find a compromise position on each that is agreeable to their client. This can be difficult: some negotiations contain issues that simply cannot be resolved in which case you have to agree as much as possible and seek further instructions from your client on the outstanding matters. When agreement is reached, it is important to keep a note of the terms of the agreement so that you have an accurate record of the terms of the negotiated settlement. It is also worth checking and double checking with the other team to make sure that you have the same understanding of what has been agreed as each point is settled. It is most unfortunate to reach the end of a negotiation thinking that there is an agreement only to find out that the other side has a different understanding of what has been agreed, particularly if there is insufficient time remaining to revisit the issue.

By the end of the negotiation, you should have reached a provisional agreement to take back to your client. Remember that you cannot agree to settle on your client's behalf—you must achieve the best deal that you can and then put this to your client to see if they will accept it.

The stages of a negotiation

Negotiation training provided me with a crucial insight into the practical aspects of the commercial world. I was introduced to the importance of several skills in such a context including the ability to empathise with the other party whilst maintaining a strong grasp on my position through calm and coherent reasoning.

Ray-Shio, King's College London

The easiest way to explain how a negotiation works is to consider the stages of a negotiation that are used by the judges in the National Negotiation Competition. These cover the extent of preparation, the proficiency of the negotiation, the professionalism of the negotiators, and their insight into their own performance. Each of the judging criteria shown in the competition scoresheet in Figure 4.5 and the skills involved will be explored in detail in the sections that follow.

Negotiation competition scoresheet

Judge

Room

Name of Negotiation Scenario

Team letter

This team's overall ranking

1 = Most effective team
2 = Next most effective team
3 = Third most effective team
4 = Least effective team

Tie-break score

Total score based on the seven judging criteria below

I - Negotiation planning

Judging from their overall performance and apparent strategy, how would you describe how well-prepared for the negotiation this team was?

1	2	3	4	5	6	7
Flawless	Outstanding	Excellent	Very good	Good	Adequate	Weak

II - Concession management

How would you describe how effective this team was in managing the time and the nature of any concessions made; holding a position or being flexible as appropriate?

1	2	3	4	5	6	7
Flawless	Outstanding	Excellent	Very good	Good	Adequate	Weak

III - Teamwork

How would you describe how effective these negotiators were in working together as a team; sharing responsibility and providing mutual backup?

1	2	3	4	5	6	7
Flawless	Outstanding	Excellent	Very good	Good	Adequate	Weak

IV - Relationship between the negotiating teams

How would you describe the way in which this team managed its relationship with the other team, either contributing or detracting from achieving the client's best interests?

1	2	3	4	5	6	7
Flawless	Outstanding	Excellent	Very good	Good	Adequate	Weak

V - Outcome of session

In light of both the negotiation and the self-analysis, **and regardless of whether agreement was reached,** how would you describe the outcome of the session in respect of it having served the client's goals and interests?

1	2	3	4	5	6	7
Flawless	Outstanding	Excellent	Very good	Good	Adequate	Weak

VI - Negotiation ethics

To what extent did this negotiating team observe or violate the ethical requirements of a professional relationship?

1	2	5	6	7
Observed		Violated somewhat	Violated	Strongly violated

VII - Self-analysis

Teams should begin this 10-minute period by addressing the following questions:

(a) "In reflecting on the entire negotiation, if you faced a similar situation tomorrow, what would you do the same and what would you do differently?"

(b) "How well did your strategy work in relation to the outcome?"

Based on this team's self-analysis, how would you describe how well the team learned from this negotiation and how adequate was their process of self-analysis?"

1	2	3	4	5	6	7
Flawless	Outstanding	Excellent	Very good	Good	Adequate	Weak

Figure 4.5 Negotiation competition scoresheet

Negotiation planning

There is a fair amount of work to do prior to the negotiation. You must start with a careful analysis of the facts in order to identify the client's issues and to formulate a strategy that will enable you to use the facts to achieve your client's objectives. Start by creating a list of the objectives and work out what your best and worst positions are on each of these. In other words, identify your best case scenario outcome and your least-good-but-still-acceptable outcome as this identifies the parameters within which you will need to negotiate. For example, Alice in the earlier scenario has stated that she wants at least £150 compensation for her injuries so this is your bottom line on this issue—anything less is not acceptable to her. What you do not know is the other end of the spectrum as she has only said that she wants 'as much money as possible'. Elsewhere in the negotiation, information was provided about the nature of Alice's injuries so you would be able to conduct research into the level of compensation that would usually be payable to give you some guidance as to what you can expect to achieve on this issue. It is always important to have some idea of the parameters of negotiation on each issue. You can plot these on a scale so that you have a visible reminder of your scope to negotiate on each point. An example of this can be seen in Figure 4.6.

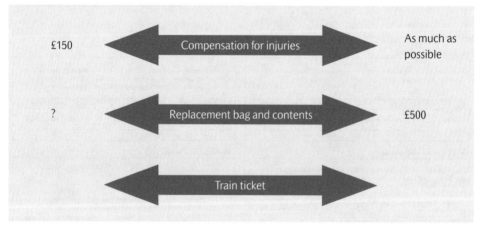

Figure 4.6 Room to negotiate on various issues

The benefit of listing the issues in this way is that you can see at a glance how they relate to each other, particularly if you plot what you have already agreed and try to offset any shortfall by aiming for a better deal on other issues. For example, if the negotiators representing Jemima refused to go higher than £175 in relation to compensation for injuries, you could see that this was towards the lower end of what you had hoped to achieve (although still acceptable to Alice). As such, you might want to try to achieve something closer to Alice's desired figure in relation to the handbag as a means of increasing the overall financial package. There are ethical issues in relation to this that will be discussed later in this section.

Research is an important part of negotiation planning as it is inevitable that there will be facts that you need to know that are not included in your instructions. This may involve the law—such as the quantum of damages for personal injury—or it may relate to other matters raised by the facts. For example, you would need to find out the cost of a train ticket from Swindon to Leeds in order to recover its cost for Alice.

The essence of the planning stage of the negotiation is the extrapolation of key information and its reorganisation into a series of inter-related goals, each of which could be satisfied by a range of outcomes. Essentially, it is a process of analysis and information management combined with an ability to distinguish between facts that are relevant and those of little or no significance. These are essential legal skills that will be important for students wishing to enter the legal profession as a solicitor or barrister. However, this ability to manage data and to sift through facts is one which will also be useful outside of the legal profession.

Concession management

Negotiation involves finding a mutually agreeable position that is some point between the desired outcome of the two parties. As such, an effective negotiation involves the timely and appropriate making of concessions—it is all about knowing what to give to the other side in order to gain something of greater importance to your client. Despite the planning that has taken place prior to the negotiation, concession management usually involves the need to think quickly and to work out how any particular concession affects the overall profile of the negotiation and whether it serves the client's interests. What will you give to get what you want and will that make your client happy? This requires that you are able to stand your ground to resist making unsuitable concessions and that you use the facts effectively to explain your position to the other team. Equally, it is important that you are flexible in suggesting ways that meet the needs of both clients: if both parties want the same thing and this is not possible, you need to be able to think of creative suggestions within the scope of your instructions that might resolve this potential deadlock. If it is not possible to divide up the pie, you will need to make the pie bigger!

There is a great skill in recognising objectives and identifying a creative way to achieve these objectives. Given the emphasis on alternative dispute resolution, this is an essential skill for those aiming to work within the legal profession. However, most forms of employment involve problem solving and the ability to respond in a timely and positive way to tricky situations with a creative and flexible solution is one that is of almost universal value.

Working in social work has made good use of the negotiation skills that I gained on my law degree. My work often involves conflict between different factions within a family and I am able to guide them towards agreement and help them to find consensus.

Kate, Southampton University

I decided not to practise law and instead took a graduate diploma in nursing and I now work as a psychiatric nurse. The ability to work through conflict in a calm way and to suggest alternative ways of resolving conflict is a key part of my role.

Dave, Southampton University

Team work

Negotiation usually involves teams of two students working together. Preparation is generally undertaken collaboratively and it is usual for students to allocate responsibility for particular aspects of the negotiation as part of the planning process. For example, you might agree that you will deal with the first issue about compensation for Alice's injuries and your partner will tackle the matter of recompense for the stolen bag. This helps to ensure that each person gets fully involved in the discussion once the negotiation gets under way and should go some way to ensuring that you are not talking over each other during the negotiation.

This may sound straightforward but it can be rather more tricky in practice. Imagine that you are listening to your partner trying to deal with an issue that you had both agreed would be their responsibility but you can see that they are struggling. Perhaps the other team has introduced factors that you did not foresee during your planning or maybe your partner has encountered a particularly hostile or argumentative opponent. Whatever the cause, you can see that they are struggling. Do you intervene? If you do, it may look like you are overriding your partner and not allowing them to play a full role in the negotiation. This would not be good team work. However, leaving them to struggle without providing assistance is also poor team work as there is an expectation of mutual backup and support. There is a fine line between interfering with your partner and abandoning them! Many students find it useful to think about how they will (tactfully) signal to their partner that they would like them to intervene and think about a form of words that can be used to precede an intervention that makes it less like a usurpation of their partner's role.

Managing communication is a central part of a successful negotiation. You will need to speak to both members of the opposing team and your partner at different points of the negotiation (see Figure 4.7) and it can be difficult, particularly if the discussion becomes heated, not to interrupt or talk over other people. However, a negotiation can become chaotic very quickly if people start talking over each other. Give some careful thought to how you will manage communications with your partner and the other team and consider what you will do to resolve the situation if the other participants become heated and start interrupting each other.

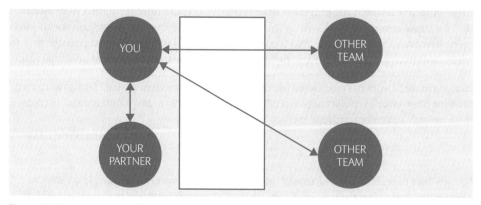

Figure 4.7 Managing communication in a negotiation

Finally, it is important to remember that team work in negotiation involves more than the distribution of responsibility for dealing with particular issues: it also necessitates the division of labour in terms of other matters such as keeping a record of what has been agreed—someone has to keep notes but it would not be professional if you were both writing at the same time—or making calculations if the negotiation involves finances.

The ability to work with colleagues in a cooperative and supportive manner that allows people to play to their strengths and bolsters their weaknesses is a highly valuable skill.

People who work well in a team are more attractive to employers as they can be used more flexibly and efficiently to achieve the objectives of the organisation. If you can work well with others, your skills can be used in a wider range of settings because they can be combined with the skills of many other employees. By working with others in a work setting, you will also be learning from them and enhancing your value to your employer. It is also a sign of professionalism to be able to work with others to achieve a common goal irrespective of your personal feelings for them.

Relationship between the negotiating teams

Negotiation is an unusual activity as it requires not only that you work in collaboration with a partner, who wants the same things that you want, but also that you form an effective working relationship with your opponents who, after all, seem to be trying to achieve the exact opposite of your client's goals. Despite this seeming opposition, it is important to remember that both sides share a common objective which is to reach an agreement that will give both parties something of what they want thus avoiding the need for litigation. A cooperative relationship that acknowledges the tension between the clients' objectives but which seeks to resolve this without acrimony between the negotiators is the best way to achieve this shared goal. This may be difficult to achieve if the other side take a hostile or aggressive approach to the negotiation but the ability to diffuse such an atmosphere is a valuable skill that can be developed through negotiation.

This aspect of negotiation will also help you to develop the ability to resist pressure as it will not always be possible to give the other party what they want without an adverse impact on your own client's interests. Any seeming lack of agreement has to be managed firmly and fairly without damaging the professional relationship between the negotiating teams.

Any number of workplace situations will involve differences of opinion or bring together people with competing goals. The ability to reconcile differences emphasises commonality and to achieve consensus out of conflict is a skill that will be valued by employers. The element of dispute management that is inherent in negotiation will enable you to experience the different strategies that can be used to manage conflict and to break deadlock.

Outcome of the session

There are a number of skills tied up with bringing the negotiation to a successful conclusion that achieves an outcome that is compatible with the client's goals and interests. It requires a good level of insight into the client's objectives and creativity in finding ways to serve these interests that are consistent with your instructions. You will need to ensure that you have covered all the points that were important to your client so you must manage your time carefully, particularly bearing in mind that the other side may raise points on behalf of their client that were not part of your instructions. You must be clear about what has been agreed during the session so you will need to summarise the points that have been concluded and draw attention to anything that is yet to be resolved. Remember that it is essential that the final outcome of the session is one that is likely to be acceptable to both clients as an unhappy client will not accept the terms of the negotiation and it will have been a pointless exercise. For this reason, it is always a good idea to check that the other team have covered all their points and have reached a provisional agreement that is acceptable to their client.

Negotiation makes great demands on your organisational skills as you have to balance all the facets of your client's case with the requirement of the other team's clients in order to find a mutually acceptable resolution within a tight time limit. As such, negotiation gives you the opportunity to demonstrate your ability to manage a complex situation and take account of a range of competing interests whilst still achieving your overall objective.

Negotiation ethics

Participation in negotiation will give you an insight into the professional framework of ethical behaviour in which lawyers operate. This is an important aspect of professional practice as it is incumbent upon all solicitors and barristers to act in an ethical way to uphold the standards and reputation of the legal profession. There is great scope for unethical behaviour within a negotiation as one way to achieve a better deal for your client is to misrepresent what it is that they would accept.

For example, if you had obtained a low sum for Alice in relation to her injuries, you might want to push for a higher sum in relation to her bag to compensate for this. However, if you said 'the value of the bag and its contents was £750' then this would be unethical as it is deliberate misstatement of the facts. Even a careless turn of phrase can give rise to ethical problems. If the other side offered you £150 as compensation for injuries and you replied 'that wouldn't be acceptable to my client' then this would also be a misrepresentation. Of course, if you simply said 'ideally, my client would be looking for more money than that' then this would be true so sometimes it is simply a matter of choosing your words carefully. Any deliberate or inadvertent falsehood is unethical and unprofessional and would be penalised by the judge in a negotiation competition.

I was asked a question about ethics at a pupillage interview and was able to draw on my experience in the National Negotiation Competition to demonstrate not just that I could comment on the problem that the panel posed but that I had some experience, albeit it in a competition rather than in real life, of recognising and resolving ethical issues.

Nick, University of Sussex

Practical exercise: ethical considerations

There are often ethical dilemmas hidden within the instructions from your client in a negotiation competition so you will need to ensure that you are able to spot these and be prepared to formulate a strategy to deal with them. For example:

- Alice has a medical report that outlines her injuries, some of which were quite serious. However, she tells you that some of these were sustained the previous day when she was beaten by her boyfriend during a drunken argument.

- Jemima tells you that she was driving whilst under the influence of prescription medication and had been told not to drive. During the negotiation, the other side ask if there was any factor that affected the quality of Jemima's driving.

- The other side ask 'what is the lowest sum that your client will accept?' You know that this is £150 but do not want to come away with such a poor settlement so you say that your client is ideally looking for a sum over £1000.

Think about the ethical consideration raised by these situations and ponder how you would deal with them.

☻ You will find some comment upon this on the Online Resource Centre.

Most industries operate within some regulatory framework and have expectations of standards of ethical behaviour. Participation in negotiation gives you an opportunity to get a feel for how such ethical requirements operate in practice and to understand the constraints that they place upon your professional practice. If you plan to work within the legal profession, you will have gained useful experience of the ethical issues that arise within law that will enable you to demonstrate to potential employers your awareness of the ethical considerations within the legal profession. If you are seeking employment in other industries, you could use your experience from negotiation to demonstrate your ability to adapt to an ethical framework and you may be able to draw parallels between the legal environment and the industry in question.

Self analysis

The national negotiation competition concludes with a period for reflection after which each team reflects on their performance in the presence of the judges. This centres around two questions:

• How well did your strategy work in relation to the outcome of the negotiation?

• In reflecting on the entire negotiation, if you faced a similar situation tomorrow, what would you do the same and what would you do differently?

The purpose of this is to ensure that students learn from their experience in the competition with a view to enabling them to improve on their performance in subsequent negotiations.

The ability to reflect on your own performance and evaluate it in a frank and honest way that picks up on areas of weakness and considers ways in which these could be strengthened is an important personal skill that is essential to self-improvement. This process of self-analysis can be exercised in a number of settings beyond the negotiation competition and will enable you to continually build upon your skills set and ensure that you are always seeking to enhance your performance.

What employability skills does negotiation develop?

Although negotiation is a common extra-curricular activity for law students and the alternative dispute resolution has a central role in legal practice, there is nothing essentially legalistic about negotiation. There will be a need to engage in formal negotiations in a range of professional settings but, more than this, the skills involved in negotiation in mustering facts and presenting these in a way that achieves your desired outcome are of wide application. This section highlights the ways in which negotiation skills are relevant to employability by using the categories outlined in Chapter 1 that have already been discussed earlier in this chapter in the context of mooting.

Practical skills

• **Problem solving.** Negotiation often involves factual situations that are outside the experience of the students taking part in the competition. For example, one recent scenario involved a dispute arising from an international space treaty and another concerned the breeding arrangements of a rare breed of donkey. Students often find it useful to investigate the factual setting to ensure that they have a grasp of the background within which the negotiation takes place but this can be complicated particularly when the subject matter is so far removed from existing knowledge.

- **Numeracy.** Negotiation scenarios often involve money and finances. It is often the case that part of a dispute involves money owed by one party to the other and these figures are sometimes complex, involving percentage profits/losses or predictions about costs. In such negotiations, the students who are able to manage the figures are always at an advantage. Remember also that finances might be at issue in negotiations involving contract formations and business arrangements as well as those involving disputes.

Personal skills

- **Time management.** As with any extra-curricular activity, you will have to manage your time carefully to ensure that your participation in negotiation competitions does not interfere with your other study commitments and deadlines. There is also a need to manage your time very carefully in the negotiation itself. You will have a limited period of time within which to try and reach a conclusion and it is up to you to ensure that all the points at issue are discussed and, hopefully, an agreement reached during that time.

- **Professional and ethical behaviour.** Professional ethics are a crucial aspect of negotiation. As the other side have no way of knowing details of the confidential facts that sets out details of your client's situation, it would be easy to misrepresent or mislead in order to obtain a more favourable outcome for your client. As such, negotiation provides an excellent opportunity to experience working within the parameters of an ethical framework and understanding how these influence professional behaviour.

- **Flexibility.** Negotiation will develop your ability to move beyond an initial strategy and to respond in a flexible manner to propositions put to you by the other side. As you only know half of the scenario, you will have to be prepared to incorporate the other party's goals into your approach to negotiation which will often mean a wide-ranging rethink of your planned strategy.

- **Planning.** Although flexibility is the key to successful negotiation, a good negotiation is based upon meticulous planning during the preparation stages. It is important that you muster all your facts and decide how to deal with them with as many alternative strategies as possible to help you to accommodate the interests that are likely to be raised by the other side.

- **Decision-making.** There are many decisions to be made during the planning stages of negotiation: what points need to be addressed, what is the range of acceptable outcomes on each point, what order will the points be taken in, and who will be responsible for doing what during the negotiation. However, by far the most difficult decisions will need to be made during the negotiation as you decide at what point to stop pushing for more and to accept the other side's suggested settlement on each issue.

- **Team working.** Negotiation is a highly collaborative activity. You should expect to analyse the scenario with your partner and to plan a strategy for the negotiation. This includes a planned division of labour in terms of which of you is to take the lead on particular points. However, the execution of negotiation is likely to involve a far more fluid approach to team working as you will need to be alert for problems encountered by your partner and to be willing and able to intervene to support them if they are struggling.

- **Verbal communication.** Negotiation requires that you are able to communicate the nature of your client's case to the other side in a clear and concise manner. You will need to be able to ask questions, using a variety of open and closed questions, in order to elicit information about their client's claim and to provide succinct summaries of what has been agreed to ensure that everyone is clear on the terms of the agreement reached.

Negotiation also depends upon your ability to listen to the other team as it is crucial that you have an awareness of what they want so that you can take it into account when formulating suggestions for a settlement.

Professional skills

- **Legal research.** The level of legal research needed to negotiate varies according to the nature of the problem scenario. Some negotiations require no legal knowledge whatsoever whereas others are based in a particular legal framework so that you will need to know, for example, the level of damages for personal injury so that you can work out what sort of figure to seek on behalf of an injured client. Remember, however, not to get too tied up with what would happen if the case went to court: a negotiation is an alternative to the strict application of the law in a courtroom setting so your legal research should guide your negotiation, not rule it.

- **Legal problem solving.** There is an element of problem solving inherent in negotiation in that you are interested in finding a resolution to a legal dispute but, as mentioned earlier, negotiation is not concerned with what the outcome of a case would be if it were heard in court. Nonetheless, it still involves the application of the law to a set of facts even if the likely legal outcome is disregarded in favour of a negotiated settlement. In essence, it is important background knowledge against which the negotiation takes place.

- **Negotiation.** It is difficult to think of any activity that will do more to develop your negotiation skills than taking part in a negotiation competition!

In conclusion, negotiation involves a range of skills that are of relevance to a career in the legal profession and which will enhance your employability in other non-law settings. Negotiation provides excellent experience in dispute management as a successful outcome is one that satisfies your client's objectives whilst still accommodating the needs of the other party to a dispute. It requires that you juggle facts with dexterity and present these in a clear manner to the other party whilst persuading them to agree to things that fulfil your client's objectives. It is a highly skilful activity that will develop your ability to manage facts and, more crucially, other people in a potentially acrimonious setting. It is invaluable for students wishing to practise law as it gives you first-hand experience of a common means of dispute resolution but it is also a fantastic (and fun) way of developing and demonstrating a wide range of the skills that will be useful in any number of professional settings and which will be valued by prospective employers.

....

I work as an estate agent and the skills that I learned by taking part in negotiation are one of the most valuable parts of the law degree for me. I often find myself marooned in the middle of the vendor and the purchasers as I try to persuade each of them to give the other just a little bit more of what they want to make a deal. Negotiation taught me to manage the facts, to look at them from the perspective of more than one party and to think about ways to present them that make them palatable to my clients.

David, Nottingham Trent University

....

Finding opportunities to negotiate

Whilst most students are aware of the importance attached to mooting as a method of developing skills and demonstrating commitment to a career in law, the benefits of taking part in negotiation competitions tend to be less well known. This is probably because nego-tiation competitions have only gained popularity in law schools in relatively recent years whereas mooting has a long-standing history as a method of inculcating key legal skills.

Opportunities to get involved in negotiation competitions tends to be more limited than opportunities to moot as many law schools have no internal negotiation competition at all and there is only one national competition. In the following sections, you will find guid-ance on how to get involved with these competitions and how to gain negotiation skills if your university does not run a negotiation competition.

Internal negotiation competitions

If there is an internal negotiation competition at your university or a training course or workshops available, be sure to take part in them. Remember that you will gain skills through participation in the training but will put these into practice in the competition so try to do both if you can find the time: it does not take long to prepare for a negotiation competition (far less than preparing for a moot) so concerns about distracting from your study time should not prevent you from taking part. Moreover, you should remember that building skills is an investment in your future career so you should try to make the time to take part in any negotiation activities that are available. In an ideal world, you should do this as soon as the opportunity arises so this could mean that you take part in negotiation activities in all three years of your studies.

If there is no negotiation competition at your university, then you could always start such a competition, either alone or in conjunction with other students to share the work-load (remember that working with others demonstrates skills in team work).

Practical advice: organising a negotiation competition

If you want to start a negotiation competition from scratch, there are certain things that you will need:

• **At least one negotiation scenario.** The negotiation scenario is comprised of sets of confidential instructions, one from each fictitious client, and may be accompanied by a set of common facts that are made known to both teams. It is possible to have a negotiation involving three or more parties but the dynamic of the negotiating relationship is trickier so it is advisable to start with a two-way negotiation if everyone is new to negotiation. The scenario will need to be distributed to the teams at least one day before the negotiation is due to take place. The organiser will need to ensure that teams are divided into two groups (one representing each party) and that the correct scenario is sent to each team.

• **A schedule of negotiations.** How many negotiations need to take place? This depends upon three factors: how many teams enter the competition, how many judges are available, and how you plan to organise the competition (a knock-out competition is likely to involve more rounds than using a points system to put the four highest scoring teams straight into the semi-final). If students are working in teams of two then four students may up a single negotiation and you can hold these simultaneously if you have more than one judge. Think about how long the negotiation will last (20 minutes should be ample for the first round provided you pick a relatively straightforward negotia-tion scenario) and be sure to give the judge(s) a break between sessions to gather their thoughts and work out the scores. It is a good idea to publish the schedule of negotiations in advance so that all students taking part are clear about the time commitment involved in the competition.

• **A set of rules that govern the competition.** It helps enormously if you can work out the rules in advance and publicise them rather than trying to deal with problems as they arise. As a minimum, your rules should specify the duration of each negotiation, the method of scoring, the timing of the rounds, whether teams can take a break, the degree of feedback provided to competitors, and the way that progression through the competition will be determined.

- **A score sheet that specifies the judging criteria.** The teams will need to understand in advance what skills are being tested and the judge will need to know how to allocate scores to the negotiations. It would be sensible (and easiest) to use the criteria that are used in the national competition but you could always create your own.

- **Facilities and equipment.** You will need to book suitable rooms for an appropriate amount of time, remembering that teams may need somewhere to wait before the competition and whilst waiting for feedback from the judges. You may want to arrange a video camera if you decide to record the negotiations and the judge will need a pen, paper, method of timing the negotiation, and water. The final should be held in a large venue and students invited to attend as this is likely to encourage participation in subsequent years.

👁 You will find some negotiation scenarios on the Online Resource Centre with an indication of an appropriate timeframe for the negotiation and its level of complexity. There are also some suggestions for rules and a sample of a score sheet.

Although it will be a wonderful opportunity to show your entrepreneurial spirit and organisational skills, there is a disadvantage to setting up a negotiation competition as it makes it harder for you to take part. Harder but not impossible. The essence of the problem is that other students might perceive that you have an advantage in that you would be able to see both sides of the negotiation in advance and you could 'fix' the draw to give yourself an advantage against a less proficient team of negotiators. The best way to deal with these problems if you do want to take part is to tackle them head on. When you first publicise the competition, make it clear that you are prepared to put the work into organising it because you want to take part and that you will deal with the issues surrounding the confidentiality of the scenarios by asking a lecturer to select and distribute them and the objectivity of the competition draw by putting names of teams into a hat and making the draw in public. Give students the opportunity to object to either of these suggestions or invite alternative solutions. In this way, you have been open about the possible problems of you taking the roles of organiser and competitor and publicised your proposed solutions so that all students who take part do so with the full knowledge of how these issues will be addressed.

Practical advice: getting negotiation experience

If all else fails and you are really keen to get some negotiation experience, you can do so provided you can find one other student who wants to get involved. You can negotiate against each other as individuals rather than in a team of two and you can use some of the sample scenarios that you will find on the Online Resource Centre. You would need to ensure that you did not give in to the temptation to peek at the other student's scenario (it will spoil your ability to negotiate if you know their side of the story) and give yourselves a set amount of time (half an hour should be fine) to reach a conclusion. To make the experience really worthwhile, you could film the negotiation and watch it back with your opponent afterwards and, having exchanged scenarios, discuss what you could have done differently.

Tell us

If you use the scenarios on the Online Resource Centre, we would be interested to hear what deal you reached and whether you think it was one that would please your client. Tell us at finchandfafinski.com/get-in-touch or @FinchFafinski on Twitter.

National negotiation competition

The national negotiation competition sponsored by the Centre for Effective Dispute Resolution (CEDR) takes place every year in the spring term, with the regional heats being held in February at four venues around England and Wales and the final taking place in April.

The competition is open to two teams of two students from each institution irrespective of whether they are studying at undergraduate or graduate level. This includes students on the CPE/GDL as well as LPC and BPTC students. The only restriction upon entry is that students may not compete more than once so you will need to think carefully about whether you want to take part whilst undertaking your undergraduate degree or to wait until you progress to the professional stage of your training.

Practical advice: when to take part

Very few universities teach negotiation skills to undergraduates although some may run extra-curricular workshops or training courses. This means that undergraduates could feel at a competitive disadvantage compared to LPC or BPTC students who will have taken a module on negotiation skills. However, as entry is limited to four students from each institution, there may be greater competition to take part at these later stages of study so it may be that you have more opportunity of being selected to take part in the national competition whilst you are an undergraduate. It is important to remember that, despite the lack of formal training, many undergraduate teams have won the competition so it is no bar to achieving success.

Progression from the regional heats to the national final is based upon the points awarded to each team over the course of two negotiations. In this competition, the lowest scoring teams are the most successful. Three teams from each of the four regional heats will progress to the final. The 12 qualifying teams receive a one-day training course at CEDR to help them to prepare for the final. The ultimate winner of the competition goes on to represent England and Wales in the international negotiation competition so it really is a prize worth having in terms of enhancing your CV and helping you stand out to prospective employers.

- National Negotiation Competition website: **www.cedr.com/skills/competition/**.
- International Negotiation Competition website: **www.chapman.edu/law/competitions/ dispute-resolution/international-negotiation-competition/index.aspx**.

Client interviewing

All legal disputes are initiated by people—either acting as individuals or as representatives of an organisation—thus dealing with clients is a central part of life within the legal profession. Clients are the legal equivalent of a doctor's patients but, unlike medical students who are taught how to deal with patients from the outset of their medical training, law students do not encounter clients during the academic stages of their legal education. Indeed, law is taught as an academic discipline in an abstract way so that students learn about legal principles and precedents rather than about the people whose lives are affected by the law and who are at the heart of every legal dispute. Client interviewing competitions seek to remedy this situation by providing some insight into the way that each case is started: with a person who arrives in a solicitor's office in the hope that their problem can be resolved. Admittedly, such competitions provided quite a limited insight into the true complexities of dealing with clients because there are no emotions involved in a simulation and nothing at stake for either the client or the solicitors but it is nonetheless an approximation of a real life situation that allows students to understand part of the day-to-day business of legal practice.

What is client interviewing?

As its name suggests, client interviewing is a practical legal skills exercise that involves a simulation of an interview with a client. The idea is that students, again working in a team of two, take on the role of solicitors to conduct a preliminary interview with a new client (played by an academic or another student) to elicit details of their problem and to formulate a course of action based upon the information disclosed during the interview. The students are given very little information about the client's problem in advance of the interview—just a few lines that capture the general nature of the issue as illustrated in Figure 4.8.

I have made an appointment for Mrs Geraldine Baker to see you tomorrow at 2pm. Mrs Baker is a new client and she has a problem with her neighbours.

Figure 4.8 A client interviewing memo

This may seem like a very small amount of information but it mirrors the situation in practice when solicitors conduct a first meeting with a new client knowing little or nothing about them other than the general nature of their problem. The person playing the role of the client will have been given a detailed account of their situation to enable them to present their problem to the solicitors and this may include instructions about their demeanour as illustrated in Figure 4.9.

The challenge involved in client interviewing is for the solicitors to find out as much of the information from the client scenario as possible so that they can propose a course of action for the client. This involves assessing whether the client has the basis for a legal claim and, if so, evaluating the strength of this claim. There is also a need to recognise non-legal aspects of the case, such as the client's distress and anxiety, and suggest avenues for dealing with these issues. All of this must be done within the time constraints of the competition and in accordance with the rules of ethical and professional practice.

⚫ You will find a video clip of client interviewing in operation on the Online Resource Centre.

Your name is Geraldine Baker. You are 45 years old and have lived at 81 Station Road in New Milton for two years since the breakdown of your marriage to your husband, Arthur. This is a terraced house in a much less desirable area than you were used to living in and you have not settled in well. You find it hard to get on with your neighbours, most of whom seem to think that you are snobbish and unfriendly. You are very much preoccupied by the unfairness of your accommodation situation and will explain this to the solicitors at length if they give you an opportunity to do so. You used to live in 'a nice house in a nice neighbourhood' until your husband left you for a much younger woman. He gave you a fair sum of money that represented half the value of the marital home which enabled you to purchase your current house but you resent the fact that he still lives there with his girlfriend whilst your standard of living had fallen dramatically. You live alone as your children, Jennifer (13) and James (12), attend boarding school paid for by their father and prefer to spend most of the school holidays in the family home with their father, his girlfriend, and their new baby. All of this causes you a great deal of anguish.

It is fair to say that you have never been on good terms with any of your neighbours and have rebuffed any overtures of friendship. The neighbours are aware that you think that they are 'beneath you' and 'common' so tend to avoid you but a problem has arisen with the people living next door that has escalated into a really nasty situation that has included damage to property and threats of personal violence. It all started six months ago when a new family, the Bells, moved into the semi-detached house adjoining your property. The Bells have three children (aged 6, 10, and 12) who like to play noisily in the garden which disturbs you whether you are outside or in the house. You complained about this about two weeks after the family moved in but were met with a very hostile reaction from the mother, Kate, who told you that she had no intention of modifying the way that her children play as it is important that they are able to express themselves and let off energy in their garden. Since then, the family have introduced more and more play equipment into the garden—a climbing frame, a trampoline and a water slide—which has increased the boisterousness of the children and the noise levels. The Bells have also had several parties to which all the neighbours and their children have been invited and these have been very noisy and lasted all day and into the early hours of the morning. Their garden is also overrun with animals: they have two dogs (that always seem to be outside and bark frequently), two cats (that dig up your flowerbeds), and numerous rabbits and guinea pigs (that are kept in hutches next to your fence and often smell). Last month, they installed a chicken run into the garden and have introduced eight chickens and a cockerel that crows at daybreak every day. You think that there must be laws that control what type and number of animals that can live in a residential garden but you do not know how to find out about this. You have complained a number of times in person but the Bells do not listen and are very rude to you.

Last week, your children came to stay and there was some hostility between them and the Bell children that involved bullying and threats of violence to the extent that your children would not go into the garden. You went round to speak to Kate Bell but she became very angry and, after an exchange of words, pushed you bodily down her front path and onto the pavement where you fell and hurt your back. You reported this to the police who called at the Bell's house but have since told you that Kate denied that this happened and they could not proceed without witnesses. Since then, you have been subjected to a hate campaign by the Bells. You have had paint stripper poured on the bonnet of your car, your tyres have been slashed, and excrement smeared on your front door. Your children were so upset that they asked to go home to their father two days early and have since said that they do not want to visit the house again. The Bell children have shouted abuse at you in the street and when you bumped into the family in the supermarket. Basically, they are making your life an absolute misery and you want it to stop. You are at the end of your tether.

Figure 4.9 A client interviewing role

How does client interviewing work?

In a client interviewing competition, a pair of students have a set period of time— usually 20 minutes—to conduct an interview that elicits details of the client's problems so that they can offer some preliminary legal advice and formulate a plan for achieving the client's objectives. In many respects, the success of the interview rests upon the effectiveness of the approach to questioning taken by the interviewers as this is the key to obtaining all the necessary information from the client. However, it can be difficult to work out what questions to ask the client as only scant information about the nature of the client's problem is provided prior to the interview. Part of the process of preparing to interview should involve speculation about what the problem might be as this will enable you to formulate questions and to consider what area of law might be involved.

Practical exercise: brainstorming the issues

The statements contained in the client memos tend to be very general. A problem with a neighbour, for example, could cover any number of different situations in addition to the rather straightforward one involving noisy children and animals that Geraldine experienced (in Figure 4.9). Test your ability to predict a client's problem from a general statement by thinking of at least three further scenarios that could have been described as 'a problem with a neighbour'.

☙ You will find some suggestions on the Online Resource Centre.

The interview will generally start with a series of questions aimed at eliciting factual details about the client—contact details, occupation, and other such necessary information. This gives you an opportunity to assess the demeanour of the client: perhaps they are relaxed and chatty or nervous and uncomfortable. You should use this stage of the interview to think about your interviewing style and ensure that it is suitable for the type of client that is in front of you. This initial stage is often a good opportunity to deal with the formalities of the interview such as its cost and duration as well as the other requirements of Practice Rule 15 (discussed in detail in the section that follows).

With the preliminaries out of the way, you can move on to the questioning stage of the interview. It is often a good idea to start by inviting the client to provide further details of their problem: something along the lines of 'I understand you have had a problem with your neighbour. Perhaps you could tell me a little more about it' would suffice. Of course, if the client does not respond to this then you will need to use closed questions—questions that require a specific response such as 'how long have you lived in your house?'—to elicit details from the client. Using a combination of questioning and listening, you should gain a good insight into the client's problem. Reflect this understanding by summarising the essence of what they have told you and check to ensure that they agree that you have captured the central points. You are then ready to offer advice and consider a way forward for the client.

The stages of client interviewing

Client interviewing taught me to think ahead at the same time that I am listening to a client and to create a mental chronology of the client's story that helps me to ask sensible questions. I was really pleased to have the experience from the competitions when I started to deal with real clients in practice.

Beth, University College London

As with negotiation, there is a national client interviewing competition for law students and most internal competitions replicate the format and judging criteria of the national competition. The judging criteria identify 11 areas in which students are expected to be able to demonstrate proficiency. These skills are discussed in the sections that follow.

Establishing a professional relationship

The relationship between solicitor and client is governed by the rules set out in the Solicitors Regulation Authority *Code of Conduct*. This identifies ten 'mandatory' and 'all-pervasive' principles that 'define the fundamental ethical and professional standards' expected of solicitors. Chapter 1 deals with client care and sets out a series of outcomes that must be achieved to ensure that the client understands the service that will be provided, how it will be delivered, and what it costs. It also provides that the client must be made aware of the steps that they can take if they are unhappy with the service provided. It then identifies a series of indicative behaviours that show that these outcomes have been achieved. You will need to demonstrate these behaviours in establishing a relationship with the client. An extract from the *Code of Conduct* is provided in Figure 4.10 to give you an idea of what is expected but you should familiarise yourself with its full requirements and think about how you will satisfy these in your interview.

Dealing with the client's matter

IB(1.1) Agreeing an appropriate level of service with your client, for example, the type and frequency of communications.

IB(1.2) Explaining your responsibilities and those of the client.

IB(1.3) Ensuring that the client is told, in writing, the name and status of the person(s) dealing with the matter and the name and status of the person responsible for its overall supervision.

Fee arrangements with your client

IB(1.13) Discussing whether the potential outcomes of the client's matter are likely to justify the expense or risk involved, including any risk of having to pay someone else's legal fees.

IB(1.14) Clearly explaining your fees and if and when they are likely to change.

IB(1.15) Warning about other payments for which the client may be responsible.

Complaints handing

IB(1.22) Having a written complaints procedure which:

    (a) is bought to the client's attention at the outset of the matter.

    (b) is easy for clients to use and understand, allowing for complaints to be made by any reasonable means.

    (c) is responsive to the needs of individual clients, especially those who are vulnerable.

Figure 4.10 Extract from SRA *Code of Conduct*: Indicative Behaviours

There is often a distinct power imbalance in the solicitor–client relationship and the onus is on the solicitor, as the professional providing a service, to create an appropriate environment in which the client feels comfortable and which is conducive to the sharing of sensitive information. The ability to establish appropriate professional relationships with a range of different individuals will be important in any employment context, particularly one that involves dealing with clients outside of the profession in which you work.

Obtaining information

Without information, you cannot evaluate the client's problem, offer advice, or do any of the other things that are part of client interviewing. In essence, the interview will not work if you are not able to obtain information from the client. You need to be able to formulate a strategy for questioning the client that will obtain a clear and comprehensive picture of their problem. This will generally need to be a combination of open and closed questions:

- **Open questions** are those which invite a general response: in essence, they give the client space to talk and allow you to find out more about the issue at hand. They are often used at the start of an interview to obtain an overview of the client's problem that is then explored in greater detail with some follow-up closed questions. For example, you might ask 'what problems have you been experiencing with your neighbour?'.

- **Closed questions** are more specific and can only be answered with a narrow range of responses, usually by answering 'yes' or 'no' or by providing factual information. For example, you might ask 'how long have you lived at your current address?' or 'did anyone witness the altercation between you and your neighbour?'. These questions are useful for obtaining the specific details. They enable the interview to control the flow of information so can be a good way to elicit details from a client who seems reluctant to provide them or is hesitant about speaking but are also a useful method of quelling a stream of detail from an over-talkative client.

You can plan a line of questioning prior to the interview but you will need to be flexible in order to adapt to the client's manner and degree of engagement with the interview. You may also find that you need to formulate a different approach to questioning if the client's problem is not one that you have anticipated.

The key skill here is the ability to create a questioning strategy that elicits relevant information in an effective manner whilst still maintaining a professional and empathetic relationship with the client. You are demonstrating your ability to balance your goal in obtaining details of the client's problem with an awareness of the client as a person rather than as a source of information. This skill will be particularly valuable in a professional setting that involves dealing with clients on a regular basis.

Learning the client's goals, expectations, and needs

It is important that you do not get carried away with the niceties of the application of the law to the client's problems but that you take into account what the client wants to achieve. The most obvious legal solution is not necessarily the outcome that the client wants or needs so this aspect of client interviewing requires that you acknowledge the context in which the legal dispute takes place. Perhaps Geraldine could bring legal proceedings against her neighbours but will this ultimately make her relationship with them better or worse? What does she actually want—a court case or a quiet life? As part of the process of advising a client, you may need to modify their expectations of what a solicitor can achieve for them. You cannot allow a client to harbour an unrealistic expectation about the strength of their claim or the likely outcome of your intervention.

You must find out what the client wants, make sure that it is realistic and then respond by tailoring your advice to fit their objectives. In an employment context, this will demonstrate your awareness of the needs of others and your ability to evolve flexible solutions that adapt to their requirements.

Problem analysis

This is the stage of the interview at which you reflect your understanding of the client's problem based upon the information that you have elicited and your appreciation of what the client hopes to achieve. You should aim to recognise both the legal issues and the non-legal elements of the problem. Ideally, you should summarise the client's problem and check whether they agree that you have captured all the important points.

This is that stage of the interview at which you demonstrate that you have untangled all the detail and got to the heart of the problem. It demonstrates your ability to distinguish between key facts and peripheral detail and to provide a concise summary of complex events. Employers will value the ability to highlight the essential issue in a clear and concise manner.

Legal analysis and giving advice

This stage of the interview involves the application of the law to the facts of the client's problem. There is a limit to how much legal advice you would be expected to give at a preliminary interview but you should be able to identify the relevant area of law and explain this to the client in a way that can be understood by a layperson and without overloading them with detail.

In any industry involving interaction with customers or other non-experts, you may need to be able to explain specialist concepts to an audience of lay people. The key skills that you are demonstrating here is your ability to be understood by people who lack your level of knowledge or expertise.

Developing a reasoned course of action

All legal disputes involve at least two options—take legal action or do nothing—and most will raise even more possibilities so you will need to be able to set out the possible courses of action for the client. Not only will you need to explain these different options, you should also provide some brief insight into the strengths and weaknesses of each course of action for the client.

The skill here is to identify all the possible alternatives and to evaluate their relative merits. This is an analytical ability that can be divorced from a legal context and deployed in any professional setting.

Assisting the client to make an informed choice

Having set out the possible courses of action for the client, you should assist them to reach a decision as to which of these is preferable, taking into account their overall situation including their emotional needs. You cannot make the decision for the client neither should you leave them to make up their minds without support and guidance. You should be able to point out the wider implications of any particular course of action, advising not only on the legal dimension but also the economic, social, and psychological consequences of their choice.

This part of the interview demonstrates your ability to see the bigger picture as you look beyond the legal ramifications of a particular course of action to consider the overall impact on the client's life. You are also demonstrating your ability to guide and counsel the client as you assist them to reach a sensible decision about the way forward.

Concluding the interview effectively

The interview should end with the client feeling that they have received the assistance that they sought and that they have made a step forward with resolving the problem that led them to seek an appointment with a solicitor. They should have a clear idea about what will happen next so you will need to be sure that they know what you are going to do, when you are going to do it, and when they can expect to hear from you. You must also ensure that they have understood what is required if there is anything that you need them to do before your next meeting such as make a doctor's appointment or send copies of documents to you.

The end of the interview will shape the impression that the client has of the service that they have received so it should be courteous, efficient, and professional. The ability to establish and maintain appropriate professional relationships is an essential aspect of business practice.

Team work

It is usual for students taking part in a client interviewing competition to work in pairs so there will be an opportunity to develop your ability to work collaboratively with others. This should involve both the preparation and execution stages of the interview. Although you will be able to work out which of you will deal with particular aspects of the interview as part of the planning process, this should not be a hard and fast division of labour but one which adapts to the interview situation as it develops as it is often the case that a client will interact more effectively with one of the interviewers. Alternatively, it may be that you need to intervene to assist your partner if they are not having any success in eliciting facts from the client on a particular issue: perhaps, as the observer, you can think of an important question that your partner has not asked or you can see a way to approach an issue that is upsetting the client differently. Think carefully about how you will deal with intervention if it is necessary as it could undermine your colleague if you do it clumsily and it may alarm or confuse the client if they feel that they are being questioned by two people at the same time. Make sure you stay engaged with the interview when you are not talking to the client: look at whoever is speaking and make notes of any important points that are raised.

The ability to work with others in an effective and professional manner is a real asset in the workplace so you should take any opportunity that arises to develop these skills and to demonstrate your ability to cooperate and collaborate to potential employers.

Ethical behaviour

The client may disclose facts which raise moral issues that you will need to address, particularly as the client is aware that their discussions with you are confidential. You will need to recognise and address any ethical issues and deal with them in an appropriate manner without being judgemental or damaging your relationship with the client. For example, if your client says 'my neighbours have accused me of beating my children' then you should not ignore this and will need to ask 'do you beat your children?' as this raises a risk to the welfare of the children that may not be something that can be kept confidential.

Ethical issues can arise in any profession. Participation in client interviewing competitions will ensure that you encounter tricky moral issues and give you an opportunity to demonstrate your professionalism in addressing them and in asking difficult questions without losing composure.

Post-interview reflection period

After the interview is concluded and the client has left, the final stage of the client interviewing competition involves a period of reflection in which the students talk to each other (in the presence of the judges) about the interview. This is an opportunity to identify any limitations in the way that the interview was conducted and to consider alternative ways in which it could have been approached that would have been stronger and more effective. There should be an evaluation of the way in which the client's problems were handled and the extent to which the client's feelings were recognised and taken into account.

Employers are often interested in your ability to evaluate your own performance. This reflective stage of the client interviewing competition will enable you to demonstrate to employers that you are able to recognise your own limitations and identify ways of strengthening your own performance.

Figure 4.11 shows a simple schematic of the key steps in a client interview and the associated skills that are being used and developed at each stage.

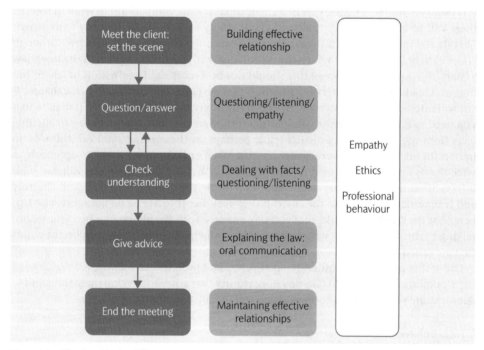

Figure 4.11 Client interviewing skills

What employability skills does client interviewing develop?

A client interviewing competition involves the use of a very general set of transferable skills in a legal setting. In other words, the skills at the heart of this activity have no necessary connection with the law or legal practice but will demonstrate your ability to deal with people and information in a way that could be adapted to any number of professional settings. This section highlights the way in which negotiation skills are relevant to employability by using the categories outlined in Chapter 1 that have already been discussed earlier in this chapter in the context of mooting and negotiation.

Practical skills

- **Numeracy.** The client's problem may require you to make financial calculations. For example, you may need to work out how much redundancy pay the client should receive or calculate the sum that they will receive if they have an entitlement to a particular percentage of profits.

Personal skills

- **Time management.** Participation in any extra-curricular activity will necessitate that you balance the time commitment involved with the need to keep up with the demands of your studies. There will also be a need to manage your time carefully in the interview itself to ensure that you conclude within the set time. This can be difficult if you encounter a particularly talkative client or one with a very detailed problem but it gives you good experience of achieving goals within tight time constraints.

- **Professional and ethical behaviour.** Client interviewing offers an excellent opportunity for you to understand and apply professional rules as you must work within the framework of the requirements of the SRA *Code of Practice*. It is also likely that you will have to address ethical issues as these are often included in interviewing scenarios.

- **Flexibility.** However well you plan your interview strategy, it is likely that you will need to adapt this to suit the needs of the client and the nature of their problem so it is a good opportunity to demonstrate your ability to be responsive and flexible.

Interpersonal skills

- **Team working.** The way in which you work with your partner will be a key component that determines the success of the interview. You need to strive for an even level of participation whilst also responding to any difficulties that your partner may encounter thus demonstrating your supportive approach to working with others.

- **Verbal communication.** Effective verbal communication is at the heart of a successful interview. You have to be able to ask questions that provide a framework for the interview and which elicit the information that you need whilst listening carefully to the detail of the answers provided. Your explanation of the law and the possible courses of action to the client need to be clear and easy for them to understand.

- **Customer service.** Interviewing is an opportunity to experience client care in action. You will have to develop a rapport with the client and ensure that you create an environment in which the client is comfortable to share sensitive information with you. The client must be treated in a professional and courteous manner that is in line with the requirements of the SRA *Code of Practice* and you should ensure that the client goes away from the interview feeling more positive than they were at the start and clear about what is going to happen next.

Professional skills

- **Legal problem solving.** Dealing with a client is the real world equivalent of writing an answer to a problem question. It requires you to focus on the relevant facts, match them to the correct area of law, and work out what will happen when the law is applied to the factual situation.

- **Interviewing.** The whole purpose of the competition is to give you an opportunity to develop your interviewing skills.

In conclusion, interviewing is not an essentially legal skill: it is a set of highly desirable employability skills that are exercised in a legal setting but which could be transferred to any situation that involves the use of questioning to elicit facts from a client. It is a valuable activity for students who wish to practise law because all solicitors and barristers have to deal with clients and to develop an effective method for extracting the relevant details of their case from them. For students who aim to work in a non-law profession, client interviewing is still a valuable activity as it provides an opportunity for you to experience fact-finding and to learn how to manage people.

Tell us

Tell us about your experiences with mooting, negotiation, and client interviewing. Did your involvement with these activities help you to get work experience or a training contract or pupillage? Perhaps you found the skills that you learned useful once you were working. Let us know at finchandfafinski.com/get-in-touch or @FinchFafinski on Twitter.

Finding opportunities to interview

As with negotiation, it is still sadly the case that some law schools do not provide any opportunities for students to learn interviewing skills or to take part in interviewing competitions. However, more and more universities are recognising the importance of client interviewing as a skills-rich extra-curricular activity so if it is not available yet at your university, campaign for it to be introduced or, better still, take the initiative and start it yourself. In the sections that follow, you will find information about internal client interviewing, including advice on how to start your own competition, and the national and international competitions.

Internal client interviewing competitions

If an internal competition already exists at your university, you should ensure that you take part. The process of eliciting information from a real person, analysing their problem and formulating some preliminary advice offers you an insight into the business of working within the legal profession and will help you to appreciate the real-world application of the law that you study. Negotiation is all about people and their problems, so being involved in a negotiation will make the law come alive to you in a way that purely academic study can never achieve.

Entry into an interviewing competition should not be too onerous in terms of the time commitment involved. You will need to ensure that you have a provisional structure in mind for the interview that covers matters such as costs, confidential and other professional matters as well as ensuring that you think about the way in which you will approach questioning but preparation is minor compared to mooting. It would be a good idea to get involved with the competition as early as possible in your academic career: consider that the first year is when you find out what it is all about and the second year is when you achieve success in the internal competition and the final year (or thereafter as a post-graduate) is when you intend to represent your institution in the national competition. Of course, it may not work out like this but it is a good objective. Alternatively, you might want to volunteer as a client in your first year so that you can see client interviewing from the 'other side of the table' as this will help you to understand what is required if you enter the competition the following year. Some students prefer to gain their practical skills experience during their first and second years to ensure that they have a wealth of experience to support their applications for work placements, training contracts, and funding for the postgraduate stage of legal education as well as leaving them time to really focus on their studies in the final year.

If no client interviewing competition exists, as with mooting and negotiation, the option is available to start one yourself which, again, shows your ability to create your own opportunities where none existed previously. Alternatively, you could raise support for the idea of a client interviewing competition amongst the student body and seek to persuade your law school to organise one for you. Either approach achieves your objective of creating an interviewing competition to enter but the first gives you more opportunity to develop organisational skills whilst the latter requires less time commitment from you.

Practical advice: organising an interviewing competition

An interviewing competition is based upon a simulated interview between two solicitors working together and a new client with a fictitious legal problem. As with negotiation, you will need scenarios, rules, judging criteria, and a judge plus you will also need someone to act as a client for each team of lawyers as well as someone to judge their performance.

⊌ You will find a pack of information about organising an interviewing competition with a selection of interview scenarios on the Online Resource Centre.

National client interviewing competition

There is a national client interviewing competition held each year and, in 2013, it attracted entries from 28 universities across England and Wales. The four highest scoring teams from two regional heats (held in London and Sheffield in 2013) are joined by a team from the institution of the winning team from the previous year's competition in the final.

Practical example: competition scenarios

The national competition focuses on a particular area of law each year to help students in their preparation. Students should think about the possible problems that could arise in relation to that area of law and decide what sorts of questions they may need to put to the clients that they encounter. This can be shaped by the memos that are sent to the teams prior to the competition in which they receive some indication of the nature of each client's problem.

For example, in 2013, the focus of the competition was serious violent crime and the client memos for the regional heats were as follows:

• You have an appointment to see Ed Barnes on Saturday 26th January. Her/his contact details: 14 Highlands Road, email address **edbarnes88@gmail.com**. S/he seems rather upset and worried. S/he says it is to do with the death of her neighbour.

> • I have made an appointment for you with Gerald/Geraldine Fisher. S/he wouldn't say exactly what was involved. However s/he did ask if you would be able to explain what was involved in being an accessory to an offence. I assured her/him that you would have that information at the interview.

The teams conduct two interviews with different clients in front of a panel of three judges who assess their performance on the basis of a set of criteria which take into account their interpersonal skills as well as their ability to handle a legal problem. The winning team will go on to represent England and Wales in the Louis M Brown and Forrest S Mosten International Client Consultation Competition. You will find further details about the national and international competitions on the following websites:

- **www.clientinterviewing.com/index.asp**
- **www.brownmosten.com**.

Skills summary

The practical legal skills activities covered in this chapter develop skills in many categories of your skills portfolio, as shown in Table 4.1.

Table 4.1 Skills portfolio: practical legal skills

Skill	Mooting	Negotiation	Interviewing
Practical skills			
Written communication skills	X		
Numeracy			
Problem solving	X	X	X
Use of IT			
Personal skills			
Time management skills			
Professional and ethical behaviour	X	X	X
Organisational skills			
Flexibility			
Planning			
Decision-making			
Interpersonal skills			
Team working	X	X	X

Skill	Mooting	Negotiation	Interviewing
Verbal communication	X	X	X
Customer service		X	X
Leadership			
Professional skills			
Legal research			
Legal problem solving	X	X	X
Drafting	X		
Negotiation		X	
Advocacy	X		
Knowledge of legal practice and procedure	X	X	X
Interviewing			X
Presentation skills			

WHERE NEXT?

Mooting, negotiation, and client interviewing offer enormous potential as ways of developing and demonstrating key employability skills. They will be of particular interest to prospective employers within the legal profession—in fact, there is rather an expectation amongst law employers that you will have done at least one of these activities during your degree—but they can be used to impress employers in any field of employment. The best advice that we can give is that you should aim to try each of these activities at least once and at the earliest possible point in your degree. This gives you plenty of time to continue with the activity if you are good at it—bear in mind that your application will stand out far more if you have represented your university in a national competition and it will take time to build up your skills to the necessary standard—and you can use it to help you get work experience in your first summer vacation if you take part in your first year. But it is never too late to get involved so make the decision to find out what opportunities exist to participate in these activities at your university and sign yourself up! If no opportunities exist, make your own by starting up an internal competition: this in itself will show your commitment to developing relevant legal skills and your leadership, organisation, planning, and team work skills.

Part III

Building employability skills

This part of the book advises you on ways in which you can build your portfolio of employability skills. Chapter 5 explores the ways in which your spare time and voluntary activities can enhance your skills before moving on to Chapter 6 which deals with vital commercial awareness and networking skills. Chapter 7 guides you through finding and making the most of work experience.

Volunteering, societies, and interests

5

INTRODUCTION

The focus in this chapter will be on the contribution that activities undertaken in your spare time can make to your skills portfolio. It will build upon Chapters 3 and 4 that explore the skills involved in academic study and practical legal activities and make suggestions as to how you can use a range of different activities to strengthen and expand your employability skills. This chapter will encourage you to dissect everything that you do outside of your study time in order to discover how skills-rich your hobbies, interests, and leisure pursuits are and to explain how these activities can be used to demonstrate the skills that are valued by prospective employers. The first part of this chapter will be structured around the employability skills identified in Chapter 1 whilst the second section will go into more detail of popular skills-rich activities.

Your time at university should not be all work and no play. Not only would this leave you feeling overworked and overtired but you will be missing out on opportunities to have fun and make friends outside of your course if you neglected the social side of university. Moreover, employers are going to want to see evidence that you are an interesting person with good social skills who has done more with their three (or four) years at university than sit in the library and read law books! So do not be afraid to use your leisure activities as a means of demonstrating to employers that you have the skills that they value and that will make you a more effective and professional employee. This chapter will help you to use activities other than studies to showcase your skills to prospective employers and suggests ways that particular employability skills can be developed to inspire students who are struggling to fill gaps in their skills portfolio.

Thinking about spare time activities

We are using spare time activities in this chapter as a broad term to cover all of the ways that you spend your leisure time. As such, it includes activities that have no obvious social elements such as hobbies pursued on a solitary basis as well as activities with a more obvious social element such as team sports. The chapter also includes things such as charitable work and other volunteering opportunities as these offer great opportunities to expand and strengthen key employability skills. In essence, it is a chapter that covers anything that is not studying, taking part in extra-curricular skills activities, or engaging in paid employment.

Practical exercise: thinking about your activities

Make a list of all the things that you do with your time that are nothing to do with law, study, or employment. This can be things that you do with other people or that you do alone and should include both organised activities and informal ways of spending your time. As you read the sections in this chapter, try to identify at least one employability skill involved in each of your spare time activities: for example,

- **Horse riding.** Keeping two horses is a lot of work. Even if I don't have time to ride, they have to be fed, watered, groomed, and mucked out every day whether or not I have exams coming up or a coursework deadline so I think that this demonstrates my **time-management skills** and my ability to juggle conflicting demands on my time.

- **Ice hockey.** I've been playing competitive ice hockey for a couple of years now and it is an important way for me to relax and let off steam as well as great exercise. In terms of employability, there is an obvious **team work** element to the sport as we have to operate as a single unit when we play and focus on what will work best for us as a team rather than our individual glory. I help to coach the youth team too which has developed my **leadership** skills.

- **Wildlife volunteer.** I work with the local wildlife trust in my spare time. The work is varied—it might involve clearing an area of woodland, nursing injured animals, or helping with fundraising or public awareness events. I can see a definite improvement in my **organisational** skills as I've been given projects of my own to coordinate and the work with the public has really strengthened my **oral communication skills** as telling people about our work is a crucial means of gaining support.

The ability to identify key employability skills that are developed by the activities that you undertake in your spare time is a good first step towards using these activities to enhance your employability. What you are doing here is identifying a skill that is valued by a prospective employer and providing evidence that you possess that skill by pointing to an activity that demonstrates that skill in action. You can, however, take this further and try to make a link between your skills and the way in which these would be valuable in an employment context:

- **Member of the drama society.** I demonstrated my flexibility and willingness to 'muck in' by building props and scenery (all through the night before our first performance) when we were let down at the last minute by others students. This would be valuable in the high pressure world of legal practice as it shows that I would be willing to help colleagues who were struggling to meet deadlines in order that a project could be completed on time.

You will find some further examples of this approach of identifying a skill, providing evidence of the skill in operation, and linking it to an employment situation on the Online Resource Centre.

In the sections that follow, you will find some suggestions of the way in which you can use your spare time to demonstrate key skills to employers. The remainder of the chapter is broken down into two parts:

- Each of the employability skills identified in Chapter 1 are considered in turn along with some examples of the sorts of activities that you should do in your spare time that would either allow you to develop a skill that you lack or to strengthen an existing skill by using it in a new context.

- You will probably notice in the first section that certain activities are used as examples several times over in relation to different skills. This is because they are immensely skills-rich activities so the second section of this chapter focuses on these activities in greater detail.

- The second section of this chapter picks out particular activities that were used as examples in the first section and explains them in greater detail including giving guidance on how to find opportunities to take part in these activities. The focus here is on participation in clubs and societies, voluntary work, and work undertaken in and around the university.

This approach is a practical solution to a problem. It would be an enormous challenge for any book to cover all of the many and varied activities that are undertaken by law students in their spare time, particularly in one single chapter, so we have provided a variety of examples of activities that should act as guidance so that you will be able to identify the employability skills in your own activities and use these to strengthen your CV and impress prospective employers.

Demonstrating skills

In this section of the chapter, the focus will be on the key employability skills that are valued by employers and the ways in which they can be evidenced by participation in spare time activities. You may find that certain activities are used as an example of more than one skill: this is a reflection of their skills-rich nature so you might take this as a bit of a pointer if you are trying to find an additional activity to undertake in your spare time in order to strengthen your skills portfolio. These activities will be discussed in greater detail in the second part of the chapter.

The skills themselves are not described in any great detail so you may want to refer to Chapter 1 if you feel that you would like further information about any of the skills covered.

Written communication skills

If you want to practise law, you will need to have excellent written communication skills as you will need to be able to capture complex legal ideas with clarity, set out legal arguments in written form, and ensure that you keep detailed and accurate records of meetings with clients and court proceedings. In other professions, you may need to produce reports, create marketing literature, produce content for the company's website, correspond with customers, or maintain written records. In essence, written communication skills will be valued by any employer so try to find evidence to demonstrate your skills in action outside of your academic studies:

- **Do you contribute to a website?** Perhaps you write content for a website as part of your involvement with a club or society or are you a regular contributor to a blog? It does not have to be a website about the law—what matters is that you are sharing things that you have written with a wide audience. And, of course, if you do contribute to a website, you could always include details on your CV so that prospective employers could see your work.

- **Do you have a role that involves regular email correspondence?** Email can be used as evidence of written communication skills because so much professional correspondence is conducted by email. This needs to be part of a formal role, rather than corresponding with friends and family. Perhaps you have a job, paid or voluntary, that includes answering emails or you are responsible for the distribution of publicity material or marketing literature for an organisation.

- **Could you write or help to write an article?** Is there an in-house student law journal at your university or could you write an article for a journal that accepts contributions from students at any university? Alternatively, could you assist one of your lecturers with an article or book that they are writing? Even if you only make research notes for them, you will still be evidencing your written communication skills and they may let you draft some content for the article or book. You may get a mention in the acknowledgements or even, in the case of an article, a credit as joint author.

Numeracy

Numeracy is important in legal practice as money, in the sense of damages, compensation, or repayment of a fine, will often be very important to your clients. You will also need to keep a track of the time spent on each case for the purposes of billing and explain your costs to your clients. At least basic competence in numeracy—mental arithmetic, percentages, and perhaps some statistical knowledge—may be required in many professions and remember that all businesses in the commercial world aim to be profitable so some degree of numeracy is likely to be required and can be a factor that relates to commercial awareness (see Chapter 6). As there are limited opportunities to develop numeracy skills as part of your academic studies, it would be useful to find examples from your spare time activities:

- **Do you have experience in handling money?** Students who have worked in shops and bars will be able to demonstrate some numeracy skills even if the work involved using a till that did most of the calculations. Be specific about the aspects of the role that involved calculations such as cashing up at the end of a shift, ordering stock, or totalling columns of figures.

- **Have you been the treasurer of a club or society?** The focus of this role is the finances of the club or society. It involves dealing with subscriptions, buying and selling merchandise, dealing with the expenses incurred by various events, and preparing the accounts of the society. As such, it offers an excellent opportunity to showcase your numeracy skills.

- **Can you use spreadsheets or statistical software such as SPSS?** Any software that involves manipulating numerical data will allow you to demonstrate your numeracy skills. You might do this in an employment context or perhaps conduct research for a dissertation that involves analysing statistics or carrying out statistical analysis.

Problem solving

This sort of problem solving skill is different from legal problem solving so it is not concerned with your ability to answer problem questions in law but your more general ability to resolve difficult situations. This is an important employability skill because unresolved problems prevent you from achieving your objectives and can lead to all sorts of strife and ill-feeling in the workplace, not to mention a possible loss of profitability. The trick here is to think of times that you have encountered a difficult situation and think about what you did to resolve it. Remember, it is not only your own problems that are relevant here—it would be just as valid to provide evidence that you have solved problems for other people.

- **Do you have a role in which you represent other people?** This could be through work experience or voluntary work that involves giving advice or support to others. It would include things such as a stint as a student rep, working as a student mentor, voluntary work such as CAB or appropriate adult, or work experience in a law firm. Roles involving the support and representation of other people would also give you good evidence of client care skills.

- **Have you been involved in a crisis situation?** Perhaps you have had to step in at short notice when someone else has been injured or suffered illness or just gone missing at a crucial time. For example, it is quite common for moot judges to drop out at the last minute due to commitments in court so having resolved this would be a good example of your ability to solve problems. Examples such as this would also support your claim to be flexible and to possess leadership skills.

- **Do you have experience of fundraising?** Fundraising for a society or charity can be hard work as people get hardened to the same old cake sales and raffles so you could demonstrate a flexible approach to problem solving by finding a creative approach to raising money.

Use of IT

Baseline IT skills—the ability to create, format, modify, and save documents, use the Internet and communicate by email—are the modern equivalent of being able to read and write so will be expected by all employers. You may also need to be able to use a database, create a spreadsheet, and operate an online diary system. Within the legal profession, there will be an expectation that you can use legal databases. Think about ways in which you can provide evidence of your IT skills:

- **Have you attended any training courses?** Perhaps you completed the Westlaw or LexisLibrary training (either online or face-to-face) or attended a course on using legal databases provided by your university. Investigate what other IT-related courses are available at your university as these are often provided free or at a low cost. Completion of such courses will support your claim to have good IT skills and you will often get a certificate that can be used as evidence that you have attended a training course. Try to choose courses that will be of value in a professional setting: for example, you may not need to use spreadsheets or general databases as a law student but these could be useful in an employment context.

- **Have you used IT in a professional setting?** It is one thing to be able to use a computer to surf the Internet, email your friends, and write essays but are you able to establish that you know how to use IT in an appropriate manner in the workplace? You could rely on any paid employment, voluntary work, or work experience that involved the use of IT here. For example, if you dealt with correspondence on a vacation scheme, this will establish that you understand email protocol and can manage professional email correspondence.

- **Have you used software in a creative way?** Perhaps you can make podcasts, produce video clips, or create web pages. Even if these skills do not seem to have any immediate relevance to life as a trainee solicitor or pupil barrister, they may be attractive to prospective employers who may see a use for these skills in marketing the company and enhancing its outward-facing image. You could try to find a law focus to demonstrate your creativity with technology: for example, you could enter the United Nations Student Short Film Competition on Human Rights.

Time management

Time management is one of a series of self-management skills that are valued by employers as it indicates that you can work in an independent and responsible manner. It is important in all professions as employers need to know that you can get the job done to an appropriate standard in a timely fashion without minute-by-minute supervision.

- **You completed your degree!** You could rely upon the successful completion of your studies as evidence of your time management skills—after all, you have had to balance your time between lectures, seminars, private study, revision, exams, and completion of coursework—but remember that this is something that every law graduate (as well as graduates in any other discipline if you are seeking work outside the legal profession) has at their disposal to demonstrate their time management skills so you may want to think of something else:

- **Do you do a lot of social activities?** You will see from the earlier discussion in this chapter, you can demonstrate your ability to manage your time by pointing to the balance of study commitments and social activities that you have maintained throughout your degree. Be sure to highlight particular achievements here: 'I have excellent time-management skills as I have demonstrated by obtaining an upper second class law degree whilst captaining the university hockey team, taking part in three external moots, and working as a student mentor'.

- **Do you have any ongoing responsibilities?** The ability to incorporate your work (or study) within the structure of a regular commitment outside of work can be more persuasive as a demonstration of your time management skills than the ability to accommodate occasional or optional activities. For example, perhaps you are responsible for caring for a child or other family member or even a pet that requires constant maintenance and attention or maybe you work as a volunteer on a regular basis where other people depend upon you.

Professional and ethical behaviour

The greatest risk associated with graduate recruitment from the perspective of an employer is that even the brightest and most successful student may not be suited to working in a professional environment. Spare time activities can be the perfect platform to demonstrate that you will be able to work effectively and professionally in the workplace and interact appropriately with colleagues and clients:

- **Have you undertaken paid or voluntary work within a regulatory framework?** Do you work in a setting where your conduct is constrained by a set of rules of professional conduct? This could be law-related or you might operate in some other setting such as caring for vulnerable adults, working with children, or in a sensitive setting such as a prison where there are strict rules of conduct. It might involve a different profession that operates within a regulatory framework such as accountancy or involve work that takes place within a strict ethos of confidentiality such as working on a crisis helpline.

- **Have you seen the law in action?** If your work experience took you into a courtroom or if you have spent a time shadowing a judge then you will have seen some of the rules of legal practice in operation. Alternatively, you may have had a role where you have been involved, even as an observer, of meetings between lawyers and their clients. Even simulation activities such as client interviewing and negotiation competitions give you an idea of the rules of professional conduct.

- **Do you take part in the running of a club or society?**Anyone who has played a role in the governance of a university society will be familiar with the need to work within the regulations set by the Student Union. If the activity of the club involves organised sport then this would be further evidence of your familiarity with operating within the constraints of a set of regulations.

Planning and organisational skills

Planning and organisational skills go hand-in-hand and, together with time management, are part of the self-management skills that are valued by employers. In essence, prospective employers want to know whether you can work with a degree of independence to achieve a task. More than any other of the employability skills, job applicants tend to make general statements that they have 'excellent planning and organisation skills' without making any attempt to provide supporting evidence so try to make sure that your application provides concrete examples of your ability to break a task down into its elements and manage it successfully to completion:

- **Have you made complicated travel arrangements?** If you have been responsible for a trip that involved several countries, a tight budget, a remote location, or a complex itinerary then you can use this to demonstrate your planning and organisation skills. The successful completion of the trip is evidence of your skills but do not be afraid to identify any problems that arose that you had not anticipated as this may highlight your problem solving skills and your flexibility.

- **Have you been responsible for organising an event?** For example, if you were the master of moot in the law society, you will probably have organised moots against other universities that involved finding a judge, coordinating the availability of the teams and judges, booking rooms, ensuring that all the cases and materials were available for the judge, and supervising the timely exchange of skeletons. Perhaps you have organised a ball or other large social event or been responsible for a fundraising project. It does not have to be a university event: even organising a stag or hen weekend would be a good example of your planning and organisational skills in operation.

- **Are you involved in competitive activities?** Taking part in any sort of competition involves working towards a distant goal so can be used as evidence of planning and organisation skills. You have to work out what standard of skill you need to take part in the competition and assess what measures you need to take to ensure you are ready to take part in the competition. Here, the success of your planning and organisation strategy was your readiness to take part rather than your ultimate success or otherwise in the competition.

Flexibility

It is important to employers in every industry that they have employees who can adapt to change and take on board new ideas and new ways of working. Flexibility demonstrates that you are not afraid of the unfamiliar and that are you able to adapt your existing skills and knowledge to new circumstances. Find evidence of your flexibility by citing examples of situations in which you have had to alter your plans, respond to change, or adapt to an unfamiliar situation.

- **Have you worked or studied abroad or moved here to study?** Finding strategies to adjust to living and working in a new country is good evidence of your flexibility as it shows you doing a familiar thing in an unfamiliar setting. If this involved use of a different language then that is all the better.

- **Have you recovered from a setback that affected your studies?** This can be a good way to turn a negative situation into a positive experience. For example, perhaps you had to repeat a year of your studies due to illness or an accident or you may have failed a module or an entire year. Rather than hoping that a prospective employer will not notice (they will!) you could be very honest in identifying the cause of the problem and then explain what changes you made to ensure that the problem did not reoccur.

- **Have you coped when plans have gone wrong?** There are all sorts of situations in life that do not turn out as you have expected through no fault of your own. Perhaps you turned up at university to find that you had not been allocated accommodation or arrived at a festival to find that the organisers had no record of your glamping booking. You can use any challenging situation as evidence of flexibility and your ability to work around problems.

Practical example: study abroad

One of the most rewarding challenges I took on during my legal education was a year-long Erasmus exchange to Maastricht University in the Netherlands. The opportunity to meet many people of a wide range of nationalities, to study a foreign legal system, to travel, and to experience a culture unlike my own was very worthwhile. Showing that you are able to take on new challenges is something that potential employers value, and gaining this international experience was very useful when applying to firms with an international client base.

Adam, Edinburgh University

Decision-making

Decision-making involves a series of other skills: analysis of a situation, identification of the options, and evaluation of the risks in order to reach an appropriate and timely conclusion. There will always be decisions to be made, major and minor, in the course of employment and, ultimately, the future of any organisation hangs on the decisions made by its employees so decision-making is a skill that will be valued in any profession.

- **What decisions did you make that influenced your studies?** Prospective employers might pick up on aspects of your studies as a means of gaining insight into your decision-making skills: for example, why you chose to study at a particular university, why you took a single or joint honours degree, what influenced your choice of final year options, or how you selected a particular dissertation topic. Think about these common questions in advance to ensure that you have something meaningful to say that demonstrates a thoughtful approach to decision-making.

- **Have you had to make an unpopular decision?** You may be able to think of a situation in which you had to make a decision that affected several people and which you knew would make at least some of those people unhappy. Perhaps you had to make a decision about a new policy or practise in a society or you were responsible for selecting players for a team sport. Decisions that affect several people and which will be unpopular with some of them are good examples as they involve more complex reasoning processes.

- **How did you decide what to do with your spare time?** It is also common for prospective employers to ask questions about your choice of spare time activities so look at what you have done and make sure that you can answer a question about why you did it. Think about each activity in turn and link your decision to participate in it to some other skill: why did you moot, what did you work as a student mentor, why did you do voluntary work with the CAB.

Team working

Team work is all about your ability to collaborate with others to achieve a goal, your willingness to support others, to contribute ideas, and to share responsibility for a piece of work. Team working skills are an essential part of working in a professional environment where it is expected that you will be able to work cooperatively with others both within the organisation and with professionals from other organisations.

- **Have you joined a group?** If you like to spend your time doing things that are usually done alone, that does not mean that you cannot use your spare time activities to demonstrate your ability to work in a team as you could join a club or society dedicated to that activity. So if you enjoy solitary activities such as fishing, bee-keeping, dress-making, or flower arranging then you can join (or start) a club or society and it becomes a group activity that demonstrates your ability to work with others. Alternatively, you could start a study group with other law students to share the burden of revision or help each other through the intricacies of land law as this would also be a good way to demonstrate your team work skills.

- **Are you part of a team?** People often think of sporting teams but there are all sorts of non-sporting activities where you will be part of a team of people working towards a single goal or engaged in a group activity. Perhaps you play an instrument in a band or orchestra, sing with a choir, or are part of a dance or drama group. You could be part of a team working for St John's Ambulance, taking part in orienteering or working towards the Duke of Edinburgh Award.

- **Are you on a committee?** It always seems surprising when university clubs and societies have difficulty in filling all the committee positions as these are such skills-rich roles that offer so much in terms of enhancing your CV. Not only do they offer an opportunity to demonstrate your ability to work as part of a team but they also provide evidence of other key employability skills such as decision-making, leadership, verbal communication, flexibility, and so on.

Verbal communication

Communication is a two-way process so it is an implicit part of verbal communication that you are skilled in listening, digesting, and questioning oral information directed towards you as well as in directing spoken communication at others. It covers one-to-one conversations as well as the dissemination of information to a larger audience in the form of a speech or presentation. Verbal communication skills are important in legal practice: you may need to be able to explain the law to non-lawyers, update colleagues on the progress of a case, brief counsel and experts from other professions, and make submissions in court.

The ability to communicate verbally in an effective, clear, and precise manner will be valuable in any employment context whether this involves daily communications with other employees, dealing with clients, or making formal presentations.

- **Do you take part in mooting or debating?** A moot involves the oral delivery of legal submissions (see Chapter 4) that can be planned in advance but which are interspersed with answers to questions posed by the moot judge. A debate may focus on legal issues but can cover any contentious subject matter. It tends to involve the structured delivery of planned oral argument but may include a right to reply to the points made by the opposition. Both are great activities for building confidence and improving oral delivery style.

- **Have you delivered a presentation?** It may have been the case that you were required to deliver a presentation on some aspect of the law during a tutorial or as part of an assessment or perhaps you made a speech to a group of students in your role as student rep or by virtue of holding an office in the law society. You might be the campus Westlaw or Lexis liaison which involves giving training sessions to new students. Any experience of public speak is valuable as it is common recruitment practice in law to be asked to give a presentation either at interview or as part of a selection centre's activities (see Chapter 12).

- **Do you a have role that involves persuasion or negotiation?** Perhaps you are a student rep or you work in an advisory capacity that involves you putting forward arguments on behalf of someone else. You might have a role where you have to manage conflict or reconcile differences. Even voluntary work that involves more listening than talking, such as Samaritans or Nightline, can be good evidence of verbal communication skills.

Customer service

Customer service embraces a collection of skills that can be summarised as a level of professional concern for the quality of service that is provided to the organisation's clients. It involves being able to listen, establish a rapport, and formulate a suitable response to issues and concerns raised by others as well as the ability to assume responsibility for ensuring that a client's needs are met in an appropriate and courteous manner. It is important in all professions: without satisfied customers, a business cannot survive, particularly given the ease with which dissatisfaction can be disseminated on the Internet and through social media. Your future employer needs to know that you will not bring the firm into disrepute by being rude, inefficient, or neglectful of its clients so try to find evidence that you are good at providing a professional service to others even under pressure:

- **Do you work in a shop or bar?** If you have a role that gives you direct contact with customers, you should be able to demonstrate your ability to provide a courteous and professional service including the ability to respond appropriately to complaints.

- **Are you involved with the committee of a club or society?** A society has a customer base in the form of its members so you can use your position on a committee to demonstrate your ability to deliver a service that meets the expectations of members and to deal with any dissatisfaction if there are perceived deficiencies in that service.

- **Do you provide a service to others as part of your voluntary work?** Any role that includes responsibility for providing something to others is appropriate to demonstrate your client care skills. Perhaps you serve meals to homeless people, give computer classes in a residential home for the elderly, or give advice on a helpline for victims of domestic violence. The provision of any goods or services involves the requirement to understand the expectations of customers and to work out what needs to be done to meet those expectations so provides good evidence of customer service.

Leadership

People often assume that you can only demonstrate leadership if you have been in charge of other people but leadership skills relate to more than just a position held and cover the ability to motivate, influence, and support others in achieving a particular goal or objective. Just because a person holds a leadership role does not mean that they have good leadership skills and so it is not necessary that you hold a leadership position in order to possess the skills that would make you a good leader. In any workplace, the ability to motivate and guide others in a calm and effective manner will be valued.

- **Are you involved in peer mentoring?** Peer mentoring schemes offer an ideal opportunity to demonstrate leadership skills. Even if you lack the confidence to take on a more formal leadership role, you may be able to work on a one-to-one basis and pass on your knowledge of the university and advice about studying to a new student.

- **Have you taken part in a student enterprise project?** Many universities have projects that encourage entrepreneurial and leadership skills. For example, 51 universities are involved with Enactus (**www.enactusuk.org**) which supports student groups in creating and managing community outreach projects. This offers various opportunities to take on roles that would enable you to develop and demonstrate leadership skills such as project management, marketing, fundraising, and corporate relations.

- **Have you started something?** If you have been the originator of an event or an activity then you will have an excellent opportunity to demonstrate leadership skills as you will have had to mobilise and enthuse others in order to convince them to turn your idea into reality. Perhaps you campaigned for study skills workshops, organised a visit to the European Court of Human Rights, arranged for recruitment partners from law firms to visit your university, or started a new society.

Legal research

The ability to use legal databases and to formulate an effective search strategy that enables you to locate relevant cases and statutes is a skill particular to the legal profession but remember that general research skills are valued in a number of professions. Legal research skills are so well evidenced by your studies and extra-curricular skills activities that it is not usually necessary to move away from these examples to demonstrate your skills.

- **Did you write a dissertation?** A dissertation is an excellent showcase for your research skills as it is impossible to gain impressive marks without conducting thorough and wide-ranging research. As a dissertation is a much longer piece of work than ordinary coursework, it necessitates a depth of research that is not required elsewhere in your studies.

- **Did you move away from the syllabus?** If you have had a reason to research an area of law that is not taught to you on the degree syllabus then you have evidence of your ability to conduct independent research. You might have written a dissertation on an area of law that was not covered elsewhere in the degree or needed to research an unfamiliar area of law as part of a work placement or in relation to voluntary work.

- **Did you take part in a moot?** It is usual for students to use participation in mooting as evidence of oral presentation skills but a good moot performance is based upon solid research. A moot involves the construction of submissions on a very narrow point of law so you have to know a lot about a little in order to succeed. In particular, a moot requires a strong ability to identify and find case law.

Legal problem solving

Although students think of these skills as limited to answering problem questions in coursework and examinations, these methods of assessment are simply a simulation of a central part of legal practice which is the application of the law to a set of facts in order to offer legal advice. So although you will have experience of answering problem questions, try to find situations in which you have applied the law in a real situation.

- **Do you work in an advisory role?** If you work for the CAB or in any other voluntary role that involves the provision of advice, you will have some experience of working out what law is relevant to a client's problems and explaining the likely outcome of the case to the client. You can also gain this experience from your participation in vacation schemes or other legal work experience.

- **Have you resolved a dispute on your own behalf?** Law students often become quite enthusiastic complainers as they realise how much of their everyday life is regulated by the law. Perhaps you have used the law to obtain a refund from a retailer for faulty goods or shoddy services or maybe you have taken an organisation to task for misleading advertising.

- **Have you campaigned for change?** Perhaps you used the law to object to a planning decision or to pressure the local council to reduce the speed limit in a residential area following a fatal accident. You might have challenged a university policy by invoking its own rules or policies.

Drafting

Drafting is a form of legal writing and tends to refer to the process of drawing up binding legal texts although you may find that drafting modules on the LPC and BTPC will cover broader issues of legal writing such as correspondence with clients and creating attend-ance notes. It is unlikely that you will find opportunities to develop this skill as part of the undergraduate degree but there may be situations in which you have drawn up a document that was intended to be legally binding:

- **Have you drafted a constitution or policy document for a society?** Every university society has a constitution that sets out its powers, objectives, and responsibilities. If you are involved with a new society at its inception, you may have had a role in drafting the constitution or you may have contributed to the amendment of the constitution if you joined an existing society. You might be involved in drawing up a policy document or creating or amending the terms of reference that apply to your post within the society at the end of your term of office.

- **Have you completed any legal forms or documents?** You may have been involved with the completion of legal paperwork either whilst gaining work experience in a law firm or if you have undertaken voluntary work that involves the provision of legal advice.

For example, you may have helped a client complete a property transfer form, a legal aid form, or advised on the drafting of a will if you have worked with the CAB.

- **Have you drawn up instructions for people to follow?** If you have organised an event, does it have joining instructions or a policy on the refund of a deposit?

Negotiation

As you will have seen in Chapter 4, negotiation is a collection of skills. It is best demonstrated by participation in a negotiation but any situation in which you have facilitated the resolution of a dispute will provide an example of your skills in action.

- **Have you taken part in a negotiation competition?** The most obvious way to demonstrate negotiation skills is to take part in a negotiation! Many universities run an internal negotiation competition for law students and there is also the opportunity for four students from each institution to take part in the annual national negotiation competition.

- **Have you facilitated an agreement between parties in a dispute?** Every time people disagree, there is scope for a negotiated resolution to the dispute. Perhaps you are involved in a club or society where members have fallen out or you may have intervened to resolve a disagreement that arose in your workplace or in shared accommodation. Work as a student rep often involves negotiation as you mediate between the student body and lecturers to find a compromise position on an issue.

- **Do you have an advisory role?** A lot of voluntary organisations exist to resolve disputes that arise between individuals and other individuals or with organisations. For example, you might volunteer at a housing advisory charity in which case you could be involved in resolving disputes between individuals and their landlords or a debt management advice centre for helping individuals to agree a schedule of repayment to their creditors.

Advocacy

Advocacy skills are a particular manifestation of verbal communication skills that involve the ability to present a coherent and persuasive argument that convinces the audience to accept your viewpoint or adopt your proposed course of action. Although it is usual to think of advocacy as something that happens in the courtroom, you could demonstrate your skills in this area in a number of other settings.

- **Have you been involved in canvassing or fundraising?** If you have canvassed for a political party or to help a fellow student get elected to a committee position, you will have used your powers of persuasion to try and convince others to give their support which is a demonstration of your advocacy skills. Similarly, fundraising can involve the need to persuade others that your cause is a worthy one that justifies them parting with money.

- **Have you represented someone at a disciplinary hearing?** Universities have provision for disciplinary hearings to investigate academic misconduct, misbehaviour in university accommodation, and breach of Student Union rules regarding the governance of clubs and societies. You may have been asked to accompany a friend to such a hearing and to assist them in presenting their case by looking at the rule it is alleged that they have breached and putting arguments that suggest that they have not done so or presenting mitigation that explains their conduct.

- **Have you been involved in mooting or debating?** These activities provide an excellent opportunity for you to demonstrate your advocacy skills. You might also consider taking part in a trial simulation as this replicates a first instance hearing so would give you experience in matters such as introducing evidence, addressing the jury, and examining witnesses.

Knowledge of legal practice and procedure

Your law degree will have given you a sound foundation of legal knowledge but there is a gap between an understanding of the law 'on paper' and an appreciation of how the law works 'in practice'. Remember that all other students will try to demonstrate this skill by reference to work experience so try to find a couple of other activities that give you a different perspective on the way the law works.

- **Have you been to court?** It is surprising how many students reach the end of their law degree without ever having set foot in a courtroom. Some universities arrange court visits for their students but other universities leave it up to the students to find their own opportunities. Try to visit as many courts as possible: magistrates' courts, Crown courts, a tribunal, the Court of Appeal, the European Court of Justice, and ordinary courts in any country that you happen to visit on holiday (even if you do not understand the language, you will get a sense for how justice is administered). Watch what lawyers do and talk to them if you get an opportunity: being at court and asking sensible questions can be an excellent networking opportunity (see Chapter 6) and could even lead to an offer of work experience.

- **Can you see the law from a different perspective?** Think about other professions that are involved in the administration of justice and see if you can gain some experience of their work. For example, you could volunteer as a support mentor with the probation service, as an appropriate adult supporting vulnerable people in police custody, as a youth offender panel member, as a court volunteer with victim support, or train as a magistrate.

- **Could you organise an event that explains procedural law?** Universities often arrange visiting speakers on various topics of interest to their students so why not suggest an event that focuses on procedural law. You could be even more proactive and offer to arrange it so that you have an opportunity to liaise with local solicitors and barristers.

Interviewing

The essence of the skill of interviewing is the use of questioning to elicit facts. This means that you need to be able to judge when to use different types of question (open and closed) and how to keep the person that you are interviewing on track if they are straying into irrelevant areas.

- **Did you take part in a client interviewing competition?** Client interviewing competitions exist to give students an insight into the issues that can arise when dealing with clients in practice. If your university runs a client interviewing competition, enter it. If your university does not have a client interviewing competition, get together with other interested students and start one.

- **Do you work in an advisory capacity?** You can only give advice once you have assimilated the facts of the problem for which advice is needed so if you have a role that involves giving advice it will also involve asking questions. This could be a voluntary role such as working for the CAB or a part of your employment if, for example, you work in customer services.

- **Have you done a mock interview?** Many universities offer mock interviews to their students to help them prepare to apply for jobs. If you have been interviewed, you have some insight into the role of the interviewer as you know what questions you have been asked. Instead of focusing exclusively on your performance, think about how you would have behaved as the interviewer and what questions you would ask if you were interviewing a candidate for a training contract or pupillage. You could even practise with other law students, taking it in turns to act as interviewer and candidate.

Presentation

A presentation is a particular form of verbal communication. The aim is for the speaker to convey information in an easily digestible form to the audience, often supported by visual information on slides or a handout. It is quite common for applicants for a training contract or pupillage to be required to give a presentation as part of the recruitment process so it is well worth ensuring that you have opportunities to practise your presentation skills.

- **Do you have a role that involves presentation?** Think about your other activities and consider whether it would be appropriate for you to give a presentation in order to share information with others. For example, if you are part of a university society, could you volunteer to give a short presentation to new students during induction week or could you give a presentation as part of a recruitment drive? If you are a course rep, you could give a (short) presentation to the appropriate student group to ensure that they are aware of your role and its relevance to them. If you have had success in student activities such as mooting or negotiation, could you give a presentation to other students about this to share what is involved and encourage them to take part?

- **Can you use PowerPoint or Keynote?** Even if you cannot find an opportunity to give a presentation during your time at university, you can ensure that you are prepared to do so whenever the need arises by making sure you can use one of the presentation software packages. You can either try to puzzle them out for yourself or attend a course if one is provided by your university.

- **Could you take part in an online video presentation?** There may be opportunities at your university to take part in an online presentation that is used for marketing purposes, perhaps talking about your course or your experiences as a student at that university. Alternatively, you could make a video clip yourself that is made available online about absolutely anything: it could even be a short clip about your mission to find a training contract. The benefit of having an online presentation is that you can include details of where it can be found on your CV so that employers can access it and see your presentation skills in action.

Tell us

Tell us what you do in your spare time and how it develops or demonstrates employability skills. Do you have an example of a way in which you used your spare time activities to impress a prospective employer? Tell us at finchandfafinski.com/get-in-touch or @FinchFafinski on Twitter.

Popular activities

You may have noticed in the sections in the first part of this chapter that the same examples were used to demonstrate several different skills. In particular, holding an office in a club or society, getting involved in work around the campus, and particular sorts of voluntary work were used on a regular basis to demonstrate key employability skills. In addition to their ability to enhance your skills portfolio, these activities have other benefits as many of them are based on and around the campus. This means that they are convenient to access and little or no cost is involved in terms of travelling expenses. Moreover, your academic referee is likely to have first-hand evidence of your involvement and will be able to write about your contribution to university life in greater detail than would be the case if there was only anecdotal evidence of your involvement with an activity.

Clubs and societies

One of the great attractions of university life is the unparalleled access that it gives you to a wide range of activities through the clubs and societies administered by the Student Union. Whatever activity you enjoy doing, there is likely to be a club or society devoted to it plus there will be any number of societies offering you opportunities to try new and exciting activities. If there is no society in existence that offers your chosen activity, you can always start one if you find other students who are interested (a very enterprising approach which will make a great addition to your CV in terms of skills such as leadership, decision-making, organisation and planning, and team work).

Practical example: societies and employability

I have been heavily involved with one of the student unions on campus, both on its Board of Management and with debating. I definitely believe these experiences made me much more confident and able to think on my feet. I worked with other students on events like Freshers' Week, which gave me an insight into budgeting and how to organise a successful social event. The skills gained throughout have been instrumental in helping me secure a job.

Katherine, Glasgow University

The majority of students join at least one club or society during their time at university so what employability skills does this demonstrate? The answer to this question depends upon two factors:

- The nature of the activity that the club provides
- Your role in the running of the club and its activities.

Nature of the activity

There are some employability skills that you can demonstrate simply by virtue of taking part in the activities organised by university clubs and societies. For example, you are showing your time-management skills by pursuing a leisure activity as well as keeping pace with your studies as you will need to balance the competing priorities involved whilst meeting deadlines. You are also demonstrating your ability and inclination to work with others by joining a club or society, particularly if the activity concerned is one that you could have done on your own. This shows that you like to join in with others and suggests that you are a congenial person who gets on with others.

Practical example: team sports

Participating in legal and non-legal activities, such as pro bono and various sports shows you have interests and dedication outside of academia. Both activities obviously require the ability to work as a team but then also give the opportunity to develop the skill of leadership, whether it is a snap judgement to pass the ball after assessing a tense situation or taking the lead in giving a presentation to a group. Through taking part in such activities I also learnt to be flexible and adaptable—things do not always go as planned (no matter how organised you may be).

Communication and team building skills gained from experience of pro bono and sport will enable me to converse and work with a wide range of people—colleagues and clients from all backgrounds. The law can sometimes seem like a foreign language, so being able to adopt a suitable language or approach, depending on who you are working with, can help make the situation more simple, workable, and often enjoyable.

Laura, Leeds Metropolitan University

Other skills are more specific to the type of activity so you will need to think about what it is that you do and try to extract the skills involved. You will have seen an example of this at the beginning of the chapter.

Role in the club

Of course, it may be the case that the activity in question does not, in and of itself, relate to any of the employability skills that you are seeking to highlight to potential employers. Nevertheless, the second way in which your involvement in clubs and societies will enable you to demonstrate these skills is by reference to your role in the club, particularly if you were part of the committee that organised the society and its activities.

Practical example: using society positions

Think about the activity at the heart of the society at which you are a member or your position in that society and try to match it to one of the employability skills discussed in the first part of this chapter. Make sure that you explain how the activity or role developed or strengthened this skill by reference to a particular attribute of the activity, using this structure:

• I was a member (or position on the committee) of the [insert society name] which strengthened my [identify skill] by [provide evidence].

Consider these examples:

• I was a member of the bee-keeping society for three years and, although I did not serve on the committee, was asked to give demonstrations of bee-keeping each year at local schools. This involved making all the arrangements for the demonstrations and recruiting helpers as well as making a presentation and answering questions asked by the children.

- As one of the four founder members of the real ale appreciation society, I was instrumental in writing a constitution for the society and completing the paperwork that led to our ratification as a new society by the Student Union. After the society was established, I took the role of vice-president which involved filling in wherever the need arose. In particular, I took responsibility for the accounts and arranging and budgeting a trip around six European breweries when our treasurer was unavailable for six months following an accident.

- I took on the role of membership secretary of the lacrosse society part way through the year following the resignation of the elected officer. This was a difficult time for the society as we were threatened with closure due to insufficient members and we did not have enough players to compete in the league. The publicity campaign that I initiated increased membership by over 200% and ensured the continued existence of the society and our return to competitive play.

Can you identify which of the employability skills are demonstrated in each of these statements? Could the statements be reworded in order to emphasise the skills involved more effectively.

⬤ You will find our suggestions for rewording the statements on the Online Resource Centre.

Student law society

Although there are any number of clubs and societies that you could join, it is worth giving particular consideration to the law society. This society is run by and for the benefit of law students and should be the focus of a number of core activities that are valuable in terms of enhancing employability skills and providing information about career opportunities. It is generally expected that students doing a law degree will join the law society in order to take advantage of activities such as mooting, court visits, and careers events that it organises. Students who choose not to do so should be aware that this is something that may be explored by potential employers at interview:

I ask applicants why they did not join their university's law society and I get annoyed with answers that offer criticism of the society as an explanation. My follow up question is 'why didn't you put yourself forward for a committee position and do something about it then?' which tends to be met with shocked silence but I am not interested in awarding pupillage to applicants who think that problems should be solved by anyone other than themselves. I want people who see a problem and want to solve it. Anything else is just not good for the future of the Chambers.

Member of pupillage committee

So the message here is that you should get involved with the law society at your university: if it is a good one, you will benefit from the activities that it offers but if it seems to be struggling then you could demonstrate a whole host of employability skills by being one of the people who try to improve it. Of course, that is not to say that you should only stand for an office in the law society if it is bad. Either way, taking on a committee position with the law society is an excellent way of developing and demonstrating a range of key skills and it shows a commitment to the furtherance of law-based activities.

The offices are filled by election every year so you can choose when you want to get involved. Most offices (other than first year rep) are held by second, third, and fourth year students. The positions available may vary between universities but could include the following:

- **President.** The main role of the president is to maintain overall responsibility for the running of the society, to manage the business of the society, and to liaise with the Student Union. Key skills: leadership and decision-making.

- **Vice-President.** The vice-president assists the president with the running of the society and supports the other officers in fulfilling their roles as and when extra assistance is needed. Key skills: flexibility and team work.

- **Treasurer.** This position confers responsibility for all financial matters relating to the society: membership fees, budgeting, financing events, sales of merchandise, the annual accounts. Key skills: numeracy and organisation.

- **Social secretary.** The Social Secretary is responsible for organising a range of social events from large formal events such as the law society ball to informal pub crawls and book sales. Key skills: organisation and problem solving.

- **Publicity officer.** The main responsibility of this role is to ensure that students are aware of the activities available through the student law society and this may involve creating fliers, maintaining the society webpage, and communicating with students through email or by announcements in lectures. Key skills: verbal and written communication, and use of IT.

- **Master of moot.** This role involves responsibility for all aspects of internal and external mooting. This may include arranging workshops for new students to encourage them to take part in mooting, organising competitions and exhibitions of mooting, and finding judges. The role offers some useful networking opportunities as it involves liaising with and taking care of visiting solicitors and barristers who come to judge moots. Key skills: problem solving and organisation.

- **Careers officer.** The Careers officer is responsible for ensuring that law students are given opportunities to find out about careers in legal practice. It may involve arranging visits to courts, arranging visiting speakers, running CV-writing clinics, or organising a Careers Fair. This role offers excellent networking opportunities too as it involves so much contact with members of the legal profession. Key skills: organisation and verbal and written communication.

Practice example: Q&A with a law society officer

Q: What made you want to get involved in the student law society?
A: I hate clichés so I will steer clear of saying something like 'I wanted to give something back'. I think what made me want to take part in the student law society is the fact that I recognised the value the society has in the lives of law students or that it can have if it's run properly.

Q: What post(s) did you hold and why did you choose those ones?
A: I held the post of legal professions officer (LPO) in my final year. I thought I could do it well as I'd had some work experience with a lobbying organisation which requires some similar skills. I also chose it because I wanted to have a more hands on position where I have a clear set of tasks rather than something general such as vice president or treasurer.

Q: What did it involve?
A: My work as LPO was focused on establishing a connection between the law society and the legal profession. This predominantly took the form of arranging trips to the Inns of Court, as the position used to be called the 'Bar liaison officer'. In addition to this however, the role included arranging talks by legal professionals (both barristers and solicitors), arranging trips to the Supreme Court to watch

a case and in my year, I created a new competition called Mooting +. This was designed to address an imbalance in Mooting which made it much more suitable to those interested in the bar and left budding solicitors without a truly marquee competition in which their natural skills would be better appreciated. I designed the rules so that in Mooting + competitors could act as either solicitors or barristers and their tasks and competences were amended accordingly.

Q: How much work was involved and did it interrupt your studies?

A: There was actually a lot of work, though to an extent this was because in any organisation you have to contribute across the board. Our committee was quite unlucky as we were unable to fill some positions right away, which meant that we had to spread the tasks between ourselves. I think in one way or another committee work will take up more time than anyone ever plans. I am sure that it did interrupt my studies at least a little—there is no way around it as it was a substantial commitment. At the same time, everyone needs a break in any event, so spending that time on committee work mitigated the interruption in my case.

Q: What were the main benefits?

A: As far as I am concerned being in the committee was pretty much an entirely positive experience. I think the main benefit to me was that I could be directly involved with the society for the first time and that was both fulfilling and just fun. I did learn a lot, both in terms of making contacts, organising things, and working with a team. It would be a useful experience for everyone in my opinion. There is no sense in beating around the bush—it's also a good thing to put in your CV. On a practical note, being a committee member meant that I had a quiet room to study in pretty much whenever I needed it, though I guess that comes under 'fringe benefits'.

Q: Has it been raised in any interviews for jobs or scholarships?

A: Yes, actually it's raised directly or indirectly every time. I'm often asked about this and other positions I've held in societies (If I recall correctly it was also briefly covered in my Inner Temple interview). When I say indirectly, I mean that talking about the committee is a good answer to many generic questions you get asked at interviews, especially about teamwork and persuasion in that context.

Emile, University of Surrey

If you are using your time on the student law society committee to demonstrate a particular skill to a potential employer, make sure that you identify a particular goal or challenge of the role and explain how you achieved or overcame it. Remember, that you want to provide evidence of your skills in actions rather than expecting a particular activity or role to speak for itself. For example:

- As the publicity officer, I designed a new website for the student law society which provided a single source of information about the committee, its policies and its activities. This ensured that the society was more visible and accessible to its members and achieved its objective of improving communication between the committee and the student body.

- My main objective as social secretary was to improve the range of events on offer with a view to making the society attractive to more students and increasing our membership. I held consultation meetings with groups of students to find out what events would be popular and responded by introducing two new social events that were less formal than the law ball and three events with a professional focus that gave members an opportunity to find out more about the legal profession and to network with local solicitors and barristers. These events were well attended and our membership increased by 12% during my year on the committee.

Practical advice: don't lie

There is an apocryphal story about a law firm who received applications for a training contract from three applicants who all claimed to have been president of the same university law society in the same year.

It has always, unfortunately, been the case that students who have not held society positions (or done other things that look good on application forms) claim to have done so. Law firms and chambers are aware of this and tend to check.

We always check. It only takes a single email to the student's academic referee, personal tutor, or any other law lecturer at the university. At a rough estimate, I would say that one in three people who claim to have held a society post have not really done so. And if someone is lying, we do not progress their application. It may seem a trivial matter but it demonstrates dishonesty and we cannot have dishonest solicitors working in our firm.

Training partner

If the student's academic reference does not mention something like a society position or participation in mooting, I tend to assume that it is untrue as these are things that a referee would mention. If the application is otherwise excellent, I might have them in for interview but I would always quiz them about the activity in question. It is dispiriting how many applicants cannot, when asked at interview, tell you any details of any moot that they allegedly took part in during their 'active participation in mooting'. Needless to say, these people do not make it to the second interview stage!

Member of pupillage committee

Voluntary work

You might like to consider getting involved in voluntary work as a way of enhancing your portfolio of skills. In broad terms, there are two types of voluntary work that you might considering doing: that which could be considered to have a legal basis and that which does not. The most obvious form of legal voluntary work would be participation in a pro bono scheme in which legal advice is provided free of charge to individuals and organisations who cannot otherwise afford it but there are other type of voluntary work that have a legal basis such as working for the Citizens Advice Bureau or acting as an appropriate adult to support young or vulnerable suspects at the police station. These sorts of voluntary work that are legal in nature will be discussed in Chapter 7 as a form of work experience whereas this chapter will focus on non-legal voluntary work.

There are numerous opportunities available to work on an unpaid basis and you may find that competition to get involved is less fierce than it is for paid employment. However, voluntary work is not always a popular option with students who are, after all, very busy and often rather short of cash so may not be attracted by the idea of devoting time to an activity that does not carry any financial reward. Of course, it is true that there are many demands on your time and your studies and paid employment is likely to take priority but do remember that one of the key objectives in attending university is to obtain a good job at the end of it. This means that you could view time spent undertaking voluntary work that enhances your employability skills as a long-term investment that actually carries more benefits than the immediate short-term gain involved in paid employment.

Practical advice: voluntary work

Voluntary work can be an excellent way to strengthen your skills portfolio and enhance your employability but you should be selective when making a decision about what work to undertake. The following are of particular importance:

- **When are you available?** One of the advantages of voluntary work is that it can be less difficult to find opportunities that fit around your availability than is the case with paid employment. You should think carefully about how much work you want to do and when you want to do it: would you prefer to make a regular commitment of a few hours each week or concentrate your efforts into a period of weeks during the summer?

- **What skills or experience do you have to offer?** Even if your objective is to strengthen your employability, remember that you must be able to make a contribution to the work of the organisation so think about what you have to offer. Of course, you may wish to learn to do something completely new and many voluntary organisations offer full training to their volunteers but you may want to use an existing skill in a different setting: perhaps your ability to use computers could be used to teach computer literacy to others or your aptitude for enthusing others could be put to good use as part of a fund-raising campaign. Remember also that the process of seeking out voluntary work will be good experience in itself as you may have to complete an application form and attend an interview.

- **What do you want to gain?** Try to think about something specific that you will add to your CV as a result of undertaking a particular piece of voluntary work. You should ensure that you will be doing something that fills a gap in your portfolio of skills or which enables you to strengthen existing skills, perhaps by giving you an opportunity to use a skill acquired in an academic context in a more practical setting.

There are a great many openings for volunteers but they can be hard to find. There are some excellent websites that can help with the task such as Volunteering England (**www.volunteering.org.uk**) or Do It (**www.do-it.org.uk**). For example, Do It has up to one million opportunities for volunteers and includes articles and advice on finding the perfect role along with a postcode searchable database of opportunities which makes it an excellent resource for students seeking voluntary work (see Figure 5.1).

Bear in mind that your opportunities are not limited to volunteering in this country so you may be able to combine your efforts to strengthen your skills with an opportunity to travel and experience different cultures. Camp America and the International Citizen Service organised by the Department of International Development are good examples of organisations that provide voluntary work in other countries. Any activity that involves travelling alone or working in a new environment demonstrates your confidence and self-sufficiency to an employer and it may be the case that voluntary work undertaking in an unusual setting is something that attracts a potential employer's attention when reading your application.

Tell us

Tell us about the voluntary work that you have done and the contribution this made to your employability skills portfolio. Did you do something unusual? What skills did it give you? How did you find out about the opportunity to get involved? Tell us at finchandfafinski.com/get-in-touch or @FinchFafinski on Twitter.

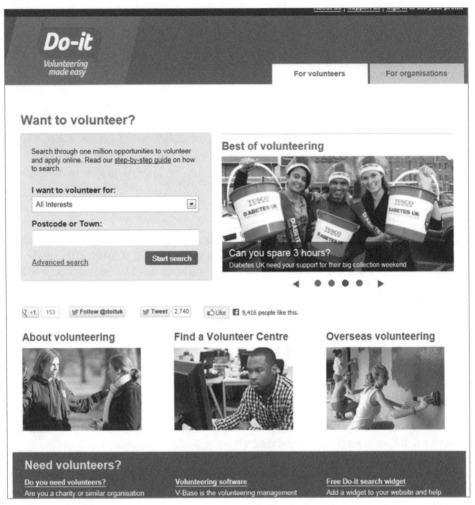

Figure 5.1 www.do-it.org.uk

Working on campus

There should be plenty of opportunities for you to undertake paid or unpaid work that contributes to the life and work of the university. This may involve a regular commitment throughout the academic year, such as work as a student mentor, or be something that occurs on a more occasional basis, such as helping out as a campus guide on university open days.

Student mentor schemes

Many universities operate a student mentor scheme in which new undergraduates are offered the opportunity to be paired with a more experienced student who will act as a source of advice and support on a variety of aspects of university life. This can be a particularly useful service for first year students, many of whom struggle to make the transition from living at home and attending school to the more independent style of university life. Most universities that run a mentoring scheme provide training for mentors and offer support in case the relationship between mentor and mentee becomes complicated; for example, if the mentee is asking for too much support or has encountered personal problems that are too challenging for the mentor. Acting as a student mentor will provide evidence of your verbal communication skills, as you pass on information about university life to your mentee, and is a valuable opportunity to demonstrate leadership skills as you take a guiding role in the relationship.

I took on a mentoring role because it was suggested by my personal tutor. I didn't think that it would be useful for my CV at all but now that I am at the stage of making training contract applications it gives me something to say that involves different skills, particularly verbal communication and creative problem solving, that I would not have been able to demonstrate so well otherwise.

Amanda, Leeds Metropolitan University

Open days and campus tours

Universities are always looking for student volunteers to assist at open days as this provides a valuable peer-to-peer insight into university life for prospective students and can make the business of visiting a university a friendlier and less intimidating experience. Student volunteers will be given guidance on what parts of the university to visit and suggestions of information that they might want to include but are then generally given free rein to take prospective students and their parents around the campus. From the point of view of employability skills, you will be demonstrating your verbal communication skills and the ability to interact well with others as well as skills of organisation and customer service as you respond to the needs of those taking part on the campus tour. In essence, this sort of volunteering makes you look helpful and friendly as well as coming across as the sort of person that likes to get involved in events that are going on around them: all attributes that employers value in the workplace.

I volunteered to work as a tour guide on Open Days because the money was quite good. I quickly discovered that I was really good at it and I really enjoyed taking prospective students round and telling them about the university. It was quite competitive between the guides as to who got the best feedback from people who had been on the tours so I put a lot of effort into planning my tour and thinking of really interesting ways to give people an insight into university life. I was actually offered more part-time work with the Events Marketing Team at my university on the back of this and that gave me the opportunity to gain even more skills.

Amir, University of Salford

Course reps and year reps

Course reps (or representatives) and year reps are interchangeable terms used at universities to describe a student who takes on a position in which they act as an intermediary between the lecturers and the student body at large. The role of these reps is to find out what issues are troubling the students and to communicate these to the academic staff at the appropriate forum, usually a staff-student committee meeting. This is an important role (useful for demonstrating your willingness to take on a position of responsibility) as it enables students to raise any concerns they have about the teaching or content of their course without doing so directly thus ensuring that issues are brought to the attention of the staff. It requires you to represent the interests of students with the staff and therefore demonstrates your aptitude for dealing with difficult situations and interacting in an effective and professional way with lecturers and your peers. As you are representing others and seeking to resolve their problems and disputes, you will also have an example of your advocacy skills in operation.

I was a course rep in my second year and I was really worried at first about looking argumentative with the staff but I actually found it really easy to speak up and put forward the views of others and to argue on their behalf, far easier than it is to argue for yourself. This was quite an eye-opener that made me far more confident that I could work as a solicitor and represent others in due course.

Dustin, Brunel University

If you have been a student rep, try to think of specific examples of issues that you tackled during your time as a course rep to demonstrate the range of your experience to prospective employers:

The main issue that I tackled during my year was the timetabling of exams which left some final year law students with three exams in a two-day period. My intervention was successful in persuading the university to reschedule these exams so that they were more evenly spaced.

Law student

I represented students who were unhappy about the teaching method of a new member of staff. I was able to mediate in the situation to help the students understand that there are a variety of different, but equally effective, approaches to teaching whilst ensuring that the lecturer concerned accommodated some of the more usual practices of lecturers in the school to assist the students to adjust to his methods.

Law student

WHERE NEXT?

This chapter did not set out to make you think that you cannot do things that you enjoy just because they do not seem to enhance your CV. Rather, its aim is to encourage you to scrutinise the things that you enjoy doing to see if they can be used to demonstrate key employability skills, particularly ones that are not covered by your academic studies or employment and work experience. It also aims to ensure that you appreciate how skills-rich certain activities can be and to encourage you to think about taking on new activities that will fill any gaps in your skills portfolio. You can still be selective about this, choosing activities that appeal to you and which fit in with the time that you have available.

Practical exercise: reviewing your skills

Look back at the first practical activity at the beginning of this chapter. Can you add to the list of activities now that you have read this chapter or find more skills in the activities that you enjoy in your spare time? You should also be able to establish a link between your activities and the employability skills that they demonstrate. Remember the formula for doing this:

- This is what I do
- This is the skill that it demonstrates
- This is how it will be useful in legal practice.

Try to make sure that every activity you do that you feel demonstrates a skill is represented on your CV. Give particular thought to identifying challenges that you encountered whilst taking part in activities and what you did to overcome them. You should also emphasise any awards or prizes that you achieved and highlight the progression of your skills either by dint of practice or by undertaking instruction.

Commercial awareness and networking

6

INTRODUCTION

This chapter covers two aspects of employability that can really help students stand out from other applicants. The first of these is commercial awareness. Commercial awareness usually features very highly on the wish list of skills for a career in law, but it is a valuable transferable employability skill regardless of career path. However, many students are unsure about what the term 'commercial awareness' actually means, or how they should go about acquiring it, developing it, and demonstrating it. This means that by taking some proactive steps to build your commercial awareness you will greatly enhance your overall employability skills portfolio. This chapter will first explain what is meant by commercial awareness and go on to provide some practical advice on how to develop it. The second aspect is networking: building effective relationships with others inside and outside the professions. The second part of this chapter will explain why networking is important, and give some pointers on how you can start networking and how to make the most of it. It will give a brief introduction to LinkedIn: an online tool for professional networking, before closing with some practical advice on making the most of law fairs.

Commercial awareness is important, since all commercial businesses exist to make a profit and all self-employed people need to earn a living. Therefore, it does not matter whether you end up working in a law firm, in-house in another business, or at the self-employed Bar: you will need some awareness of the business world in which both you and your clients exist. Networking is important as it enables you to build a list of useful contacts and connections, within which you can find opportunities and establish relationships within the legal profession. Such relationships will stand you in good stead in your search for employment and beyond. In addition, your first-hand interaction with members of your network will enable you to hear directly what is going on in their businesses and therefore will also enhance your commercial awareness. The two activities therefore go hand-in-hand.

Commercial awareness

Put simply, commercial awareness requires some knowledge of the business or financial context in which firms, transactions, or situations exist and operate. Therefore, in order to demonstrate this, you will need to have a basic level of understanding of the factors that underpin and influence successful businesses: how they work, what their employees do, how they are organised, and the issues that they face.

Commercial awareness is important to careers on both sides of the traditional legal professions:

- As a solicitor, you will be providing legal advice that will have some sort of financial dimension (particularly if you become a commercial lawyer). At the very least you will need to be aware of what your clients need, why they need it, and how much they are prepared to pay for it. As your career progresses to more senior positions within the firm, you will become more deeply involved in decisions that will have a commercial impact on your own firm's business. If you demonstrate the capacity for developing new client relationships, or, in time, new products or services, then you will be a good acquisition for a law firm. Remember the Legal Services Act 2007 opened up competition in the legal marketplace and introduced alternative business structures (ABSs): as such, commercial competitiveness is crucial for all law firms. Firms of solicitors are traditionally structured as limited liability partnerships (LLPs). You can find out what this means on the Companies House website at **www.companieshouse.gov.uk/infoAndGuide/llp.shtml**.

You will find more on ABSs in Chapter 8.

- As a barrister, you will be responsible for the commercial aspects of your own practice and the impact of that on your chambers. Of course, commercial barristers will need to demonstrate higher standards of commercial awareness.

Many students will think that they are not commercially aware, but commercial awareness is an employability skill that can be developed just like any other, as your experience, research, and learning continues. In order to develop your commercial awareness, there are a number of activities that you can undertake:

- **Develop your knowledge of current business issues.** You can do this by reading a business newspaper (or the business section of a serious newspaper) regularly. Sign up for alerts from the financial websites, listen to radio financial programmes, or watch business programmes on television. This does not have to be dull. You can start to develop your interests in financial and commercial matters by focusing on stories that relate to your own interests. For example, if you are an avid football supporter, look to see what transfer or loan deals are being done in the January transfer window and start to think of the commercial aspects of each of them such as player salaries, investments by clubs looking for promotion or trying to avoid relegation, or the need for clubs in financial difficulties to sell players. Thinking about the commercial aspects of something that interests you should build your curiosity in other commercial areas and start to build your skills in analysing situations from a commercial perspective. When you next read a business article that interests you, think beyond the main business or financial effects to the legal, social, or political implications that could arise (or have already arisen). Analysing a few stories in depth is preferable to a superficial knowledge of many.

- **Develop your knowledge of the commercial issues facing the legal professions.** You can develop your knowledge of the commercial environment and pressures facing the legal community by reading the legal press and subscribing to news alerts from them. You should also consider how the general state of the economy may affect the professions and whether any proposed reforms may have a positive or negative effect.

Practical exercise: commercial awareness

Have a look at the story in Figure 6.1.

| Home | News | In Practice | In Business | Features | Opinion | Blogs | Moving On |

Peers pursue low-cost arbitration service

Monday 04 February 2013 by **John Hyde**

A group of four peers will this week make the case for an arbitration service for defamation cases.

In an amendment to the Defamation Bill to be debated tomorrow, the Lords want to follow the recommendation of the Leveson report and push forward a low-cost arbitration service.

Courts would be encouraged to take into account whether claimants or defendants have chosen to use the service when awarding costs and damages.

Even successful parties may be ordered to pay all the costs of proceedings if they have unreasonably refused to use an available recognised arbitration service.

The lord chief justice would establish a Defamation Recognition Commission to appoint an independent regulatory board to provide the service.

Figure 6.1 *The Law Society Gazette*

You will see that the story concerns a proposed arbitration service for cases that involve defamation. It mentions the impact on costs for both claimants and defendants and the introduction of a new Defamation Recognition Commission. Think about the commercial implications of this, should it go ahead, and then consider the following questions:

• What impact would this have on law firms that specialise in defamation cases?

• Is it right that the law should impose a financial penalty on those who refuse alternative dispute resolution?

☺ Compare your thoughts with those provided on the Online Resource Centre.

• **Understand how law firms operate.** You should make sure that you understand how firms of solicitors and chambers operate: how they are structured, how they find and retain clients, and how they make and spend their money. In anticipation of your interview, research the market/sector in which you are looking to be recruited, and the main competition. You can also gain useful insight by talking to practitioners at events or open days.

- **Think about your own commercial experience.** It is likely that you already have some awareness of commercial issues, even if you might think otherwise. If you have had work experience outside the law, then think about how the organisation that you have worked for is organised and how it operates. Who are its customers? What is it trying to achieve? How well does it manage? If you have helped to run a university society, you will have encountered objectives, members (customers), finances, and policies in some form: all of which are key components of a commercial operation. Even if you have just sold some textbooks via online auction, you will probably have made some commercial decisions—how many other similar books are for sale, how much have they sold for, where should you set your asking price, how much should you charge for postage and packing?

An important point to note is that there is a distinction between 'awareness' and 'knowledge': many students fret that they need to grasp the minute details of the commercial world, but, as a trainee or pupil, they will not be expected to know everything from the outset. So, employers will not expect you to have comprehensive commercial knowledge or fully developed commercial skills: these can only be achieved after substantial commercial experience. However, they will expect you to have a genuine and demonstrable interest and understanding of business issues, the concepts of the commercial world, and the context in which legal services are provided.

Some suggestions of sources that you can investigate and which offer useful insight are listed in Table 6.1. Not all of them will suit you, but do try some. As you read, watch, or listen, think about the commercial context/impact of the features you encounter, just as you did in the practical exercise earlier in this chapter.

Table 6.1 Some useful sources of commercial information

General press	*The Times* (the law supplement is published on Thursdays)
	The Daily Telegraph (particularly the Saturday edition)
	The Guardian (also has a law supplement)
	The Financial Times
	The Economist
	BBC News website (**www.bbc.co.uk/news**)
Legal press	*The Lawyer*
	Legal Week
	Law Society Gazette
Television	BBC News
	Channel 4 News (a longer format gives time for more in-depth reporting)
	Newsnight
BBC Radio 4/World Service (also on iPlayer)	Today Programme
	Global Business
	World Business Report

Networking

Love it or hate it (and opinion seems to be split amongst law students), networking is important. It gives you the opportunity to make an impression upon people who may, directly or indirectly, provide career opportunities to you. More than this, however, it is an important employability skill in its own right as the ability to make useful professional contacts thereby generating business or forging valuable mutually beneficial working relationships is a significant part of professional life. In essence, it is the skill of making the right impression and creating a network of professional contacts that can further your career or the business prospects of the organisation for which you work.

So how can networking help you as a law student and what opportunities exist for you to network within the legal profession?

Why network?

You already have a network. It is your family, friends, fellow students, lecturers, and anyone else that you associate with on a regular basis. It may be that you can use this network to create employment opportunities: perhaps a family member works as a solicitor or a lecturer will recommend you to one of their contacts for work experience. However, in order to find opportunities that will strengthen your career prospects more effectively, it would be useful to expand your network of contacts to include people working within the legal profession.

You may think that networking is unnecessary—surely the 'its not what you know but who you know' era has long gone and everybody has an equal chance to apply for work experience, training contracts, and pupillage. This is certainly true to a degree, particularly in relation to advertised opportunities but there are two ways in which networking can nonetheless be advantageous:

- It can alert you to opportunities that are not advertised. Not all firms routinely offer work experience and there are certain opportunities, such as shadowing a judge, that tend to be available if asked for but not advertised as such. Meeting people and asking them whether opportunities are available is a great way to create something that would not have otherwise existed.

- It can give you the edge over other candidates if someone at a firm or chambers can endorse your application on the basis of having some personal knowledge of you. It takes some of the gamble out of the appointment process if you have managed to create a positive impression on someone who works for the firm or chambers in question.

Practical example: the value of personal knowledge

Brian Clough, England footballer and controversial manager who led Nottingham Forest to consecutive European Cup victories in 1979 and 1980, once famously said 'we were a good team on paper. Unfortunately, the game was played on grass'.

This gap between how a person seems 'on paper' and how they actually perform in practice is a perennial problem for employers. As the chair of a pupillage committee at a London chambers put it 'students these days seem to get a great deal of help with their applications so it is very often the case that an applicant who appears brilliant on paper is considerably less so in person when they turn up for their mini pupillage'.

If you are known to somebody at the law firm or chambers to which you are applying for work experience, training contract or pupillage, they can comment on their experience of you as a person, confirming or contradicting the impression that you have given in your paper application. Therefore, it cannot hinder your prospects of success if you build up a series of contacts and use these to strengthen your applications. For example, if you are able to write 'I met Mrs James at our university pro bono dinner and she suggested that I apply to your firm for work experience due to my interest in employment law' then it implies that the person in question formed a favourable opinion of your capability and suitability. Of course, this may not be true and Mrs James may have said this to be polite but a quick question to her is all that is needed. A response 'oh yes, he was so well informed about recent cases and seemed very personable and enthusiastic' is likely to make your application stand out from another applicant who is equally good 'on paper' but who presents more of a gamble for the law firm because have no basis upon which to judge whether they will live up to the promise of their paper application.

Finding networking opportunities

You can network anywhere that you meet someone who is involved in the legal profession. There are obvious places to do this—you will always find solicitors, barristers, and judges at court—but part of your networking strategy should include ensuring that you are ready and able to network if you should have a chance encounter with a lawyer in an unexpected place. In essence, you should be able to get stuck in a lift with a lawyer for five minutes and come away having made a useful contact to add to your network (plus a promise of work experience if you have done really well).

This leads on to another facet of successful networking: you must ensure that you make a positive impression. This requires some prior thought and preparation. It is not enough (for most people anyway—some people are just naturally good at creating opportunities out of nothing with no prior thought) simply to bumble your way through a conversation with any solicitor you happen to meet and expect to come away with two weeks' work experience in your pocket! Bear in mind the following points as they will help you to network successfully and with confidence:

- **Be able to start a conversation.** It will usually be up to you to initiate contact so you need to be able to introduce yourself in a way that creates a good first impression. Practise your handshake and introduction until it feels natural and appears confident.

- **Think about what you want to say about yourself.** This will depend to a degree on the situation in which you meet the other person and what you want to achieve. For example, if you meet a barrister who has come to your university to judge a moot, it is not necessary to say 'I am a law student at the University of x' but you would want to say this if the encounter took place at court. Formulate some stock sentences that you can combine that capture who you are and what your interest is that are appropriate to the situations in which you might encounter lawyers. You will find some suggestions on the Online Resource Centre.

- **Keep the conversation going.** As it was you that initiated contact and are the one that wants something from the conversation, the onus is on you to keep it flowing. Moreover, it provides an instant demonstration of your verbal communication skills. Open questions are useful—these are questions that require information as an answer rather than a one word response so try questions such as 'what makes x a good place to work?' rather than 'is x a good place to work?' and 'what sort of work experience would be most useful?' rather than 'should I get more work experience?'. You can create a list of questions to help you maintain a conversation as part of your preparation for networking.

- **Ask for suggestions.** Remember that creating contacts is not the only purpose behind networking. It can also be a great source of inspiration and guidance in terms of your future career. All solicitors, barristers, and judges have already achieved what you want to achieve so do not be afraid to ask them for advice.

- **Build your network.** The person you are speaking to already has their own network of legal contacts so try to tap into it by asking for suggestions of other people that you could contact. You can then start your initial email by saying 'x suggested that I contact you because…' as this personal recommendation is more likely to elicit a positive response.

- **Remember names.** It is no good sending an email that starts 'I met someone who works at your firm who suggested that I get in touch with you and ask about work experience' because you have forgotten the name of your contact. An inability to name the person you spoke to does nothing to strengthen your approach and it looks very unprofessional.

- **Make contact.** Ask for a contact email address and get in touch with the person shortly after meeting them to thank them for their help and to follow up on any other relevant points: for example, you may have offered to send them your CV, asked for further information about a case they were handling, or asked for details of someone to contact about work experience. Keep your email short, polite, and relatively formal as well as ensuring that it is well presented and free from errors.

- **Keep in touch.** Make a note of who you have met and what it is that you want to achieve from networking with them and follow up your initial contact after an appropriate period of time. You could update them on significant achievements or on developments that are relevant to what you discussed, for example:

  ○ You may remember that we discussed my dissertation on family-friendly maternity policies as it was relevant to one of your cases. I am pleased to say that I have received first class marks for my dissertation, thanks in part to the sources that you suggested: please do let me send you a copy by way of thanks as it contains a summary of some recent European developments that might be of interest to you.

  ○ When we met, you suggested that I contact your associate, John Garvey, with a view to securing work experience given my interest in environmental law. I did as you suggested and am pleased to report that I will be working with him for six weeks over the summer. I wanted to let you know and to thank you for the suggestion.

- **Provide a point of reference.** Make life easy for your contact by providing a short statement that will help them to remember you. Something like 'you judged a moot at my university last week and we talked about European consumer law' or 'we met at your firm's open day and you suggested that I contact you about the case you are working on about criminal liability for sporting injuries'. If the person you contact cannot remember speaking to you, they are less inclined to answer so it can be useful to provide a reminder.

Tell us

We'd like to hear about your best (or worst!) networking experience. Tell us at finchandfafinski.com/get-in-touch or @FinchFafinski on Twitter.

The final point to consider is where you can go to meet people to add to your network of professional contacts. It can be a good idea to start in an environment where you feel comfortable as you are more likely to be calm and confident when meeting people in familiar surroundings. Does your university have a law fair where you can meet local solicitors and barristers or perhaps there are links between your law school and a particular local chambers or law firm that leads to some shared events? These events organised for your law school are the obvious place to start networking. Alternatively, you may find that local solicitors or barristers visit your school to give talks about the legal profession or to judge a moot or your student law society may arrange a visit to one of the Inns of Court. These are all good networking opportunities where the lawyers that you meet will be expecting to talk to students about the legal profession.

As you grow in confidence, you can expand the scope of your networking operation. Investigate the possibility of attending an open day or insight event at one of the large law firms. These are designed to give law students an insight into the operation, work, and ethos of the firm and are an excellent opportunity to meet practitioners and build contacts within the legal profession. They are often targeted at students in their first year so it is important to look out for these opportunities at an early stage of your studies.

Practical example: open days and insight events

Addleshaw Goddard has two one-day events for first year students held during the Easter vacation: one in London and one in their Leeds office. These provide students with an insight into the firm's practice areas and life as a trainee solicitor. There will be an opportunity to meet partners, trainees, and the graduate recruitment team and a session that helps students to think about the process of applying for a training contract with hints on how to make your application stand out from others.

DLA Piper host three one-day insight days for first year students during June each year. These introduce students to the firm and to life as a commercial lawyer. As well as offering an opportunity to meet partners, associates, trainees, and the graduate recruitment team, the days offer advice on how to develop commercial awareness and share the secrets of making a successful application.

Eversheds offer a different sort of experience to first and second year law students with their Big Deal event that takes place in March each year in their London, Birmingham, and Leeds offices. This gives students the opportunity to work in small teams on a simulated multi-agency international deal which includes experience of brokering an agreement, creating a marketing strategy, holding a press conference, and negotiating in the boardroom. Students work alongside experienced lawyers and the event is a great insight into the commercial reality of legal practice.

Court is an obvious place to meet legal practitioners but remember that they are there to work so they may be rather busy or preoccupied when you try to engage them in conversation. Watch proceedings and try to predict good times to approach people—this may be a matter of trial and error so try not to be daunted if someone you approach is brusque and does not want to speak to you but learn from this and time your future approaches differently. The added advantage about approaching a solicitor or barrister at court is that you can ask about the case that you have just seen them working on as a way of engaging them in conversation.

I was sitting in the magistrates' court out of interest one summer and there was a case about a lady who had been picking wild mushrooms and was charged with theft. I asked the solicitor who represented her about this as I was genuinely curious as I had thought that things growing wild did not fall within theft and he offered to have coffee with me and explain it. We had a really good discussion and I ended up with an offer of two weeks' work experience starting the following day without even having to ask for it!

A further opportunity for networking arises during any work experience that you have secured. Not only will you meet practitioners working for the particular firm or chambers but it is possible that you will meet other solicitors and barristers as you go about your work. Be sure to explain to them that you are a student on work experience and try to add them to your network. Express an interest in their work and ask if there is an opportunity for work experience with them. This can be a good strategy:

I spent the week of my mini pupillage at Snaresbrook Crown Court on a trial involving drugs and weapons. My advice is that you should get involved and be friendly with the other side—they may offer you a mini pupillage after if you show enough enthusiasm: it happened to me!

Practical example: networking schemes

Pure Potential organises events for students wanting an insight into the legal profession that includes networking advice and opportunities, guidance on applying for vacancies for vacation schemes and training contracts, as well as a visit to a leading London law firm. You will find further details on their website: **www.purepotential.org/events/pp-law**.

City Solicitors' Education Trust Summer School is a residential skills-training event to be held at Queen Mary University of London. It includes group and individual structured sessions on making a successful application, confident networking, and the commercial background to legal practice while providing business and social networking opportunities. Students will meet senior representatives and graduates from leading law firms as well as visiting the firms' offices. Further details are available online: **www.cset.org.uk/?page=cset-summer-school**.

City Law for ethnic minorities organises a two-day event to facilitate networking between eligible students and representatives of top City law firms. The event includes real business activities and law case studies to provide insight into the legal profession. It also includes the opportunity to meet graduate recruiters and develop essential skills and interview techniques for vacation schemes and training contracts. For further details, see: **targetjobsevents.co.uk/city-law-for-ethnic-minorities**

LinkedIn

There is a theory known as six degrees of separation which surmises that everyone is six or fewer introductions away from anyone else in the world. In other words, any two people can be connected through 'friends of friends' in a maximum of six steps. There is an associated game known as 'Six Degrees of Kevin Bacon' in which the goal is to link any actor to Kevin Bacon through no more than six connections (two actors are connected if they appeared in a film, television show, or commercial together). For example: Stefan Fafinski appeared with Professor Brian Cox on a show with the British Science Association in 2006; Brian Cox and Jonathan Ross appeared on Stargazing Live; and Kevin Bacon appeared with Jonathan Ross on Film 2005. Therefore Stefan's Bacon Number is 3 (Fafinski—Cox—Ross—Bacon).

LinkedIn (**www.linkedin.com**) is a social networking site for professionals. It enables individuals to create a profile and contact network and to grow it through introductions to the contacts of their contacts. It is essentially a professional manifestation of Six Degrees of Kevin Bacon.

However, this does not mean that you are instantly going to get connected to the managing partner of each of the major firms or the heads of chambers in the City. If you choose to use LinkedIn, there are some basic principles that you should follow:

- **Keep it professional.** LinkedIn exists as a professional directory. It has different norms to other social networking sites and you should use it in a way that reflects that standing.

- **Build your profile.** Add the details of your academic and employment history. Unlike a static CV, LinkedIn allows you to continually update your activities and to demonstrate the steps that you are taking to build your employability skills portfolio.

- **Build your network.** Start with people that you know: fellow students and academics. Add people that you meet both online and offline in whatever context. However, do not send out a huge number of speculative requests to connect with people that you do not actually know. Not only is this ill-mannered, but can be quite irritating for the recipient. If you build a good network, not only will this show that you are not afraid to network, but your network may also be useful to your employer in the future.

- **Seek recommendations.** LinkedIn allows you to receive recommendations for your work. Therefore if you have had a successful work experience, pupillage, or placement, ask if your employer would be willing to write you a positive recommendation endorsing your position on LinkedIn.

- **Join groups.** There are a huge number of interest groups on LinkedIn. You should consider joining those that are linked to your university and law school. Then look to see if there are relevant groups for legal areas in which you are interested or would like to work. If there is no group that suits exactly what you are seeking, then think about starting one: this will demonstrate entrepreneurial skills. Do not hold back from joining groups in areas outside the law: this will show that you can relate and engage with people with similar interests but different backgrounds.

Overall, LinkedIn is a useful networking tool, if used professionally and carefully. You can find us on LinkedIn at **www.linkedin.com/in/stefanfafinski** and **www.linkedin.com/in/dremilyfinch**.

Law fairs

Law fairs are a great networking opportunity for you to meet practitioners, current trainees, and graduate recruiters and to find out more about their firms. They are usually held on campus in the autumn term. Not only are they an opportunity for you to find out more, they also offer recruiters the first opportunity to meet you face-to- face in a setting that is a lot less formal (and intimidating) than an interview.

To make the most of a law fair:

- **Think about your practice area.** This chapter will have enabled you to have, at the very least, a rough idea of the sorts of areas that you would ultimately want to practise and why. If you are able to communicate this to recruiters from firms involved in those areas, then this will demonstrate that you have already started preparing for success.

You will find more detail on various areas of legal practice in Chapter 8.

- **Find out who's going and do some research.** You should find out what firms are attending and draw up a plan of those that you think will be most interesting for you to meet. There will probably not be enough time for you to talk to everyone, so be focused. When you know which firms you will be approaching, do some preliminary research into who they are and what they do. Even at this early stage, recruiters do not appreciate explaining what their firm does or giving out very basic information that could easily have been found on the firm's website homepage.

- **Be confident and personable.** Being armed with a little knowledge about your preferred areas of work and the firms you are meeting should give you some confidence. Always give your name, as firms often pro-actively approach impressive candidates after a fair. Try to be as natural as possible (for more advice on this, see the section in Chapter 12 on interview technique) and ask suitable questions about the firm. These could include the culture of the firm, the style of training and the structure of the training contract, or the opportunity for travel (but only for firms with overseas/multiple offices!). Whatever questions you prepare, ask them of all the firms you meet. That way you will have a consistent framework for evaluating them afterwards.

- **Talk to trainees.** Do not overlook the value in talking to current trainees. While you will want to be memorable to recruiters (for the right reasons), trainees will be able to give you first-hand accounts of the reality of training in that firm.

- **Be patient.** Law fairs can be quite chaotic places and queue jumping can happen. Stay calm, wait patiently, and be polite. These professional characteristics can—and are— noted by recruiters, just as negative behaviour is also noted.

WHERE NEXT?

By following the advice in this chapter, you should find that you have demystified two of the areas that students are often concerned about. Commercial awareness and networking are two key skills that, if properly developed and demonstrated, will greatly enhance your employability skills.

The next chapter looks at a more practical way of building your employability skills with concrete examples to back them up: work experience.

7

Work experience

INTRODUCTION

This chapter focuses on all aspects of work experience. It explains the importance of work experience for law students and the benefits to be gained as well as outlining the different kinds of work experience available. It covers work experience in a law firm, mini pupillages, and other less common opportunities such as marshalling a judge that will add variety to your work experience portfolio as well as outlining opportunities for law-related voluntary work. It includes advice on how to find and apply for work experience and how to make a good impression during your placement. The chapter concludes with guidance on how to find opportunities to undertake the various types of work experience including advice on how to write an effective speculative application.

Students tend to recognise that it is important that they gain work experience but often lack understanding of what work they should do, how to find it and, crucially, when to do it. This lack of awareness can lead to a situation in which students leave it far too late, only thinking about work experience in their final year when the reality of the end of the degree is looming. Of course, it is not too late but there is a limit to what can be done in a year, especially when this has to be combined with the demands of final year studies. This chapter will encourage you to think about work experience from the very first day of your degree (if not before) and explain what you need to be doing to ensure that you have a portfolio of varied and relevant work experience as well as a degree when you graduate.

Benefits of work experience

There is a strong link in most people's minds between work experience and employment. In other words, it is usual to think that the benefit of work experience is that it will help you to get a job or, in the case of law students, a training contract or pupillage as an interim step that will enable you to enter the legal profession as a qualified solicitor or barrister. Obviously, this is an important factor but work experience is not only valuable because it enhances your employability; there are a range of other benefits to be gained:

- **Development of skills.** Work experience with a solicitor or barrister will help you to understand how the law in practice differs from the academic study of law. You will start to develop the skills that you will need as a legal practitioner such as working under time pressure, dealing with clients, and other aspects of professional life. This will demonstrate to prospective employers that you have an aptitude for working within the legal profession and, just as important, the glimpse that it affords into legal practice will increase your confidence in your ability to do the job of a solicitor or barrister.

- **Career decisions.** How do you know that you want to be a solicitor rather than a barrister or that you want to practise commercial law in a large City firm rather than family law in a high street firm? You might think that you know what type of legal career you want but undertaking a diverse range of work experience will enable you to make a more informed decision about your future career objectives. This will help you to target particular vacancies that fit your desired specifications (size of firm, area of practice etc.) and this will strengthen your application as you will have a basis to demonstrate to potential employers that you are looking for a particular kind of practice based upon your work experience rather than blindly applying for every training contract.

- **Confidence.** In order to succeed at interview and other stages of the recruitment process, you need to come across as a person who is confident in the workplace and in your interactions with colleagues and clients. Few people achieve this confidence without experience in a professional environment. Work experience gives you the opportunity to become familiar with working practices within a law firm, chambers, or other workplace, to develop a professional outlook and to gain confidence in handling the situations and people that are part and parcel of employment in a professional setting.

- **Commercial awareness.** The business of working within the law is a world away from its study at university level. Work experience will enable you to understand the commercial reality of legal practice and give you an understanding of the operation of the legal profession. This is important because it is sadly often the case that academic success is not necessarily an indicator of potential to work effectively in an employment setting. Work experience gives you the opportunity to demonstrate that you can work well with others (colleagues and clients) and within the procedural parameters of legal practice.

- **Interview practice.** The process of obtaining work experience often mirrors the process of applying for training contracts and pupillages in that you will need to locate appropriate vacancies, complete an application form, and attend an interview. As with anything, you should get better at these things with practice so you are polishing your application and interview skills ready to apply for training contracts and pupillages every time you apply for work experience. You will learn what works and what does not work on the basis of your successful and unsuccessful applications and you may find that you receive feedback on your application and interview that helps you to improve subsequent performances.

- **Networking.** Work experience will give you the chance to make good contacts within the legal profession that might help you to find further work experience opportunities so you should strive to make a good impression on everyone that you encounter. You may also find that you further your prospects of gaining a training contract as a result of undertaking work experience as some of the larger law firms use their summer placement schemes as part of the recruitment process.

As you will see from this list, work experience offers benefits far beyond its role in bolstering your CV. It gives you insight into the world of legal practice that will enable you to make informed decisions about your future, strengthen your prospects for success with future applications, and gives both you and prospective employers confidence that you can operate in a professional setting. However, the most immediate driving force that should create an impetus for you to seek out work experience is that you will be competing for training contracts or pupillage places against students who have work experience. Do not put yourself at a disadvantage.

I was able to get various work experience placements though throughout my degree and also several mini pupillages. These helped in many ways. Firstly, I was familiar with an office environment before starting my job which made me feel much more confident on my first day. I was also able to gain an insight into how a law firm works in practice, first-hand experience of dealing with clients and attending court and colleagues and also an understanding of various legal terminology and procedures. Secondly, I was able to judge which career path I wanted to take by observing both solicitors and barristers at work. In short, work experience taught me a whole range of things that you simply cannot learn at law school.

Lizzie, law graduate

Practical advice: diversity in work experience

Keep these benefits in mind when making applications for work experience to ensure that you target a range of different opportunities to ensure that your work experience portfolio is diverse as this maximises your opportunity to develop the whole spectrum of employability skills. Try to find a mix of large and small law firms, City and provincial practices, and different areas of specialisation as well as working for different lengths of time: you will get a different insight into legal practice working for a month than you will for a week. Not only will this variety give you a breadth of experience that will impress prospective employers, you will gain a greater insight into the sort of work that you most enjoy which will help you to make decisions about your career path.

Don't panic

Are you worried about work experience? Perhaps the experience described in the following practical example sounds familiar to you:

Practical example: worried about work experience?

The whole work experience thing took me by surprise in my second year. Up until then, nobody had mentioned it all and then, all of a sudden, all of my friends were talking about what work experience they had lined up. I was the only person, or so it seemed, that hadn't done anything plus they were all telling me it was too late to do anything now. The received wisdom was that if I didn't have it by now, I wouldn't get any this year and if I didn't do it in my second year then I wouldn't get any in my final year. And, of course, without work experience then I had no chance of getting a training contract. So I felt as if my chances of a career in law were finished and I was only halfway through the second year of my degree. It was pretty depressing. Foolishly, I didn't do anything about it—largely because I didn't know what to do—but then, in the final year, I was talking about it to one of the lecturers. She told me that it was never too late and sat down with me for about an hour to put together a plan of action which I followed and, by return of email, I had my first piece of work experience! I ended up fitting five different pieces of work experience into my final year. And, yes, I did get a training contract so all the fear-mongers who said that it wouldn't happen because I didn't have work experience in a City firm in my second year were wrong.

Ryan, University of Law LPC

Unfortunately, Ryan's experience is not uncommon. Many students do not appreciate the need to start finding work experience until quite a late stage of their degree as not all universities are active in pointing this out to students. This can lead to a feeling that you have 'missed the boat' if everyone else has work experience and you do not but remember, it does not matter what point you are at in your studies—or even if you have already graduated—it is never too late to start looking for work experience. Do not measure your work experience (or lack of it) by comparison with other students: whether or not they have work experience is of no relevance whatsoever to your situation so concentrate on working out a strategy for finding work experience rather than worrying about what other students are doing. Similarly, try not to be too influenced by the urban myths that circulate about work experience: there is no magic time or type of work experience that will open the door to a training contract or pupillage. It is simply the case that the earlier you start, the more work experience you can acquire during your degree and this will have an obvious impact on the strength of your training contract and pupillage applications.

So if, like Ryan, you feel that you have left it a bit late, try not to worry. Despite not looking for work experience until a late stage of his degree, Ryan secured a fair amount of work experience in his final year and was successful in obtaining a training contract. You will be able to find work experience that will help you on the way towards a training contract, pupillage, or other career path of your choice if you follow the advice and guidance set out in this chapter.

Before then, though, we are going to look at three common reasons that students panic about work experience:

• I don't know how to get work experience

• I don't know what to do on work experience

• I don't have any work experience.

It is often the case that the third problem—not having done any significant work experience—is a consequence of one (or both) of the first two problems. Students often fail to acquire any work experience either because they simply do not know how to go about gaining work placements or they are so worried that they will not know how to do the work that is required of them that they avoid doing work experience altogether. Each of these problems has the potential to lead to the same outcome— you will complete your degree without work experience and be at a competitive disadvantage to other students in the competition for a training contract or pupillage. Even if you decide that you do not want to practise law, the lack of experience in a professional working environment may be a significant impediment to the development of any alternative career.

So how can each of these three problems be avoided or overcome?

I don't know how to get work experience

It is most unfortunate that so many students miss the work experience boat because they do not know how to go about securing work placements. It seems to be the case that universities differ enormously in the level of help that they give students with finding work experience and the degree to which they publicise the help which is available so it is important that you take the initiative when it comes to seeking out work placements:

• **Act sooner rather than later.** It is never too early to get work experience; in fact, some students do this whilst at school and turn up at university with three or four law-based placements under their belts. The sooner you start, the more experience you can acquire.

- **Ask everyone for help and advice.** If other students have work experience, ask how they obtained it. Ask your personal tutor for guidance and visit the careers service at your university. See if any one amongst your family and their friends has any useful contacts in the legal profession. If solicitors, barristers, or judges visit your university, try to find an opportunity to ask for their advice or, even better, ask for a day or week of work experience with them.

- **Find out what your university offers.** More and more universities are offering support to students looking for work experience so see what services are available and use them. There may be a database of work experience that you can search on the university website or there may be a person in the law school whose role it is to offer career guidance or someone within the careers service that specialises in law placements.

- **Do it yourself.** Do not rely on the university to provide work placements —a great many do not do this at all and, in any case, there are far more opportunities available than are made available through your university. Make it your responsibility to find your own work experience. Carry out a search on the Internet to find solicitors or barristers in the locality or area of specialism that interests you. There is no magic to this: just type 'solicitors in Guildford practising family law' or 'solicitors in Bournemouth offering work experience'. Get the name of a specific person and send them a short email introducing yourself and asking for work experience.

Practical advice: finding a named contact

If you are making speculative enquiries to a law firm where you have no existing contacts, it is important to direct your request to a particular person rather than using a general enquires form or email address. Look on the firm's website to see if they specify how enquiries for work experience should be made. In the absence of this, telephone the firm and ask for the name of the person to whom requests for work experience should be directed. Alternatively, look under the 'people' link on the firm's website to identify a particular individual with expertise in your chosen field and contact them directly.

I don't know what to do on work experience

For some students, fear of the unknown deters them from making an attempt to gain work experience. This is perfectly understandable: after all, work experience takes you out of your comfort zone as a university student and launches you into a pressured work environment full of busy people. However, it is self-defeating to let this uncertainty hold you back from undertaking work experience as you will never find out what a solicitor or barrister does unless you venture into the workplace. Moreover, without work experience, you are limiting your opportunities to develop and demonstrate employability skills which will be instrumental to your career prospects in the future irrespective of whether or not you practise law.

Practical advice: overcoming your fears

Think about what worries you about taking on work experience. Make a list and be as specific as possible—there's no point in listing something general like a concern about looking silly—you will need to work out what it is that you think that you could do (or not do) that would make you look silly. Once you have a list, look at each item and think about how to avoid the problem from arising or how you would deal with it if it does arise. If you cannot think of solutions, book an appointment with a personal tutor or a careers advisor and ask for their help. Once you have worked out a strategy for dealing with problems, you should feel more confident about making a foray into the workplace.

⚉ Have a think about these common concerns about work experience expressed by law students and consider how you would advise someone to overcome them. You will find our suggestions on the Online Resource Centre.

- I don't know what to wear
- I'm worried that I'll make a mistake with something that will have serious consequences for a case
- I'm afraid that I won't know how to do something that someone asks me to do
- I might run out of things to do and just be hanging around getting in the way
- I might not understand what people are talking about when they discuss cases.

Tell us

Tell us about your concerns regarding work experience and what, if anything, you did to overcome your fears. Contact us at finchandfafinski.com/get-in-touch or @FinchFafinski on Twitter.

Most people feel nervous when going into a new and unfamiliar environment but try not to let this deter you from seeking work experience. After all, it is only by going into the workplace that you will come to understand what it requires of you and therefore become more confident. Everybody you encounter was once new to the firm and new to the practice of law so they will remember this and not expect you to have skills and knowledge beyond your experience. It is very unlikely that you will be asked to do anything particularly complex and if you are in any doubt whatsoever then you should always express this and ask for help. You are there to learn and the firm has offered you work experience to help you learn so do not be afraid to ask for help or clarification of your instructions.

Practical advice: an easy introduction

If you are really anxious and this is stopping you from trying to find work experience, try these suggestions to ease your way into a work placement.

- **Attend an open day.** Many firms have open days to inform law students about their work and to explain what they can expect to do during a work placement. This will give you a chance to see what a firm is like and get an insight into what you will be doing if you apply for work experience.
- **Start with shadowing.** Explain that you are inexperienced and that you would like to shadow a solicitor or barrister—that is, follow them as they go about their daily work—for a short time, even a couple of hours will do. This will allow you to get the feel of the firm and an idea of what work they might require from someone on work experience.
- **Go to court.** Dress smartly, sit in on a few cases, and identify the solicitors and/or barristers involved. At an appropriate time, start a conversation in which you tell them that you are a student and ask if they have ten minutes to tell you about the case over coffee. This will give you an opportunity to ask for a day (or more) of work experience with them.

Each of these three suggestions gives you some exposure to a firm by taking you into their offices or establishing a link with a solicitor before you apply for work experience. This will take some of the unfamiliarity out of the situation and help you to take your first steps in the legal work environment.

I don't have any work experience

Let's imagine that it is almost April in the final year of your degree. Your exams are looming and you have just been told the date of your graduation ceremony. Other students are boasting about training contracts that they have secured or have a list of impressive work experience that spans several pages of their CV. You, however, have no work experience at all.

Whilst this is not the best situation you could be in, all is not lost. You will have the summer vacation after graduation and before starting the LPC or BPTC to gain relevant work experience plus there will be opportunities available for work experience once you start to study for these professional qualifications. Moreover, you could always take a year out before commencing the next stage of your studies to work as a paralegal which will both give you an in-depth insight into the legal profession and earn money to pay for the LPC or BPTC.

See Chapter 9 for further details on working as a paralegal.

The sections that follow will provide guidance for all students, irrespective of the stage of your studies, on how to find work experience. Before then, you might find it useful to read the section on getting started as this answers some commonly asked questions about work experience.

Getting started

This section of the chapter will cover some preliminary matters about work experience that answers the three questions most commonly asked by law students such as:

- When should I start applying for work experience?
- What sort of work experience should I do?
- How much work experience am I expected to have?

Before addressing these questions, we will deal with a more fundamental issue which is to define what we mean by work experience in this chapter.

What is work experience?

There is a general and a specific answer to this question. In general, work experience refers to any experience of the world of employment so would refer to any full-time or part-time jobs that you have had irrespective of the nature of the employment or the industry within which you worked. It could also refer to unpaid employment such as voluntary work. So the answer to the question 'what work experience do you have?' could be 'I worked part-time for two years in the Student Union bar and I volunteered at a hostel for homeless people for three months in the summer as part of my Duke of Edinburgh award'. However, in this book and in the context of university life as a law student, work experience refers to a more specific type of activity: it is work undertaken, paid or unpaid and irrespective of its duration, in an environment that gives you insight into working life within the legal profession. This might involve:

- Temporary work on a part-time or full-time basis in a law firm
- A mini pupillage with a barrister

- A vacation scheme involving a structured placement of one or two weeks in a large law firm that usually takes place in the summer vacation prior to the final year of study
- Other work in a law firm
- A placement for a longer period, usually six months or one year, which forms part of the assessable component of the degree, often referred to as a sandwich year
- Voluntary work in a pro bono centre or advice centre
- Shadowing a judge or other legal professional for a day.

These are common forms of work experience undertaken by law students but are by no means the only activities that you could undertake. In essence, any work that gives you direct or indirect experience of working within the legal profession or dispensing legal advice will be relevant to your objective of maximising your employability within the legal profession at the end of your degree. Do not be afraid to look for work experience other than with solicitors and barristers: sometimes opportunities exist in unexpected settings:

....

I'd left it too late to apply for summer vacation placements so I applied for a job at the magistrates' court working with the victim liaison team. To be honest, I only did this because it paid quite well for a summer job and had a vague connection with law but it was fascinating. I learned an enormous amount about criminal practice and procedure and decided that I wanted to specialise in criminal law. Talking to the solicitors at the court was really helpful too and it was actually very easy to get work experience with those that I'd met at the courts so it turned out to be a really wonderful opportunity.

Stephanie, De Montfort University

....

Of course, you may decide that you do not want to practise law—sometimes students do this as a direct consequence of undertaking work experience and finding that it is not for them—but the experience of working in a professional environment and the skills you gain will be valuable irrespective of your ultimate career destination. If you are undecided about your career path, you may also find the section on non-law work experience later in this chapter useful.

In the next section, there is some guidance to help you to start planning the timing of your work experience. This is important as students (as the earlier examples illustrate) often fail to realise how early some applications need to be made, particularly for vacation placement schemes at large law firms.

When should I start applying for work experience?

Today.

Start planning your strategy for finding work experience right now. It is never too early to start making preparations for work experience and the earlier you start, the more opportunities there will be available to you. If you have left it rather late to arrange work experience (anything after the Easter vacation of your second year falls into this category) then you need to get moving on your applications as soon as possible. In the sections that follow, you will find advice tailored to the different stages of your academic studies.

Irrespective of whether you are in your first year or final year, you will need to think in a realistic way about how much time you have available to undertake work experience. Take into account the demands of your lectures and tutorials, the amount of private study required, and the timing of coursework and exams plus any paid employment commitments in order to reach a reasoned decision as to whether you could undertake work experience in term time. Even if you have only a few hours spare a week, it might be possible to find an opportunity that fits into your availability. Other than this, consider the three holiday periods: could you do one week at Christmas and another at Easter with more time devoted to work experience in the longer summer break? Making decisions about when you want to undertake work experience is an important factor in the timing of applications.

Another factor that ties in with your availability is the location of your work experience. If you are aiming to work in the holidays then it is likely that you will want to target law firms and barristers working near your home rather than in the vicinity of the university (assuming that you study somewhere other than your home town). This can be advantageous especially if you live in an area where there is no university offering a law degree as these firms are less likely to be overwhelmed with applications than firms located in areas where there is a university with a law school.

Tell us

Resolve to make one application for work experience every day for a month. One application a day will not take you long to research, compose and submit. Get in touch to let us know how many days it took you to achieve success. Tell us at finchandfafinski.com/get-in-touch or @ FinchFafinski on Twitter.

Hopefully, you are convinced that you should start making applications right away so in the next section you will find some guidance on the sort of work experience that you should aim to acquire at each stage of your studies. This is a suggested approach only, to help you to get started, it is not the only approach and the overriding principle is that all work experience is valuable.

What sort of work experience should I do?

As was explained earlier in this chapter, relevant work experience for those considering a career in the legal profession covers any time spent working with a solicitor or barrister as well as any other situation involving the giving of legal advice, the administration of legal rules, or participating in the operation of the justice system. This gives you a great deal of choice of potential work experience. However, the range of options available can be problematic in itself as many students say that they do not know what sort of work experience to undertake and that this uncertainty puts them off making applications.

- I didn't know what to do about work experience so I did nothing at all.
- It seemed like other students knew something that I didn't know about what to do and where to apply. People kept talking about placements they had done and I had no idea how to go about getting work experience myself so I felt more and more left behind.
- I knew we were supposed to get work experience but where from? Do I look for vacancies somewhere or approach firms directly and ask for work experience? If I approach firms directly, how do I know who to contact? Do I write a letter or send an email? I thought that there might be some sort of protocol involved that I'd breach by accident and make myself look silly.

The overriding theme from these quotations from law students is that they had grasped the general idea that it was important for them to gain work experience but that the specific details of how to go about finding and securing work experience were unclear to them. This uncertainty leads far too many students, as the first quotation here illustrates, to do nothing at all. In the sections that follow, you will find some suggestions of the sort of work experience that you should target in each year of your degree along with guidance on how to go about obtaining work experience.

First year

Many students do not think about work experience at all in their first year—after all, it seems like graduation and career choices are a long way off in the future—but it pays to start gaining work experience at the very earliest opportunity. Think about it like this: if you leave it until the second year of your law degree, you will be at a competitive disadvantage compared to other applicants at the same stage of their studies who have already gained work experience as employers are more likely to offer placements to students who have already demonstrated their commitment to a career in law and have proved that they can operate in a professional environment. In particular, you will find it difficult to get accepted onto one of the vacation placement schemes in your second year in the absence of any prior work experience that demonstrates your commitment to a career in law. However, you should not be deterred if you have no prior legal work experience as some firms are prepared to consider work in other environments as relevant work experience:

Work experience is always useful as it consolidates skills that you practise at university, but it doesn't need to be legal. A candidate who has been working part time through their studies or who has had a summer job, will also be using those competencies we are looking for in suitable applicants for the vacation scheme.

Amelia Spinks, Field Fisher Waterhouse

Although many firms operate a vacation placement scheme for second year students, very few have comparable schemes for students in the first year of their studies. There are some exceptions such as the Pathfinders scheme introduced by Linklaters in 2011 to provide work experience for first year law students.

Practical example: pathfinder at Linklaters

The Pathfinder scheme is a two-day programme created by Linklaters to provide first year law students with an early insight into the work of a global law firm. The programme introduces the firm's work, culture, direction, and strategy and provides opportunities for students to work with existing trainees as well as opportunities to develop important skills.

Day 1. Students attend a range of workshops aimed at developing team working, networking, and commercial thinking skills. There is an overview of the recruitment process from the Graduate Recruitment Team that includes hints and tips on applying for the summer vacation scheme and training contracts. The evening social event provides an opportunity for you to get to know others on a more informal basis.

Day 2. Students will shadow a trainee and observe work and life in a leading commercial law firm as well as receiving a personal impact master class which will help you to stand out from the crowd when making future applications.

You will find more information on the Pathfinder scheme at Linklaters on their website: www.linklatersgraduates.co.uk/our-schemes/pathfinder.

There are actually very few placement schemes that are open to students in the first year of their studies so you must be prepared to be proactive and find your own opportunities for work experience by making speculative approaches to law firms. This means that you need to contact a firm directly, usually by email although you could write a letter or telephone, and find out whether they will be prepared to offer you a period of work experience. You can either use the Internet to search for law firms in a particular location (near to your home or to the university is usual) or you can consult a directory such as the Legal 500.

Practical advice: your first application

Because you are in the early stages of your studies with no prior work experience, a solicitor or barrister is likely to have reservations about offering you work experience. You are unlikely to know what to do so it is possible that you will be more of a hindrance than a help in their busy day. Here are some suggestions to help you to make a successful application:

- **Ask for work of limited duration.** Stipulate the dates that you are available and ask for one or two days' work within those dates whilst indicating a willingness to work for a longer period should this be required. This strikes a nice balance between not posing too great a burden on a busy employer if you prove to be a hindrance whilst offering to help out for a longer period of time if they can find a use for you.

- **Acknowledge your inexperience and stress your enthusiasm.** Include a sentence in your letter or email that highlights the reason for your application at this early stage of your legal studies. This could be something that indicates your keenness to experience legal practice or a link between the area of practice in question and a subject that you have studied in your first year. Applications have greater success if they appear tailored to a particular work experience opportunity rather than seeming as if you have taken a scattergun approach by targeting any firm that might take you.

- **Suggest tasks that you could carry out.** As you are inexperienced, some firms may wonder how much supervision you will need and what you will be able to do so make some suggestions. You could shadow a solicitor, do some administrative tasks, carry out research, or take notes at court. Make it clear that you are happy to do anything at all but including some specific suggestions may help a firm to think of work they could ask you to do.

- **Make it clear that you do not expect to be paid.** This lets the employer know that you are looking for experience rather than money and that even if you prove to be a nuisance at least it will be for free!

- **Think about the technicalities of writing.** Your letter or email should be relatively short and to-the-point—no more than one side of A4 if typed—and impeccable in terms of its written style, grammar, spelling, and punctuation. Use your application as an advertisement for your writing skills and attention to detail. Write to a specific named person rather than the more general 'to whom it may concern' and provide contact details so that they can get in touch with you.

⚈ You will find some examples of successful applications for work experience written by first year law students on the Online Resource Centre. Have a look at these to see how these have been drafted.

Tell us

Tell us if you followed this advice and were successful in obtaining work experience. Let us know so that we can share your story (using a pseudonym if you wish) to encourage other students. Send us a copy of your application email and we will feature the best ones on the Online Resource

Centre and in the next edition of the book. Contact us at finchandfafinski.com/get-in-touch or @ FinchFafinski on Twitter.

The guiding principle in your first year is that you should be open to any work experience opportunities that are available even if it is not what you had hoped to achieve or if it is not in an area of law that you anticipate that you might like to practise. This is because all work that you do in the legal environment will help you to develop important employability skills and the experience may strengthen your application for other placements that are more in line with your plans and preferences in the future. Besides, it may be that the two days that you have been offered working with, say, an aerospace lawyer actually sparks an interest and influences your future plans. After all, until you have tried various types of legal work, you can only speculate about what it is that you want to do and what you will enjoy so a great many students actually find that work experience expands their ideas of the possible areas of practice available within the legal profession. The final reason that you should seek out many and varied opportunities for work experience as early as possible in your studies is that it will help you to acclimatise to the professional working environment and ensure that you combat any nerves associated with entering into the workplace. By the time that you graduate, you should be confident that you have the skills necessary to survive and thrive in the workplace.

Second year

....

I felt I gave myself a major advantage in my second year by making sure to get some work experience in my first year. It gave me the chance to get to grips with the basics and the hidden formalities associated with the legal profession, ensuring my second year could be focused on truly assessing the broad range of areas I had the opportunity to experience and seeing what truly suited my tastes.

Ben, law graduate

....

The second year of your studies is the optimal time to undertake work experience. You have a full year of legal study behind you so you have at least some idea of how the law works and how to undertake legal research but you are not yet facing the pressured final year of your studies. Ideally, you will have undertaken some work experience in your first year and can use this as the basis to make decisions about applications for further placements in your second year. If this is the case, you can make a targeted search for work experience that strengthens and complements that which you have already undertaken. Do this at the beginning of your second year (or as soon as possible thereafter) so that you have time to source suitable work experience and make applications.

Practical advice: reviewing your work experience

Start by listing your work experience thus far using categories such as the area of law practised, the size of the firm, and the duration of your placement and add to that a list of the skills and experience that you gained during the placement.

Can you see any pattern to your placements? Have you achieved sufficient variety in your work experience and are you finding examples of each of the key employability skills? Is there anything that you have not done that other students seem to be doing on work experience: attended court, sat in on a client conference, drafted legal documents etc? Compare your list with your skills audit to check whether there are gaps that need to be filled and then you can target placements that will give the missing skills and experience.

Have a look at the example in Table 7.1. What advice would you give to a student with this work experience about the sorts of placements they should target during their second year? There are three different placements of varying duration in firms of different sizes involving a fair spread of activities but all involve working in family law. This is fine if you are absolutely convinced that your future lies in family law practice but if not, variation would be advisable. After all, how do you know that you would not enjoy criminal law, corporate finance, or personal injury practice if you have not tried it?

Table 7.1 Examples of different types of work experience

Area of Law	Size of Firm	Duration	Skills/Experience
Family	Small firm (four solicitors, no trainees)	2 days	Shadowing a solicitor specialising in care proceedings, attending client meetings, doing general administration, and drafting emails to clients.
Family	Small firm (4 partners, 12 solicitors, one trainee, two branches)	1 week	Assisting the trainee solicitor working in the family department with all aspects of her role. This included two days spent in court for a custody hearing and drawing up some papers relating to financial settlement.
Family	Department in large national firm with over one hundred employees, four trainees, and six offices.	2 weeks	The first week was spent carrying out research for a case on removal from the jurisdiction and preparing a summary of the precedents for the team working on the case. The second week involved shadowing a family solicitor including two days in court dealing with a contentious adoption case and sitting in on four client conferences.

Once you have an idea of the work experience that you wish to obtain in order to strengthen your skills portfolio, you can start to make targeted applications to appropriate firms. Do this as early as possible, preferably before Christmas in your second year, especially if you hope to obtain a summer vacation placement with a large law firm. As a rule of thumb, you should apply for work experience at least two months before you want it to take place. Of course, there is nothing to stop you making approaches at any time—there have been instances of students sending a speculative email of enquiry and being asked 'can you start on Monday?'—but applying well in advance allows you to plan your work experience strategy more effectively. Some law firms and barristers' chambers only accept applications for work experience at particular times of the year. For example, the application period for most summer vacation schemes runs between November and the end of January and applications made outside of this period would not be considered. However, many smaller law firms will consider applications for work experience whenever they are made so do not be afraid to make speculative approaches.

I have a broad range of work experience including two mini pupillages in London and Hull, a week working for the Government chambers in Guernsey, a week marshalling with a Crown Court judge, continued employment as a volunteer with the Youth Justice and Probation Services, and eight weeks in paid employment as a legal researcher for a high street firm assessing the viability of the renewable energy sector as a legal market. I have had the opportunity to experience criminal and civil work, right through to international public and commercial law. Apart from helping me to decide which areas of practice I might be interested in, my circle of contacts has expanded dramatically and my view of the profession has matured significantly.

Ben, law graduate

If you are in your second year but have no work experience, you really must get started. It is unlikely that you will secure a place on a summer vacation scheme without prior work experience and even if you are not interested in this type of work experience, you do need to start gaining some experience to ensure that you are prepared for the business of finding a training contract in the future. Remember, some students will secure training contracts in their second year so if you have still not got any work experience then you are putting yourself at rather a disadvantage. But all is not lost: there is still time to make applications and gain experience, especially if you target smaller firms who are less likely to have rigid timeframes for applications.

Practical advice: make five applications today

If you are in your second year and have no work experience, resolve to try and find at least one placement today. Decide where and when you would like to work and formulate an email based upon the advice given in the previous section of this chapter. Identify five potential employers and email them today.

Tell us

Tell us whether you were successful at finchandfafinski.com/get-in-touch or @FinchFafinski on Twitter. Good luck!

Final year

Your primary focus in your final year should be on your studies and ensuring that you obtain the grades that you need to secure the best possible degree classification. However, unless you are in the fortunate position of having secured a training contract, you should still give some time and thought to the matter of work experience. The level of attention that this requires will depend upon how much work experience you have already acquired.

For students with a solid foundation of work experience gained over the previous two or three years of study, the emphasis in your final year should be on adding value to your portfolio of work experience. This could be targeting work experience that will fill a gap in your employability skills or by adding something unusual that will help to make your application stand out to prospective employers. This does not have to interfere with your study time: you could simply ensure that you find and secure such an opportunity for work during the summer following graduation.

Practical advice: finding unusual opportunities

If you want your application to stand out amongst the many others that employers will receive, try to have at least one piece of work experience on it that is a real conversation point: something above and beyond the usual run of work experience.

- **Law work in another country.** You could seek work experience in a law firm in another jurisdiction during the summer vacation (remember practical considerations, though, such as the cost of travel and accommodation and the possible need for a visa). If it is not an English-speaking country, you should emphasise your proficiency in another language (valuable as some law firms value language skills), or your ability to work in an unfamiliar setting where you are not conversant in the language. There are numerous opportunities for law work experience abroad in countries such as China, Ghana, and South Africa at www.projects-abroad.co.uk or you could seek an internship with a capital defence lawyer representing prisoners on death row.

- **A different perspective on the law.** Try not to think of the law only in terms of legal representation. You could seek work experience that allows you to see the law from a different perspective such as working in a local authority legal department, volunteering as a prison visitor, training as a magistrate, or by assisting an MP to draft a Private Members Bill.

Tell us

Tell us about your unusual work experience. What did you do and did it work in making your application-to-interview rate more successful? Contact us at finchandfafinski.com/get-in-touch or @FinchFafinski on Twitter.

For students with little or no work experience, the emphasis in the final year should be on acquiring any work experience that you can manage to fit in provided that this does not interfere with your study commitments. Remember that you have the entirety of the summer holiday after graduation to undertake work experience and that you have the option of taking up employment as a paralegal for a year (or more). Of course, the option of working as a paralegal is not limited to students with insufficient work experience: it is a really great opportunity to experience the day-to-day life in legal practice whilst earning money so many students choose to do this before commencing the LPC.

How much work experience am I expected to have?

This is a difficult question to answer as it requires the quantification of something that is, in reality, unquantifiable, rather like students who expect a straightforward numerical answer to the question 'how many cases should I put in my contract coursework essay?'. The answer, in both cases, is 'it depends' and 'as much/as many as you need'. A more helpful, although equally imprecise, answer is that you should have sufficient work experience to demonstrate to prospective employers that you have a commitment to a career in law and that you have set about gaining a good insight into the working life of a legal professional and the skills involved in legal practice.

Practical example: how much work experience?

We asked practitioners how much work experience they would expect students to have at the end of the degree. As you will see, there is no precise answer to this but their responses do identify a number of factors that you might want to bear in mind when making decisions about work experience.

. . . .

Ideally, students should have some work experience gained in each year of study. I don't think there is ever too much.

Variety is more important than quantity. Students should not keep returning to the same firm, unless there is a training contract on the horizon, because repeated experience of the same sort of work adds nothing that wasn't demonstrated by their first stint at the firm.

At least one longer period—a month or more—is useful as it means that students will have been exposed to more complex aspects of practice and have become used to the daily rhythm of life in a law firm.

I think that there is an important balance that students need to strike between sampling a variety of different types of legal work and doing too many different things. It is all very well and good to have a range of different work experience but you need to be able to explain why you did the things that you did otherwise you just look aimless.

. . . .

The extent to which you are able to demonstrate these things from work experience will depend not upon the number of different work placements that you have undertaken but instead upon the extent to which these placements afforded you with an opportunity to expand your knowledge and understanding of legal practice. For example, the duration of a work experience placement varies from a single day to several months. It is obvious that you will gain a far greater insight into the day-to-day work of a solicitor or barrister if you work with them for a month than you will from working for a week. You will be better able to follow the progression of cases and to learn the procedural steps involved if your work experience lasts for a longer period of time. As such, you could say that you gain more experience from a one month placement than you would from four one-week placements. Of course, you could counter-argue, as all good lawyers should, that four one-week placements demonstrates your ability to adapt to new working situations and new colleagues so there is merit in both. The key point really is to try and ensure that you have at least one lengthy period of work experience undertaken over the summer vacation as well as shorter periods of work. The other factor to bear in mind when selecting work experience is to aim for a degree of variability.

In summary, you should measure the extent and adequacy of your work experience on the basis of the range of opportunities that it has afforded for you to gain essential lawyering skills and experience of the legal environment rather than by counting the number of work placements completed. It should be a qualitative, rather than quantitative, exercise. Aim to gain as much work experience as you can manage within the time constraints of your studies and any necessary paid employment but try to make sure that you vary the sort of work placements that you do to ensure that you build up a portfolio of varied experience of different kinds of legal practice.

Types of work experience in law

The majority of students setting out upon a law degree do so with the aim of entering the legal profession as either a solicitor or a barrister. Of course, it may be that you change your mind during the course of the degree and embark on an entirely different career or that you simply chose law out of general interest as a good solid academic degree with no plan to practise law. However, unless you have actively and definitely ruled out any possibility that you will want to work within the legal profession, the most obvious type of work experience that you should gain will come from working with a solicitor or barrister. There are a number of forms that this may take, as you will see in the sections that follow, and you should also consider other forms of legal work experience such as voluntary work and marshalling a judge to build up a varied portfolio of experience that will give you plenty of opportunities to enhance your employability skills and impress prospective employers.

Mini pupillage

A mini pupillage is work experience, usually for one or two weeks, with a barrister although some barristers do offer a single day mini pupillage as a snapshot of life in chambers. This usually involves working with a particular barrister to observe every facet of their work and may also include talks about life as a barrister and social events. A mini pupillage may include a piece of assessed work and may be part of the selection process when recruiting for pupillage.

Practical example: what is it like?

Each chambers will have a different approach to the nature and content of a mini pupillage and much will depend upon what work the supervising barrister is doing at the time.

- **Falcon Chambers, London**. On arrival, you will be given an introductory talk and assigned to your mini pupilmaster who will ensure you see a variety of work. Each afternoon, there will be a talk from one or more members of chambers and clerks on different aspects of life at the Bar (applying for pupillage, life at the Bar, the running of chambers). We aim to give you the opportunity to meet as many members of chambers as possible during the course of your visit and there will usually be an informal gathering with some of our barristers and clerks on the last day. www.falcon-chambers.co.uk

- **Guildhall Chambers, Bristol.** Undertaking a mini pupillage provides an opportunity to experience all elements of life as a barrister including being in court, observing conferences with lay clients and instructing solicitors, and drafting legal documents. Mini pupils will also have the opportunity to talk with members of chambers and ask them questions about their profession and the pupillage application procedure. www.guildhallchambers.co.uk

- **No 1 High Pavement, Nottingham.** A mini pupillage will consist of one week shadowing one or more members of chambers at court, in the Robing Room, and in chambers. The student may be allowed access to counsel's papers but will not be required to prepare any written work. The student may be allowed to sit in on conferences when counsel deems it appropriate and the client consents. www.1highpavement.co.uk

---

Tell us

Tell us about your mini pupillage. How did you secure the mini pupillage and what work did you do? Contact us at finchandfafinski.com/get-in-touch or @FinchFafinski on Twitter.

....

The benefit of mini pupillage varies enormously depending on the set you are with and the supervisor you are given. I had one week at a commercial mega-set where I sat in the office of a leading junior. In effect, it was a week of one-to-one tuition and the work I was involved in was first-class. It was a fantastic experience. I had another mini where my role was to simply spectate from a distance. This was much less beneficial, but still useful—if only to rule out applying to that chambers.

Rupert, law graduate and barrister

....

For students wishing to practise law as a barrister, it really is essential to undertake at least two, preferably more, mini pupillages as it will be extremely difficult to succeed in the competition to secure a pupillage without this experience. Some chambers will not accept a pupillage application from students who have not undertaken a mini pupillage whilst some will not accept applications unless students have undertaken a mini pupillage with them. For students who wish to practise as solicitors or who are undecided about their destination after graduation, there is no reason not to do a mini pupillage: it is an excellent addition to your work experience portfolio and it will give you an insight into the life of a barrister which will help you to make decisions about your career path.

Practical example: good etiquette whilst on a mini pupillage

We asked several barristers to tell us what a student can do to make a good impression during a mini pupillage:

....

If you are given a piece of written work, make sure you give it the time, care, and attention it deserves—it may be filed and re-assessed when the chambers is deciding whether to give you a pupillage interview. And finally, number your paragraphs as barristers do when advising.

Pupillage Committee, 5 Essex Court

....

....

Resist the temptation to fill silences; don't forget the barrister you are shadowing is working, not simply entertaining you for a day. Take notes, remember details, and always offer to help carry papers. A quiet, intelligent mini-pupil who pays attention and asks sensible questions will always make a good impression.

Aiden Briggs, Ely Place Chambers

....

....

First of all, he or she should turn up on time! If we have arranged to meet at court, he should find out in advance where the court is, the name of the case, and which courtroom it is to be held in. Be enthusiastic, be willing, and appear to be interested.

Astra Emir, barrister

....

Minis are difficult because students need to balance being interested and engaged while also taking a step back to allow the barrister they are shadowing to get on with the job. How can students do this?

1. Save all your questions for after the hearing when the barrister will no longer be focused on the case and should be more relaxed.

2. Make sure that you have read all the information available on the website so you don't ask unnecessary questions.

3. Never offer legal advice, particularly in front of a client—unless asked.

4. Look the part. Dress smartly and conservatively. Bring a counsel's notebook, a pen, highlighter. Take a note of evidence/submissions during a court hearing.

Assessed and non-assessed mini pupillages

Many mini pupillages are non-assessed in that they exist to give students an insight into the working life of a barrister without any formal exercises to measure their aptitude for the law and legal practice. Other mini pupillages include some form of written and/or oral assessment that aims to contribute to the selection process by identifying students who are suitable for consideration for a pupillage. For some chambers, this is a crucial part of recruitment.

Practical example: assessed mini pupillage

- Mini pupillages are a vital part of our applications process. Accordingly, no pupillage will be offered at **Blackstone Chambers** unless the applicant has undertaken an assessed mini pupillage.

- At **Brick Court Chambers**, assessment is by a written task that tests the writing skills and analytical ability of students with a view to identifying those who could potentially be offered a pupillage.

- Students undertaking a mini pupillage at **Keating Chambers** are usually asked to complete a written mini pupillage exercise and, if practicable, an advocacy exercise during their time in chambers. This provides students with an opportunity to discuss their work with a member of chambers and identifies promising candidates for pupillage.

In reality, the distinction between an assessed and non-assessed mini pupillage is not great. The work will be the same and all students will be observed with a view to considering whether or not they would be suitable for pupillage at that chambers. So there is an element of assessment to all mini pupillages; the only real difference is whether or not there is a formal written and/or oral exercise that is used for evaluative purposes.

Some [chambers] will set a piece of work, others will run moots or advocacy competitions. Often it will be even more informal and members of chambers will simply send feedback to the Pupillage Committee about how the student performed.

Pupillage Committee, 5 Essex Court

Finding mini pupillages

As with work experience in a firm of solicitors, the opportunities for mini pupillages may or may not be advertised. Advertised vacancies can be found in a number of ways and a speculative application (discussed earlier in relation to work experience with a solicitor) can be made to chambers which do not advertise mini pupillages.

In terms of identifying existing opportunities, you could consult one of a number of online resources that will provide details of chambers with pupillages on offer as these will often also include details of the availability of mini pupillages. For example, the Pupillage Gateway is operated by the Bar Council as the portal through which all pupillage applications are made but the information about each chambers includes details of whether or not mini pupillages are available. Accordingly, a search can be made for chambers that offer mini pupillages in any particular location so, for example, you could search for chambers in the Midlands offering mini pupillages which, at the time of writing, would alert you to only one option with St Mary's Chambers in Nottingham (see Figure 7.1).

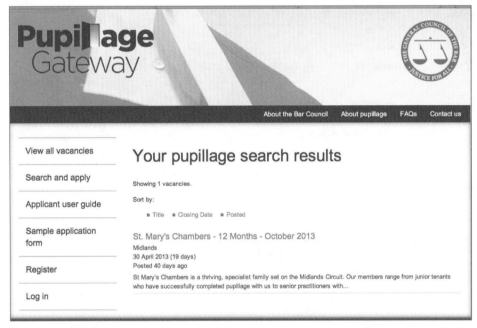

Figure 7.1 Pupillage Gateway

The limitation to this method of finding mini pupillages is that it presents only a partial picture of the opportunities available at any point in time. The Pupillage Gateway is designed to facilitate a search for pupillages, not mini pupillages, so you are using the database to find chambers that offer mini pupillages from amongst those that are currently advertising pupillages. As such, it will not assist you to identify mini pupillages available at chambers that do not have current pupillage vacancies. So it is not a perfect method for identifying mini pupillages but it is at least a starting point.

There are two further alternatives. Firstly, you could take a more methodical approach by compiling a list of all chambers within a particular area and checking their websites one by one to ascertain whether they offer mini pupillages. There are a number of resources that offer listings of barristers and chambers. For example, you could use Legal Hub (**www.legalhub.co.uk**) to list all chambers in a region or narrow your search by reference to the area of law practised to create a list of possible sources of mini pupillages. For example, if you searched for chambers in the Midlands with specialism in crime (see Figure 7.2), you would obtain a list of ten chambers spread across the Midlands (see Figure 7.3).

Figure 7.2 Legal Hub search

5.	No 8 Chambers	Birmingham B4 6DR Tel: 0121 236 5514	Arbitration; Capital tax; Care proceedings; Chancery (land law) ...
6.	Equity Chambers	Birmingham B4 7LR Tel: 0121 236 5007	Common law (general); Corporate fraud; Crime; Employment ...
7.	1 High Pavement	Nottingham NG1 1HF Tel: 0115 941 8218	Corporate fraud; Crime; Licensing
8.	Cornwall Street Chambers	Birmingham B3 3BY Tel: 0121 233 7500	Care proceedings; Children; Commercial law; Common law (general) ...
9.	Regent Chambers	Stoke On Trent ST1 1HP Tel: 01782 286666	Care proceedings; Chancery (general); Common law (general); Corporate fraud ...
10.	KCH Garden Square	Nottingham NG1 5BH Tel: 0115 941 8851	Care proceedings; Chancery (general); Commercial litigation; Commercial property ...

Figure 7.3 Legal Hub search results

Secondly, you could carry out a general search of the Internet using the search term 'mini pupillages' in combination with your preferred geographic location and/or area of legal practice. Although this approach may seem more generic than using a specialist database, it actually offers a couple of advantages. For instance, you can be more specific about the geographic location of where you are looking for work; the searchable databases tend to divide locations to mirror the circuits in which barristers work whereas you can narrow this down to a particular town by carrying out a keyword search on the Internet. Moreover, the professional databases tend to carry details of chambers that subscribe to their services so could return fewer results than a general Internet search as the following example illustrates.

Practical example: internet versus database search

Imagine that you are interested in crime and are looking for a mini pupillage in Nottingham. You would identify two opportunities by using the Legal Hub search:

- KCH Garden Square
- 1 High Pavement.

However, a keyword search of the Internet would identify the following additional possible sources of a mini pupillage at chambers in Nottingham that deal with crime:

- 23 Essex Street
- Trent Chambers.

It is always worth supplementing a database search with a more general Internet search to ensure that you find all the possible opportunities for a mini pupillage in your preferred areas (legal and geographic).

Once you have identified a list of chambers of interest, you can check their website for information about the availability of mini pupillages and the application procedure. In the absence of any specific information, you will need to make a speculative application (see earlier discussion in relation to work experience in a firm of solicitors). As many chambers require that applications are made by the submission of a CV and a covering letter, there is unlikely to be much difference between a response to an advertised mini pupillage and a speculative application.

Practical example: methods of securing mini pupillage

Rebecca Morgan has undertaken three mini pupillages, each of which was obtained in a different way:

St Albans Chambers, St Albans: I contacted the chambers directly. They didn't have a formal application procedure and they were able to accommodate me very quickly.

One Paper Building, London: I sent an online application using the Pupillage Gateway.

4 Breams Buildings, London: I used contacts at the chambers that I had made through taking part in an advocacy course at university.

Bear in mind that barristers can be overwhelmed with applications so you may need to be persistent and make a large number of applications:

I focused on doing mini pupillages because I knew I wanted to train to become a barrister. They can be difficult things to organise as the competition is often fierce, particularly for placements out of term time. I sent out over 30 letters and arranged 5 mini pupillages at chambers that undertook work in different areas.

Rupert, law graduate and barrister

I did get daunted by my lack of success at first but was determined to persevere. It paid off and I eventually obtained three mini pupillages at different chambers but I think that I made about 60 applications to get them.

Suranne, Middlesex University

I got fed up with receiving no response or getting cursory rejection emails so I decided to go and sit in the chambers and talk to barristers in person. I'm quite personable and I was convinced that the direct approach would work and it did. I have to admit that the clerk was quite surprised when I explained what I was doing but I said that I was quite happy to sit in a quiet corner and wait all day if necessary until one of the barristers had time to chat to me. To my surprise, the Head of Chambers came to see me after ten minutes and had a chat. He said he was impressed by my enterprising nature and made me an offer of a two-week pupillage there and then.

Adam, University College London

Pegasus Access Scheme

This is a social mobility initiative launched by the Inner Temple in association with 56 partner chambers that gives students from under-represented groups that may face obstacles in entering the legal profession an opportunity to undertake a mini pupillage. The scheme gives preference to students who have participated on the following programmes:

- Pathways to Law
- Social Mobility Foundation
- Warwick Multicultural Scholars Programme
- Inner Temple Schools Project.

If you are eligible, it is well worth taking part in the scheme as it is a good source of short (two to five days) mini pupillages and reasonable expenses incurred in taking part are also covered. Students who have not taken part in one of the four programmes may still apply if they meet certain criteria and will be considered for any additional places that are available. There is more detail about the scheme and its eligibility requirements on the website: **www.pegasus.me**.

Applications should be made between September and October and involves a short application form and a personal statement of no more than 500 words that sums up why you want to be a barrister and how the scheme will help you achieve this as well as detailing any work experience or extra-curricular activities that demonstrate your interest in the Bar and your academic achievements on your degree.

Vacation placement schemes

Many of the larger law firms offer work experience to second year law students by way of formal vacation scheme placements, generally during the Easter and summer holidays. This is a programme of work experience and other activities—talks about the firm, skills workshops, and social activities—spanning one, two, or three weeks that allows students to experience daily life as a solicitor whilst giving the firm an opportunity to assess the suitability of the students for a future within the legal profession. Indeed, many firms use the vacation scheme as part of the recruitment process.

Practical advice: vacation schemes and training contracts

The vacation schemes run by the larger law firms are regarded as the Holy Grail of work placements both because of the way that they are structured around the needs of the students and because they are so often used as part of the process of recruitment for training contracts.

- At **Nabarro** '[a]lmost all our trainees (95%+) come to us through our multi award-winning vacation schemes'.

- 'Our internships are one of the primary means of selecting candidates for a career at **Simmons & Simmons**. They provide us with the chance to test your suitability for a training contract. They are also a unique opportunity for you to get to know our firm, decide if we are the best firm for you and for you to prove your potential during your time with us.'

- At **Pinsent Masons**, '[a] good 70% of our trainees regularly join us after experiencing the working environment first-hand, through our summer placement programme…If you gain a placement, it's because we're already thinking of you as a potential trainee. And over the course of the placement, we'll do our best to give you every chance to prove us right. That's why placement students don't need to make a separate application for the training programme. If you've already gained a placement, in our eyes you're already in the running'.

Due to the link between the placement and training contract recruitment, the quality of the work experience provided and the reasonable rate of pay (around £250 a week), competition for these places is fierce. Applications are generally made towards the end of the autumn term and into January and the application process often mirrors that used for training contracts so you should expect to complete an application form with some testing questions on it as well as a telephone and/or face-to-face interview plus other recruitment tools such as psychometric tests and assessment centres.

The recruitment process used at Field Fisher Waterhouse is depicted in Figure 7.4.

Do not be deterred by this rigorous recruitment process: it is excellent practice that will stand you in good stead when it comes to making training contract applications. Some firms such as Field Fisher Waterhouse offer detailed feedback to unsuccessful applicants that reach a certain stage of the process so it is also an opportunity to learn how to strengthen future applications.

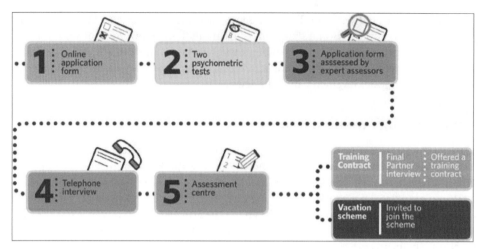

Figure 7.4 Recruitment process at Field Fisher Waterhouse

Practical advice: placement applications

You will find detailed advice on all aspects of the application process in Chapter 11. For now, though, there are some points to bear in mind in relation to your application for a place on a summer vacation scheme.

- **Research**. Set aside an hour or so each week in the autumn term of your second year to carry out research into firms offering vacation schemes so that you can make an informed decision about where to apply.

- **Tailor your application**. A generic application is obvious to recruiters and is rarely welcome. Draw on your research into the firm to tailor your application to its specialisations, ethos, and approach to work experience. List at least three things about the firm and its vacation scheme that attracts you and find a way to work these into your application.

- **Take your time**. Make a list of deadlines for applications in your diary and include a reminder one week before the deadline. Print a copy of the application form as soon as it is available and give yourself time to work out answers to the questions and reflect upon them so that you can make any necessary changes. Most firms require electronic applications either direct by a form completed on their website or via an electronic application system such as Apply 4 Law (**www.apply4law.com**) so check to see if applications can be saved once they have been started.

- **Give full answers supported by evidence**. Some of the questions will be challenging but you must write a complete answer as best you can. You should always substantiate your statements: do not claim to be a good team player unless you can make reference to a specific time that you have worked well with others.

- **Get help**. Show your application to someone from the careers service or your personal tutor and seek their advice on how it can be improved.

- **Check it for errors**. Silly mistakes and grammatical errors condemn your application to the bin so be meticulous in checking the accuracy of your finished application. It can help to get someone else to read it for you—we tend to see what we think we have written so it can be easier for someone else to spot your mistakes. In particular, take care that you have not copied and pasted something from one application into another that is unsuitable: for example, like a section on 'why I want to work for x' without realising that you have not changed the name of the firm.

- **Stick to the deadline**. Late applications will not be accepted even if the reason for lateness is not your fault. Remember that online applications may create a high volume of traffic through the firm's website in the final hours before the deadline so aim to submit your application a few days early, just in case the server goes down under the pressure of applications.

- **Do not be afraid to update the firm on new developments**. If, for example, you win the internal negotiation competition after you have applied for a place on a vacation scheme, there is nothing to be lost by contacting an appropriate person in the firm and asking to update your application with this piece of new information. You should only do this with significant pieces of information.

There are no limits to the number of applications that you can make nor, for that matter, to the number of vacation schemes that you can attend. If you have been offered a place on four, five, six, or however many different schemes then, provided that the dates do not clash, there is nothing to stop you taking up all of the offers. After all, each scheme is with a separate firm and will be structured in a different way with its own approach to work experience so there will always be something new to learn at each firm and you will be building up an excellent portfolio of work experience at some of the biggest law firms.

Practical example: what is it like?

It is difficult to offer a description of what you can expect on a vacation placement scheme as each firm will do things differently but, in general, you can expect to be supervised and given appropriate tasks to do as well as being offered opportunities to take part in social activities, presentations, and workshops as these examples show:

The vacation scheme at **Macfarlanes** aims to provide a two-week snapshot into life as a trainee. You will spend each week in a different department, working with a partner, assistant solicitor or trainee, on real work such as drafting a letter (and working through the draft with the solicitor or trainee) or carrying out research on a live issue for a client.

At **Blandy & Blandy**, you will shadow a different trainee on each day therefore experiencing five departments in the week and, wherever possible, accompany a trainee to court for a hearing or tribunal.

At **Mayer Brown International**, students assist a partner or senior associate on real deals to gain first-hand experience of life in a City law firm. You will sit in two departments and attend presentations on different practice areas to give an insight into the breadth of the firm. There are plenty of social activities including a trip to one of the European offices.

The placement scheme at **Olswang** gives students an insight into the firm's work, culture, and ethos and an opportunity to experience the life of a typical trainee solicitor. You will normally be placed in two different departments during the placement under the supervision of an associate or trainee and given work from a variety of fee-earners within the group. There is a structured timetable of talks, skills workshops, and social events.

The **Simmons & Simmons** three-week summer vacation schemes are designed to make you really feel a part of our firm and get a genuine insight into what it is like to work with us. Working alongside a partner or associate— who will supervise, direct, and coach you—you'll also be matched with a current trainee to help you to settle in. This support will ensure that you get the most out of your time with us and get involved in a host of exciting and challenging projects.

You'll be included in every aspect of working life, from departmental events to firm-wide training sessions, as well as research, drafting, minute taking, and meeting arrangements. You could also work directly with our clients. You and other members of the vacation scheme will also be assigned a project, which will be presented to members of the firm at the end of your stay. In addition, we hold a full programme of lectures, skills sessions, and social events.

Tell us

Tell us about your summer vacation placement. Was it a good insight into life as a solicitor and did it help you to make a decision about working at the firm in the future? Contact us at finchandfafinski.com/get-in-touch or @FinchFafinski on Twitter.

Practical example: on placement at Bircham Dyson Bell

You will spend two weeks with us, gaining valuable experience with two of our legal departments. We aim to give you as much practical experience as possible, plus the opportunity to experience first-hand how our solicitors and partners work.

In each of the departments you will be allocated a supervisor, one of our partners or senior associates, so you have support and guidance during your time with us. You will also have a nominated buddy, one of our current trainees or newly qualified solicitors, so you can hear their experience first-hand.

Additionally, a range of organised activities including a networking event, trainee social and legal research exercises will make your time with us enjoyable as well as insightful. We hope during your time with us you will make friends and we encourage those on the programme to arrange informal activities to build relationships and network further. **www.bdb-law.co.uk**

Anyone who wants to practise law as a solicitor, particular in the larger City and commercial law firms, should consider applying for a place on at least one vacation scheme. They are designed to provide a good insight into the operation of the firm so will help you to decide whether it is a place that you would like to apply for a training contract as well as strengthening your CV.

Practical advice: researching law placements

It would be unrealistic to think that you will have time to apply for every placement scheme that is available so you will have to find some basis to decide between the different placement providers. You can use the Internet to find details of their placements and to get a feel for what they offer as well as finding reviews written by students who have undertaken placements and who are giving their impressions. Another option would to be to consider firms that have won awards for their placements. There are a number of accolades that could be awarded.

For example, the National Council for Work Experience gives awards on an annual basis to organisations that offer outstanding work experience to students and graduates with particular emphasis on the extent to which the placements offer opportunities for the development of employability skills. For the first time in 2012, a separate award was introduced for the best placement provided by a law firm and this was won by Nabarro.

The law firms short-listed for an award in 2013 are:

- Baker & McKenzie
- Bircham Dyson Bell
- Nabarro (winner)
- Pinsent Masons
- Shearman & Sterling
- Simmons & Simmons (highly commended).

You will find more details of the awards and the judging criteria as well as a wealth of information on work experience in a range of industries on their website **www.work-experience.org**.

Finding vacation schemes

Practical advice: placements and training contracts

Be aware that some firms only consider applications for training contracts from students who have undertaken work experience with them whereas others will offer some shortening of the recruitment process to placement students such as a direct route to interview. Some firms will automatically consider all students who undertake work experience for a training contract and will incorporate an interview into the placement. Even if this is not the case and there seems to be no link between the placement and recruitment for training contracts, it is inevitable that the insight that the firm has gained into you as a prospective solicitor during the placement will be a factor in the recruitment process. As such, you should treat the placement itself as it is one long interview!

Remember that the placement is also a chance for you to get the feel of a firm and to decide if you think that it is a place where you would be comfortable working on a longer term basis. If you dislike the work, your colleagues, or the general atmosphere and find yourself counting the days (or hours) until the end of your placement then it would not be a good idea to apply for a training contract at that particular firm. Try not to worry—law firms differ enormously so there is bound to be a different firm where you feel more at home.

In essence, it is advisable to secure a work placement at any firm where you feel that you would consider applying for a training contract. It will give you an insight into the firm and the firm an insight into you which could work to your advantage in the recruitment process. Of course, you do not have to aspire to work at a firm in order to apply for a place on its vacation scheme: they offer excellent work experience that will strengthen your employability skills and enhance your CV.

Despite these benefits, many students do not even try to secure a placement thus they miss out on one of the best work experience opportunities. This was surprising so we asked students why they did not apply for a place on a vacation scheme. The answers that we received fell into two categories:

1. **Lack of awareness about placement schemes and the application process:**
   - I didn't realise that there were any formal schemes so I just applied to work with a local solicitor to get work experience
   - I knew that vacation schemes existed but didn't know where to find out about them

- I didn't realise we'd have to apply so early so I didn't start thinking about it until the Easter break and by then I'd missed all the closing dates.

Lack of awareness about vacation schemes, their availability, application process, and the timing of applications is a major factor that causes students to miss out on the opportunity to secure a placement. We have sought to tackle this problem by gathering information on the schemes that exist. Table 7.2 provides an extract from a fuller table that can be found in Appendix A that identifies the vacation schemes available in England and Wales along with information about the number of vacancies, location, and duration of the placement and whether or not it is a paid placement. We have included details about the application process but not the deadline for applications as these can change from year-to-year and it is important that you are not misled by out-of-date information. However, we have included a link to the vacation placement areas of each firm's website so that you can find more information including the closing date for applications.

Table 7.2 Extract from Appendix A

Firm	Placements Available	Application Process	Duration	Location	Pay per Week
Jones Day www.jonesdaycareers.com/offices/office_detail.aspx?office=4&subsection=11	60	Online application plus covering letter	2 weeks	London	£400
K & L Gates LLP www.klgates.com/careers	8	Online application plus interview	2 weeks	London	£300
Kennedys www.kennedys-law.com/uk/careers/graduates/summerplacements/	12	Online application plus telephone interview and online ability test	2 weeks	London	£275
Kirkland & Ellis International LLP http://ukgraduate.kirkland.com	20	Online application	2 weeks	London	£250

The application window tends to be open from November to mid- or late-January (although a few deadlines are in February or March) so you should start thinking about vacation schemes and deciding where to apply at the start of your penultimate academic year. The application process can be quite challenging—some firms use the same questions for placements as they do on the training contract application forms— so you should ensure that you have plenty of time to prepare your answers.

Practical advice: plan your applications

Print out the application forms for vacation schemes well before the application deadline and familiarise yourself with the sort of questions that are asked.

Take time to research the firms so that you can tailor your application accordingly: there is usually a question about why you want a placement at that firm and the answer 'I'm not fussy as long as I get work experience' is not a good one (even if it is the truth).

Think about your skills and experience and identify gaps that may jeopardise the success of your application. You will then have time to rectify the situation before you start to complete the application forms.

You will find further information on all aspects of the application process in Chapter 10 and suggestions on the time-management of applications in Chapter 2.

2. **Anxiety or uncertainty about applying for or undertaking a work placement:**

- We were always told how competitive it was to get places and my first year grades were not great so I assumed I'd be unsuccessful

- I had a look at the application forms and they asked really difficult questions that I didn't know how to answer so I gave up and didn't apply

- All the placements are in really big law firms and I found that really daunting plus I don't know how to do any of the things that they would want me to do so I was worried that I'd be really out of my depth.

It is true that competition for places on a vacation scheme can be fierce but you should not let that deter you from making an application; after all, if you do not apply then you will certainly not get a place whereas you are at least in with a chance if you submit an application and your prospects of success increase the more applications that you make.

Practical advice: successful applications

There are over 2000 places available on vacation schemes offered by different law firms each year so there is no reason whatsoever why your application should not be one of the successful ones. There are some things that you can try to improve the chances of success:

- **Start early.** Take time to research each firm and put together a thoughtful and polished application. It is better to make ten good applications than it is to make 50 hurried ones that contain mistakes or lack attention to detail.

- **Target schemes with early closing dates.** The earlier the closing date, the sooner you will find out whether your application has been successful. An unsuccessful application is an indication that something needs to be developed so you will have time to make changes and to strengthen subsequent applications.

- **Spread your applications.** Some firms receive more applications than others so ensure that you target a range of different placement opportunities to maximise your chances of success. For example, work experience at well- known City law firms is highly sought after whereas unpaid placements in smaller firms or in more remote locations may receive fewer applications.

It is also true that the application process can be challenging and time-consuming but it replicates the process used for training contract applications so just putting an application together and discovering whether it was successful is a useful learning experience in itself. You will also see from the table of placement opportunities in Appendix A that the application procedure varies from firm to firm so you can gain experience of different recruitment practices: CVs and covering letters, application forms, telephone and face-to-face interviews and other selection processes such as psychometric tests, verbal reasoning, and aptitude tests.

You will find advice about all aspects of the application and interview process, including how to tackle challenging questions, in Chapters 11 and 12.

Practical advice: overcoming anxiety

It is fair to say that the majority of students feel apprehensive about undertaking a work placement, particularly for the first time. By and large, it is fear of the unknown that is really daunting. What work will I have to do? What shall I wear? What will I do if I don't understand something? Where do I go on the first day? The best way to overcome your fears is to turn the unknown into the known. In other words, make a list of the questions that are bothering you and set about answering them. You will find plenty of information about the vacation scheme on the firm's website or you can contact the person responsible for placement recruitment to ask if you are unsure about anything. Anecdotal accounts from other students may also be reassuring.

Tell us

If you were worried about undertaking a work placement, did your concerns make applying for work experience more difficult? Did you go ahead despite your worries and, if so, how did you deal with your anxieties once you started work? Tell us at finchandfafinski.com/get-in-touch or @FinchFafinski on Twitter.

It is only natural to feel a degree of nervousness about trying something new in an unfamiliar setting but the only way to overcome this is to take the plunge by undertaking work experience and finding out for yourself what it is like to practise law. After all, unless you abandon your aim of practising law, you are going to have to set foot in a law firm for the first time at some point so it would be a good idea to do it as early as possible as this will help to familiarise you with legal practice and you will soon gain confidence in the professional environment.

Remember that vacation schemes exist to give students at exactly your stage of legal studies some experience of work within the legal profession. In other words, they are designed to be a supportive and informative experience rather than something that puts you off working in law forever. Careful thought is given to the work that you will be given to ensure that it is appropriate and you will have support and supervision at all times. It will be expected that you will need clear instructions and that you may need to ask questions so try not to worry that you will be lost and unable to work out what to do. It is impossible to outline the precise details of what you will be doing during a placement as each firm has its own approach but you could expect to do some or all of the following:

- **Office-based work** such as undertaking legal research, drafting documents, and completing legal forms
- **Work with clients** such as attending meetings, taking notes, and drafting correspondence
- **Court-based work** such as attending hearings, making notes, liaising with counsel, or other professionals such as expert witnesses or social workers
- **Presentations** on the organisation and work of the firm to give you an insight into its operation on a wider scale

- **Workshops or seminars** to enhance your practical skills such as advocacy, negotiation, client care, or presentation skills
- **Group activities** undertaken with other placement students such as working on a case together, creating a business plan, or putting together a report or presentation
- **Social events** to enable you to meet the various people who work at the firm: trainees, associates, partners, and administrative staff.

You may find an outline of the activities that make up the placement on the firm's website or be sent a schedule of activities once you are accepted on the vacation scheme.

In summary, vacation schemes have a great deal to offer in terms of structured work experience, insight into the operation of the legal profession, the opportunity to network and build up contacts as well as offering the possibility of a head start in training contract applications. Be aware that the application process is time-consuming and often involves answering challenging questions so start early in your second year (or third year if undertaking a four year degree) and give careful thought to the different ways that you can provide evidence of your aptitude for law and employability skills in your application.

Remember that you can take part in more than one vacation scheme: in fact, with careful planning and successful applications, you could fill the entire summer vacation with a series of placements at different law firms. If you aim to do this, it can be a good idea to create a diagram that shows the dates of the various placements that you have applied for so that you can see where gaps exist and to ensure that you do not end up being double booked. If you are going to aim to complete several placements, bear in mind that you need to add variety to your work experience portfolio so, once you have one or two placements confirmed, think about applying for others that differ in some way: size or location of the firm, area of practice, activities offered as part of the scheme etc. Remember also that some firms offer the opportunity to work overseas for some or all of the placement and that this can also add a point of interest to your CV that demonstrates your confidence in working in different environments.

....

I was really determined to get a place on a vacation scheme with one of the big City law firms. I wanted to know what legal practice was like in that sort of firm. and I did think that having an impressive firm on my CV would help me to stand out from other applicants when it came to training contract applications. I did a lot of research on the vacation schemes offered by various firms and created my own 'top twenty' placements to target. I resolved to write one application each day but it turned out to take me a bit longer than that at first as I was determined to get it right and some of the questions were really challenging and I knew that it was important to research the firm and find a way to show that I had done so in my application and that was not always easy. I made a point of finding a way to weave at least two points about the firm that were not taken from its website into my applications. My strategy paid off and I ended up with four offers, two of which unfortunately clashed with each other but, in any case, I did manage to fill my whole summer with work at three top law firms. One of these offered a fast-track into the interview stage of training contract applications for students who had completed the vacation scheme which was a bonus.

Jack, University of Leeds

....

Other work experience in a law firm

Not all law firms operate a vacation placement scheme but that does not mean that it is not possible to secure work experience with them by making a direct approach to the firm. As they do not operate such a structured scheme, smaller law firms can be more flexible in offering work experience at different times of the year for varying durations and may be amenable to an offer of help one day or even one afternoon a week on a regular basis.

If you want to work in a solicitor's firm that does not operate a vacation placement scheme, you will need to make a proactive approach to them requesting work experience. According to the Law Society's annual statistical report, there are 10,202 private practice law firms operating in England and Wales (as of 31 July 2011) which means that there are plenty of sources of work experience in solicitors' offices so, with a little patience and perseverance, you should be able to secure a placement.

Aside from learning more about the day-to-day operation of a law firm, gaining work experience during university gives you a wide range of transferable skills which can be really useful. Helping draft legal documents, learning to deal with clients, and even getting to grips with legal software are all things you will experience if you undertake work experience or summer placements at a law firm. On top of this, the interpersonal skills you pick up from working in this environment and the attention to detail you will develop are really useful in a wider context. Even if you choose to pursue a career in a non-legal sector, all of these skills are universally highly valued by employers.

Adam, Edinburgh University

Finding work in a law firm

The first step in making a speculative application for work experience is to identify a firm to approach. This should not be difficult as every solicitor, with the exception of those that operate a formal placement scheme, is a potential source of work experience. You may have preferences such as the location of the firm (taking into account where you will be living at the time and where you might reasonably travel each day) and the area of legal practice. Having considered these factors, it is a straightforward matter to search the Internet using keywords (for example, solicitors in Bournemouth practising criminal law) or to consult one of the databases of law firms that exist such as:

- www.lawsociety.org.uk/find-a-solicitor/
- www.waterlowlegal.com/directories/solicitors.php
- www.justicedirectory.co.uk.

Take time to make thoughtful and deliberate choices about the firms that you target for work experience rather than simply showering every firm in the local area with copies of your CV. Remember that you should assess the sufficiency of your work experience by its breadth and the extent to which it has enabled you to develop and demonstrate key employability skills rather than by its quantification. In other words, do not accumulate work experience for the sake of it but because it adds strength to your skills and experience portfolio in some way. This means that you should evaluate your work experience, looking for gaps and omissions and then target work experience opportunities that allow you to fill these gaps. For example, you might seek to work in different practice areas, to vary the size of firm in which you have worked, or to expand your skills by working with solicitors who specialise in alternative dispute resolution, asset recovery, or international shipping law. Make every speculative application with a purpose in mind and make this clear in your approach to the law firm as this will highlight the reason for your interest in the firm.

Practical advice: tailor your application

A speculative application should appear to have been written specifically for the firm to which it has been sent. Take the time and effort to research the firm and find out something about it that explains why you want to work with them: an area of law, an approach to practice, a complex or high profile case that they have handed, a particular solicitor that you have seen in action. Look at the firm's website to find out more about what they do and read the solicitor's profiles to see what area of law they practise and what cases they have handled recently and then try and find a link between the firm and your own interests and experience.

- I have undertaken several placements in criminal law firms but would really like to add to this experience by working with your firm due to many cases that you have handled involving witnesses with repressed memory syndrome. I read the article on these cases that was published on your website as part of my extended project in criminal evidence and would really appreciate the opportunity to work in a firm that has so much experience with this issue.

- Having completed work experience placements in City firms, I find myself increasingly disinclined to practise corporate law and drawn to the more personal work of the high street solicitor. In particular, I notice that your firm specialises in contested care proceedings cases and I have a real interest in this area of law due to my experiences last summer doing voluntary work in a children's home.

- I have a passionate interest in technology law and your firm is leading the way in its work with the use of intellectual property as a means of protecting software innovation. I would like to combine my interest in law and technology in my future career so would value the opportunity to work within a leading technology law firm.

Remember, you are more likely to be successful in your search for work experience if your speculative application makes it clear that you want to work for the firm in question for a reason rather than simply wanting any work experience that is available. The message that you should try to communicate is 'I want work experience with your firm' rather than 'I want work experience wherever I can find it'.

Tell us

If you made speculative applications, what did you write and were you successful? How many applications did you make and what was your success rate? Did you write letters or send emails? Tell us at finchandfafinski.com/get-in-touch or @FinchFafinski on Twitter.

Many students are reluctant to make speculative approaches to law firms in their quest for work experience and instead apply only for advertised opportunities, assuming that all firms who offer work experience will publicise information about this and that a formal application process will exist. This is not the case at all and a great many firms that do not operate a formal placement scheme or otherwise advertise that work experience is available are nonetheless happy to oblige if they are contacted with a request for work experience. In fact, it is only a very few law firms who have a blanket policy of refusing requests for work experience: most firms will try to accommodate students seeking work experience although some firms, generally smaller ones, are not able to do so on a regular basis. This is understandable. Law students, however keen and capable, cannot be left to work unsupervised when undertaking work experience and the business of providing supervision, explaining what needs to be done and checking work can be so time-consuming that it cannot be accommodated in a busy office. However, even if a firm does not offer work experience on a regular basis, your speculative application might be so impressive that they decide to make an exception or it may be that they are so busy at the time that your application arrives that they are in need of an extra pair of hands. So, in essence, it is always worth making speculative applications. Law firms that do not advertise work experience may still be prepared to offer some and there may be less competition for the opportunities available than is the case with the formal work placement schemes.

Another factor that deters many students from making speculative applications for work experience is a lack of understanding about various practical matters associated with making an unsolicited application:

- **How do you apply?** Is the best approach by letter, email, telephone call, or just dropping in to the law firm and asking in person? This is a difficult question, in many ways, and the answer depends upon the preferences of the person who you ask for work experience. Some solicitors would say that email is the medium of professional correspondence so should be used whereas others indicate that they are more likely to read and respond to a letter sent in the post. Equally, a telephone call or personal visit can work really well if the timing is right and you make a good impression but could be badly received if you call or arrive at a particularly busy or stressful moment. The sensible approach, then, would be to use a combination of methods. Why not combine postal and email approaches and see which works best for you? You could always make a follow up telephone call if you do not receive a reply after two weeks but mention in your letter or email that you intend to do so. Dropping into the firm on the off-chance that you encounter the right person at the right moment is probably a bit of an unpredictable method: if you really want to take a direct approach, then taking advantage of a chance meeting at court might be preferable (although your ability to produce a copy of your CV at the drop of a hat might raise a few eyebrows).

- **Who should you ask for work experience?** Is it the senior partner, the solicitor who you want to work with, or the person responsible for recruitment at the firm? Again, somewhat unhelpful, the correct answer here is also likely to vary from firm to firm. Some law firms have a dedicated person or team of people who deal with all aspects of recruitment including work experience whereas this function will be fulfilled by the partners in other firms. You want to be sure that your application reaches a person who has the power to make the decision about work experience so you should check the firm's website to see if it specifies a person responsible for recruitment. In the absence of this, telephone the firm's general enquiries number and ask for contact details for the person to whom requests for work experience should be directed. Make sure that you find out the person's name as well as their role within the firm: an application that starts 'Dear Senior Partner' or 'Dear Head of Human Resources' is not impressive because you could quite easily have discovered the name of the person who holds that position. You should also bear in mind that people are more likely to ignore a letter that turns up on their desk if it is addressed to Sir/Madam than they would if the letter was addressed to them by name.

- **What information should go into a speculative letter?** How much detail should you include and what sort of information? How long is too long and how short is too short? Let's deal with length first as that is a straightforward matter. One side of A4—one-and-a-half at most—is sufficient to capture the essential information. A speculative letter is not a summary of your academic achievements or an opportunity to outline career aspirations but a concise and to-the-point advertisement of your suitability for a short period of work experience in the firm. It should start with a statement of purpose, be followed by one paragraph that explains your interest in the firm and another which highlights the skills and experience that will enable you to make a contribution to the firm and conclude with your thanks and with any further details that might be pertinent such as whether or not you expect to be paid, when you are available, and how you can be contacted. An example of a speculative letter is provided in Figure 7.5.

You will find further examples of letters that have been sent successfully by students on the Online Resource Centre.

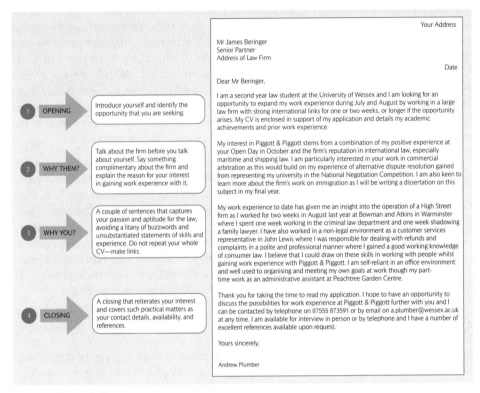

Figure 7.5 Speculative letter

- **What supporting documentation should be included?** Are you going to send a CV along with your speculative letter and, if so, how long should it be? And what about other documents like a transcript of your grades or a reference from previous work experience? The usual approach is to send a short (two to three page) CV that captures your qualifications, experience, and achievements. This should include the grades that you have achieved in your studies thus far obviating the need to include a transcript. Some students feel that the transcript provides substantiating evidence of their grades but most employers state that they prefer speculative applications to be kept short and easy to navigate without any unnecessary additional material. The same arguments apply to sending a reference with your application: many employers are just too busy to wade through pages of different information and will be more receptive to a short and to-the-point application that contains only essential information. However, if there is some defect in your profile that the reference addresses, it might be worth attaching a short open reference from a previous employer: for example, 'My grades so far have been in the 2.2 bracket but I have a far greater aptitude for the law in practice than I do for its academic study as the attached reference from Law Firm & Co indicates'. It can also be a way to strengthen your application if your previous speculative approaches have been unsuccessful. You will find further guidance on overcoming unsuccessful applications later in the chapter.

Hopefully, by addressing these common questions, you will feel more able to grasp the nettle and start to make some speculative approaches to law firms with the aim of securing work experience.

Treat your speculative application as a piece of marketing literature aimed at marketing you to a law firm as a potential employee. With this in mind, you need to ensure that your letter and the accompanying CV are polished, professional, and wholly free from errors. Remember that the ability to use language in an effective and accurate manner is essential for a solicitor so the misuse of language and errors in grammar and punctuation in your application suggest that either you do not know how to write correctly or that you could not be bothered to check your application before submitting it. Neither of these gives a positive impression to a prospective employer and may well be the factor that convinces the firm to discard your application. The employer's perspective on a poorly constructed application can be seen in the thoughts expressed by John Redwood MP in relation to the quality of applications for work experience and internships that he received:

> I have been sifting through CVs and application letters…Many of the ones I have been reading about have degrees. They send in CVs which start with similar paragraphs that they have been taught to write. They usually claim to be excellent at team working, brilliant communicators, and to offer good leadership. They are all highly motivated, enthusiastic, pro-active with strong organisational and problem solving skills. The rest of the CV sometimes belies the standard phrases of the opening. Some are unable to write a sentence. There are usually spelling and typing errors— understandable in the rush of everyday communication but glaring in a considered and formal document like a CV. One example produced the following second sentence to the application: 'I fill the experience I have gained in past employment will put me in good persian for this role'.

Sandwich placements

One way to ensure that you are guaranteed to gain relevant work experience during your degree is to select a course that includes one or more work placements as part of the programme of study.

- A thick sandwich course is one in which the student spends an entire year, usually the third, away from university in one or more work placements.

- A thin sandwich course involves two six-month placements with each placement taken in a separate year of study.

There are a number of advantages to undertaking a sandwich degree. Firstly, as already noted, it guarantees that you will have work experience at the end of your degree. Moreover, this is of a prolonged nature as you will work for at least six months, if not a year, in a single work environment thus getting a far greater insight into ordinary life in legal practice than is possible in a two-week placement. In fact, many students find it strange to return to university after their placement year as they are so used to working that they feel as if they are already qualified. A longer placement will ensure that you are given more responsibility and get far more experience at doing the job of a lawyer than would otherwise be possible. A further advantage is that universities offering a sandwich degree tend to find the placements for you thus removing the pressure on you to find your own work experience opportunities. Finally, this period of work in the law environment offers wonderful networking opportunities as you meet other solicitors and barristers so you should build up some good contacts. You will get to know the people at your placement very well so should obtain a good reference that will support your application for training contracts and may even put yourself in the running for a training contract with your placement firm.

I spent a year working at Minter Ellison, one of the 'Big Six' law firms in Australia and it was the most amazing experience. I am actually quite a shy person so I really tried to challenge myself by applying to do my placement year halfway around the world in a country where I knew nobody and had no knowledge of the law. I can remember landing in Australia and thinking 'I must be mad' and there was just a little part of me that wanted to find the first flight back to England. But everyone was really friendly and I soon got in the swing of the work. The legal system is not dissimilar to our own and the law itself often works on similar principles so I was not as out-of-my-depth as I feared. It has done wonders for my confidence and it was always something that I was asked about at interview and I have no doubt at all that it was instrumental in me receiving offers of not just one but two training contracts!

Jenny, University of Leicester

Practical example: Work experience case study

The biggest dilemma for students is how to stand out. Employers want evidence that you can enter a job role and hit the ground running; good grades are not enough and this is particularly pertinent within law. I chose what is known as a sandwich course at Brunel University; a law degree that specifically incorporates work experience within a law firm, over two six-month periods, so that when I finished my degree I obtained an LLB with professional development.

Brunel has fostered a number of close links with the legal community in London, so finding a placement in London is relatively easy. You perfect your CV with the help of the careers team and then you register your interest with whatever firms take your fancy. Brunel has a list of employers ranging from high street solicitors to chambers willing to provide six-month placements, practising everything from criminal law to commercial law with some firms offering a generous salary and others seeking passionate students willing to work for free. As I was unable to secure a paid placement in London, I went in search of my own placement in Birmingham.

I already had links with the Birmingham legal community through work experience so I approached the criminal defence firm who had taken me on previously and pitched the following: A law student, who already knew the firm, had a good grasp of criminal law and better still was willing to work free of charge. With legal aid as it is free labour is welcome labour but a general willingness to pitch in where needed and contacts within a firm will go a long way too.

I spent six months at this firm working closely with the solicitors and with a set of chambers that the firm instructed exclusively. As an aspiring criminal barrister I had hit the jackpot; I attended everything from conferences with clients to week long trials with the offences ranging from theft to attempted murder. This placement gave me a unique insight into various types of advocacy at an early stage of my legal career.

The greatest benefit of this scheme? If you prove yourself, you will be given real responsibility which is something you will not gain whilst on a mini pupillage or vacation scheme. Brunel University ensure that any placement they authorise will include quality legal work; making a good cup of coffee is not included in the job descriptions. I represented the firm whilst in court meeting defendants and barristers and that sort of experience is invaluable. I drafted witness statements, proofs of evidence, submitted legal aid forms, took notes during trials to be used during closing speeches by counsel, and was responsible for my own caseload.

The experience I gained made studying criminal practice and litigation on the BPTC a lot more understandable as I had real experiences I could relate the material to. When it came to legal scholarship and pupillage interviews, the panels always wanted to know about my work placement and it made for a good talking point, gave me the opportunity to emphasise my practical experience in conjunction with my academic knowledge, and enabled me to demonstrate that I knew yet more hard work lay ahead.

My time at the criminal defence firm continues to be a focus in interviews and employers are often intrigued by the addition of 'with professional development' on my CV. Many of the skills that I have gained you simply cannot gain whilst on conventional work experience but are necessary for fee earning positions within legal firms. Firstly managing your own caseload: prospective employers will always want to know how many files you handled and this experience will make you incredibly employable. Following that is file management, working to strict court deadlines and procedure and working on files from inception to completion is something employers want to avoid having to train you in if possible.

Even basic skills such as already knowing how office telephones work, how to make a photocopier hole punch and staple documents, and being comfortable dealing with all manner of people in a professional setting enables an employer to sleep easy and have confidence in the fact that not only do you have experience of the more complex processes but you also have the basics down to a fine art.

Most of all this type of experience shows your dedication to law and will make entering the legal market a little less formidable.

Lyndsay, Brunel University

Voluntary work

Any work undertaken without remuneration falls under the heading of voluntary work but the focus in this chapter is on voluntary work with a legal emphasis. There is a section further on in the chapter on pro bono work. This is a particular form of voluntary work in which legal advice and/or representation by a solicitor or barrister is provided free of charge to individuals and organisations that cannot afford it but there is other voluntary work that touches base with law and the legal system that you might also like to consider as a means of gaining valuable work experience and strengthening your employability skills. In the sections that follow, there will be a consideration of work of various kinds within the legal system or involving legal advice or issues. This is a guide only and you should remember that there are many other opportunities available. If you undertake other kinds of voluntary work with no hint of law about them, you will find a discussion of how to use this to strengthen your skills portfolio in Chapter 5.

Practical advice: voluntary work

Volunteering can be a good way to gain law-based work experience and strengthen key employability skills so it would be a useful addition to your CV. It also indicates that you are the sort of person who will expend time and effort on an activity that does not carry a financial reward: something that is of particular importance given the emphasis on corporate social responsibility. You might want to check what activities a particular law firm or chambers is involved with prior to applying to them and see if you can tie your own voluntary work in with their corporate social responsibility agenda.

I believe work experience provides the opportunity to develop a multitude of transferable skills such as communication, time management, professionalism, and learning to adapt to a goal centred environment. For me, with my work in a children's charity, not only have I developed the above skills (particularly strong non-verbal communication skills) but I have also developed the skill of understanding my own personal approach to goals and how I individually manage situations. This is important as it means I can structure my work accordingly (as far as I am able) to ensure quality and efficiency on all my tasks.

Catie, Southampton University

Citizens Advice Bureau

The Citizens Advice Bureau (CAB) is a charitable organisation that provides free advice on legal and financial matters to members of the public. Some of the issues that it encounters on a regular basis involve giving advice about managing debt, accessing benefits, and dealing with disputes with landlords and employers. It also advises on consumer complaints and problems associated with immigration and asylum. As you can see from this, a great deal of the work of that CAB is legal in nature so it is an excellent opportunity for you to gain experience in dealing with legal disputes thus strengthening many of the professional skills that are important in legal practice. For example, you may be involved in drafting a letter or court documents for a client or need to engage in legal research to inform the advice given to a client. You might negotiate with a landlord on behalf of a client or use your advocacy skills to represent the client's interests at a hearing to determine their entitlement to benefit. As you will be dealing with members of the public who have come to the CAB for help, this will also give you experience in customer service: a very important skill that students often struggle to demonstrate to prospective employers. There may also be opportunities to develop numeracy skills as many of the cases involve debt management.

- Have a look at the Citizens Advice Bureau website for further information and details of the training programme for volunteers: **www.citizensadvice.org.uk/index/join-us.htm**.

Appropriate adult service

The role of an appropriate adult was created by the Police and Criminal Evidence Act 1984 as an additional means of safeguarding the rights of children and vulnerable adults in police custody. It is not a substitute for legal advice and you would not be expected or permitted to give legal advice but instead to assist the person who has been arrested to understand what is happening and to support them during the period of their detention and questioning. It will be important that you are familiar with the rights of a detained person (these are set out in the Codes of Practice attached to the Police and Criminal Evidence Act 1984) and that you understand the duty of the police to treat the suspect in a fair manner. You may also need to facilitate communication between the police and the person who has been arrested, be present whilst the suspect is searched, fingerprinted, or during any identification procedure as well as when the police review decisions about detention or charge the suspect.

- Have a look at the National Appropriate Adult Network website for further details including a map that will show whether opportunities are available in your area: **www.appropriateadult.org.uk**.

Youth offender panels

People under the age of 17 who commit offences that will not justify the imposition of a custodial sentence are referred by the courts to youth offender panels as part of the restorative justice initiative. This consists of a member of the youth offending team and two volunteers from the local community. The panel acts as a neutral party and discusses the offence with the offender, their parents and, wherever possible, the victim with a view to formulating a suitable remedy that becomes part of a contract to ensure that the offender makes reparation to the victim or the wider community and addresses the causes of their offending behaviour.

The Youth Justice Board offers training for volunteers which consists of a three-day foundation programme focusing on young people and crime followed by four days of training that explains the work of youth offender panels and the role of panel members. The role will give you a good insight into the operation of restorative justice as well as a sound knowledge of issues surrounding young offenders. You will need to be an objective and balanced listener and have the ability to formulate a solution to the problem that suits both the offender and the victim.

- You will find more details of the work of youth offenders panels and the training programme on the Youth Justice Board website: **www.justice.gov.uk/youth-justice/ workforce-development/working-with-volunteers/training-for-volunteers**.

Victim support

Victim support is a national charity that provides free confidential support and advice for victims of crime and their families as well as running a witness service at every criminal court to support those who are called to give evidence in criminal cases. There are a number of roles available for volunteers and there is a good general training package for volunteers plus the opportunity to undergo further specialist training in areas such as sexual offences, hate crimes, and homicide. There is no requirement that volunteers have any legal knowledge but the role involves knowledge of the operation of the criminal justice system. The opportunity to work at a court as part of the witness service might be particularly useful for law students and give rise to some useful networking opportunities.

- Details of the work of victim support volunteers and the application process are available on their website: **www.victimsupport.org.uk/Get-involved/Volunteering/ Being-a-volunteer**.

Prisoner advice service

There are over 80,000 people in prison in England and Wales. The prisoner advice service is a charity committed to ensuring that these prisoners have access to legal advice and are kept informed as to their rights whilst they are in prison. Volunteers support the work of employed caseworkers and solicitors in communicating with prisoners and advising on penal law, criminal law, and human rights issues. This work provides a good insight into the operation of the custodial system as well as an opportunity to see the law in action.

- You will find further details of the work of the Prisoners Advice Service and volunteering opportunities on their website: **www.prisonersadvice.org.uk/volunteer.html**.

Magistracy

You may have been to a magistrates' court to watch a case or whilst undertaking work experience with a criminal solicitor and so seen magistrates in action but did you realise that there is no reason why you, as a law student, should not sit as a magistrate? Magistrates are ordinary members of the community with no legal knowledge who are trained to adjudicate in criminal cases that are not sufficiently serious to be heard in the Crown Court. Anyone aged 18 to 65 can apply to be a magistrate but they are particularly keen to appoint younger people. Magistrates sit in panels of three so the decision-making responsibility is shared and there is a good programme of training and preparation for new members plus the support of a more experienced mentor for the first two years. This is a great opportunity for law students to gain familiarity with the workings of the criminal justice system and to observe the work undertaken by solicitors in a magistrates' court.

- There is further information about the work of magistrates and the qualities required in volunteers plus details of the application process on the government website: **www.gov.uk/become-magistrate/what-magistrates-do**.

Finding voluntary work

If you are interested in voluntary work, you may already have a type of work or particular voluntary organisation in mind in which case it is likely that you have sufficient information to investigate whether opportunities exist. If, however, you have no prior interests or associations with particular work or organisations then you can use one of the voluntary work resources that will enable you to explore what volunteering opportunities are available.

There are a number of organisations that exist to allow organisations looking for volunteers and people interested in voluntary work to find each other. Do-It is one of the leading volunteering websites that has details of over one million different voluntary work opportunities both in this country and overseas (**www.do-it.org.uk**).

Do-It has a searchable database that will help you find opportunities based upon a combination of the location, the nature of the work, and your availability as well as a wealth of informative resources to help you to understand more about the types of voluntary work available.

Practical example: finding voluntary work

One of the categories of voluntary work available through Do-It is law and legal support. This would always be worth investigating as it might turn up some interesting law-based opportunities that you had not previously considered. For example, if you were looking for law-related voluntary work in the Reading area, you would have the following options:

- Working as a mentor to support sex offenders in the community on a one-to-one in partnership with the police and probation service
- Sitting as a panel member on the Thames Valley local security improvement panel that meets quarterly and examines cases relating to racially aggravated and religious crime, homophobic, and disability hate crime
- Working on the front counter of a police station where you would deal with enquiries over the phone or face-to-face, receive and record documents, and undertake a range of administrative activities
- Acting as a trustee of the Citizen's Advice Bureau therefore undertaking a legal responsibility for the organisation and running of a local branch, ensuring its objectives are met and its financial position is sound.

Any of these would make a useful addition to your portfolio of work experience.

⚫ Think about how you would use each of these four opportunities to demonstrate key employability skills to prospective employers. You will see our thoughts on this on the Online Resource Centre.

Do not feel that you have to find voluntary work of a legal nature in order to enhance your skills portfolio. Remember that almost every activity that you can think of is regulated by the law one way or another so there will be an opportunity to find a legal perspective in most forms of voluntary work if you look for one. Alternatively, you might find a way to carry out non-law work in a legal setting or simply undertake work that has no link with the law whatsoever and instead highlight the skills involved, especially those which you have had little opportunity to develop during your studies. The quotations that follow give you an insight into how students have used their voluntary work to impress employers:

- **Finding a legal perspective.** I volunteered at an animal rescue centre. It was quite a small local charity and I really enjoyed the work. One day, knowing that I was a law student, one of the trustees asked me some questions about charity law and the way that it worked that led to me preparing a paper for the board of trustees about their legal duties. It was strange because I hadn't enjoyed trust law when I studied it but putting together a paper for the trustees really brought the subject alive and made me realise its real-world significance. So I had an unexpected opportunity to use the law and I was able to emphasise this on my CV.

- **Non-law work in a legal setting.** I was looking for voluntary work that would give me a break from law and my studies and would make use of my skills as a musician but then I found something that combined the two and I ended up doing music therapy and song writing workshops in an immigration detention centre. Not only was it an amazing experience, it was something that I got asked about a lot at interviews, including the one for my Bar scholarship, which was successful, so I think it really caught the interest of people reading my applications.

- **Emphasising the skills involved in non-law work.** I am passionate about old buildings and worked as a heritage volunteer for a week each summer when I was at university. I still had plenty of time left for legal work experience and I felt that it gave me an opportunity to show that I was a well-rounded person with plenty of interests besides the law. On my CV, I emphasised how I learned to work well with others and lead a small team on a restoration project as well as the importance of being methodical and able to work without supervision so that my interest had some resonance to working life.

Tell us

Did you undertake any voluntary work? Did it involve the law or was it an unrelated area of work? How did you use it on your CV and in job applications? Were employers interested? Tell us at finchandfafinski.com/get-in-touch or @FinchFafinski on Twitter.

Pro bono work

The phrase 'pro bono' refers to work undertaken by professionals who do not charge a fee for their services. It originates from the Latin phrase pro bono *publico* which means 'for the public good' as the public is benefitted by the availability of free services that they need but could not otherwise afford. In relation to lawyers, pro bono refers to legal advice and representation undertaken free of charge. Much of the pro bono legal work in England and Wales is coordinated by the National Pro Bono Centre which is a 'hub' for pro bono charities such as LawWorks and the Bar Pro Bono Unit.

- www.nationalprobonocentre.org.uk/
- www.lawworks.org.uk/

- www.barprobono.org.uk/
- www.thefru.org.uk/.

The work of each of these organisations and the volunteering opportunities that they offer to law students will be considered in the sections that follow. There will also be a discussion of other pro bono opportunities such as those arranged through your university.

LawWorks

LawWorks is a charitable organisation that provides free legal advice to individuals and community groups who cannot afford to pay but who do not qualify for Legal Aid. It is the leading pro bono organisation for solicitors and has links with over 100 law firms and organisations with a significant in-house legal department such as Aviva and Tesco. By and large, LawWorks coordinates pro bono opportunities for qualified solicitors but there is a section on the website that lists volunteering opportunities that are open to students:

- **www.lawworks.org.uk/current-student-volunteering-vacancies**.

LawWorks is keen to encourage law students to get involved with pro bono work and has a separate branch devoted to this: **www.studentprobono.net**. This provides help and support for student pro bono projects within universities. You can use the Student Pro Bono website to find out what is happening in your own university or to get inspiration from schemes in operation at other institutions if you wanted to set up your own pro bono project.

Bar Pro Bono Unit

The Bar Pro Bono Unit provides legal advice from barristers by acting as a clearing house that matches individuals and groups in need of legal advice but unable to afford it with a barrister with appropriate expertise. Although it does not offer opportunities for student volunteers to get involved with case work, there are a number of ways that you can participate in the work of the Bar Pro Bono Unit thus gaining valuable experience and demonstrating your commitment to working within the legal profession.

- **Administrative work.** The unit has some limited volunteering opportunities for students in an administrative capacity. This would enable you to demonstrate your skills in organisation and planning and give you a valuable insight into the 'behind the scenes' workings of the legal profession. These roles are based in the London office and requires volunteers who can commit time during working hours. You can register your interest for this role on the Bar Pro Bono Unit website.

- **Fund raising.** The unit organises the Law School Challenge in which teams of five students compete to raise the most money for the unit. The winner is the team that raises the most money and the prize is an audience with a judge, lunch at one of the Inns of Court, and visits to a city law firm and the pro bono centre. There is also a prize for the most creative approach to fund-raising. There are some great networking opportunities for the winning team but all participants could use this as a way of demonstrating their entrepreneurial spirit and to highlight skills in team working, organisation, leadership, verbal communication, and decision-making.

- **Bar in the community.** This is a match-making service that brings together solicitors, barristers, and law students wishing to undertake voluntary work with organisations that are in need of help. It is organised by region and covers a wide range of organisations seeking assistance of various kinds so you can be sure to find something that suits your expertise, skills, and interests. Not all of the work is legal in nature but remember that you are seeking to develop your transferable skills so do not be deterred from a volunteering opportunity that has no legal content provided that it offers an opportunity to strengthen your skills portfolio.

Free Representation Unit

The Free Representation Unit (FRU) provides legal advice and representation for individuals at tribunals and in appeals against a tribunal decision, mainly in the areas of employment law and in relation to decisions involving social security. Volunteers are given training and, under supervision, undertake responsibility for the entire management of a case from initial interview to tribunal representation and all the stages in between thus offering a really great opportunity to develop a full range of professional skills.

Students are accepted as volunteers provided they are able to travel to London regularly and are at an appropriate stage of their legal education, which varies according to whether you wish to train to deal with employment or social security cases:

- **Social security** volunteers must either be in the third year of an LLB, have reached May in the penultimate year of an LLB, or be a GDL student

- **Employment** volunteers must either be an LLB graduate, have reached May in the final year of an LLB, or be an LLM or GDL student.

FRU operates a four-stage recruitment process involving attendance at a training day, a test based upon interpretation of a statute and its application to a factual scenario, observation of a tribunal, and an office induction session. There are examples of the test on the FRU website: **www.thefru.org.uk/volunteers/tests**.

Once accepted as a volunteer, you would be allocated a client and take responsibility for the entire conduct of the case so you would interview the client, take instruction, liaise with the other party or their representative, negotiate settlements, draft witness statements and other documents, and represent the client at tribunal. In essence, this would give you hands-on experience of work within the legal profession and an opportunity to develop skills in customer service as well as a whole host of professional skills such as drafting, negotiation, and advocacy that can be quite hard to demonstrate within the confines of academic study.

In-house schemes

A number of universities have established their own pro bono schemes or law clinics, often working in conjunction with local solicitors and barristers, so make sure you find out what is available at your own institution and get involved if such a scheme exists. If there is no in-house pro bono scheme, perhaps you could think about exploring the possibility of establishing one as this could be used to demonstrate any number of employability skills—leadership, organisation, decision-making, planning, and problem solving—as well as giving you access to the benefits of taking part once the scheme was up-and-running.

Practical example: Cardiff University pro bono centre

There is an excellent pro bono scheme at Cardiff University that works with local law firms to offer a range of volunteering opportunities to its students that includes working at an asylum centre in Cardiff, providing advice on healthcare issues as part of the NHS Continuing Healthcare Scheme, and working with the Welsh Rugby Union to provide free legal advice to Welsh rugby clubs.

Marshalling

Marshalling (sometimes called shadowing) describes the process of following a member of the legal profession as they go about their working life and is usually used to refer to sitting with a judge in court. This will be in the county court, Crown Court, or the High Court: it is not usually possible to shadow Court of Appeal or Supreme Court judges. Most judges who are prepared to be marshalled by students will be quite keen to explain things to you and will try to involve you with as much of their work as is possible in the context of the case. You may read skeleton arguments and case summaries, hear submissions being made in court, and discuss proceedings with the judge. Some judges will comment on litigation techniques that you have observed, explain the procedural intricacies of the case, and outline what they expect to happen to the case in the future. All-in-all, it is a very informative experience.

Practical advice: marshalling a judge

Try to ensure that your work experience includes at least one example of marshalling as this gives you a view of the operation of the legal system from a different perspective. Do not forget that you are not limited to marshalling in this jurisdiction: why not try to sit with a judge in a court in a different country if, for example, you have a work placement abroad or even if you visit another country on holiday.

Tell us

Tell us about your marshalling experience. How did you go about getting it and how did it enhance your employability skills? Contact us at finchandfafinski.com/get-in-touch or @FinchFafinski on Twitter.

....

I undertook some judicial marshalling at both Chester Civil Justice Centre and also at Nottingham Crown Court. I was able, during the work experience, to view a number of very different civil and criminal hearings from full trials to interlocutory applications. I found that sitting with experienced Circuit Judges allowed me to become familiar with the processes involved in a number of different hearings. I also found that sitting with the Judge gives the opportunity to hear a professional, unbiased, and knowledgeable opinion from somebody in possession of all the facts. I also found it useful as Judges can give their opinion on the future of the legal professions and also give you hints and tips as to the best way to put forward an argument in Court, they were particularly good after a hearing at pointing out the techniques of advocates which they found most convincing. Some of the best career advice I got was from Judges.

Josh, law graduate

....

Once you are on the BPTC, you should find it relatively easy to get some shadowing experience as the Inns of Court tend to make arrangements for this and, in any case, you will have many opportunities to meet judges at events at your Inn so could make your own arrangements with them directly. You may also find that your BPTC provider organises marshalling opportunities for its students so keep a look out for information about this.

If you want to experience the legal proceedings from a judicial perspective whilst still undertaking your undergraduate studies, you will probably have to make your own arrangements to do so. There are a number of ways that you could do this:

- **Contact the court.** Write a letter or email to the clerk of the court or the court manager at the court you wish to attend (one that is not in a university town is less likely to be overwhelmed by requests) and ask if there are any marshalling opportunities available. You could also go to the court and ask about this in person.

- **Make use of any contacts.** Many lecturers are also practitioners or have been in the past so ask if they know any judges who might be amenable to offering you some marshalling experience. Equally, think about whether any of your family or friends has a connection with a judge that you can use to ask for experience. If you happen to encounter a judge at a work placement or, for example, if they come to judge a moot, you can ask them directly. Never be afraid to ask: the worst that can happen is that they will say 'no' and they might say 'yes'.

- **Attend court and watch a case.** Make a note of the name of the judge and write directly to them (care of the court) explaining why you found the case interesting and what it was about their comments that grabbed your attention and asking if you might be able to sit with them for a day (or two) in the future.

Obviously, any written contact with a judge, their clerk, or other court personnel must be meticulously polite and scrupulously well written, grammatical, and free from errors. Remember that this letter is marketing you to the recipient so make sure that it does a good job. Equally, if you are fortunate in securing some marshalling experience, remember that the court is a professional environment and dress (and behave) accordingly. This includes addressing the judge as Your Honour (or other appropriate title according to the judge's status) unless you are explicitly invited to address them otherwise.

Making the most of work experience

If you have been able to obtain work experience, make sure you make the most of the opportunity that it offers. Even if it is not the sort of work experience that you really wanted, remember that it will still be an opportunity to develop your skills, network, and see the legal profession in action. The experience that you gain on this placement may help you to secure the one that you really want next time.

Create a favourable impression

It is important that you leave your work placement having made a positive impression on everyone that you have encountered. You want to leave the firm having made people think that you are exactly the sort of person that they want to work for them in the future, either on a further work placement, as a trainee, or far in the future once you are qualified. Moreover, you should leave the placement with at least one person who will act as a referee for you to support your future applications. Having a good reference from a work placement will help you to get future work placements as employers can see from the get go that you are not going to be a nuisance and might actually make a positive contribution.

Practical example: making an impression

We asked solicitors and barristers for examples of things that students had done during a work placement that created a particularly favourable impression. They also provided some good examples of things that students on work experience should not do:

- I like students who show a genuine enthusiasm for the work we do. Some of them set about even the most mundane tasks with excitement whereas others act as if you are putting upon them if you ask them to send a fax.

- If I ever see a student checking their watch, I send them home so that they can do whatever it is that they would rather be doing than being at work. If they come back the next day with a better attitude then that is fine otherwise I end their placement early. I am too busy to waste time with people who are not committed to making the most of their placement with us.

- Students should be presentable, polite, and prepared to work. A good level of initiative is handy as there isn't the time to guide them through every step of the work that we give them.

- The most impressive students are the ones who have got into the mind-set of a lawyer and do more than they are asked. Delivering good work is a given, but the most impressive will be thinking about clients, communicating, meeting deadlines, and going out of their way to get to know people around the firm.

- I remember a student who would email me every evening with a short summary of what he had done that day and any questions he had about the day's work. It always ended with an invitation for me to point out anything that he had done wrong or could have done better and asked if there was anything that I'd like him to prepare or read up on for the next day. I was hugely impressed by his methodical approach to work and his determination to really learn and improve his performance.

- I was most impressed by a student who turned up on the first day to find us in the midst of a crisis. I managed to point him towards a desk, show him the facilities and give him a two sentence summary of what the problem was before dashing off to a meeting. He joined us shortly afterwards bringing a tray of coffee and a notepad. He stayed unobtrusively for an hour or so before disappearing. I found him two hours later glued to his computer screen and expected him to be fiddling with email or something but he was actually reading up on the area of law that prompted our crisis as it was unfamiliar to him and he wanted to be able to understand our discussions.

- My most overwhelming memory of a student on work experience was not a good one. A young lady who scowled a lot and inexplicably refused to take her coat off at all on the first day and refused to photocopy a document on the basis that she was 'here to learn how to be a solicitor not to do secretarial work'. I am a patient man but I eventually gave up on the third day when we were in court and I had to collect her at the end of the day from the coffee shop where she'd been reading a magazine because there was nothing for her to do while I was in action in the courtroom.

Be proactive in finding tasks

It is likely that you will be assigned to work with one particular person who will supervise your work and allocate tasks to you but do not sit around doing nothing if you complete your work and your supervisor is not available to give you more work to do. Ask other people to see if there is anything that you can do to help them with their work. It can help if you are specific about the timeframe that you have available so that they understand what sort of work you could undertake. For example, you might say 'Mr X has been held up in court for the rest of the day and I've finished drafting the document that he wanted so is there anything that I could do for you for the rest of the afternoon?'.

Practical advice: finishing tasks

One of the things that students often say worries them about work experience is knowing what to do when they finish a particular task. Tackle the problem before it occurs by asking your supervisor how they would like you to fill any spare time:

- What would you like me to do when I've finished this?
- Are there any general tasks such as filing or copying that I can do if I am at a loose end?
- Should I offer to help anyone else in particular if I complete my work and you are not available?
- Are there any areas of law that I should research for you if I find myself with spare time?
- How would you like me to occupy my time if I finish the work you have given me and you are not around to ask?

If nobody has any work for you, find some for yourself. Check through what you have already done and make sure it is perfect and then do some further research on the law relevant to a case that you are working on or read the previous day's judgments from the Court of Appeal, perhaps preparing a case note on any that seem relevant to the work of your supervisor or others working in the firm. Do something so that your time is occupied with relevant work. Under no circumstances should you start sending personal emails, surfing the net, or updating your Facebook page!

Keep your skills portfolio in mind

All work experience is useful but try to ensure that you maximise its value to you by keeping an eye on the skills that you possess and have already demonstrated and the skills that you still need to develop. Make sure that you have a clear idea of areas where you need to focus your attention and try to target work experience opportunities that will enable you to build on hitherto undemonstrated skills.

- If you have not had an opportunity to demonstrate numeracy skills, try to obtain work experience in a financial or associated environment. Perhaps you could target insolvency practitioners or apply to HM Revenue & Customs for a work placement.
- If you have not yet had much experience of litigation, target work placements in areas of practice that involve a high degree of court work such as criminal law and family law. Alternatively, see if there is any work experience available that will enable you to attend tribunal hearings: employment law, immigration, and social security law are good areas here.

Practical advice: list your skills

Check to see which of the employability skills you can demonstrate by means of work experience. Make a list of your work experience and think carefully about the extent to which each placement gave you an opportunity to develop each of the employability skills that you need to be able to demonstrate to employers. Remember that you need to be able to point to specific examples of the skills in operation so jot down particular activities that provide supporting evidence. This will help you to see which skills you still need to be able to demonstrate so that you can target work experience accordingly.

Ask for feedback

It can be difficult for you to know whether or not you are doing a good job because you have so little experience of the workplace so be sure to ask your supervisor, or anyone else who gives you a task, for feedback. Always check that you have completed every task to their satisfaction, asking them to give you an opportunity to rectify it if it is not satisfactory or requesting that they show you how to improve it.

Employers do have fairly high expectations of law students so you should also ask for general feedback on your performance from your supervisor at regular intervals: is the speed of your work satisfactory, are you making too many mistakes, is there anything that you need to improve or do differently? It is important that you find out what is wrong and that you try to put it right. This may mean that you need to accept criticism. Try not to get defensive or upset if the feedback that you receive is negative. Nobody is trying to hurt your feelings: they are trying to help you to understand how you could improve your performance and develop the skills that you need to practise the law. Of course, they may do this in a way that is a bit blunt or tactless but remember that they have nonetheless still taken the time to try and help you to improve. The best way to deal with negative feedback is to thank the person giving it to you and assure them that you will address their concerns. You should then check again in a few days' time to see if they have noticed an improvement.

It is very easy to say 'thank you for pointing that out. I didn't realise that I was working so slowly but I'll certainly try and speed up now that I know what you expect'—you can always cry at home later or rant to your friends over a drink!

Practical advice: references

Ask for a reference after every piece of work experience to build up a selection of different referees. You can then select the ones that are most suited to subsequent vacancies. If you are struggling to get more work experience, ask for an open reference from a previous placement and attach it to your applications.

Get involved

Work experience is a networking opportunity as well as a chance for you to gain an insight into the workings of the legal profession. Make sure that you talk to as many people as possible and that you leave them with a good impression: ask questions about their work and seek their advice whilst being careful not to make too many demands on their time. By and large, people like it when others are interested in them so asking questions, particularly work-related ones, can be a good way of getting to know people working at the firm. One of the skills that employers want prospective employees to possess is the ability to get on with others and to integrate smoothly within an existing team so use your work experience as an opportunity to develop and demonstrate this skill.

Talk to people at all levels—partners, salaried lawyers, trainees, and paralegals—and find out what goes on in different departments so that you can build up a picture of the firm that goes beyond your own direct experience. Remember, just as the firm is evaluating you to see if you would be a good investment as a trainee, so you are assessing whether the firm would be a supportive and challenging place to undergo your training. With this in mind, you should get involved with any social activities that are going on as it will give you the chance to get to know people on a less formal basis and it is a further opportunity for them to get to know you.

Keep a record of your work

Remember that you are undertaking work experience to help you to secure a training contract or pupillage in the future so it would be a good idea to keep a detailed record of the work that you do so that you can have this to hand when completing applications. It will be useful to get into the habit of doing this every day so that there is less chance that you will forget details of your work. Take particular care to record specific tasks undertaken and areas of law that you have encountered.

In terms of your future employability, it would be useful to tie your work experience in with your skills audit so look on a regular basis to see what links you can make between the work you are doing and the skills that are valued by prospective employers. This can also help to remind you of the need to ensure that you maximise the benefit of your work experience: if you see that you are not gaining any experience of a particular skill that you had hoped to strengthen, you could make a specific enquiry about whether there is any work available that would give you an opportunity to do so. If no such opportunities exist, you can try to target work experience in the future that will enable you to fill this gap in your skills portfolio.

WHERE NEXT?

You cannot have failed to have noticed that this chapter is rather long. However, the justification for its length is that work experience is a very important topic and there was a lot of advice that we wanted to impart about it, particular as it is something that is a cause for concern for many students. Hopefully you will now have a much clearer idea of the different sorts of work experience that you could undertake, what they are likely to involve, and where you would go about finding opportunities to do them. If we were to distil the entire chapter down into three pieces of advice, it would be these:

- Do not let your understandable anxiety about going into a strange environment hold you back from applying for work experience. It is the best way to find out what solicitors and barristers actually do on a daily basis and your skills and confidence will grow as a result. But you do have to take that first step. Why not follow Jenny's example (see earlier) and apply to do something that frightens you? Jumping in at the deepest possible end can be a really good way to overcome your nerves because everything that you do thereafter seems easy by comparison. Alternatively, make it easy for yourself by thinking of the least threatening type of work experience possible and using that as a starting point to build up to more challenging things.

- It is never too late to start looking for work experience but make a decision not to delay any longer. We were serious when we said that you should start today—that advice applies whether today is the first day of your degree or you are reading this chapter on the morning of your graduation. So make a plan and start putting it into action.

- Be persistent. There are a lot of law students looking for work experience so be prepared to stick with it in the face of fierce competition. You might find it useful to look at some of the other chapters in this book for more advice on ways that you can strengthen your skills portfolio and make your application for work experience the one that really stands out.

Part IV

Focusing employability skills

This part of the book is concerned with focusing your employability skills towards your chosen career. Chapter 8 covers the traditional next steps for careers in legal practice—training contracts and pupillages—followed by Chapter 9 dealing with other law-related jobs and Chapter 10 looking at non-law work in a legal setting, non-law work with a degree of legal content, and careers with no legal context or content whatsoever.

Training contracts and pupillages

8

INTRODUCTION

This chapter discusses the final stages of professional training necessary for students who wish to practise in one of the two traditional branches of the legal profession: the training contract for solicitors and pupillage for barristers. This chapter should be read in conjunction with Chapter 11 which covers the actual application process and Chapter 12 which deals with interviews and assessment centres. If you are considering either a training contract or pupillage, then you will need to reflect on the area of legal practice that you wish to pursue. This chapter will guide you through many of the specific areas of legal practice before explaining the structure, content, and purpose of training contracts and pupillage and concluding with a discussion on finding funding.

Obtaining a training contract or pupillage is the last obstacle that must be overcome before you can begin practising law. The training contract or pupillage gives you the opportunity to begin working as a solicitor or barrister and to further develop your skills and knowledge in a working environment. You can think of them both as apprenticeships in which you really begin to learn your trade as a practising lawyer. In return, the firm or chambers in which you are employed will have the opportunity to assess your personal performance and to evaluate your prospects of a full-time contract or tenancy on completion. This chapter helps you to make the best-informed decision on where to apply and enables you to focus your employability skills portfolio towards opportunities that suit your desired area of legal practice.

Choosing an area of practice

There are many different law firms and sets of chambers and it would be neither possible nor desirable to apply to them all. This raises the question as to where you should apply and the most sensible way to start building your shortlist is by area of practice. However, before you can do this, you need to give some thought to what area of law you would wish to work in. In our experience, students tend to fall into four categories:

- **I know exactly what I want to do.** You may have a very clear idea of your preferred areas of law. This makes selecting application targets quite straightforward. However, being absolutely dead set on a particular area can narrow the options quite significantly, especially if it is quite niche. In addition, you may have made your decision without thinking through (or even being aware of) some of the alternatives.

- **I'd be happy with x or y but certainly not z.** You might have a shortlist of desired practice areas with some others that you know you definitely do not want to do. This widens the net of possible applications whilst eliminating others. It has the advantage of a contingency, should your first choice not come to fruition.

- **I don't care as long as I get a training contract/pupillage.** You may not be especially bothered about the particular specialism of the firms or chambers to which you apply. You might think that getting a foot through the door is all that matters and that you can always move around within the profession after qualification. While this keeps your options entirely open, remember that your applications and interview responses must demonstrate your interest in the specific opportunity (even though this might not be your actual viewpoint). You can run the risk of being caught out as insincere or uncommitted: therefore you would be better off taking a more focused approach and seeing if there are particular areas that might appeal more than others.

- **I haven't got a clue.** If you have no idea regarding a specialism, it would be a good idea to look at the different areas of practice that are available and try and say 'yes, no, or maybe' to each. This should help you to form a focused application strategy.

Whichever of these categories you identify with most closely, you should take some time to consider carefully the range of practice areas which would suit you so that this can inform your choice of application targets. There are, however, a multitude of options, as Figure 8.1 shows! The sections that follow will give you a brief overview of many of these areas and illustrate the nature of the work and the employability skills required for success.

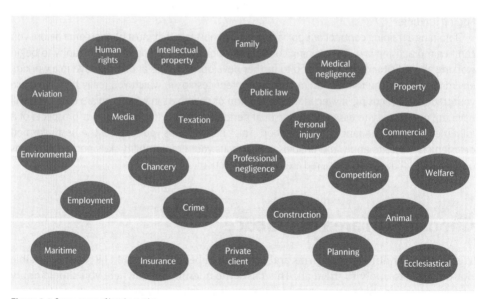

Figure 8.1 Some areas of legal practice

These descriptions are not exhaustive: instead they are there to illustrate the wide range of different opportunities and the key differences between them. As you read through them, think also about the sort of law that you have enjoyed doing on your studies. Do you prefer topics that are governed by complex legislation, or are you more comfortable with taking a general set of principles and applying them to different scenarios? Also consider whether you would prefer 'steady' work that is less likely to be affected by the general economic climate (such as family law) or that which will depend on the state of the economy (such as property law). You should think about the kind of work would be most likely to suit you since, although it is not impossible to change your area of practice once you have finally qualified, you will find it difficult to move somewhere with a different specialism if you have not undertaken any relevant work during your training contract or pupillage.

Although there are, of course, similarities between the areas of law covered by solicitors and barristers, the nature of the work varies to reflect the different expertise of the two branches of the profession. The descriptions are therefore broken down into solicitor and barrister areas of practice.

Solicitors—commercial law

The term 'commercial law' is very broad and covers many different fields of activity with a single common thread: they all impact on the world of business. Aspects of commercial law include:

- **Corporate.** Corporate lawyers are involved with corporate transactions such as mergers and acquisitions, taking companies public (listing them on a stock exchange), venture capital investments, and joint venture agreements. On a more routine basis, corporate work can include company and partnership formations, directors' service agreements, and shareholder agreements. General corporate work often requires specialist input on, say, taxation, property, employment or finance, so an effective corporate lawyer will require excellent commercial awareness and team working skills. As with many aspects of the commercial world, deals and transactions may have very pressing deadlines, so the ability to work long hours and to deal with pressure is key to success.

- **Banking and finance.** Banking and finance solicitors are primarily concerned with the legalities of financial transactions on behalf of banks, investors, or corporations. They will typically work through the entire lifecycle of a transaction, from planning and structuring through to completion. This may involve negotiating and drafting funding agreements and associated documentation as well as dealing with the regulatory aspects of the transaction. Complex transactions may require input from other parties including accountants and tax advisors. This will require good team working and communication skills. In addition the commercial pressure to conclude a deal on a certain date will require flexibility, an ability to work under pressure, and an expectation of working long hours.

- **Contract.** Commercial contract law is concerned with negotiating and drafting contractual agreements. These could be concerned with any area of business, such as terms and conditions of business, development, or outsourcing. Clients will typically include both public and private sector organisations. This type of work requires excellent negotiation and drafting skills and the commercial awareness to understand the client's business, to reflect the client's needs in the final negotiated agreements, and to identify and mitigate commercial risk.

- **Property.** Commercial property law involves the leasing, selling, development, and purchase of commercial land and buildings and all associated issues (such as planning and management). This area of law will typically involve managing a number of cases simultaneously and will therefore require excellent organisational and time-management skills as well as the ability to work independently.

- **Employment.** Employment lawyers advise companies on all aspects of employment law and the duties and liabilities that arise from the relationship between employee and employer. This can encompass drafting employee and sub-contractor agreements and associated employment policies (for example, sickness, absence management, grievance, or home-working) to ensure that they comply with the requirements of the complex body of employment legislation. In addition, employment lawyers are engaged by companies to deal with issues including redundancy, dismissal, and business restructuring and may be required to represent the employer in an arbitration or mediation or in the Employment Tribunal. This area requires good negotiation, drafting, and advocacy skills.

- **Insolvency.** Insolvency lawyers are involved with corporate bankruptcy, liquidation, administration, and business restructuring. They can act as advisors to companies or their creditors or other stakeholders. This will often involve working closely with accountants and bankers. Insolvency practice requires flexibility and a good sense of commercial awareness.

- **Litigation.** When commercial relationships and agreements go wrong, they can ultimately end up in litigation. That said, commercial litigators will also be involved in forms of alternative dispute resolution to avoid the need for court. This will involve understanding, advising, and representing their client's position in meetings and correspondence with the opposition. It will also require the ability to assess and communicate the client's prospects of success and may involve instructing a barrister and attending court or an arbitration hearing. The role requires well-developed negotiation, mediation, and advocacy skills.

Solicitors—private client

- **General private client.** Private client work spans a whole range of topics concerning an individual's private affairs, such as inheritance and tax planning, will-writing, and the administration of assets held in trust. It can also include advising the elderly on private nursing care and welfare matters. Very often, a private client will stick with one solicitor or firm for life, so it is important to demonstrate good interpersonal and communication skills and to understand the client's personal needs as well as the legal framework within which those needs can be most effectively realised.

- **Residential property.** Residential property work concerns the buying, selling, and leasing of houses. It involves drafting and reviewing contracts, investigating title to the property (and dealing with any difficulties that arise, such as restrictive covenants, or lack of rights of way), working with the solicitors for the other party, together with mortgage lenders and the stamp duty office, to ensure that funds are transferred properly upon completion of sale, and that the property registers are properly updated. Residential property lawyers often deal with a significant number of cases at once, so organisational and time management skills are important, as well as the ability to communicate with individuals for whom buying a home might be their first encounter with a solicitor.

- **Family.** Family law covers a wide range of areas. As well as the matters arising from divorce proceedings (such as the negotiation of financial orders or access/visitation rights for children) it can include dealing with pre-nuptial or cohabitation agreements, injunctions in situations involving domestic violence, or care/welfare proceedings for children. Family lawyers need to have excellent interpersonal and client care skills, with the ability to maintain a professional detachment from what are often very emotive situations.

- **Personal injury.** Personal injury (PI) lawyers bring claims on behalf of those who have suffered loss or damage as a result of another's negligence, or defend such claims, tending to specialise on one side or the other. They can specialise further depending on the nature of the negligence, such as medical or motoring. Cases will involve working with insurers and medical experts and can take a long time—often measured in years—to reach a settlement. PI work requires the ability to engage objectively with issues that are often very distressing for the claimant.

The Bar—areas of practice

As with solicitors, there are many distinct areas of practice at the Bar. These include:

- **Commercial.** The majority of commercial litigation arises as a result of a contractual dispute of some kind, although the subject matter of the contract can vary enormously. There is a strong focus on ADR since the majority of cases settle before reaching court. Cases can be extremely large and complex and may include an international element. Excellent commercial awareness skills are essential. There are limited prospects for oral advocacy, with the majority of the work requiring legal research and documentary analysis skills. Successful commercial barristers are, however, very well paid.

- **Chancery.** Chancery law is concerned with the exercise and application of equitable principles to contemporary situations. These principles can apply to a very broad range of legal issues. 'Traditional' Chancery work includes matters such as trusts, property, charity, and probate, whereas 'commercial' Chancery focuses more on commercial equitable areas including company law, banking, pensions, financial services, and insolvency. Chancery cases can be very complex, contain an international dimension, and often involve a great deal of research and analysis of paperwork. There is little oral advocacy but, as with commercial law, successful practitioners are well rewarded.

- **Public law.** Public law practitioners deal with cases that involve the exercise of power by government bodies and other public authorities (such as local authorities, prison authorities, and NHS trusts). The public nature of such cases means that they often attract a great deal of public and media interest—the Leveson inquiry is a good example—although the vast majority of public law cases are much more low-key, involving local matters on immigration, planning, or education. Many cases involve judicial review in the Administrative Court which has the authority to set aside a decision made unlawfully by a public body, or order that it be reconsidered. There are good opportunities for oral advocacy, particularly in specialist tribunals. Advocacy skills coupled with a good interest in current affairs are essential.

- **Employment.** The Employment Bar handles cases that arise from the breakdown of relationships between employers and employees. As such it can cover matters as diverse as discrimination, industrial action, whistle-blowing, workplace harassment, unfair dismissal, and redundancy. There is a strong emphasis on dispute resolution out of court. Disputes that cannot be resolved using ADR are normally settled at the employment tribunal which is less formal than court. This will allow plenty of opportunity for advocacy, although the accessibility of the tribunal system may mean that the other side is a litigant in person. More complex or higher-value cases will involve barristers on both sides. Employment practitioners need very good interpersonal skills since cases are frequently emotionally-charged: it is important to empathise with the client, but to be able to construct a case dispassionately. There can be a great deal of travel, since cases are heard in the tribunal closest to where the parties to the dispute are based.

- **Crime.** For most lay people, the criminal Bar is the area of practice most commonly associated with 'being a barrister': it is most often depicted in television and film dramas, and the notoriety and content of the highest-profile reported cases catch the public imagination. Criminal barristers are instructed to prosecute or defend those accused of crimes in the criminal courts. Typically, practitioners begin with minor road traffic and other offences along with bail hearings and pleas in mitigation in the magistrates' courts before progressing to more serious offences in the Crown Court. Since criminal practice necessitates a great deal of advocacy from the outset, advocacy skills are essential, particularly in cases where there has been little time for preparation. There is often a significant amount of travel involved and clients can be, frankly, unpleasant. In addition, recent cuts and reforms to legal aid are a significant threat to the Criminal Bar. With the exception of white-collar fraud cases, which still pay well, criminal practice is probably the lowest earning category of professional practice. Yet for some, the excitement of courtroom appearances, interaction with a jury, and securing a conviction or acquittal can, and do, outweigh many of the perceived downsides.

- **Family.** Family law barristers deal with the consequences of the breakdown of relationships (marriage, civil partnership, and cohabitation) and associated issues of finance, children, or domestic violence. A strongly developed emotional resilience is essential since cases can require the disclosure of sensitive and intimate information as well as having to give unwelcome news to clients who are in an emotionally-charged state. Custody hearings may require input from expert witnesses such as child psychologists. The work involves advocacy as well as client conferences and drafting agreements. Competition for places at the Family Bar is intense and mini-pupillages are essential (since the lower family courts sit in private, there is no other opportunity to witness family proceedings).

Practical exercise: what area of law do you want to practise?

This exercise is designed to get you thinking in a structured way about the areas of law in which you would like to practise. Remember that it is important for you to consider and reflect on your own preferences and priorities: for example, if you do not especially relish the prospect of travelling around the country from court to court, then employment work or criminal work at the Bar may not be for you. Of course, there may be compromises that you are willing to make, but you should do this in an informed way, rather than once you are 'in the job'.

⚲ You will find a worksheet on the Online Resource Centre that asks you a number of questions about yourself, your personal priorities and your studies. Take some time to think carefully about your answers and the areas of law that you have studied, encountered on work experience, or read about in this chapter. You will also find a commentary on the Online Resource Centre which will give some suggestions based on your answers. Of course, this sort of exercise cannot give you tailored career advice. It should, however, enable you to reason which areas are worthy of further investigation and therefore to start to work out where to apply. There are other factors that you might also like to bear in mind, such as location, size, and client base, which are covered later in this chapter.

Training contracts

The training contract is the last step in the process of qualifying as a solicitor. It is generally a two-year full-time period of paid practical experience, typically undertaken in a firm of solicitors (although there other organisations authorised to take trainees). The training contract process is regulated by the Solicitors Regulation Authority (SRA). On successful completion, a solicitor can be admitted to the Roll of Solicitors and may apply for their first practising certificate.

Content of the training contract

The SRA requires trainees to be given at least three different practice areas of substantive English law, including both contentious and non-contentious work. If an employer is not able to do this, it must arrange secondment to another firm to complete the training. The placements in the different areas of practice are often referred to as 'seats': for example 'my first training seat was in residential property, followed by a seat in family': typically a trainee will undertake four six-month seats. This will cover the three practice areas required by the regulations, plus the opportunity for a trainee to return to the seat in which they would most like to work once qualified. Typical work will include research, drafting, correspondence with clients and other solicitors, and attending meetings with clients, although the nature of the cases in which trainees are involved will depend on the size and practice focus of the firm. In larger firms, trainees can be part of a large team working on a complex case; in smaller firms, trainees can have responsibility for smaller cases (under the supervision of an experienced solicitor).

The Professional Skills Course

In addition to the work experience, trainees must complete the Professional Skills Course (PSC). The training firm will pay the course fees and must grant study leave for trainees to attend the course. The PSC comprises three compulsory core modules (advocacy and communication skills, client care and professional standards, and financial and business skills) plus a number of elective modules chosen to suit specific areas of interest under the broad headings of practice skills, contentions skills and non-contentious skills. Alternatively, Higher Rights of Audience training can be taken in lieu of PSC electives for solicitors who are planning a career in litigation. The PSC totals 12 days of training, with eight days spent on core modules and four on electives.

Developing your skills

You should make sure that you document your activities throughout the training contract. There is no set way of doing so, and individual training firms may have their own requirements. However, there is an excellent template available from the SRA, which encourages trainees to document:

- The case
- The task
- The skills involved
- Lessons learned from the task.

The SRA provides a set of practice skills standards in its guide *Training Trainee Solicitors: Guidance to the SRA Regulations on Training Contracts*. The practice skills that it identifies as being relevant to practice as a solicitor are:

- Advocacy and oral presentation
- Case and transaction management
- Client care and practice support
- Communication skills
- Dispute resolution
- Drafting
- Interviewing and advising
- Legal research
- Negotiation.

The SRA form also has space to log any professional development undertaken (including courses attended) and to note any professional conduct issues that arose in relation to any of the work undertaken.

You can find this form at **www.sra.org.uk/documents/students/training-contract/ recordform.pdf**.

Trainees must have three formal appraisals during the training contact (one in the first year, one in the second year, and one at the end), but it is common good practice to have an informal appraisal at the end of each seat to help keep track of your skills development and overall progress.

Part-time training

It is possible, but not common, to undertake a training contract on a part-time basis. The period of training cannot exceed four years, and so part-time trainees are required to work a minimum of two-and-a-half days per week. The length of the training contract is determined by the number of days per week spent on training (counted in half days). Additional hours made up by overtime and weekend working is not counted against the overall contract term.

Employers do not have to offer part-time training contracts, so it is often harder to find a firm that is willing to allow part-time training.

Pay

Trainees must be paid the minimum salary set by the SRA. For 2013/14, the minimum annual salary for trainee solicitors in Central London is £18,590 and £16,650 for trainees working elsewhere in England and Wales. Commercial law firms in the City can offer starting salaries of up to £50,000. Remember, though, that the cost of living in London is much greater than in the rest of the country.

Types of law firm

Once you have an idea of the sort of work that you want to do, you then need to think about what sort of firm you would want to do that work in and the clients that you would be working with. Law firms vary by size from the enormous commercial law firms advising multi-national organisations through to small high street practices dealing predominantly with members of the public. Most firms tend to fall into one of the following categories (although this list is not exhaustive and there can of course be exceptions):

- **International.** International firms tend to be huge concerns with thousands of staff. They handle international business, commercial, and financial law, with multiple offices throughout the world. It follows that there are often good opportunities for travel. Clients are typically global companies across a range of industrial sectors. Examples include Clifford Chance, which has offices in 24 countries and annual revenues of around £1.3 billion, and Linklaters which has offices in 19 countries and has a turnover of around £1.2 billion.

- **US firms.** Some larger law firms, such as Baker and McKenzie from the USA have offices in London dealing with the same types of work as the UK international firms. They also offer training contracts, but do not generally take on as many trainees as their UK based counterparts.

- **Major City.** Major City firms typically undertake commercial work for UK public companies. Many such firms will deal with international cases using established associations with overseas firms. City firms tend to have solicitors working in teams on substantial engagements with various professional service staff offering backup.

- **National.** National law firms provide a range of different legal services across the UK through a network of regional offices. They often arise through the merger of one or more successful regional firms.

- **Regional.** Regional firms typically consist of one or more offices covering a particular geographic area. Clients include local businesses and private client work (that is, acting for private individuals on a wide range of legal matters such as wealth management, wills, trusts, and probate).

- **Niche.** Some firms have a very clearly defined specialism in one or more areas such as shipping, charity, intellectual property, or insurance. Some niche practices are unable to offer sufficiently broad training to meet the SRA regulations on training contracts. If they can, you need to be absolutely sure that this is the right practice area for you, as, by their very nature, there are no real opportunities to move into different areas within a niche firm.

- **High Street/Legal Aid.** High Street firms deal primarily with individuals on private client work, such as residential property, employment law, family law, wills, and probate.

Generally speaking, the larger the firm, the more training contract places are offered. You may also therefore wish to consider whether it would suit your personality better to be one of many trainees or one of a handful. A further point to consider is that the larger the firm, the more support services are available. In smaller firms, the support and research services are fewer (or may not exist at all) and therefore you will need to be more suited to working independently. Think about whether either of these alternatives is more attractive to you.

Alternative training contract providers

Although firms of solicitors offer the vast majority of training contracts, there are other organisations that are authorised to take on trainees and thus provide alternative routes to qualification as a solicitor. Opportunities here are more limited, simply because there are fewer contracts available. The most common alternatives are:

- **Government Legal Service.** The Government Legal Service (GLS) (**www.gls.gov.uk**) provides legal services to the British government. It comprises around 2,000 qualified lawyers and trainees and advises government departments, agencies, and other public regulatory bodies. In 2013, the GLS had 30 to 35 trainee places available (most starting in 2015) although these places include opportunities for pupil barristers as well as trainee solicitors. Most places are available in the Treasury Solicitor's Department in London and offer four six-month seats over two years. At the time of writing, the first year legal trainees' salary is in the range of £23,900 to £25,000. The second year salary range is £25,300 to £27,000.

- **Crown Prosecution Service.** The Crown Prosecution Service (CPS) (**www.cps.gov. uk**) prosecutes criminal cases that have been investigated by the police in England and Wales. Like the GLS, it employs both solicitors and barristers. It runs a Legal Trainee Scheme (LTS) which, in 2013, offered ten training contracts or pupillages.

- **Local authorities.** Local authorities employ around 4,000 solicitors and trainees across England and Wales. They have their own professional body—Solicitors in Local Government (**www.slgov.org.uk**) which is separate from, but recognised by, the Law Society. Individual local authorities may offer training contract vacancies, but there is no national recruitment scheme or central list of local authority training contract vacancies. Local authorities that have been granted permission to employ trainees can be found on the SRA website. Vacancies are usually advertised in the national press or in relevant journals such as *The Law Society Gazette*. They may also be advertised on the SLG website. The types of local authority legal work are varied and can include commercial law, administrative law, social care, consumer protection, environmental law, highways and planning, education, and housing.

- **In-house.** In-house solicitors are employed by large non-legal institutions, such as banks and professional services firms. Some of these have the ability to offer training contracts which will be advertised in the national and legal press, and through specialist recruitment agencies.

- **Alternative Business Structures.** Alternative Business Structures were introduced by the Legal Services Act 2007. They allow non-lawyers to invest in, own, or run law firms, subject to approval from either the Solicitors Regulatory Authority or the Council for Licensed Conveyancers.

There are currently 179 ABSs licenced by the SRA (**www.sra.org.uk/absregister/**): these include Co-op Legal Services, Russell Jones and Walker (which is foreign-owned), Direct Line, and BT. ABSs were designed to stimulate competition and provide more consumer choice while the regulatory bodies continue to ensure that lawyers are able and competent to provide legal advice regardless of the business structure in which they do so: all ABSs must have at least one manager who holds a current practising certificate. With the exception of Co-op Legal Services, few of these organisations currently offer training contracts or pupillages, although this may change in the coming years. Although the business model in which legal services are offered is different in an ABS, there may be very little day-to-day difference in the nature of the work between an ABS and a traditional firm of solicitors. Therefore the core employability skills that firms currently look for in their trainees will be the same in an ABS, regardless of the structure of the working environment.

Timeline for applications

The majority of firms offering training contracts recruit two years in advance, so law students should apply at the end of their second year as an undergraduate, and non-law students should apply in their final year. The closing date for training contract applications at many firms is 31 July each year, but you should double check the deadlines at the firms that you wish to apply to well in advance.

Look back at Chapter 2 for the detailed application timetable. Chapter 11 contains detailed guidance on putting your application together. Chapter 6 has further information on law fairs and networking.

Pupillages

Pupillage is the final stage of training to be a barrister. It is undertaken after the Bar Professional Training Course (BPTC) and combines the vocational training that you will have acquired with practical work experience in a set of barristers' chambers or with another Authorised Training Organisation (ATO). Pupillage usually lasts for one year, starting in the September or October, one year after being accepted. It is formally divided into two six-month periods, known as 'sixes':

- **First six.** During the first six, you will be assigned a pupil supervisor. The first six is non-practising. This means that you are not able to accept instructions other than 'noting briefs'. In these, you get sent along to court to take a note of proceedings in which your client is not otherwise represented but is interested in the outcome. You will typically spend your first six shadowing your pupil supervisor, reading their paperwork and observing them in court, undertaking legal research, and drafting court documents and opinions. Provided that you have passed the BPTC you may undertake your first six without having been called.

- **Second six.** After successful completion of the first six you will be issued with a provisional qualification certificate and a practising certificate (provided that you have registered for a second six) by the Pupillage Compliance Section of the Bar Standards Board. This will mean that you will be able to take instructions on your own account, as long as your pupil supervisor or head of chambers has given you permission. The whole of the second six must be done after your call.

Getting pupillage is highly competitive: there are roughly six times as many applicants as there are places. Therefore, it is vital that you make your pupillage application as strong as possible. Even if you have already had a mini pupillage at the set to which you are applying, you must make sure that they remember you from your application. If you have not had a mini pupillage there, your application is the first opportunity that you will have to make a positive impression. The Bar Standards Board requires that all pupillages are advertised and that each set of chambers makes its recruitment decisions against a transparent and published pupillage policy document. Chambers which 'tap in' pupils to an unadvertised pupillage are in breach of the equality code and such pupillages may not be registered by the Bar Standards Board—which would mean that there would be no practising certificate or qualification certificate at the end of it.

Chambers are required to fund pupillage with at least £12,000 (split into £6,000 for each six). The financial award can be more (and often is) and the pupil may also earn money from case work during the second six. Decisions about tenancy are usually made about ten months into pupillage: decisions might be based simply on a pupil supervisor's assessment of a pupil's abilities, or the pupil might have to take part in a formal exercise. Some sets of chambers take on every pupil with a view to making them a tenant if they perform well.

Chapter 11 covers the process of researching and putting together an application, and Chapter 12 deals with interviews and other recruitment practices.

Finding pupillage opportunities

The Bar Code of Conduct stipulates that *all* vacancies for pupillages must be advertised on a website designated by the Bar Council, which is the Pupillage Gateway at **www.pupillagegateway.com** (see Figure 8.2). This opened in March 2013 and allows candidates to view all vacancies, or to narrow their selection using various search criteria.

A complementary free online resource that also allows you to search for pupillage opportunities is the Pupillage Pages at **www.thepupillagepages.com** (see Figure 8.3).

Both sites allow you to search for available pupillages in various practice areas and to focus your search by variables such as location, type of application, size of chambers, minimum degree classification, and typical value of pupillage award. It also gives details of application deadlines.

You should also check the websites of chambers in which you are interested. Increasingly, chambers also use social media, particularly Twitter, to provide short updates on their activities and also to issue alerts when pupillages or other such opportunities become available (see Figure 8.4).

If you use Twitter, it would be useful to follow the feeds of interesting chambers and the Inns of Court.

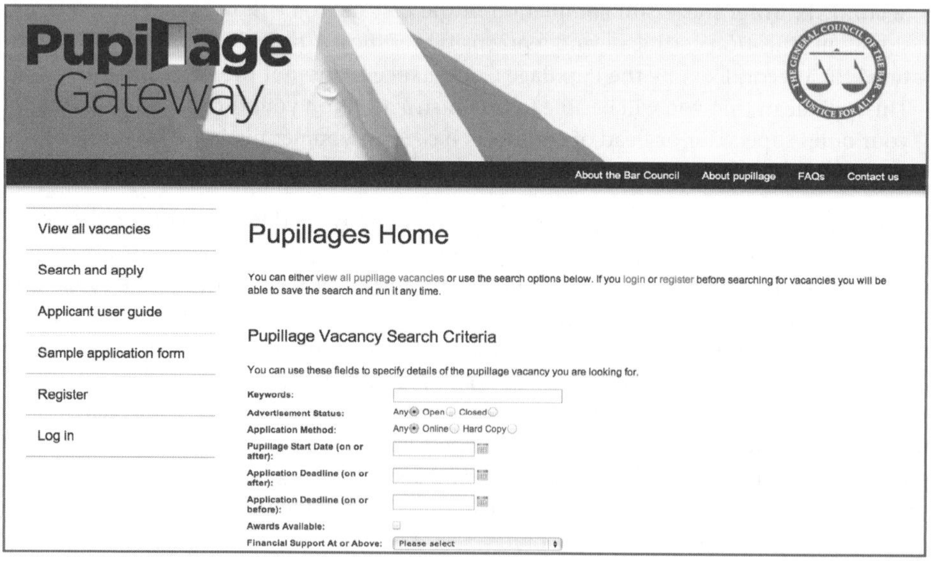

Figure 8.2 Pupillage Gateway

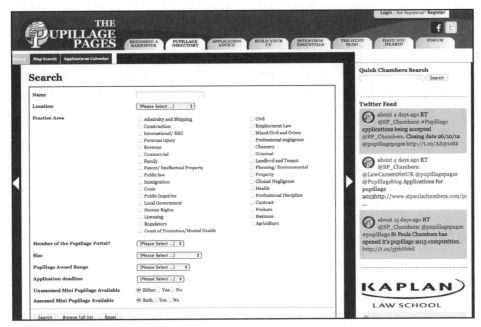

Figure 8.3 The Pupillage Pages

Figure 8.4 5 Essex Pupillages

Choosing pupillages

The Pupillage Gateway online application system allows you to select your choice(s) of pupillage up to a maximum of 12. It is vital that you research your chambers carefully. You must make sure that your skills and experience are aligned as closely as possible with the areas of practice within that chambers. You should also make sure that you spend as much time as you can on finding the right sets. Remember that if you are successful, then you will spend the first part of your professional working life as a member of the set and it is important that you choose potential sets that give you the greatest likelihood of fitting in successfully.

Unless you have a personal contact at a set that you can talk to directly, or have had a mini pupillage there, it is likely that the primary resource that you will have to research chambers will be their websites. A note of caution: remember that the marketing focus of a set's website will be instructing solicitors and clients. As such, the impression that is given by a superficial glance at the site may well be quite different from a detailed study of the members of chambers and their particular experience.

Ensure that the chambers that you choose have a significant practice in your chosen area. You can only really do this by looking in depth at the profiles of the members of chambers. Some websites might claim that they can take a particular type of instruction, even though they only have one or two barristers who can specialise in that area. If you are keen on a particular area of work, then you must be sure your chosen chambers has substantial expertise in that area so that you maximise your chances of receiving instructions in your preferred area in your early years in practice. You might also want to look at the types of cases that the chambers handle, or the chambers ranking in that area. One useful website that may be able to assist can be found at **www.chambersandpartners.com/ UK-Bar** (see Figure 8.5). This is a free service that enables you to search rankings in around 70 practice areas.

Don't take the website at face value. Every chambers will tout itself as a master of all trades, with practitioners who are somehow experts in everything from defamation to dilapidations. Look at members' reported cases and their mentions in Chambers & Partners—this is a much better indication of where a chamber's strengths really lie. Don't be afraid to mention one or two particular barristers whose practices you would like to emulate, especially if you can later recall cases in which they were involved.

Aidan Briggs, Ely Place Chambers

It is likely that there will be more than 12 sets that provide services in your chosen specialism, so you may want to evaluate chambers using other factors that are important to you. Matters that may influence your choices could include location (although certain

Figure 8.5 Chambers and Partners

practices only operate in London, sets covering general areas such as criminal or family law also exist outside London), value of pupillage award, and your ultimate chances of tenancy. Chambers may mention the prospects of success on their website. You may also want to look at the profiles of recent tenants to see if there are any particular themes that might encourage or dissuade you from applying. While chambers will always want to remain open to any outstanding application, the only evidence you have as to their recent preferences are the inferences you can reasonably draw from their recruits: in particular, look at their academic history. Is there a tendency to prefer applicants with an LLB or the GDL/CPE, or do most have an LLM?

Make sure that you take enough time to do your research and select a good cross-section of chambers at which you think you have reasonable prospects of success and that, if you were successful, you think you would be happy.

Timetable for applications

Law students should apply during their final year as an undergraduate, and non-law students should apply while undertaking their conversion. Table 8.1 shows key dates. Pupillage vacancies that are not administered through the Pupillage Gateway may

Table 8.1 Key dates for pupillage applications

1 March	Pupillage Gateway opens. You can access it to browse vacancies and to see a generic sample application form.
1 April, 11am	Submissions windows for applications opens.
30 April, 11am	Submissions window for applications closes. No new applications or amendments to existing applications are possible.
June—July	First and second round interviews.
August—September	Offers of pupillage are made to successful applicants.
September (following year)	Pupillage commences.

operate to a different timetable. However, all pupillages are advertised on the Pupillage Gateway and will indicate whether any exceptions to the mode of application or timetable apply.

Have a plan. Know which chambers you are going to apply to well in advance of the system opening. Use all twelve of your possible applications on the online system. Be realistic about your choices—look at the calibre of the recent tenants at your target sets and compare their CVs to yours.

Rupert Jones, barrister

Look back at Chapter 2 to see how this fits into your overall timetable. Chapter 11 contains detailed guidance on putting your application together.

Third sixes

Once pupillage has been completed satisfactorily, barristers are able to practise independently as tenants in chambers. However, if a pupil has not been offered tenancy after pupillage has been completed, they can go on to take a 'third six' pupillage, usually at a different chambers to the one at which they completed their first and second six.

Unlike the first and second six pupillages, the third six pupillage application system is unregulated although chambers are encouraged to advertise third six vacancies on the Bar Council website at **www.barcouncil.org.uk/for-the-bar/careers,-recruitment-and-vacancies/third-six-pupillage-vacancies/**. Some chambers will only advertise on their website. Other members of chambers and clerks can also be great sources of information on sets offering or considering third six pupils.

Chambers may also consider outstanding speculative applications.

Third six applications are generally made by CV and covering letter.

Chapter 10 deals with compiling CVs and covering letters.

The general advice in Chapter 10 applies to third six applications, but you should also ensure that you give detailed examples of the work undertaken in the first and second six and highlight the skills that you have developed throughout pupillage. You should also secure a solid reference from the set at which you did pupillage to enable you to answer the obvious question from third six recruiters: why were you not taken on at your pupillage chambers?

There is no set timetable for applying for third sixes, although the market is most active between June and August when tenancy decisions are usually made.

Finding funding

One of the important considerations facing many students seeking a training contract or pupillage is funding. The LPC and BPTC courses are rather expensive with fees up to £16,885 (depending on the course provider and pattern of study) and this does not include accommodation or living costs (although it does include course materials and professional registration fees). There are a number of options open to students to fund this stage of their legal training:

- **Self-funding.** Some students (or their parents) are able to pay the course fee and associated costs of studying. Think carefully before committing to self-funding as completion of the LPC or BPTC is no guarantee of a training contract or pupillage.

- **Loans.** It is possible to obtain a career development loan from many of the high street banks to pay for a professional training course such as the LPC and BPTC as long as the provider is on the government's Register of Learning Providers (see **www.ukrlp.co.uk** for details).

- **Sponsorship.** The offer of a training contract, particularly from one of the larger law firms, may be accompanied by the additional benefit of sponsorship through the LPC. This may involve payment of course fees plus a contribution towards living expenses for the duration of the course. This may mean that the law firm will stipulate a particular LPC-provider. You will find details of law firms that offer sponsorship in Appendix B.

- **Scholarships.** A number of organisations provide scholarships and bursaries that may cover all or part of the costs associated with undertaking the LPC or BPTC. Some of the scholarships available are covered in more detail in the sections that follow.

Training contract provider sponsorship

From the point of view of law students who wish to qualify as solicitors, the ultimate goal is to secure a training contract. However, there is a flip side to this situation as law firms are also keen to secure good students to train as future lawyers. For this reason, many law firms offer to pay LPC course fees and provide a sum of money to contribute towards living costs during the LPC year. By offering an attractive package of benefits, law firms believe that they will attract the brightest students and select the best of these for a training contract.

You may think that competition for a training contract is so fierce that there is no point in applying for a funded training contract as you will have no chance. It is true that there are more students looking for training contracts than there are training contracts available but there are many funded training contracts available each year and they have to be awarded to somebody so there is no reason why, if you take all the right steps to ensure your application is competitive, that it should not be you.

Practical example: number of applicants

How many applicants do you think that there are for each funded training contract vacancy? You might be surprised to find that there are fewer applicants for each vacancy than you imagine. For example, Howell Lovells is a leading London law firm that pays LPC fees and offers a £7000 maintenance package to support students during the LPC year. It receives approximately 1500 applications each year. Of these, it interviews about 300 students and recruits 75 applicants.

- There is a *one in five* chance of getting an interview
- There is a *one in four* chance of getting a training contract if you are interviewed
- Overall, you have a *one in 20 chance of success* if you apply for a funded training contract.

Of course, in order to apply for a funded training contract, you have to know that it is available. There are various ways that you can identify sponsored LPC places— you could check the web pages of individual law firms, focusing particularly on larger firms as these are more likely to have funded training contracts available or use a resource such as the *Training Contract Handbook* or the Target Jobs website (**http://targetjobs.co.uk/career-sectors/law-solicitors**). However, for ease of reference, we have compiled a list that is as comprehensive as possible of the firms offering at least a contribution to course fees as part of the package for trainees and it is organised as an alphabetical list in Appendix B. You will see an extract from this in Table 8.2.

Table 8.2 Funded training contracts—excerpt

Firm	Training contracts available	Requirements	Starting salary	Sponsorship
Addleshaw Goddard www.addleshawgoddard.com/graduates	35	2.1 3 Bs at A-level (excluding General Studies)	£37,000 (London) £25,000 (Leeds and Manchester)	LPC fees plus £7,000 (London) or £4,500 (elsewhere) maintenance
Allen & Overy LLP www.aograduate.com	90	2.1	£38,000	LPC fees and £5,000 maintenance
Arnold & Porter LLP http://arnoldporter.webfactional.com/career/london-trainees/index.html	2	2.1	US firm market rate	LPC fees plus unspecified maintenance

Firm	Training contracts available	Requirements	Starting salary	Sponsorship
Ashfords LLP www.ashfords.co.uk/ graduate_recruitment	12	2.1 preferred but applicants with a 2.2 may be considered	Unspecified	£9,000 towards LPC fees
Ashurst LLP www.ashurst.com/ trainees/	40	2.1	£38,000	LPC fees plus £6,500 maintenance

The funding available varies from a partial contribution of a few thousand pounds towards the cost of the LPC fees to a package that covers the entirety of the fees plus a maintenance grant of up to £10,000. You may find that some firms do not specify the value of their maintenance grant, stating that it is 'to be confirmed', 'under review', or is simply 'competitive'. If this is the case, you can contact the person responsible for graduate recruitment to ask for more up-to-date information—do not be embarrassed to do this: you are considering committing two years of your life to a firm so it is reasonable to find out what they are providing in return.

Practical example: finding information

You will find that some law firms have websites that are more user-friendly and easy to navigate than others. If you are struggling to find information about training contracts including any sponsorship that is available, try the following links:

- Recruitment
- Graduate opportunities
- Careers
- Join us
- Working here
- Our trainees.

You may find that some firms that do not offer sponsorship to their trainees may make interest-free loans available to cover the fees and expenses of the LPC year. Moreover, some firms have discretionary funding available which means that they do not routinely offer sponsorship but may do so if you can make a persuasive case that you cannot undertake the LPC without financial support. Do not be afraid to do this: after all, if they like you enough to offer you a training contract, they may be prepared to offer sponsorship rather than risk losing you to another law firm.

Course provider scholarships

There are various ways in which institutions that offer the LPC and/or BPTC provide financial support for students undertaking these courses. Many institutions offer discounted fees to their own graduates, offer a discount for early payment, or have payment schemes to spread the cost of the course. Some institutions even run competitions in which the prize is a fully funded LPC or BPTC place:

- **BPP (in conjunction with Lawyer2B).** The competition is based upon the submission of a 1500 word article that explores how a graduate can best be prepared for a job as a trainee solicitor. For further details, see: **www.bpp.com/university-college/l/external-award-schemes#Lawyer2B.**

- **Oxford Brookes.** This is an essay writing competition. Applicants must write a 1000 word essay which discusses this statement: 'Changes to public funding are compromising access to justice'. Further details are to be found on their website: **www.law.brookes.ac.uk.**

It is quite unusual to find course fees as a competition prize but, of course, it would strengthen your CV as well as making a significant contribution to the cost of your professional training year if you were to enter and win such a competition. It is more usual, however, for students seeking financial support to obtain this by way of a scholarship offered by the institution that they plan to attend. In Table 8.3, you will find details of the scholarships from course providers for the LPC and BPTC that were on offer at the time of writing.

💧 You can find up-to-date details of competitions and scholarships on the Online Resource Centre.

Table 8.3 LPC/BPTC course provider scholarships

Name of Award	Value	LPC or BPTC
BPP www.bpp.com/university-college/l/university-college-scholarships		
Principal's Scholarship	Full fees	Either
Senior Academic's Scholarship	£1000–£3000	Either
Law School Dean's Scholarship	£5000	Either
Cohen Scholarship (GDL students only)	£2500	Either
Director of BPTC Programme Scholarships (London and Leeds only)	£3000	BPTC
Director of LPC Programme Scholarships	£3000	LPC
City University www.city.ac.uk/law/courses/applicants-zone/scholarships-application		
CLS Bar Professional Training Course Scholarships	£3000	BPTC
CLS Legal Practice Course Scholarships	£3000	LPC
Rosie Keane Memorial Scholarships (female students only)	£5000	
Kaplan Law School www.law-school.kaplan.co.uk/law-courses/lpc		
Diversity Scholarship	15% discount	LPC

Name of Award	Value	LPC or BPTC
Pro Bono Scholarship	15% discount	LPC
Excellence Scholarship	15% discount	LPC
Manchester Metropolitan University www.law.mmu.ac.uk/scholarships/		
LPC Scholarships	£3000	LPC
BPTC Scholarships	£4000	BPTC
Nottingham Trent University www.ntu.ac.uk/nls/courses/fees_scholarships/index.html		
Competitive Scholarships	£2000	Either
Pro Bono Scholarship	£2000	LPC
Mooting Scholarship	£2000	LPC
Commercial Practice Scholarship	£2000	LPC
University of Law www.law.ac.uk/lawscholarships		
LPC Full Scholarship Scheme	Full fees	LPC
LPC Scholarship Award	£4000	LPC
LPC Lunar Awards Scheme	£3000	LPC
BPTC Full Scholarship Scheme (Bloomsbury and Birmingham only)	Full fees	BPTC
BPTC Scholarship Award (Bloomsbury and Birmingham only)	£4000	BPTC
BPTC Platinum Awards Scheme	£3000	BPTC

Inns of Court scholarships

All prospective barristers must join one of the four Inns of Court before embarking on the vocational stage of their training; in fact, you will not be able to commence the BPTC unless you are a member of an Inn. Each of the Inns offers scholarships to support its student members during the BPTC.

You do not have to be a member of an Inn to apply for its scholarships but you must join before the application deadline on 31 March in order to receive any award that has been offered to you.

It is essential that you remember that you must join one Inn and apply for its scholarships. It is not permitted to make multiple applications so you cannot apply for scholarships at all four Inns and then join whichever one offers you funding. The Inns share information and circulate the names of students who have applied for scholarships to prevent this happening and any student who does this will be refused an award at all four Inns.

Gray's Inn

The Honourable Society of Gray's Inn gave away over £830,000 in scholarships, awards and prizes in 2012. Of this, £660,000 took the form of scholarships for BPTC students as set out in Table 8.4.

Table 8.4 Gray's Inn Scholarships

Award Name	Number given	Amount awarded
Birkenhead Award	1	£20,000
Bedingfield Scholarships	9	£18,000
Prince of Wales Scholarships	11	£15,000
Other named awards	14	£14,000
	9	£13,000
Total Awarded	44	£660,000

The application deadline is the first Friday in November of the year before you wish to start the BPTC. For many students, this means that you need to apply in November of your final undergraduate year. Application forms can be found on the Gray's Inn website and applicants must submit the completed form and two written references. It is important that you chase up your referees yourself as the Inn will not contact them and neither will they shortlist candidates whose references have not arrived. This can require careful management as you will need to check (well before the deadline) to make sure that your lecturer has done this without annoying them (try to remember that yours is not the only reference that they need to write at this time of the year).

Shortlisted candidates will be interviewed the following year in late February or early March. The interview is usually conducted by a three-person panel of benchers and senior members of the Inn who will ask you questions about your application. You may be given a discussion topic upon arrival at the interview upon which you may be asked your opinion such as whether the freedom of the press is more important than individual privacy.

The criteria used for awarding scholarships at Gray's Inn is fourfold:

- **Intellectual ability.** This is the ability to conduct legal research and give written advice as demonstrated by your exam performance (school and university), the interview, and any other relevant experience.
- **Motivation to succeed at the Bar.** Applicants should demonstrate a sound knowledge of the profession and the operation of the courts and be able to show that they have taken steps to acquire the personal skills required of a barrister.
- **Potential as an advocate.** The focus here is on the applicant's oral and written skills so emphasise any experience in public speaking such as mooting, debating, and participation in mock advocacy exercises.
- **Personal qualities.** The qualities that are valued include self-reliance, independence, integrity, reliability, and the capability to work effectively with colleagues, clients, and the chamber's staff.

Practical exercise: demonstrating criteria

Many of the questions that you are asked at interview will be prompted by the information provided on your application so it stands to reason that you should strive to ensure that your application provides evidence of the four assessment criteria. Check that it does by taking four different coloured highlighter pens and allocating one colour to each set of criteria. Go through a printed copy of your application form (before it is submitted) and think about which criteria is illustrated by each of your answers and colour it in accordingly. You will then be able to see at a glance whether each of the criteria is demonstrated sufficiently in your application and make adjustments to your answers if there is an imbalance.

- You will find more information about the application procedure on the Gray's Inn website: **www.graysinn.info/index.php/scholarships/bptc-scholarships-awards**.

Middle Temple

The Honourable Society of Middle Temple awarded over £1million in scholarships in 2012. In 2011, it awarded 172 scholarships for BPTC students, the highest of which was £15,000. The criteria for making awards is as follows:

- **Intellectual ability.** The ability to conduct legal research and give written advice as demonstrated by performance in school and university examinations, the interview and, where appropriate, other experience.

- **Motivation to succeed at the Bar.** Knowledge of the profession and the courts, and steps taken to acquire the personal skills required of a barrister will be taken into account.

- **Potential as an advocate.** Both in oral and written skills.

- **Personal qualities.** Those required by members of the Bar include self-reliance, independence, integrity, reliability, and the capacity to work effectively with clients, colleagues, and chambers' staff.

Practical example: application questions

In addition to questions focused on factual details about your education and experience, application forms are likely to contain other questions designed to explore your personality and character. These examples are taken from the 2013 application form for Middle Temple scholarships, each of which has to be answered in no more than 250 words:

- What question would you most like the panel to ask you?
- Give an example of when you have demonstrated integrity
- Give an example of a situation when you had to overcome adversity or disadvantage
- Give an example of something which you have done which has made you proud of yourself
- What do you think your greatest strength is which will enable you to succeed at the Bar?
- What is a weakness you would need to overcome in order to become a good barrister?

Tell us

What questions were you asked at your scholarship interview? What answer did you give and did you obtain a scholarship?

Tell us at finchandfafinski.com/get-in-touch or @FinchFafinski on Twitter so we can build up an online reference list for other applicants looking to apply for scholarships.

The Honourable Society of Lincolns Inn

In 2012/13, Lincolns Inn awarded £1,237,500 million in scholarships. There are up to 70 scholarships of between £6000 and £18,000 and up to 40 bursaries of up to £3000 each available. The scholarships awarded in 2013 are set out in Table 8.5:

Table 8.5 Lincoln's Inn Scholarships

Award name	Number given	Amount awarded
Lord Mansfield Scholarships	11	£18,000
Lord Denning Scholarships	62	£15,000
Tancred Scholarships	2	£15,000
Marchant Scholarship	1	£15,000
Mary MacMurray Scholarship	1	£6000
Kennedy Scholarships	4	£6000
Cassell Scholarships	4	£6000
Thomas Moore Bursaries	12	£3000

Awards are based upon merit and the majority of applicants with a 2:1 or above are invited for interview and some candidates with a 2:2 will be interviewed if sufficient merit is revealed in their application and references. The criteria used as the basis for granting awards are as follows:

- **Intellectual strength.** Usually evidenced in large part by real excellence in performance at university.
- **Confidence and sensitivity.** A confident person capable also of being sensitive to other people and to the situation with which they are dealing.
- **Motivation.** High motivation and drive with evidence of serious commitment to some aspect of work at the Bar through, for example, mooting and mini pupillages.
- **Complete integrity.**
- **Articulateness.** A high level of intelligent articulateness: a confident but perceptive person who knows what they are talking about.

Inner Temple

The Honourable Society of the Inner Temple awarded £982,500 in scholarships in 2011, making awards to 119 of the 371 applicants. They plan to award scholarships to the value of £1,428,000 in 2012. The number of awards made each year is not fixed but are typically as set out in Table 8.6.

Table 8.6 Inner Temple Scholarships

Award name	Number given	Amount awarded
Peter Taylor Scholarship	1	£20,000
Stephen Chapman Scholarships	1	£18,000
Princess Royal Scholarships	5	£17,500
Major scholarships	Up to £1,043,000 available	
Other named awards	16	£100 - £1500
Total Awarded	102	£1,428,000

There are also 50 awards of £150 from the Duke of Edinburgh Award to cover the cost of the Inn's fees for admission and call. No separate application is required for this as it will be automatically covered in all other scholarship applications.

Students must complete an online application form which is available on the Inner Temple website and submit this by the deadline which is usually around the beginning of November. The application must be accompanied by two academic and one personal reference. Inner Temple interview every eligible applicant for a scholarship with the interviews taking place late in March. As part of the interview, students are given an unreported case to study for 30 minutes and are asked questions about it during the interview. Awards for scholarships are based upon merit and for exhibitions on a combination of merit and need (so it is advisable to complete the financial section of the application) and the following criteria are applied:

- **Intellectual qualities.** The ability to analyse complex information and identify essential points, judgement, perceptiveness, and memory. These qualities can generally be evidenced by academic achievements.
- **Motivation.** Applicants should have a very high level of drive and determination and a commitment to appropriate aspects of work at the Bar.
- **Relationships.** The ability to get on with a wide range of people is important as is diplomacy and the ability to sustain relationships.
- **Character.** Calmness under fire, the ability to work hard for long hours and against deadlines, sound personal values, and integrity.
- **Impact.** Articulateness, persuasiveness, confidence, ability to suit conduct to occasion.

Recent statistics on awards are shown in Table 8.7.

Table 8.7 Inner Temple Scholarship statistics

	2008	2009	2010	2011	2012
Applicants	205	299	371	365	376
Interviews (applicants minus withdrawals)	193	276	317	321	342
Awards	98	107	119	101	102

Diversity Access Scheme

The Law Society operates a Diversity Access Scheme (DAS) which provides promising prospective solicitors with work experience opportunities, professional mentoring, and assistance with the LPC course fees. It is open to students who have encountered exceptional obstacles that make their goal of qualifying as a solicitor an especial challenge. These obstacles may be financial, social, educational, or personal in nature or may relate to a disability or chronic health condition.

Applicants are asked to provide details of the nature of the obstacles they have faced or overcome, their financial circumstances, their reasons for wishing to enter the legal profession, and the extent to which they have developed the skills relevant to becoming a solicitor through vacation placements, work experience, paid employment, voluntary work, or personal commitments. Applicants are also required to submit an essay so that their ability to conduct legal research and put together a legal argument can be evaluated. The most recent essay addressed the question: 'Are the provisions for the compulsory removal of an individual from the UK to a foreign state satisfactory?'.

In 2012, there were 113 applicants to the DAS of which 30 were successful.

- You will find further details of the DAS and the application procedure on the Law Society website: **www.lawsociety.org.uk/about-us/law-society-charity/diversity-access-scheme/**.

WHERE NEXT?

This chapter has provided an introduction to a selection of the different areas of legal practice that could be followed as a solicitor or at the Bar together with guidance on the structure and format of the training contract and pupillage. It should have helped you to narrow your focus on the area of law that you would ideally like to practise should you wish to pursue a career in either of the traditional branches of the legal profession.

It may be that you are still unaware of the alternative career paths that can be followed with a law degree. The next two chapters look at other law jobs after graduation and non-law careers: they are there to make you aware of the whole range of career opportunities that exist for law graduates.

Alternatively, you may by now be absolutely ready to apply for a training contract or pupillage, in which case Chapter 11 takes you through putting together an application, matching your employability skills to the requirements of the employer, and communicating them as effectively as possible to give you the best chance of progressing to interview, which is dealt with in Chapter 12.

9 Law jobs after graduation

INTRODUCTION

Although it is usual to think of 'law jobs' as being limited to work as a solicitor or barrister, there are a number of other career options for law graduates that will make good use of your legal knowledge and the skills acquired on a law degree without the need to complete the professional training courses or to find a training contract or pupillage. This chapter will focus upon work as a paralegal, legal research roles, and other law support roles such as legal advisors. It will outline the sort of work involved and the skills that are needed to do it successfully as well as detailing how to find opportunities to apply for such jobs. It also considers the merits of undertaking further academic study. This chapter explores these types of work both as career destinations in their own right and also in terms of the value that they offer to a graduate who still aims to qualify as a solicitor or barrister in the future.

Do you know what you are going to do after graduation? If you have secured a training contract or pupillage during your undergraduate studies then the answer is likely to be an unqualified 'yes' but other students might find the answer to the question rather less straightforward due to a number of issues: cost of the professional training courses, the elusive nature of the training contract or pupillage, or just uncertainty about whether or not to go into practice. Or perhaps you have already completed the LPC or BPTC but you have not managed to secure a training contract or pupillage. If you are in the position of having graduated or being about to graduate with a law degree but not being sure about what to do then this chapter will identify a number of law-focused career options that you could pursue on a temporary or permanent basis. They may turn into a job that you love and decide to keep doing, a temporary stop gap that gives you time to think about what to do next, or a means of gaining more work experience that helps you achieve your ultimate objective of qualifying as a solicitor or barrister.

Thinking about law jobs

As you will have read in Chapter 2, there are a whole range of jobs with a strong law focus that you can pursue after graduation without committing to a training contract or pupillage. Although there tends to be an assumption that all law students will move straight on to take the LPC or BPTC immediately after graduation, there are various reasons why you might not want to do this:

- The professional training courses are a big financial commitment, not forgetting that you have to pay for accommodation and living expenses during the year, and may seem like an enormous risk without the security of a training contract or pupillage already in the bag. Work for a year in a legal setting would give you more work experience which may improve your prospects of success with training contract or pupillage applications plus it is an opportunity to earn money to pay for the LPC or BPTC.

- The professional training courses prepare you to work as a solicitor or barrister but do not offer a great deal in terms of preparation for other career paths so it may not be a good decision to undertake such a course unless you are confident that you really do want to practise law. By working in a law environment for a longer period of time, you will get a clearer idea of what legal practice involves and be in a position to make an informed decision about whether or not it is a career that appeals to you.

- You might need a break. After three (or four) years at university studying law, the prospect of further (and more intensive) study on the professional training courses might be an unattractive prospect. Alternatively, you may feel that you need a bit of breathing space after your degree before you have to make serious decisions about what to do next. In either case, a period of time spent in the workplace seeing the law in action may give you the respite from study that you need before embarking on the LPC or BPTC.

Such jobs may be career paths in their own right or they may be a step on the path to qualifying as a solicitor or barrister. In the sections that follow, you will find information about a range of employment possibilities that would make use of your legal knowledge and legal skills in a legal setting. There are any number of law-focused jobs that you could consider but the focus in this chapter is on paralegal work, research and advice roles, and teaching opportunities.

Paralegal work

One of the uses of the prefix *para* is that it denotes that something is different from but analogous to the thing that it precedes; for example, paraphrasing involves the rephrasing of a sentence so that the words used are different but the meaning is still the same. Following this, the term 'paralegal' is used to describe someone who is different to a solicitor but who does much of the same work. So a paralegal is someone who works alongside a solicitor (think of them working in *para*llel) but whose job status is different to a solicitor despite carrying out work of a similar nature (in the same way that a *para*military force is not officially recognised as a military force although its behaviour is military in nature). You may also find this role referred to as a legal executive. There are three main types of paralegal work:

- **Fee-earning paralegal work.** This refers to support work within private practice that involves undertaking tasks that can be billed to a client whether this involves working on case files carrying out administrative tasks, conducting due diligence, or taking notes at court or during a client conference. It is the commonest form of paralegal work and that which is most analogous to the ordinary work of a solicitor in private practice.

- **Professional support paralegal work.** This form of paralegal work involves working alongside a professional support lawyer and undertaking research, collating news, and producing updates and legal bulletins to keep lawyers up-to-date with legal developments.

It may involve writing articles for publication in professional journals or on the firm's website.

- **In-house paralegal work.** Working in-house refers to a law department that operates within a non-law organisation. As such, an in-house paralegal will focus on the sort of law that is relevant to the organisation in which it is based: the work of an in-house team in a media firm, for example, will be very different to the sort of in-house legal work involved in investment banking.

It is well worth considering seeking work as a paralegal if you want to practise law after graduation but feel that you need to gain more work experience to help you to secure a training contract or pupillage and, of course, it is an opportunity to earn money as well as a chance to experience the day-to-day life of a law firm. Most paralegal contracts are for six months or a year so you will get a far more detailed insight into all facets of legal practice than is possible on a two-week work placement and this will enable you to strengthen your application for a training contract or pupillage:

After a year's practical experience, you're a hundred times more useful on day one of a training contract.

James O'Connell, Institute of Paralegals

In addition to its value as a means of gaining work experience that might improve your prospects of securing a training contract or pupillage, it is important to remember that work as a paralegal is a career option in itself and so may be of particular interest to students who want to get straight into the workplace after graduation. If this prospect appeals to you, it might be worth considering undertaking training to enhance your prospects of finding work as a paralegal. This is discussed later in this section under the heading 'training and accreditation'.

What does the work involve?

The general answer to this question is that a paralegal works to assist the fee-earning solicitors and, as you would expect, takes on much of the background work involved with managing cases and dealing with clients. This can be quite administrative in nature so do not be surprised to be filling in forms and gathering documents together but the precise nature of the work will vary according to factors such as the area of law and the size of the law firm. You can see quite a contrast between the work required in Table 9.1 which details the responsibilities of two paralegal vacancies that were advertised at the time of writing.

Table 9.1 Typical paralegal vacancies

Criminal paralegal at Kingsley Napley	Litigation and commercial dispute resolution paralegal at Eversheds
• Researching points of law and other factual issues through the use of legal databases, textbooks, and other appropriate sources.	• Provision of full secretarial, PA, and administrative support.
• Gathering researched information into bundles for fee-earners to review.	• Managing the workflow of typing, making appropriate use of the firm's outsourced service.
• Case administration and document management.	• Highly proactive and responsive diary management.

Criminal paralegal at Kingsley Napley	Litigation and commercial dispute resolution paralegal at Eversheds
• Analysing, collating, and summarising large quantities of information including reviewing evidence for cases. • Attending meetings with clients, conferences with counsel and court appearances and taking detailed notes. • Liaising with police, prosecution, and court.	• Organising extensive international travel, business trips, itineraries, and events. • Management of emails and correspondence. • Organising internal and external meetings, to include co-ordinating reports and agendas. • Preparation of presentations and pitch documents. • Acting as liaison point for clients and colleagues. • Dealing and screening calls, delivering a positive client experience. • File opening/closing. • High volume billing and problem-solving. • Paper and electronic filing.

Although the lists of responsibilities give you some idea of the tasks you might encounter as a paralegal, you might get more of a sense of what is involved from Ellena's account of her work as a paralegal: she has worked in two different departments in the same law firm and her experience demonstrates the varied nature of paralegal work.

Practical example: work as a paralegal

I started work as a family paralegal where my main duties were assessing clients and determining their eligibility for legal aid, taking their instructions, and completing forms and correspondence in relation to their cases. I was involved in briefing counsel and sitting behind counsel at court as well as representing clients at case conferences. Sometimes I would be directed to attend court and assist at very late notice and have to meet the client knowing little or nothing about their case. The urgency that came with family law was very exciting but also challenging and the working day could be long.

I transferred to the dispute resolution department where the work and pace was entirely different to family law but the skills I learned and developed have been transferable. I deal with commercial disputes, commercial and residential property disputes, and insolvency cases. I assist several senior fee earners and will soon have my own work that falls under the small claims track. Most disputes are resolved without going to court so the position is mostly office based—one case was listed for a two-day trial but was settled the day before as the opponent agreed to pay our client's costs. All the work is privately funded and so I spend a lot of time 'marketing' the firm at business events in the area to get the firm's name out there and ultimately attract more clients.

Ellena, University of Surrey

Recent graduates often worry whether they will be able to manage the work that is expected of them as a paralegal. This is a perfectly reasonable concern—after all, it is quite a shift from being a student into paid employment in the legal profession. However, the expectations of the law firm will vary according to the level of experience that they ask for in applicants: if you apply for an entry-level position, they will assume that you have minimal previous experience in practical law so you will be given work that is suitable for you as well as assistance with unfamiliar tasks. If you have gained a good level of work experience during your degree—perhaps you secured work in a law firm every summer or completed a placement year in a law firm—then you may be able to rely on this experience to get a more advanced paralegal role and it is likely that the law firm will expect you to be able to carry out some of the routine work of legal practice without the need to explain this to you. Provided you have been honest about your level of work experience during the application process, there is no reason why an employer should expect more of you than you are able to do.

How to find work as a paralegal

There is a consistent level of demand for paralegals to work in law firms alongside qualified solicitors with many of the larger law firms maintaining large teams of paralegals on a permanent basis: according to the Institute of Paralegals, 44% of the fee-earning legal population are paralegals.[1] The majority of posts are advertised by legal recruitment agencies who have been retained by law firms to find suitable applicants for their vacancies.

Practical example: legal recruitment agencies

Not all legal recruitment firms deal with a high volume of paralegal vacancies so it can be advantageous to approach firms that have a specialist paralegal advisor or team of advisors. They will be in a better position to advise you about the sort of vacancies that will suit your skills, experience, and interests as well as suggesting ways to ensure that you are attractive to a prospective employer.

- **Chadwick Nott** are a leading national legal recruiter with dedicated paralegal consultants who understand the needs of candidates and, as true specialists in paralegal recruitment, are committed to nurturing their careers. www.chadwicknott.co.uk/Pages/Paralegals-Legal-Execs.aspx.

- **Taylor Root** offer a specialist paralegal team that have built fantastic relationships with Magic Circle firms, Silver Circle firms, leading regional firms, and niche boutique firms, giving candidates access to the most sought after and prestigious roles available. www.taylorroot.com/uk/paralegal/.

Tell us

Tell us about your experience as a paralegal. Did you approach a law firm directly or did you use a recruitment agency? Was the agency helpful? What benefits did you feel were attached to using an agency? Tell us at finchandfafinski.com/get-in-touch or @FinchFafinski on Twitter.

The difficulty that you may encounter when seeking work as a paralegal is that many law firms do not use agencies to recruit entry-level paralegals: that is, individuals wanting to work as paralegals who have little or no previous experience in legal practice. This does not mean that you will not be able to find work as a paralegal: just that it might not be easy to find your first position through an agency (although they are a good way to find subsequent paralegal vacancies). There are, however, a number of other options:

---

1. Carman, D. (2011) 'The Paralegal Path: Why Law Grads without a TC Should Try a Paralegal Role', <http://www.legalweek.com/legal-week/analysis/2042987/paralegal-path-graduates-training-contracts-consider-paralegal-position>.

- **Rely on your work experience**. Taylor Root suggest that recent graduates can rely upon any time spent in a commercial law environment such as placements and vacation schemes (but not pro bono work) as relevant work experience. Even work in a non-law professional services environments such as insurance or banking may suffice. Paralegal advisors at recruitment agencies will be able to discuss the nature and extent of your work experience and decide whether they will be able to place you with an employer. Taylor Root also offer advice to students without sufficient experience (see Figure 9.1).

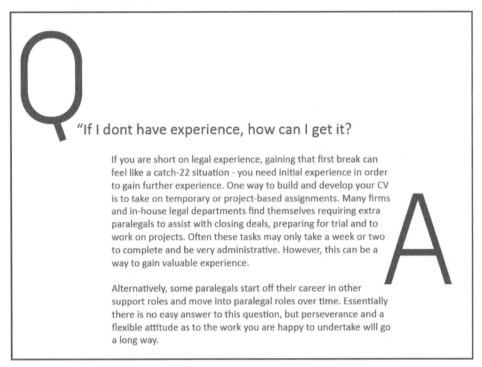

Q "If I dont have experience, how can I get it?

If you are short on legal experience, gaining that first break can feel like a catch-22 situation - you need initial experience in order to gain further experience. One way to build and develop your CV is to take on temporary or project-based assignments. Many firms and in-house legal departments find themselves requiring extra paralegals to assist with closing deals, preparing for trial and to work on projects. Often these tasks may only take a week or two to complete and be very administrative. However, this can be a way to gain valuable experience.

Alternatively, some paralegals start off their career in other support roles and move into paralegal roles over time. Essentially there is no easy answer to this question, but perseverance and a flexible attitude as to the work you are happy to undertake will go a long way.

Figure 9.1 Taylor Root

- **Make direct approaches to employers.** Andrew Land at Law Staff Legal Recruitment suggests that it can be advantageous for law graduates with less than two years' work experience to approach employers direct to seek work as a paralegal. Visit the websites of law firms to see if they have any vacancies or to find out their policy on paralegal recruitment or simply make a speculative application to firms that interest you irrespective of whether or not they appear to have vacancies. Law firms are inundated with applications from recent graduates but do not let that deter you from making applications: Ellena (see earlier) made 50 applications before getting the interview that secured her a job as a paralegal. Remember, if you decide not to apply because you feel doomed to failure then you give yourself a 100% guarantee that you will not get work as a paralegal so try not to be daunted by the level of competition but just concentrate on making targeted applications that highlight your suitability for work as a paralegal.
- There is advice on finding entry-level paralegal work on the Law Staff Legal Recruitment website: **www.law-staff.co.uk/news/post/1-free-advice--starting-a-career-in-law** (see Figure 9.2).

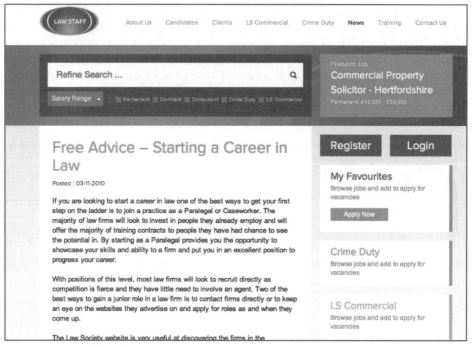

Figure 9.2 www.lawstaff.co.uk

- **Use your network.** Looking for work is a great test of your networking skills. During the course of your studies, you should have started to establish links within the legal profession: you should have met some solicitors and barristers through work experience or mini pupillage, at law firms or chambers open days, or through their visits to your university. Make use of your network in your search for paralegal work by asking these contacts if they can recommend you to anyone who is looking for a paralegal. Remember to outline your availability and to summarise your skills and experience just in case your contact does not remember this from your previous encounters and attach a short CV so that they can send this on to colleagues who might be interested in paralegal support. This can be a very effective method of securing work as a personal recommendation is often more compelling than an unsolicited application.

I wanted work as a paralegal close to my home town so that I could live with my parents and save money for my LPC. I tried making speculative applications but it didn't get me anywhere so I had to try a different approach. I made a list of professional people that I knew, either directly or by a family connection, and composed a short email to each person on the list, being sure to personalise each one, asking if they had any suggestions of someone that I could approach for work as a paralegal. It felt a bit cheeky so I started each email with an apology and kept the emails short. It was surprising how much difference that personal link made. I got a reply from every email, which compared very favourablly to the less than 50% response rate to my speculative applications, and almost everyone made at least one suggestion of someone that I could contact. One person even offered me work to keep me going until I got paralegal work so I was able to boost my CV by working in an advertising agency for three weeks until my networking paid off and I found work in a regional branch of a national law firm.

Lucy, Cardiff University

Practical example: entry-level paralegals

It can be difficult to get work as a paralegal immediately after graduation as advertised vacancies often specify that applicants must have at least six months' experience and making speculative applications can be a bit 'hit and miss'. Law recruitment firm BCL has set up a dedicated service that brings law firms and graduates together with a view to facilitating recruitment of entry-level paralegals. Simply complete the online application and upload your CV and employers can access your details and make contact if they have a vacancy that would suit you.

Law firms say:

....

Having used BCL Graduates, I was able to download 10 relevant CVs and have since arranged interviews. I found BCL Graduates easy to use and unique. It definitely saved me a lot of time in our recruitment process and I would recommend it to any firm looking to hire graduates.

Andrea Parry, HR Manager, Barnetts Solicitors

....

Law graduates say:

....

I would really recommend taking the time to sign up to this site. I was contacted about a clinical negligence paralegal position at Hempsons within a few days of signing up. The support provided by BCL Graduates was absolutely fantastic. I was kept fully informed throughout the whole process and given help with my interview preparation and I genuinely felt as though I could get in touch with any queries or worries that I had. I now have a paralegal job in the area that I have always wanted to work in and this is down to BCL Graduates.

The service is really great because it appreciates that the majority of graduates will lack legal work experience which is a massive barrier in trying to secure a paralegal opportunity. In terms of advice in using BCL Graduates, I would say that you should make sure that you fill out the objectives section as thoroughly as possible. It enables you to demonstrate what areas of law you want to work in which will help the recruitment team find jobs that are suitable and interesting for you.

....

See Figure 9.3 for a screenshot of the BCL Graduates website.

Training and accreditation

Some students undertake work as a paralegal as a step on the way towards a training contract or pupillage but it can be an attractive career option in itself: it allows you to get working in a law environment straight away so that you can make use of your law degree and start earning money. If you are considering work as a paralegal as a long-term career option, it might be worth considering training with one of the organisations that provide courses for paralegals as this can expand the type of work that you would be able to undertake and make you a more attractive prospect for employers.

Figure 9.3 BCL Graduates

Practical example: training as a paralegal

There are three organisations in England and Wales that provide accreditation and/or training for those wishing to work in a legal support role as a paralegal or legal executive. Obviously, there are costs associated with this but at a lower level than the LPC and BPTC as the courses tend to be modular and they are specially designed to prepare you for paralegal work. Between them, the three organisations have in excess of 35,000 members:

- **Institute of Paralegals (IoP).** The IoP administers a route to qualification as a paralegal which means that it does not offer its own courses but works with other institutions that offer such training to ensure that they provide qualifications of an appropriate standard. You will find a list of approved course providers on the IoP website: www.theiop.org.

- **National Association of Licensed Paralegals (NALP).** The NALP offers nationally recognised paralegal qualifications. For law graduates, this takes the form of a Diploma in Paralegal Practice which focuses on procedural law and which covers six units: civil litigation, corporate and business structures, criminal procedure, matrimonial procedure, conveyancing, and succession. There are also special research awards in 13 areas of law that can be studied in addition to this qualification to facilitate a degree of specialisation. The courses can be studied on a distance learning basis. For further details, see www.nationalparalegals.co.uk.

- **Chartered Institute of Legal Executives (CILEx).** CILEx is the professional association and governing body for legal executives and other paralegals. It offers legal education and training. For law graduates, there is the Graduate Fast-Track Diploma which builds on your legal studies and involves completion of two Level 6 Practice subjects and the Level 6 Client Care Skills course. Further details can be found on the CILEx website: www.cilex.org.uk/study.aspx.

There are differences between paralegals and legal executives that you need to appreciate. A legal executive does work in a paralegal role in the sense that they provide support to qualified solicitors but the term paralegal is one that can be used by anyone who works in a legal support role whereas only those who have trained and qualified by CILEx can refer to themselves as legal executives. So a person who works as a legal executive has undergone a structured programme of education and training in order to qualify as a legal executive whereas anyone, with or without a law degree can work as a paralegal.

Licensed conveyancers

There is an alternative route into legal practice that does not involve undertaking the LPC or BPTC and completing a training contract or pupillage and that is qualifying as a licensed conveyancer. A licensed conveyancer is a specialist property lawyer who works to facilitate all kinds of property transfers and transactions. The work includes drawing up all the documentation needed to process the sale or lease of a property or land, carrying out the necessary Land Registry searches, and advising on all aspects of the property transaction. Conveyancers also ensure that properties are not encumbered with covenants, easements, or mortgages and check whether they are likely to be affected by land developments, flooding, or subsidence. Conveyancers also deal with the transfer of mortgage funds and payment of stamp duty as well as ensuring that clients can satisfy money laundering safeguards.

The Council for Licensed Conveyancers offers several different routes to qualification and, as you will see from Figure 9.4, the accredited academic route offers law graduates the opportunity to bypass the first stage of training. This essentially involves a training course, which can be undertaken online by distance learning or study part-time at a college

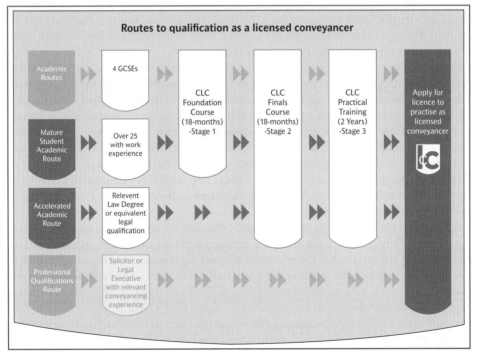

Figure 9.4 Qualification routes for licensed conveyancers

offering conveyancing courses (if you have already completed the LPC, you will be exempt from some of the modules). This is followed by a practical stage of employment-based experience under the supervision of an experienced conveyancer before a licence to practise is issued which qualifies you to start your own conveyancing business.

For further details, and for updates to the qualification routes after the first quarter of 2014, see the Council for Licensed Conveyancers website: **www.clc-uk.org**.

Research assistant

A research assistant, as the job title suggests, provides assistance to a researcher in carrying out a research project. This assistance may take many different forms, depending on the nature of the project, but is likely to involve many of the skills that you have developed during your law degree:

- Identifying literature on a particular topic
- Using legal databases to locate statute and case law
- Reading primary and secondary source material and extracting key points
- Summarising and analysing the law
- Organising and collating documents
- Finding the law in other jurisdictions.

It is possible that you will be required to work on a new area of law that you have not studied or that you would need to carry out tasks that you have not previously encountered such as setting up a series of interviews, writing a questionnaire, or managing data that has been collected but the researcher that you are assisting will be able to provide guidance on unfamiliar tasks and to answer your questions. Remember, though, that you will be expected to show some initiative in working out what to do and to be able to work quite independently on completing the necessary tasks.

The most usual places for graduates to find work as a legal research assistant are within universities or at the Law Commission. These tend to be temporary vacancies rather than permanent positions so they can be an ideal stop-gap for law graduates who are looking for a short-term position that will add to their skills portfolio. Research assistant vacancies of this nature tend to be advertised on **www.jobs.ac.uk** (see Figure 9.5) which is an academic recruitment website as well as on the Law Commission or university websites. Other organisations may need research assistants for law-based projects on a temporary or permanent basis but these are too varied to detail here so you would need to explore the possibilities by using a recruitment website such as **www.indeed.co.uk** or by carrying out a general search for legal research jobs on the Internet.

For students who are seeking work that will enhance their prospects of securing a training contract or pupillage, a position as a research assistant can be an excellent way of strengthening research skills. The ability to conduct legal research is an essential skill in legal practice as both solicitors and barristers have to be able to identify and locate the relevant law as well as to understand, explain, analyse, and apply it. This means that you must be able to find the law when you know it exists (if, for example, you are told to find section 9 of the Copyright, Design and Patents Act) but also to be able to find out whether any law exists that covers a particular situation (if you were asked to find out whether there

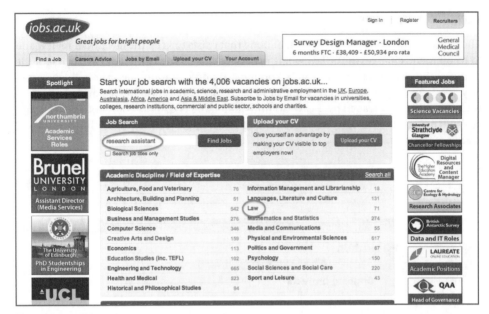

Figure 9.5 www.jobs.ac.uk

was any law that stipulated that a driver must stop when directed to do so by a lollipop lady). As Susie's account of her time as a research assistant highlights, it is a role that really stretches and improves your research skills.

Practical example: research assistant in a university

I worked as a research assistant for one year after graduation to give myself time to look for a training contract as I didn't want to start the LPC without one plus I wanted to earn some money. I thought that working as a research assistant in a university would be just like being a student but I was very much mistaken. For a start, you have to actually do things properly and that means reading cases rather than picking up the main points from the textbook and you have to be fast and accurate in the way that you work. It was a steep learning curve in terms of the volume of work and I quickly realised that life as a student preparing for three tutorials a week was incredibly easy compared to my workload as a research assistant. But it was an amazing experience and I ended up giving a paper at a conference about the work that we had done and being the co-author of one of the articles that came out of the research. More than that, it helped me get a training contract: I was able to use it at interview to really highlight the quality of my research skills and my ability to organise my work and to be proactive in working through problems. Once I was working, it was clear that I was much faster at finding the law than other trainees and that I had a far more creative approach to working around problems: I could think of alternative ways to do things whereas the other trainees tended to try one approach and then get stuck if it didn't work. I think it was the best way that I could have spent the year and that it helped me to stand out from the other applicants for training contracts as well as making me more efficient once I started work.

Amira, Leeds Met

Law Commission

The Law Commission is an independent body that exists to keep the law under review and to recommend changes in the law where necessary. It is divided into four categories for the purpose of conducting legal research: commercial and common law, criminal law, property, trusts and family law, and public law (see Figure 9.6). It also has a statute law repeal team. Each team is headed by a Law Commissioner and is comprised of both lawyers and research assistants who carry out a number of research projects falling within the subject matter of the team.

Figure 9.6 Law Commission

Every year, usually in January, the Law Commission recruits research assistants for a fixed period, generally one year, to start in September. Applicants must have a good degree (this usually means a 2.1 or first class degree) and be able to demonstrate skills in legal research, legal knowledge, communication (written and oral), and policy analysis. The salary is around £25,000.

Practical example: working at the Law Commission

Working as a research assistant is fascinating. After four years of studying law and hearing (and writing) seemingly endless criticisms of it, I'm able to make a (very small) contribution to its reform. Being at the heart of the law reform process is exciting for anyone who has read about the law or who has an interest in politics. There are meetings with government officials, senior judges, and eminent lawyers, as well as an opportunity to write material which ends up in Commission publications.

Research assistants are given a number of tasks, depending on the needs of the team. A typical day might involve writing research minutes on a particular area of law or procedure, dealing with correspondence coming into the team, or proofreading documents prior to publication. I've been lucky enough to have an opportunity to draft a piece of work which is going to be published alongside the Commission's consultation paper on contempt of court. Freedom of Information requests are also the responsibility of research assistants.

So, what sort of skills might a research assistant need? Clearly, a good knowledge of the area of law in question is essential. In addition, researchers must have a keen eye for detail—a missed case or statutory provision at the start of a project may cause the whole argument to unravel further down the line. The ability to explain difficult concepts clearly—both face to face and on paper—is also crucial, as is a willingness to work closely with the other members of the team. Researchers also have to be able to drop what they are doing and familiarise themselves with a new area of law at short notice.

http://publiclawforeveryone.wordpress.com/2012/11/13/what-law-graduates-do-1-the-law-commission/

See the Law Commission website for details of their vacancies and to find out about the application process: **http://lawcommission.justice.gov.uk/working-for-us.htm**.

Remember that research skills are general skills rather than law specific. In other words, the skills that you learned when carrying out legal research during your degree can be used to research outside of the legal discipline so you could consider work as a research assistant in a non-law setting. You will find more about this in Chapter 10 on non-law careers.

Legal assistants

The work that falls into the category of legal assistant is extremely diverse. There are a wide range of different roles available that can be filled by law graduates. Although these may offer long-term career options in themselves, the focus in this section will be on the benefits of work as a legal assistant to a longer-term objective of qualifying as a solicitor or barrister.

Due to the immense variability of the jobs that fall into this category, no attempt to generalise about the nature of the work or the tasks involved will be made. Instead, an illustrative list of current (at the time of writing) examples are provided in Table 9.2 with an observation as to how such a role would contribute to your skills portfolio if you were trying to secure a training contract or pupillage.

Table 9.2 Legal assistant roles

Legal helpline advisor working at Irwin Mitchell solicitors	Commentary
The role involves the provision of preliminary legal advice on any area of law to callers that are entitled to use the service. The advisor is responsible for undertaking research in order to provide clients with advice that includes the discussion of options available, potential remedies, and the risks involved in the various courses of action available.	With close similarities to the ordinary work of a solicitor in private practice, this role would help you to demonstrate your aptitude for assessing a client's problem and formulating advice that outlines a choice of reasonable courses of actions. It would enable you to demonstrate good client care skills.

(Continued)

Table 9.2 (*Continued*)

Legal assistant in a regulatory and professional discipline department	Commentary
The work involves assisting with prosecutions for breaches of professional discipline particularly within the medical profession. It includes assessment of papers received on instruction, taking statements from witnesses, liaising with clients, and preparing bundles for hearings.	The focus on 'behind the scenes' case preparation would highlight your organisational skills and would be especially useful experience if you aim to specialise in litigation. There is good experience in dealing with clients and witnesses as well as useful exposure to procedural aspects of legal practice.
Legal assistant at EA Games	**Commentary**
Working as part of the legal team for the world's largest video game publisher, this role includes responsibility for researching and reporting on developments in European and domestic trademark law, and drafting competition terms and conditions and legal correspondence.	Interesting work experience for anyone interested in practising intellectual property law or working as an in-house lawyer. The commercial setting will allow you to demonstrate commercial awareness. The role involves research of domestic and European law and the opportunity to use this research in a practical way in the drafting of documents and reports.
Legal assistant at SkyMediator	**Commentary**
This is a new post in a recently created company that exists to offer advice to victims of airline problems such as cancellation, delay, and overbooking and assist them in their claim for compensation. The role involves liaising with clients, drafting correspondence, managing settlement and court case administration, legal research, and billing.	This is a standard legal advice role that involves eliciting information from clients and assisting them with their claim so is good experience from a private client perspective. There is a good deal of routine legal paperwork involved and an element of claim negotiation that would give you good case management experience.
Administrative assistant in the legal department at Oxford University Press	**Commentary**
This position supports the work of six lawyers in the legal department by dealing with correspondence, organising meetings, managing billing, and completing standard trademark licences, powers of attorney and piracy letters.	Perhaps less legal content than the other roles outlined here but a good opportunity to demonstrate organisational skills and an insight into the operation of a commercial organisation as well as experience with legal correspondence.
Assistant to the Company Secretary in a FTSE 250 company	**Commentary**
The role focuses on the provision of support across a number of commercial projects and bids for pan-European services. It includes written analysis of documentation and research on a range of legal and commercial issues to support strategic decision-making on growth plans and profit initiatives.	Although the legal focus may not seem obvious from the details provided, the role was open only to applicants with a law degree. A very good role for developing commercial awareness and for gaining experience in business transactions.

These vacancies represent just a fraction of those available at present that were discovered by using the search term 'legal assistant' across several law-based recruitment websites:

- www.simplylawjobs.com
- www.totallylegal.com
- www.thelawyer.com.

I was successful in securing a position as a Judicial Assistant in the Court of Appeal. This is a 6-month, fixed-term position. My time as a Judicial Assistant has been challenging but immensely rewarding. The job gives you incredible access to those holding the most senior positions in judicial office and the opportunity to discuss the cases with the constitution and the opportunity to understand how the Judges reach their decisions. As legal work experience goes, I do not think it can get any better than this!

John, law graduate

I worked as a Legal Assistant at an international pharmaceutical company for two years after graduation. The work was varied and some of it involved familiar areas of law such as contract but some was totally new to me like the patents and licensing work but it was fascinating to see the law in operation within such a complex industry. I really understood what it meant to work under pressure by the end of the first month and I felt much more confident within the workplace. The experience seemed to help me in my search for a training contract—I got more interviews and proceeded further with all my applications and I did finally get an offer—funnily enough, with a firm that does a lot of work in the pharmaceutical industry!

Cara, University of Bristol

Teaching law

There is a great demand for law teaching due to the popularity of the subject with students. In 2012, according to the Higher Education Statistic Agency, there were 73,455 students enrolled on undergraduate law programs on a full-time basis (making it the second most popular degree choice after business and management) and 13,154 taking law at A2 level (figures published in *The Guardian*). By the time you complete your law degree, you will have acquired a great deal of knowledge about a wide range of areas of the law so you may be able to use this to teach law to others either at university, college, or school. However, it can be tricky to secure a teaching position immediately after graduation without any further training or experience so you may need to think about undertaking further qualifications if you decide that this is an attractive career path. The qualifications that you will need will depend upon the age group that you want to teach and whether you want to teach in a secondary school, a further education institution, or a university.

Teaching law in school

In order to teach in a state-maintained school at GCSE level in England and Wales, you will need qualified teacher status (QTS). For students with a law degree, this can be achieved by undertaking a Postgraduate Certificate in Education (PGCE) which includes a period of practical experience in a school. It is possible to teach in an academy or public school without a teaching qualification but, in practice, one is usually required.

As law is not part of the national curriculum and is not a popular subject at GCSE, there is no law-based route through the PGCE but it is possible to take a PGCE in citizenship which covers many issues that you will have covered on the law degree. It is useful to remember, however, that you do not have to have a degree in a subject in order to teach it: the possession of a degree qualifies you to take this route into teaching but you can then go on to specialise in any area of your choosing.

There is a section in Chapter 10 that deals with teaching in schools where you will find a more detailed discussion of the routes to qualification and the options available.

Teaching law at college

Law is relatively popular at A-level with 13,154 students taking the subject at A2 level in 2013. Whether this level of interest is maintained remains to be seen as there are signs that an A-level in law is not viewed positively by universities: it is often described as a 'soft' subject involving 'learning and churning' (thoughtless repetition of remembered facts) rather than analysis and critique and many law schools consider that it is actually disadvantageous for students on a law degree to have A-level law as it oversimplifies complex concepts. Irrespective of these views, demand for A-level law has remained consistent and is likely to continue as many students find it useful to have a taster of the subject as a means of assessing whether they want to study it at degree level.

Practical example: teaching A-level law

I applied for a job teaching A-level law at the local college more in hope than expectation because I had no teaching experience but, to my amazement, I was offered the job. I then had an absolute panic because I didn't know how to go about teaching but there was a pretty good structure in place at the college that set out what had to be covered in each class and they offered training for people new to teaching—although I have to say that this didn't start until I'd actually been there for about four months.

I was very nervous before my first class but I actually found it much easier than I had expected to go in and say 'right, this is what we are doing today' and to split the students into activity groups and so on. I was worried that I wouldn't know enough about the law to teach it but it hasn't been a problem and I've realised that it doesn't matter if I get asked a question that I can't answer because I can just tell the students that I don't know and then I find out before the next session.

The college hours are quite flexible so I have been able to keep doing bits and pieces of work experience in law firms because I had not given up my dream of qualifying as a solicitor. I started making training contract applications earlier this year and felt so much more equipped to go to interview in the belief that I was actually ready to do the job and I think that this showed in my confidence at interview. I was able to explain how teaching had prepared me to work as a solicitor by drawing parallels between my job and the work experience I had done and the interview panels seemed really interested. The interviews felt so much more positive than the ones that I'd had straight after graduation where I felt so out-of-my-depth just being at interview so I'm not surprised, looking back, that I was never offered a training contract then. This time round, after four years of teaching and with over twenty different stints of work experience under my belt, I was offered a fully funded training contract at a national firm on only my third interview so I start the LPC in September.

Sarah, University of Derby

Teaching at A-level is a good option for law graduates who may lack confidence to teach undergraduates or who find the idea of teaching in a secondary school at GCSE rather daunting. A-level students study law at a more basic level but have chosen to continue education once it ceased to be compulsory so should be keen to learn. It used to be the case that you could teach at A-level without any formal training or a teaching qualification but there is increasingly a requirement that A-level teachers have a PGCE PCET (a Postgraduate Certificate in Post-Compulsory Education and Training) which leads to the Qualified Teacher Learning and Skills status (QTLS).

You will find more information about qualifications needed to teach at various levels in Chapter 10.

Teaching law in university

There are two main options in terms of teaching law at university:

- Working as a sessional lecturer to undertake teaching and teaching-related activities for a fixed period of time
- Working as a lecturer with a full portfolio of teaching, research and administrative responsibilities.

Sessional teaching

Sessional teaching is very much a temporary role as it involves working for a single university 'session', generally an academic year. As such, it is a good option for a law graduate looking for temporary work teaching law as a means of earning money and expanding their skills portfolio with teaching experience.

Sessional lecturers tend to be involved mostly with module delivery rather than course design which means that they do face-to-face teaching of material that has been devised by other lecturers: so you might be asked to take tutorials but it is less likely that you would be expected to write tutorial questions. You need no qualifications or teaching experience to work as a sessional lecturer but, obviously, if you do have any relevant work experience to offer then your chances of finding work of this nature are strengthened. It need not be formal teaching experience but could include any position where you were involved in disseminating information to others and taking a leadership role. Although it might seem daunting to be involved in university teaching soon after graduation, you would most likely be taking tutorials with first year students who have no preconceptions about how tutorials ought to be conducted. In any case, you have plenty of experience of tutorials from the student perspective so you will not find it difficult to adjust this to take on the lecturer role.

Have a look at **www.jobs.ac.uk** (searching under 'law') for temporary teaching jobs or contact the Head of School at the university of your choice directly to find out if there are sessional teaching opportunities.

University lecturer

If you are contemplating a long-term career as a university lecturer, you will probably need to take a postgraduate course—an LLM or a PhD is most usual although some universities may consider applicants who have taken the LPC or BPTC —as very few lecturers are appointed these days without a postgraduate qualification.

Doctoral research leading to the award of a PhD often involves opportunities to teach; in fact, many universities regard the ability to disseminate knowledge about your subject as part of the skills that are involved in the acquisition of a PhD. If you are in receipt of a university scholarship or bursary, there is likely to be an expectation that you will teach in return so you may be appointed as a Graduate Teaching Assistant (GTA). The teaching load is likely to be light—usually around four contact hours each week—and it is likely to involve teaching first year students. You may be expected to mark formative coursework and to carry out other administrative work such as invigilating exams or organising moots.

Practical example: teaching at university

I am just finishing my first year as a PhD student. I have funding that pays my fees and gives me money for living expenses and, in return, I take tutorials in contract and English Legal Systems, both first year subjects. I started my PhD straight after my undergraduate degree so I had no teaching experience but there was a one-week course for new PhD students to help us to prepare to teach and the module leaders of both my courses were very approachable and keen to make sure that I understood what to do in the tutorials. I was worried about not knowing the answers so I did a lot of reading—far more than I'd ever done for my own tutorials as a student—and about not being able to get the students to do what I wanted them to do but both worries turned out to be unfounded. Of course it felt a bit strange leading the tutorial at first but the students just accepted that I was in charge like any other lecturer and I soon got used to it.

I didn't really enjoy marking the coursework because I agonised over each essay for a long time trying to make sure that I got the right mark but it turned out that, like all new lecturers, I had been far too harsh and critical of weaknesses and omissions and didn't give nearly enough credit for good points. I think that's something that I'll need to work on this year!

I do plan to become a university lecturer when I complete my PhD. The idea of working in a university really appeals to me particularly the research aspect and writing articles that will be published in journals. I do enjoy teaching—far more than I thought that I would—but I can see that it is much harder work than I thought it was when I was a student. I could never understand why lecturers said that they were too busy to see students outside of office hours but now I see all the background work and preparation that is involved in teaching.

James, Nottingham University

You will find university lectureships and PhD opportunities advertised on **www.jobs.ac.uk** or on the website of the Times Higher Education: **www.timeshighereducation.co.uk**.

Further study

Although it is not work in the sense of paid employment, a further option that is attractive to many students is the possibility of undertaking further academic study after graduation. This may take the form of a taught LLM, an LLM by research, or a PhD.

LLM (taught or by research)

An LLM usually takes the form of a one-year taught postgraduate course (although you can, at some universities, complete an LLM by research) leading to the award of an LLM (Master of Laws) degree.

The majority of students undertaking an LLM opt to take a taught course although it is still possible, at some universities, to take an LLM by research. A taught LLM is a one-year (full-time) postgraduate course involving 180 credits of study broken down into modules of 15, 30, and 60 credits. Some universities stipulate that 60 credits are gained by the completion of a dissertation to demonstrate advanced research skills.

The range of modules available varies from university to university so it would be advisable to check the online prospectus carefully to ensure that your chosen institution offers modules that interest you. An LLM by research generally involves the production of a 30,000 word thesis as this is regarded as the equivalent in study hours of 180 taught credits.

There are four types of LLM that you could consider, each of which offers something different in terms of how it could be used to enhance your prospects of success in securing a training contract or pupillage (see Table 9.3).

The cost of postgraduate study is not inexpensive as course fees range from £5,000 to £12,000 and there is very little funding available. You might find that you can get a professional studies loan to fund the cost of the course fees and some modest living expenses but remember that these loans have to be repaid quite promptly after the course is complete. With these costs in mind, it would be judicious to think carefully about the value of postgraduate study in the context of its role in your future career plans.

There are various reasons that might motivate you to consider studying for an LLM after graduation:

- **To bolster a disappointing degree classification.** Many students who graduate with a lower second class degree (2.2) decide to improve their academic profile by acquiring an LLM as many firms or chambers specify that applicants for training contracts or pupillages must have at least a 2.1 in order to be considered. There is some debate on the merits of this approach with some employers preferring an applicant with a 2.2 and a good range of work experience to a student with a 2.2 and a postgraduate qualification whereas other employers admit that they would not consider a student with a 2.2 however good their work experience. In light of these opposing viewpoints, it might be that the best course of action is to combine your year of study with further work experience so that both strands of your profile are strengthened simultaneously. You may also want to consider a practice-based postgraduate course (see Table 9.3) as you should be able to secure a place on the LPC with a 2.2 and then improve your academic profile with an LLM.

- **To gain a qualification from a 'better' university.** Some students perceive a degree of snobbishness in the legal profession that favours certain universities over others. This can be demoralising for a student who has worked very hard and achieved a good degree but who feels disadvantaged as a result of the university that they attended. Try to remember that graduates from every law school in England and Wales are securing training contracts and pupillages so some of the perceptions about prejudice are simply outdated. However, it may be that you have a real yen to have a qualification from one of the more prestigious universities and feel that it will make your application stand out in which case there is no real reason not to take this option. Remember, though, the importance of combining academic excellence with a good range of professional skills gained through work experience: in other words, add a postgraduate qualification if you want to but do not expect it to open doors on its own.

- **To demonstrate expertise in a particular area of specialisation.** If you are committed to working in a particular area of law then it could help your prospects of gaining work in that field if you enhanced your knowledge of the relevant law by taking a specialist LLM. This is particularly so if it is a niche area of practice or an area of law that you did not have the opportunity to study during your undergraduate degree. You should, of course, be

Table 9.3 Types of LLM

	What is it?	For example	Benefits	Drawbacks	Sell it to employers
General	A general LLM allows students to select modules from the choice of those available without any requirement that they fall within the same broad area of law or that there is any link between them.	You could select three 60-credit modules on, say, commercial arbitration, child law, and civil litigation and write a dissertation on the reform of coroner's courts.	You can select subjects that interest you or that fit with the area of law that you want to practise to demonstrate greater knowledge. The spread of subjects available means that you can offer a degree of expertise in a number of areas.	Some students say that a general LLM feels no different to an additional year of undergraduate study. It could be said to be a missed opportunity to specialise in a particular area of law.	You could mention the personal challenge of achieving a postgraduate qualification as well as the development of core study and legal skills beyond undergraduate level. There may be links between the modules studied and the area of practice that you wish to enter.
Specialist	A specialist LLM enables students to focus on a particular area of law thus studying it in greater depth and detail. It is essentially a closer look at a particular subject.	If you took, say, a medical law LLM, you could choose from modules such as medical negligence, consent, death and dying, reproductive technology, medical ethics, and mental health law.	It offers the opportunity to gain a real depth of knowledge in the subject of your interest, allowing you to develop a far greater claim to expertise than undergraduate study.	If you cannot find work in the area of your specialisation, you have to look outside of this in which case you may feel that you have wasted expertise. It is also a visible reminder to employers that you wanted to practise in a particular area of law but could not find work in it.	Emphasise depth of knowledge and the extent of your expertise which demonstrates your commitment to working in that particular area of law. You can also highlight the opportunity to develop skills acquired on the LLB to a much higher standard.
Practice	Practice-focused LLMs have grown in popularity in recent years as an 'add on' to the LPC or BPTC.	Having completed the LPC or BPTC, you could write a dissertation on some area of legal practice covered	It is a way to gain an academic qualification in addition to a professional qualification and it offers an	There is less study involved than with a traditional LLM and there is no corresponding opportunity to develop	The focus on legal practice in the dissertation could make your research of real practical interest to employers. Think

	What is it?	For example	Benefits	Drawbacks	Sell it to employers
	Essentially, the credits gained by studying the LPC or BPTC count towards the LLM but are 'topped up' by additional study, usually a dissertation.	on the professional training course. Some institutions offer the option of a shorter dissertation in conjunction with a taught module.	opportunity to demonstrate advanced research skills and knowledge of a particular area of legal practice.	knowledge. In essence, you are limited to the skills and knowledge involved in producing a dissertation which may not enhance your profile a great deal especially if you produced a dissertation at undergraduate level.	carefully about topic choice and try to find an area that is topical and of relevance to the area of law that you want to practise.
Research	An LLM by research has no taught element. Students formulate a proposal for a program of research, much like a dissertation, and write a thesis of approximately 30,000 words under the guidance of an academic supervisor.	You can conduct research on any topic of your choice providing that it has sufficient academic rigour to satisfy the requirements of postgraduate research. Recent examples include the future of jury trials and an evaluation of liability for war crimes in international law.	This is a real opportunity to develop depth of knowledge and to conduct a research on a topic that is of real interest to you plus the large-scale nature of the project is a real challenge for your legal skills.	The focus of your research will be narrow and you may miss the camaraderie of a taught course.	Even if the subject matter does not have much relevance to prospective employers, you can focus on the skills involved in managing and completing a large-scale piece of research and, in particular, working with minimal supervision. The ability to conduct independent research is important in practice so make sure that you highlight the way in which your research skills developed during the year.

aware that you may still not find it straightforward to secure a training contract or pupillage in your chosen specialist area: a specialist LLM may help you to demonstrate commitment to that area of law and a level of knowledge greater than many other applicants but it is no guarantee that you will be successful in your applications. You may have to widen your search to include training contracts and pupillages outside of this field of law, in which case you will need to be able to explain to prospective employers your change of interest.

- **As a stepping stone to a career as an academic.** If you have aspirations to undertake doctoral research with a view to working as a university lecturer, a taught postgraduate course will give you a taste of academic study at a higher level and may help you to secure a PhD place. Most universities now require new lecturers to have (or be in the process of acquiring) a PhD so you might want to consider an LLM to improve your chances of finding a funded PhD place.

If you are interested in finding out more about further academic study after your undergraduate degree, have a look at the LLM Guide which covers study in England and Wales and in other countries: **www.llm-guide.com**.

Doctor of Philosophy (PhD)

A PhD is a higher qualification than an LLM and it is undertaken over a longer period of time—usually three years—and involves a program of research that leads to the production of a thesis that makes an original contribution to legal knowledge. The thesis can be anything from 60,000 to 120,000 words, depending upon the regulations of the university at which it is undertaken.

The majority of students who work towards obtaining a PhD do so with a view to working as an academic in a university (or some other research-focused institution) rather than entering into legal practice. Although the successful completion of a PhD involves a great many relevant legal skills, it is not regarded as a qualification that enhances an applicant's prospects of gaining a training contract or pupillage. In essence, it could be used to demonstrate skills relevant to a career as a solicitor or barrister but it would be very unusual for a student to work towards a PhD with the aim of enhancing their attractiveness to employers in the legal profession.

If, however, your objective is to pursue a career as a university lecturer (discussed earlier), a PhD is a valuable, almost indispensable, qualification. It demonstrates research, writing, and analytical skills of the highest order and establishes you as an expert in a particular field of law.

If you are interested in undertaking doctoral research, then you will find more detailed information about this in *Getting a PhD in Law* (Hart Publishing 2011).

WHERE NEXT?

There are any number of opportunities available to graduates with a law degree other than qualifying to be a solicitor or barrister. Some of these are closely allied with the legal profession whereas other roles use law in a wholly different way. There are plenty of options available so you should be able to find a role that suits you.

If you are looking for a job on a temporary basis while still working towards the goal of qualifying as a solicitor or barrister, try to think about how the roles that you apply for will help to strengthen your skills portfolio. It is true that your objective may be to secure a job that will earn money to pay for the LPC or BPTC but remember that you will be improving your chances of achieving your ultimate objective if the job also adds to your attractiveness in terms of securing a training contract or pupillage. Unusual opportunities exist and can make your application for a training contract or pupillage really stand out from the rest so it can really be worth taking time to have a thorough look around at the different positions that are available.

Practical advice: choosing a temporary job

There is a vast array of law-based temporary work that you could do whilst waiting to take the LPC or BPTC or whilst searching for a training contract or pupillage so try to make sure that the jobs that you apply for make a positive contribution to your portfolio of work experience. Look at the job description and identify at least three ways in which performing this role would enhance your CV:

- Does it allow you to develop a new skill that you have not yet managed to demonstrate? Skills such as client care, drafting, and commercial awareness can be particularly difficult to demonstrate as a result of academic study so look out for work that offers you the chance to gain these skills.

- Will you be able to strengthen an existing skill by applying a skill gained at university in a professional setting? Perhaps you entered the negotiation competition and can use those skills in practice or you can tailor your academic research skills to operate in a practical context.

- Does the job include doing the tasks that lawyers do? Will you be able to have direct contact with clients, witnesses, or experts in other professions? Perhaps there will be opportunities to attend court or to prepare documents.

- Is the work relevant to the area of law that you want to practise? This can be especially useful if you want to work in an area of law that was not covered on your degree.

Non-law jobs

INTRODUCTION

Chapter 9 outlined a number of law-based career options other than qualifying as a solicitor or barrister. This chapter will continue to explore alternative career paths by looking at a range of non-law jobs. It may seem strange to include a chapter on non-law careers in a book that is aimed for law students but not every student taking a law degree wants to enter a legal profession and not every student who wishes to practise law will end up being able to do so. This chapter acknowledges that reality by exploring the other career options for students with a law degree other than qualifying as a solicitor or barrister. It does this by classifying all other employment opportunities into three categories: non-law work in a legal setting, non-law work with a degree of legal content and, finally, careers with no legal context or content whatsoever.

For some students, the matter is straightforward: they started the law degree with no intention of practising law and this position did not change during the course of their studies. Other students start and finish with an unwavering commitment to entering the legal profession. For these students, the only dilemma is whether or not they will be able to secure a training contract or pupillage. Given the level of competition in terms of entry into the legal profession, even students with a determination to practise law may not be able to do so. It can therefore be a sensible precaution to work towards a career in law whilst also keeping your mind open to the possibility of other career paths. Finally, many students start a law degree without any clear plans about entering into practice or change their minds during the course of their studies. In other words, for all students taking a law degree, a non-law job is at least a possibility if not a positive career choice. For this reason, you should read this chapter to find out about non-law career paths and how best to prepare for them during your study of the law.

Thinking about non-law careers

Just because you have a law degree, do not think that this means that there are no career options open to you other than a career as a solicitor or barrister.

According to the Hardee Report, which was commissioned by the UK Centre for Legal Education in 2012, almost one-fifth of students who start a law degree in England and Wales do so with no intention of entering the legal profession. By the end of the law degree, approximately half of law students have decided on some other career path or, at least, have made the decision not to practise law even if they have not yet decided on an alternative career path. So if you have decided that legal practice is not for you then you are not alone. You will find a discussion in Chapter 2 of the factors that many students consider when deciding whether or not they are suited to legal practice.

> By the time of final exams, I couldn't bear to look at another case. The thought of doing more exams, and not joining the workplace immediately, was not an attractive one. I had done various work experience projects in various sectors and had a pre-existing relationship with one of the Big Four accountancy firms; it seemed natural to look at all the options available to me—the advantage of a more varied work experience.
>
> Thomas, Oxford University

Alternatively, you may still have this as your ultimate career goal but have decided to explore other career options for a period of time in order to build up your employability skills and improve your prospects of securing a training contract or pupillage in the future.

> There are benefits to considering working towards a non-law career. It can provide the opportunity to gain more pay more quickly, which you can use towards paying for your LPC later or part time. There is more opportunity to prove responsibility and leadership skills. You will have developed different skills and experience which will make your training contract application more interesting.
>
> Jennifer, law graduate

You will find a discussion of law-related career options in Chapter 9 and this chapter will consider a selection on non-law jobs that you might consider after graduation. Obviously, we cannot go into detail about every other possible career path but we will be exploring a range of possibilities that fall into three broad categories:

- **Non-law work in a law context.** This section will cover careers in which the tasks performed are not legal in nature but are performed in a law environment such as a legal secretary (administrative work in a law firm) or a witness liaison officer (working in the criminal courts).
- **Non-law work with legal content.** This covers careers in which the understanding and application of a particular area of law is needed on a regular basis such as a social worker (who applies social welfare law) or a career in human resource management (using employment law).
- **Non-law work with no legal context or content.** This includes careers where there may be a legal framework that regulates how the job must be done, such as the regulatory framework of professions such as dentistry and accountancy, but where this is very much a peripheral part of the role as well as careers with no legal basis whatsoever.

Each of these three categories will be considered in the sections that follow with guidance on how to explore different career options and how to make the best use of the skills and knowledge acquired during the law degree to gain entry into these professions.

Work in a law context

The focus in this section is on non-law work that takes place in a legal environment. What is a legal environment? By this, we mean the locations where the law 'happens' such as law firms, courts, prisons and such like as well as jobs that are part of a legal framework such as the criminal justice system. It is something of an arbitrary definition and some people may categorise certain jobs differently: for example, some people would consider that work as a police officer was law work in a non-law setting but we have taken into account the full spectrum of responsibilities of a police officer when categorising it as a non-law job and have taken account of its context within the criminal justice system. So this category of careers has the common theme of being part of the mechanism of criminal or civil justice.

Legal secretary

If you like the idea of working in a law firm without being involved in legal practice then an administrative position might be attractive. The role of the legal secretary has rather diminished in recent years as the work that was traditionally done by a legal secretary—typing documents, dealing with correspondence, completing forms, liaising with clients, and organising appointments—tends to be done by solicitors themselves or have become part of the responsibilities of a paralegal. Nonetheless, there are still opportunities available for legal secretaries to provide administrative support for a solicitor or team of solicitors within a practice. The sorts of duties that would be expected include answering the telephone, passing messages to the relevant fee-earner, scanning, copying and faxing documents, file management, and making arrangements for meetings and travel. Depending on the size of the law firm, there may be a requirement to complete legal documentation and accompany fee-earners to meetings with clients and barristers or to attend court.

There is no requirement that a legal secretary should have a law degree—it is an administrative support role rather than a legal position—but many law firms are recognising how attractive the role may be to prospective solicitors and are adding the phrase 'may suit recent law graduate' to their advertisements. The role may be described as a legal assistant or an administrative assistant rather than a legal secretary. Most of the law recruitment firms include sections on their websites for administrative support vacancies so this would be the place to look for opportunities to work as a legal secretary.

- Find out more about work as a legal secretary on the Institute of Legal Secretaries website: **www.legalsecretaryjournal.com/?q=a_day_in_the_life_of_a_legal_secretary**. This website also provides details of training opportunities for legal secretaries.

Barrister's clerk

Many people misunderstand the nature of the work of a barrister's clerk as the title 'clerk' is often taken to refer to a relatively junior administrative role. In reality, a barrister's clerk is responsible for the business management aspects of running a barrister's chamber; this involves making administrative arrangements, organising the workload of barristers, marketing the chambers and ensuring that its finances are in order. In light of the responsibility attached to the role, some chambers have relabelled the position of barrister's clerk with titles such as administrative officer or practice manager.

The role of barrister's clerk is best understood by considering the range of areas of responsibility that it includes:

- Allocating cases that come into chambers to particular barristers taking into account their expertise, level of experience and availability

- Estimating the timetable of the case, organising meetings to ensure its smooth progress, liaising with instructing solicitors and calculating the fees to be charged for work on the case

- Supervising junior barristers, helping them to establish a reputation and acquire an area of expertise

- Marketing the chambers, networking with solicitors and taking other proactive measures to ensure that the chambers maintains a steady flow of work

- Planning the workload of the chambers by keeping track of meetings, court dates and other events and maintaining a schedule for each barrister

- Keeping up-to-date with professional regulations and organising training to ensure that all barristers are fully compliant with the requirements of the profession and that all necessary accreditation documentation is current

- Being alert for legal developments that affect the practice areas of barristers in chambers and organising training events and seminars to promote the range of areas of specialisation in chambers

- Making arrangements such as ensuring that case files reach the correct court and documents are delivered to barristers in other chambers as well as making travel arrangements for barristers

- Maintaining the law library and assisting barristers to locate statutory materials and case law.

As you can see from this range of duties, a barrister's clerk will need a high level of organisational skills, excellent communication skills, and the ability to prioritise tasks and manage time effectively. There is no requirement for a barrister's clerk to have a law degree but a law graduate would have the advantage of understanding the operation of the legal system and have an insight into the scope of each barrister's area of expertise which might make aspects of the job easier. Barrister's clerks usually work in teams and a large chambers may have a delineation between junior and senior clerks. Training is provided 'on the job' from senior or more experienced clerks and there is the possibility of undertaking further study to gain the BTEC Advanced Award in Chambers Administration for Barrister's Clerks.

Family mediator

A family mediator works with couples who are divorcing or separating to help them communicate and resolve issues in a constructive manner. The role involves meeting with each of the parties separately to identify their concerns and priorities and then conducting joint meetings with a view to guiding the parties towards resolution of disputed issues. There are often complicated and emotional issues such as distribution of marital property, financial support following divorce, and care and custody of children. There may be a need to speak to the children of the marriage to ascertain their views and ensure that their feelings can be taken into account.

The work may be based in court, at a family mediation centre or within a law firm. There is no requirement that family mediators have a law degree or any legal knowledge as the role does not involve giving legal advice. However, an understanding of family law and the operation of the legal system would provide useful background knowledge, especially as the role involves liaising with solicitors and attending court. Many of the skills acquired during a law degree will be valuable in this role: objectivity especially in emotive situations, fact-management, creativity in problem solving, and negotiation skills.

Training is needed to qualify as a family mediator as well as some previous work experience, paid or voluntary, within the support services sector. This involves completion of a training course provided by one of the six organisations approved by the Family Mediation Council (listed in the following paragraph) that covers such matters as mediation skills, conflict theory, and family law followed by a period of at least ten hours' supervised work alongside a qualified family mediator. Once qualified, there is a requirement to complete ten hours' continuing professional development (CPD) each year and to have regular supervisory meetings with a mentor. Mediators wishing to undertake publically funded (legal aid) work must also undergo an Assessment of Professional Competence recognised by the Legal Services Commission.

The six training providers seem to vary in terms of the eligibility for undertaking their courses and in the way that the training is structured and provided so it would be worth taking some time to investigate all six organisations to determine which program is best suited to your experience and qualifications.

- ADR Group: **www.adrgroup.co.uk/product/33/become_a_family_mediator** (see Figure 10.1)
- College of Mediators: **www.collegeofmediators.co.uk**
- Family Mediators Association: **www.thefma.co.uk/train-as-a-mediator**

Become a Family Mediator

How to Become a Family Mediator
Follow our training programme to become a Family Mediator recognised by the Family Mediation Council, Bar Council and the Law Society of England and Wales.

Family Foundation Training - Option 1

The fast track course is run over six days. It is delivered over two weekend modules with long days starting from 9.00 and running through to 19.00 or even 19.30 dependent on numbers.

The first three days of intensive training is followed by a written assignment. The second three days will be followed by two written assignments and successful completion will enable trainees to begin co-mediating and to apply for membership of ADRg Family Register

CPD: 52 Hours SRA, 33 Hours BSB

Family Foundation Training - Option 2

The seven day course is delivered over two modules, the first of which includes a Saturday, and aimed at those who would like to minimise time out of the office/their busy schedules.

The first five days of intensive training during which a short written assignment must be completed and followed by two written assignments.

Successful completion of the last two days will enable trainees to begin co-mediating and to apply for membership of ADRg Family

CPD: 52 Hours SRA, 33 Hours BSB

Figure 10.1 Example of family mediator training courses (ADR)

- Law Society: **www.lawsociety.org.uk/accreditation/specialist-scheme/family-mediation/**
- National Family Mediation: **www.nfm.org.uk/index.php/nfm-training-home**
- Resolution: **www.resolution.org.uk/events.asp?page_id=24**.

Witness care officer

This is a role within the Crown Prosecution Service (CPS) that centres on providing support and guidance for victims of crime and witnesses before and during a criminal trial at which their evidence will be presented. The witness care officer provides a single point of contact for victims and witnesses thus providing a level of continuity and a source of information that recognises and respects their role in the prosecution process. An important part of the role is to conduct a Needs Assessment on each victim and witness to ensure that measures can be put in place during the trial that will enable them to provide the best quality evidence for the court. Witness care officers need to liaise with the police, lawyers, and other professional service providers to ensure that the case progresses smoothly and to ensure that the needs of witnesses are met. As you might expect, the role includes providing support and information at court, both before and on the day of the trial.

Practical example: witness care officer

When I finished the LPC, I decided that I didn't want to go into practice but I did want a job that kept me involved with the law. I had encountered witness care officers at court when I did work experience with a criminal solicitor and had learned a lot about their job and I felt that their work in finding ways to make witnesses feel safe to give evidence was an important part of ensuring that prosecutions were successful.

The most important part of my job involves finding out about witnesses and their feelings about giving evidence so that I can assess what measures they need in order to feel comfortable giving evidence. This can be quite challenging as some witnesses are so intimidated by the idea of coming to court that they don't want to talk to anyone that they consider to be in a position of authority so I have to be very patient and sympathetic whilst still keeping an appropriate distance and not getting too involved in their case. A lot of my work involves practical things like finding a translator, counsellor or child minder for a witness.

Over the past three years, I have seen a lot of trials and found out a lot about criminal practice and procedure at trial and plea management hearings, so much so that I now feel that I'm ready to get a training contract so that I can work in criminal practice. My job has given me a lot of skills that I didn't have before that I think will help me to get a training contract. My advocacy skills will have improved no end as a result of watching so many trials and learning so much about questioning witnesses and presenting arguments to the jury. I am used to working with all sorts of different people: police, social workers, solicitors, barristers and, obviously, victims of crime as well as third party witnesses. I am used to taking statements, preparing reports and prioritising my case load and, most importantly, I can see the role that people play in the criminal justice system.

David, University of Westminster (2010)

- You will find more information about work as a witness care officer and the other administrative jobs within the CPS on their website: **www.cps.gov.uk/careers/ business_administration_careers/witness_care/**.

Police, probation, and prison

The police force, probation service, and prison service are all part of the criminal justice system and offer an interesting and structured career path for law graduates with an interest in law enforcement. Each organisation makes provision for a graduate career path but it is important to note that neither the probation service nor the prison service guarantee that you will be appointed to a permanent post at the end of the training period; you will merely be eligible to apply for relevant vacancies. By contrast, at the end of the three-year training period within the police force, you will be allocated a role based upon your aptitude and performance.

Police force

The police are at the frontline of law enforcement, investigating crime and dealing with perpetrators and victims of crime on a daily basis. According to the Surrey Police website: 'any working police officer would probably tell you that their job is a complex mix of excitement, danger, compassion and paperwork'. The standard route into a career as a police officer involves the completion of a two-year Initial Police Learning and Development Programme (IPLDP). Each police force determines the precise breakdown and content of its training programme so they will vary to a certain degree in the detail whilst all covering the same essential elements. Table 10.1 sets out the training programme for police officers in the Surrey police force by way of example.

Table 10.1 Police training programme

Internal Training 10 weeks	Students will be taught legislative and practical skills. The training includes operationally based and assessed role plays, an interview skills course, and opportunities to work in the community as well as lessons from experienced police officers.
IT Training 2 weeks	Students are taught how to use the Surrey police computer systems.
Tutoring Phase 10 weeks	Students are trained by the Street Duties Tutoring Unit to develop skills in an operational environment dealing with day-to-day incidents working in Response teams and Neighbourhood teams. There is an opportunity to carry out interviews and low-level investigations. At the end of this period and subject to satisfactory progress, the student will be awarded Independent Patrol Status.
Independent Patrol Status 2 years	Students are now eligible to work alone. This is the stage at which students will complete a Level 3 Diploma in Policing to demonstrate that they have the skills necessary to perform the role of a police constable to an acceptable standard.

Independent Patrol Status lasts for two years, during which time students will be supported by a PC assessor. It includes the following attachments:

- Response Strand—12 weeks
- Investigation Strand—11 weeks
- Neighbourhood Strand—11 weeks

After 56 weeks, the Diploma in Policing should be complete and all areas of police business should have been experienced. It is at this stage that students will receive their permanent posting, taking into account their preferences and the needs of the force.

At the two year point, appointment as a police constable is confirmed.

The police force is organised on a regional basis with each area operating its own recruitment and training programmes for police officers so you should check the details on the relevant force's website.

- You will find a list of the regional forces as well as links to the non-geographic branches of the police such as the British Transport police online: **www.police.uk/?view=force_sites**.

The Metropolitan Police force makes provision for graduate entry and training by way of the Graduate Development Programme (GDP) and the Accelerated Graduate Development Programme (AGDP) (see Figure 10.2). Both programmes require applicants to have a 2.1 degree in any subject and there are other eligibility criteria covering nationality, residency, business, and financial status and medical and fitness as well as compliance with the police policy on tattoos and body piercings.

- There is a comprehensive FAQ section on the graduate entry programmes on the Metropolitan Police website: **www.metpolicecareers.co.uk/graduates/faqs.html**.

Probation service

The probation service operates within the criminal justice system to provide supervision of adult offenders who have been sentenced to a community penalty by the courts or who have been released from prison on licence. This amounts to approximately 170,000 offenders each year. Probation officers work with offenders for the duration of a non-custodial sentence with a view to ensuring that they understand the impact of their offending behaviour and to achieve their rehabilitation and reintegration into society. They may organise unpaid work for offenders or supervise their attendance on drugs or alcohol treatment programmes. An important part of the probation officer's role is to prepare pre-sentence reports on convicted offenders that outlines the background of the offender and their offending so that an informed sentencing decision can be made and to carry out a risk assessment to ensure that public protection is taken into account.

Until April 2010, the graduate route to qualification as a social worker involved taking the Graduate Diploma in Probation Studies. This route is no longer available to new applicants who must instead qualify through the Probations Qualifications Framework (PQF) whilst working as an unqualified Probation Services Office (PSO). Progression through the advanced stages of the PQF is contingent on acquisition or possession of a relevant degree; that is, a degree in criminology, police studies, community justice, or criminal justice. A joint honours degree with law and any of these subjects would be likely to suffice but it would depend upon the level of relevant content. The best course of action if you are unsure as to whether your degree would suffice for the basis of progression through the PQF is to contact the relevant Probation Trust for further information.

Graduate development programme	Accelerated graduate development programme
Year one Probationer training and completion of the IPLDP. Participation in action in learning sets training to expose you to key strategic challenges in policing.	**Year one** Operational grounding, probationer training and completion of the IPLDP.
Year two A series of operational placements within the following borough operational command units: – Investigative: intelligence-led approaches to local crimes. – Police response: fast-paced immediate response to 999 calls. – Partnership: building relationships within the local community and working with people to to solve long-term local issues.	**Months 12–18** Completion of segment examinations plus NPIA modules covering leadership & self and leadership & teams. You could be promoted to the rank of sergeant at the end of this period.
	Months 18–30 You take part in the core leadership development programme which includes two-to-three intensive residential courses. Training at this stage focuses on strategic leadership, community policing, and team building. At the completion of this period, you will take your inspector examinations.
Year three Focuses on leadership, management, and strategic development. Completion of a volunteering project to develop community links and enhance key personal skills. At the end of the programme, you will recieve a strategic or operational posting that will enable you to apply the operational policing experience, leadership skills, and change management theory that you have learned.	**Months 30–36** Focus is on leadership development and executive skills required for senior positions within the police force and the completion of operational command simulation exercises. You could be promoted to inspector at the end of this period.

Figure 10.2 Graduate Development Programmes at the Metropolitan Police

- If you are interested in training as a probation officer, you should visit the Ministry of Justice website to find a list of the regional Probation Trusts, each of which has its own website which includes details of its recruitment processes: **www.justice.gov.uk/about/ probation/probation-trusts**.

When applying for work within the probation service, previous experience in working with offenders and other groups with difficult or challenging behaviour is likely to be welcomed and this can be acquired by undertaking relevant voluntary work (see Chapter 5). This could include voluntary work with youth groups, in prisons, as a police community support officer or any experience in working with people with drugs, alcohol, or mental health problems.

Prison service

Although it is common to think of the purpose of prison as being the incarceration of offenders, this is only one of three objectives of the prison service: it also aims to prevent the risk of re-offending and to provide safe and well-ordered environments in which prisoners are treated humanely, decently, and lawfully. There are various career options within the prison service that contribute to the pursuit of these objectives but the opportunity that may be of particular interest to law graduates is the National Offender Management Service (NOMS) graduate programme.

Practical example NOMS graduate programme

The programme starts with a six week course at the training centre in Rugby. This prepares you for your first post as prison officer. The training includes basic control and restraint methods including use of handcuffs and search techniques. The last week of training involves shadowing an officer in the prison where you will be posted after which you take on the role of prison officer yourself.

Over the next 12 to 18 months, you will gain experience and be given more responsibility as you progress to supervisor officer level. This is followed by a move to another prison to take up the role of custodial manager in which you take over the management of a group of staff. Finally, you will move into the middle-management governor-grade role as operational manager which puts you in charge of an entire area of the prison.

Upon completion of the programme, usually after two or three years, you will be able to apply for a managerial post within the prison service.

Unlike the more specific requirements of the Probation service, it is possible to qualify for the NOMS graduate programme with a 2.1 degree in any subject. Applicants must also satisfy the civil service national rules, be prepared to be flexible in terms of work location and mobility and be able to pass the medical and fitness tests required. In addition to this, certain personal characteristics should be demonstrated by potential applicants:

• Resilience, integrity, and decisiveness, even under intense pressure
• The ability to get on with people from all walks of life and to stay calm in emotionally charged situations
• A determination to exceed targets that have been set for you
• The ability to bounce back if things go wrong and to be adaptable when faced with unpredictable people and situations
• A commitment to rehabilitation
• Strong and compassionate leadership with confidence in your own ability.

There are some excellent resources on the NOMS graduate programme on the Ministry of Justice website that includes a series of video clips of various prison service personnel talking about their roles and experience. There are also resources that allow you to assess your leadership skills and to test out your response to a problem situation that you could encounter when working in a prison (see Figure 10.3).

• www.justice.gov.uk/jobs/prisons/on-offer/graduate-programme.

Non-law work with legal content

There are a number of careers that could not be considered to fall within the legal profession, however broadly defined, nor involve working in a legal environment but which

Figure 10.3 www.justice.gov.uk

nonetheless require a comprehensive knowledge of a particular area of law. These are jobs that would be suitable for a law graduate and offer a career path that would enable you to make good use of the knowledge and skills gained during a law degree. These tend to be careers that involve the application and enforcement of a particular regulatory regime: in other words, they involve putting a particular area of law into practice within some other profession. Entry into these careers may involve further education and training but you would at least have something of a head start due to your understanding of the law and the way in which the legal system operates.

Trading standards officer

A trading standards officer is employed by the local council in a public protection capacity to advise on and apply consumer law. This involves dealing with matters such as counterfeit goods, product labelling, and weights and measures as well as ensuring that there is compliance with the law relating to age-related sales and, somewhat anomalously, certain animal welfare issues. So a trading standards officer may do some or all of the following:

- Carry out checks in pubs to make sure that they are selling full measures of spirits and take samples to determine whether the drinks have been watered down

- Organise a sting operation to catch traders selling alcohol or cigarettes to under-age children

- Scrutinise the wording of advertisements of products for sale to ensure that they are not misleading or false

- Visit markets and car boot sales to make sure that counterfeit goods are not being offered for sale.

The objective of the role is to protect consumers and businesses by investigating complaints, facilitating compliance with the law by carrying out inspections of trade premises, and initiating prosecutions for breach of the law. The role has quite a significant investigative element as it involves gathering evidence to support a prosecution and it may require this evidence to be presented at court.

The Trading Standards Institute (TSI) has established a qualification framework that operates within the industry and this has a route that is tailored to law graduates as possession of a qualifying law degree confers exemption from two elements of the professional qualification framework: (1) legal systems and (2) contract and tort. The TSI Academy offers a blended learning option for achieving the necessary qualifications or it is possible to undertake a qualification at Teesside University, Manchester Metropolitan University, or Nottingham Trent University.

- Find out more about the qualifications necessary to work as a Trading Standards Officer and the modular approach to achieving these qualifications at the TSI Academy website: **www.tradingstandards.gov.uk/products/tsiacademy.cfm**.

Immigration officer

This is a role based within the Border Agency that focuses on control of entry into the UK at airports, seaports, and the Channel Tunnel. As it is concerned with an individual's eligibility to enter the country, an interest in and understanding of immigration law would be valuable and the ability to undergo an objective evaluation of the evidence and reach a reasoned decision is important. There is a possibility of working with one of the specialist teams within the Border Agency and focusing on issues such as forged documents, trafficking, or intelligence gathering or in gaining expertise in issues such as enforcement or asylum claims.

Immigration officers undergo a nine-week period of training which starts with five weeks in the classroom and is followed by four weeks of operational coaching. They are expected to be able to grasp the niceties of immigration law and its associated regulations and policy requirements. Training in interview techniques is provided and the initial period of employment is undertaken under the supervision of an experienced immigration officer. There is no graduate recruitment scheme within the Border Agency but it is part of the civil service so it is one of the options for graduates recruited through the Fast Stream Scheme (the graduate entry route to the civil service).

- All vacancies for immigration officers and other roles within the Border Agency can be found on the recruitment section of the Border Agency website: **www.ukba.homeoffice. gov.uk/aboutus/workingforus/currentvacancies/**.

Tax inspector

HM Revenue and Customs (HMRC) is the government department responsible for collecting tax from individuals and businesses in the UK (around £468 billion each year) and for administering the National Insurance system, dealing with Student Loans and the tax credit system as well as ensuring that businesses comply with minimum wage requirements. This is an area which is heavily regulated by legislation and so would suit a law graduate with business-orientated interests.

The Tax Professional Development Programme is designed for graduates from any discipline although the ability to understand and apply the law would be useful as much of the work involves ensuring that businesses and individuals are complying with the law regarding taxation. A legal background might also be useful as there is the possibility of preparing cases for tax tribunals. It takes four years to complete the Tax Professional Development Programme, at the end of which you would be qualified as a tax inspector. The alternative would be to consider HMRC's Management Fast Track which focuses on policy, advisory, or strategic management training and prepares you for a qualification with the Chartered Management Institute (CMI).

Social work

The role of a social worker is to work with people who, for whatever reason, are in a vulnerable position and help them to support themselves in a way that is appropriate to their needs and circumstances. Many social workers work for the local authority but they may also be employed by hospitals, charities, or community-based organisations. Social workers form professional and supportive relationships with the client and also engage with their families as well as agencies who may have a role to play in the client's life such as the police, the medical profession, schools, residential care facilities, and the probation service. Social workers tend to specialise in working either with adults or with children:

- **Adult services.** There are a range of situations in which adults may need the support of social services so a social worker who specialises in adult care may be dealing with the elderly, offenders, drug addicts, and people with mental health problems or learning difficulties.

- **Children and young people.** Social work with young people often centres on difficulties in the family unit so they may work to provide support so that families can stay together or oversee the removal of the child which may involve foster care, work in a children's home or managing the adoption process. It also involves intervention if children experience problems at school, get into trouble with the law, or face difficulties at home as a result of illness in the family.

Social workers must be registered with the Health and Care Professions Council and must hold a recognised qualification in social work. For law graduates, it is possible to achieve the necessary qualification by undertaking a two-year postgraduate course that combines 100 hours of university teaching and 100 hours of workplace training and assessment. There is a strong law element to social work and you will find that various areas of law are covered in the course: social welfare law covers aspects of family law, mental health law, education law, housing law, and the law concerning access to welfare benefits.

Practical example: social work

I was looking for a career that would allow me to use the law to help people in quite a direct way and so social work seemed an obvious choice. I worked as an unqualified social work assistant at my local authority for a year just to make sure that it was the right job for me and then took a Diploma in Social Work at which was half university teaching and half work placements. There was a fair amount of law covered which I did find quite straightforward even the topics like welfare and mental health law that I hadn't covered on my degree.

I work in adult services now, specialising in adults with mental health problems and so I do actually use the law quite a lot on a daily basis as it is a very regulated area. I feel a lot more confident that my understanding of the law is correct because of my legal background and I am often asked to explain legislation and regulations to my colleagues because of my knowledge of the law. I also find that it helps when dealing with court proceedings because I have a good understanding of what is going on.

So I wouldn't say that you need a law degree to be a social worker but that I have got to grips with the legal framework of social work a lot better because of it.

Kate, Southampton University

Human resources

The human resources department within an organisation deals with all aspects of the business that relate to employees with the overall objective of 'creating, implementing and managing efficient processes to ensure a happy workforce' (Lawrence Carter, Reed in Partnership). This can include recruitment, health and safety, training and education, creating policies on pay and conditions, liaising with unions and employee groups, promoting equality and diversity in the workplace as well as dealing with disciplinary issues. It is a career where a good knowledge and understanding of employment law is an essential element and where other areas of law, such as equality legislation and health and safety law, may be relevant.

It is possible to obtain entry level work as a human resources assistant without any specific training or experience but if you wanted to progress within the human resources profession you may need to consider further qualifications. Most medium and large organisations have a human resources department, some of which offer graduate entry schemes. You might also want to consider the HR Fast Stream within the civil service (discussed later in the chapter).

Practical example: human resources

Midway through my second year, I realised that not only did I not want to apply to study for my LPC, I was unsure as to whether I wanted a career in the legal field at all. I decided to focus on completing my degree, and once I graduated, was faced with the situation facing so many graduates—'what do I do now, and how do I get a job'.

I considered the options that I had, what skills I had obtained, and what I had learnt from my degree. In hindsight, I can recognise the benefits of my degree with regards to employability as opposed to graduates of different disciplines. It really is so much more than the first step on the ladder to the eventual goal of practising law. Not only did I graduate with an excellent academic foundation to build a career on, but I gained a broad skill set that has relevance in fields as diverse as politics, finance, business or even journalism.

I considered what areas of law I was most interested in. Despite having not taken employment law as an elective in third year, I have always had a strong interest in workplace law. I considered where I could take this, how I could progress. Accordingly, I undertook a voluntary unpaid placement with a large public service organisation within the human resources team. Since that placement, I have had numerous roles in different organisations, culminating in my current role as a HR Assistant within a medium sized company. My law degree has held me in excellent stead with regards to progressing within the HR field. I use the skills I gained at university every day in my working life.

Taking a brief snapshot of a typical day in the office, I draw upon the skills gained from my degree in so many different ways:

- Interviewing a candidate with a disability—My understanding of the legal system ensures that I can keep abreast of employment law developments, whilst my lateral thinking skills and problem solving skills ensure my actions and my decisions represent best practice, in that I meet the demands of statute, the organisation and the individuals concerned.

- Report writing and general administration—Effective record keeping and statistical analysis is one of the key issues in delivering HR services, and my ability to present myself clearly and articulately both orally and in writing is a vital part of this. Accordingly, my attention to specific details, time management skills, ability to prioritise and keep to deadlines are all skills gained from my degree that I use every day at work.

- Training the management team on conducting back to work interviews after staff sickness—My evaluation skills and ability to explain complex information clearly ensures not only that I'm able to understand the law and data behind effective absence management and the effect this has on business goals, but I can present and transfer such concepts to the managers ensuring effective delivery of HR services.

- Advising on employee relations issues—My reasoning and ability to understand complex legal theory gained from my academic understanding of the law has ensured that not only do I understand the statute and case law behind employee relations issues, but I can ensure that the advice I give leads to resolution of issues that covers all bases, in that all actions are within the parameters of the law, and the goals of the company are met. My ability to toe the fine line that HR must sit as an impartial advisor, where the goals are to ensure best practice, meet legal requirements, protect staff and the organisational interests, all fundamentally stem from my skills gained through studying for my law degree.

Siobhan, Brunel University

Non-law careers

This final section of the book covers careers that have very little, if any, legal content. Obviously, there are a great many careers that fall into this category so we have had to be very selective and have chosen to focus on career paths that seem well suited to the skills that students will have acquired during a law degree. For example, we have selected examples of careers that are suitable for those with good oral (teaching) and written (journalism) communication skills and those that would make use of your research skills (research assistant). We have also looked at career options that offer a structured approach to training and development, such as the civil service. There has also been an emphasis on opportunities to pursue any number of alternative careers hence the inclusion of graduate training schemes and conversion courses. The overall aim is to give you an insight into the possibilities rather than a complete and comprehensive guide to every possible career path.

Civil Service Fast Stream

The Fast Stream is a graduate recruitment scheme within the civil service that allows employees to amass experience of a range of government departments and types of work within a short period of time. The Graduate Fast Stream is open to graduates from any academic discipline with at least a 2.2 degree but there are also specialist streams for graduates with certain degrees or with particular interests:

- **Analytical Fast Stream** for economists, statisticians, social researchers, and operational researchers
- **HR Fast Stream** for graduates with an interest in the HR profession
- **Technology in Business Fast Stream** for gradates with a strong interest in technology and its application in a commercial setting
- **European Fast Stream** is for graduates from any discipline with an interest in a career in the EU institutions in Brussels
- **Northern Ireland Fast Stream** offers graduates of any discipline a career path in the Northern Ireland civil service.

The Graduate Fast Stream is divided into four options that offer different career opportunities and you will need to indicate the options that interest you the most as part of the application process. These four options are Central Departments, the Diplomatic Service, the Houses of Parliament, and Science and Engineering and all but the last of these are open to law graduates.

Central Departments

Work in the Central Departments covers every major government department except the Foreign and Commonwealth Office so you could work in the department dealing with health, education, transport, justice, defence, the economy, and so on. Given the diversity of departments and roles within them, the first two years of the Fast Stream in the Central Departments is divided into six-month postings to ensure that you develop a broad portfolio of skills and experience. One of these postings is likely to be in a different part of the country and you should also expect a short secondment to a small or medium enterprise or a charity. This shift of department and activity is designed to ensure that you face new challenges on a regular basis and that you experience different situations and objectives. The work will involve a range of different activities with a combination of operational delivery and policy development in addition to opportunities to develop skills in management of people, finance, and projects and to develop commercial awareness.

After two years, you will transfer to another department where you will undertake two longer postings for the remaining two years of the Fast Stream programme. This provides a depth of experience that balances the breadth provided by a variety of different placements in the first two years.

Diplomatic service

The diplomatic service is the part of government that maintains relationships with the governments of other countries, develops foreign policy, and deals with a range of transnational issues such as terrorism, international peacekeeping initiatives, and the global economic environment. The first two years of the Fast Stream are spent in the Foreign and Commonwealth Office's headquarters in Whitehall with one year devoted to a policy issue, such as defence, and one year spent on service delivery, such as provision of assistance to British citizens incarcerated abroad. This is followed by a three- or four-year overseas posting in one of the 200+ embassies, high commissions, or consulates where there will be a chance to get to know the country and its culture.

Competition for the Diplomatic Service Fast Stream is fierce with almost 100 applicants for every vacancy. For this reason, applications are not considered unless the diplomatic service is listed as your first choice option. Contrary to popular belief, you do not need to be fluent in a second language to work in the diplomatic service but an aptitude for languages would be useful. There is an opportunity to spend the second year of the Fast Stream acquiring a hard to master language such as Mandarin or Arabic and intensive tuition is provided if an overseas posting requires the proficiency in a particular language.

Houses of Parliament

The Houses of Parliament Fast Stream is focused on providing support to the work of the House of Lords and the House of Commons, their Committees and individual MPs. It is an obvious choice for law graduates who have an interest in the political process, constitutional affairs, and public policy especially as it may include opportunities to scrutinise drafts of legislation and to brief MPs prior to debates thus giving them a direct role in the legislative process.

The first year of the Fast Stream will usually be spent either as a clerk in the Chamber and Committee Services Department in the House of Commons or as a clerk in the Committee Office of the House of Lords. Subsequent roles may include work on a Select Committee, secondment as a private secretary to a senior MP or providing support for international Parliamentary assemblies such as NATO or the Council of Europe. There is always an opportunity to work at evening sessions when the Houses are sitting carrying out duties such as taking formal minutes of proceedings or undertaking division duties when MPs vote.

- There is a detailed account of roles and responsibilities in the Houses of Parliament Fast Stream online: **www.parliament.uk/documents/jobs/Fast-Stream-booklet-FINAL-2012.pdf**.

Application process

Careers in the civil service are popular and so, as you might expect, the application process for the Fast Stream is lengthy and challenging (see Figure 10.4). However, there are opportunities to practise the online tests and an online example of the e-Tray exercise to help you to understand what will be expected of you and a comprehensive guide to what to expect if your application proceeds as far as the selection centre.

Teaching

The focus in this section is on a general career in teaching, concentrating on training to teach in a primary or secondary school. If your interest is in teaching law, this will generally take place at A-level or in a tertiary education setting and you will find a discussion of the options for doing so in Chapter 9.

Other than A-level, law is rarely taught in schools. There is a GCSE in law but it is not popular, probably due to the need to over-simplify legal concepts in order to teach it at that level. Therefore, if your objective is to teach in a school, you will probably need to accept that you will not be teaching law. That is not necessarily a problem: the postgraduate route into teaching requires you to have a degree in any subject, not in the subject that you want to teach, but you will need to find another subject that you want to teach once you are qualified.

The Postgraduate Certificate in Education (PGCE) is the traditional method of entry into the teaching profession for graduates. This is a one-year full-time course that focuses on teaching you to teach rather than on the subject that you intend to teach but the PGCE courses are linked to particular subjects. In other words, you could take a PGCE in geography or a PGCE in mathematics, both of which would cover certain common areas of teaching practice and theory but which would differ in terms of certain skills that are specific to the

REGISTRATION
Register online to access the secure application area.

SELECT FAST STREAM SCHEME
Once you have made your selection, you have a certain number of days to complete each of the stages that follows. Time starts as soon as the preceding stage is complete and unused time cannot be carried forward.

ONLINE SELF-ASSESSMENT TESTS
These verbal and numerical reasoning tests are for your benefit so that you can assess your own performance and rate your chances of success.
You have 7 days to complete these tests.

ONLINE PRACTICE TESTS
These tests are optional but give you an opportunity to practise the tests that you will undertake in the next stage and which will be used to determine whether or not your application succeeds.
You have 7 days to complete these tests.

ONLINE SELECTION TESTS
Verbal reasoning, numerical reasoning, and competency questionnaire.
You have 7 days to complete these tests.

OPTIONS SELECTION AND ONLINE APPLICATION FORM
If you pass the online selection tests, you will have 7 days to complete each of these stages.

SUPERVISED e-TRAY EXERCISE
This takes place at regional test centres on particular dates that will be sent to you if your application has progressed to this stage. There is an example e-tray exercise online that will help you to understand what is expected:
http://faststream.civilservice.gov.uk.

SELECTION CENTRE
There is a one day selection centre event in London. Have a look at the selection centre guide for more information: http://faststream.civilservice.gov.uk.

FINAL SELECTION BOARD
An additional stage for applicants to the House of Parliament or Diplomatic Service Fast Stream.

Figure 10.4 Civil service application process

teaching of those particular subjects. For teaching at secondary school level (ages 11 to 16), there is an expectation that you will possess a degree that is related to your chosen area of teaching specialisation. As there is no PGCE in law, what are the options for a law graduate?

- A PGCE in citizenship would qualify you to teach citizenship in secondary schools where it is part of the National Curriculum at Key Stage 3 and 4. The entry requirements are a degree with a significant element of social studies, politics, or law.

- Subject Knowledge Enhancement (SKE) courses are available to enable graduates without a degree in the subject that they wish to teach to achieve an appropriate level of knowledge and understanding to embark on a PGCE in that subject. For example, if you have an A-level in maths, you should take SKE mathematics which you could then follow with a PGCE in mathematics. SKE courses are currently available in chemistry, computer science, design and technology, mathematics, modern languages, and physics.

- Take a PGCE in a particular subject where you feel you have at least a fair level of competence and education (to A-level standard) at a university that includes SKE as part of the PGCE.

The alternative would be to take a PGCE Early Years (3 to 7 years) or PGCE Primary (5 to 11 years) which qualifies you to teach younger children at primary school level and which is not allied to any particular subject specialisation. Primary school teachers are expected to demonstrate a sound, basic knowledge of all the subjects in the curriculum for Key Stages 1 and 2 (see Table 10.2).

Table 10.2: Key Stages 1 and 2 National Curriculum

Core subjects	English
	Mathematics
	Science
Non-core foundation subjects	Design and Technology (D&T)
	Information and Communication Technology (ICT)
	History
	Geography
	Modern Foreign Languages
	Art and Design
	Music
	Physical Education (PE)

Practical example: primary teaching

I didn't know what I wanted to do at the end of my law degree other than I was sure that I didn't want to practise law. I went to a careers fair and just had a wander around looking at all the possibilities to see if any of them appealed to me and I was really taken by the idea of teaching. I had a lot of help and advice from the Teaching Line at the Department of Education and realised that I should get some practical experience of working in a school so I got involved with School Experience Programme that gives you up to ten placement days to watch classes and talk to teachers. I also arranged my own placements by contacting schools directly and, after a lot of thought, I decided that I wanted to teach at primary school level so I enrolled for a PGCE in Early Years teaching (children aged 3 to 7) and actually got a really good bursary to help with my fees and expenses. The course included two stints of teaching practice in different schools and a separate placement that allowed me to pursue my interest in teaching children with Special Educational Needs. My work now is so far removed from my early career plans to work as a solicitor but it was the right choice for me. I felt quite well prepared to train to be a teacher after having completed a law degree. In particular, my verbal and written communication skills were quite advanced compared to some of the other students on my course and I was very much more confident about my ability to conduct the research needed to prepare for my classes than I would have been without the background in research that my degree provided.

Sarah-Louise, University of Leicester

- You will find more information on a career in teaching on the Department of Education website: **www.education.gov.uk/get-into-teaching**.

Working as a researcher

In Chapter 9, there was a discussion of employment opportunities in the area of legal research. It is important to remember, however, that research skills are generic: that is, the ability to formulate a search strategy that enables you to locate target material is one that can be applied to almost any subject matter. In addition to being able to find material, you will have developed the ability to evaluate whether it is relevant and to extract key information from it. The law degree will also have equipped you with good written and oral communication skills as well as an ability to organise your own work and to make progress towards goals without constant supervision. So, in essence, you are well qualified to work as a research assistant in a great range of settings other than law.

As with all the sections in this chapter, the range of work opportunities for a research assistant are too diverse to detail them all but the following will give you a flavour of the sort of work that you could do in this area as they are selected from amongst the vacancies for research assistants that were available at the time of writing:

- **Research Assistant at the BBC** in the Audience Measurement Department responsible for analysing television ratings data to identify trends and explain programme performance.

- **Research Assistant at the Royal Academy of Arts** in the Development Department to assist with fundraising initiatives by creating biographical profiles of potential corporate and individual donors.

- **Research Assistant at the Mental Health Foundation** to support a project that focuses on the needs of male offenders in Parc Prison and includes the collection and analysis of data and the production of research reports.

- **Research Assistant at the Celesio Group**, a leading healthcare services provider that includes Lloyds Pharmacy, to find and collate data from various websites about particular products to facilitate a price comparison and to make business recommendations based upon these findings.

Practical example: work as a research assistant

I worked as a temporary research assistant for a well-known charity after graduation for six months as part of a small team of researchers. Our objective was to collect data that would allow an informed decision to be made about the likely success of a fundraising campaign. Each team member was given a different fundraising event to evaluate and we had to search the Internet to collect data about similar fundraising initiatives, when they had taken place, how successful they had been and how they were advertised. We had to supplement our Internet findings with information from other sources such as the archives of the local newspaper and by conducting telephone research. I had to compile a written report on my findings and prepare a thirty minute oral presentation for the board. I thought that the job sounded easy when I started but I was astonished at how it stretched my research skills— it is so frustrating trying to find information on the Internet that you know must be there somewhere but you can't find it—but I soon got the hang of thinking laterally and coming up with different search strategies. I was really proud of my final report especially because I knew that it could make a real difference to the fundraising strategy over the coming year for that charity.

Matthew, Bournemouth University

Journalism

A career in journalism could prove to be a good option for a law graduate as, in many ways, it involves processes that are very familiar: research and the communication of the results of that research in written or oral form. Journalism involves the dissemination of factual events to the public whether by written, audio, or visual means and there is an increasing emphasis on online dissemination. It can be communicated to the public in general or targeted at a specialist audience and includes subject matter such as news, business, entertainment, politics, sports, science, technology, and arts. The diversity of subject matter and the centrality of core skills of research and communication make it a *very* popular career choice for graduates of all disciplines so previous involvement in activities such as the student newspaper or university radio might be a real advantage.

There are three possible routes into a career in journalism: employment or training on the job, further study at postgraduate level to learn about the media industry, or working as a freelance journalist.

Employment or training schemes

You could apply for work or for a place on a training scheme within the media industry. You could look at the websites of newspapers, magazines, and television companies, remembering to look at regional as well as national organisations. Expect to start at a very junior level: for example, most newspaper editors start out as sub-editors or staff writers and spend a great deal of time proofreading articles written by others rather than producing your own work. As a law graduate, you might want to consider drawing on your specialist knowledge by seeking employment with one of the law periodicals such as the *Solicitor's Journal, the New Law Journal, Counsel*, or the *Estates Gazette*.

Postgraduate qualification

Competition is fierce for graduate entry jobs in journalism so you may wish to improve your prospects of success by taking a postgraduate qualification in journalism. This may be a general course, covering all forms of journalism, or it may allow you to specialise: for example, the Diploma in Journalism at Cardiff University has three variations depending upon whether you are interested in broadcast media, newspaper, or magazine journalism. Such courses cover all aspects of journalism such as production and design work thus broadening the scope of your employment possibilities beyond publication. Most courses have excellent links with the media industry and may involve opportunities for work placements as part of the course.

Freelance work

A freelance journalist is not connected to any particular newspaper or magazine but instead works independently to produce articles that are offered to newspapers or magazines for publication. This may involve coming up with an idea for an article in advance and offering it to editors to see if they are interested or writing the piece up front and sending it out to editors. The former is more usual but the latter might be more successful as a strategy until you are established as a freelancer. You should research your target publication by looking at the style, length, and subject area within which they publish and aim to cover a topic which has some currency in terms of its newsworthiness. Finally, remember that your expertise is in law but that does not limit you to writing for an audience of solicitors and barristers: you could write about legal issues in a way that is aimed at a general non-law audience.

- If you are interested in a career in journalism, you should look at **www.journalism. co.uk** as this has an excellent range of resources including advice about how to get started in journalism and how to get published as a freelancer.

Graduate training schemes

There are all sorts of career opportunities that you may not have considered that you might find attractive and one good route into a new career is through a graduate training scheme. These are programmes run by large organisations that provide structured training and development to graduates spread across one to three years (although two years is most usual). In essence, it is on-the-job training that gives you the opportunity to start earning at the same time as developing the skills and knowledge necessary for a career within a particular industry. Graduate training schemes are available in a range of industries across the public and private sector so can be an excellent route into employment in industries such as banking, insurance, retail, marketing, and media as well as the utility companies and organisations such as the NHS and local government.

A graduate training scheme is not the same as a graduate job. A graduate job is one that requires that applicants possess a degree, sometimes in a specified subject, but that lacks the structured approach to training and development of a graduate training scheme. You may find graduate jobs in smaller organisations that cannot commit the resources to offering a formal training scheme but which nonetheless offer some opportunities for career progression and development. Graduate training schemes often operate on the basis of a series of placements in different parts of the organisation to ensure that trainees are given an insight into the various aspects of the business.

The recruitment process differs for graduate jobs and graduate training schemes. Graduate jobs may be advertised at any point in the year with the start date of the job corresponding with the organisation's needs. Graduate training schemes tend to be advertised well in advance of their start date: many schemes have a deadline as early as November in your final year with a start date of autumn the following year. The application process tends to be more protracted involving several stages: you may be required to make a paper application followed by a telephone interview, a face-to-face interview, psychometric tests, and attendance at a selection centre. Just as is the case with law firms and training contracts, an organisation offering a place on a graduate training scheme is investing a great deal in the person appointed so it is only reasonable to expect a detailed and careful recruitment process aimed at selecting the best applicants.

You will find more information about recruitment processes such as interviews (telephone and face-to-face) and selection centres in Chapter 12.

Finding training schemes

There are various ways to find out about the availability of graduate training schemes. You could look online as there are a number of graduate recruitment websites that will have details of some of the graduate training schemes available or you might want to do your own searches, especially if you have an idea of the organisation or industry in which you want to work. You might find details of graduate recruitment schemes in the employment sections of the websites (and print versions) of quality newspapers. By far the best method of finding information about graduate training schemes is to attend a careers fair.

🌐 Visit the Online Resource Centre to find links to graduate recruitment websites.

Careers fairs

A careers fair is an event that brings together organisations who are looking for employees and individuals who are looking for employment. These may either be general careers fairs or focus on a particular industry: for example, your law school may well organise a law careers fair that will be attended by a combination of law firms, barristers chambers, and non-law organisations with a significant in-house legal department. General careers fairs may be organised by your university or you could attend a national graduate careers event:

- The London Graduate Fair: **http://autumn.londongradfair.co.uk**
- National Graduate Recruitment Exhibition (in London and Birmingham): **www.gradjobs.co.uk/recruitment-exhibitions**
- Autumn Graduate Fair: **www.autumngradfair.co.uk**
- Bright Festival: **www.brightnetwork.co.uk/festival**.

If your university does not organise its own career fair, you might be able to attend one that is organised by another university: be sure to ask in advance though, as some universities do not permit anyone other than their own students to attend.

Practical advice: careers fairs

Attend a careers fair if one is organised by your university. Not only may it give you inspiration if you are unsure what career path to pursue but you will benefit from the opportunity to get a real feel for an organisation or profession by speaking to people who are involved in it. This is particularly true in relation to graduate training schemes as these are usually advertised by people who are currently training or who have recently completed the training and they are in an ideal position to give you a trainee perspective of the firm, its scheme, and the profession more generally.

I found a place on a graduate training scheme by attending a careers fair. I was taken by how approachable the people from Yorkshire Water were and how much the two girls I spoke to seemed to have enjoyed their time on the graduate scheme. I hadn't thought about a career in accountancy before attending the event and I hadn't realised that I'd be able to do a finance-based scheme with a law degree. Even though I picked up application details of seven different schemes and applied for them all, it was the Yorkshire Water one that really stuck with me so I was thrilled to be invited for interview and from there to selection centre and ultimately to be offered a place on the training scheme. There is a really clear career structure that is set out from day one and a very positive atmosphere around the place so I felt enthusiastic about my future career from the very first day that I started. There is a lot of law in financial regulations so I feel like my degree was a good way into my career in finance and accounting.

Emma, Exeter University

I went to the National Graduate Recruitment Exhibition in London with no clear idea of what I wanted—I was just interested to see the sorts of careers that might be open to me. I was amazed by the choice and variety—it really opened my eyes to the possibilities. I was also heartened by the friendliness of many of the employers and their willingness to answer questions. I came away with several application packs and a lot more optimism for my future career than I had when I arrived. Part of this was due to the workshops that were available at the exhibition—I went to one on CVs (identifying several faults in mine in doing so) and to a mock assessment centre event that proved to be really helpful when I reached the section centre stage with one of my applications. I was ultimately successful in my application for the Virgin Media Graduate Business Programme which is not something that I would ever have thought of doing if I hadn't gone to the recruitment fair.

Mark, Plymouth University

If you do attend a graduate careers fair, there are a number of issues to consider:

- **What will you do when you get there?** You could just turn up and wander round in the hope that something catches your eye (as both Emma and Mark did) but this is quite an inefficient way of spending your time. After all, there will be so many organisations at the fair that you cannot hope to visit every stand so it would be worth taking a rather more structured approach to the event to make the most of the opportunities that it provides. Take time to read through the list of exhibitors and decide which ones you want to visit or, at least, which ones you do not want to visit. Prioritise the list and make sure that you focus on visiting these priority employers even if that means that you have to wait to speak to someone. If you are provided with a map of the event (this would usually be the case) then you can use this to plan a route around the event that allows you to visit all the stands of interest rather than wasting time trudging backwards and forwards across the arena.

- **How much can you reasonably fit in?** Take into account the time that you are likely to arrive (especially if you have to make a long journey) and the time that the fair closes. How many stands can you visit in the time available? If you assume that you will talk to someone on the stand for about ten minutes then you may think that you can visit six an hour but this is unrealistic: you have to find the stand, make your way through the crowds and wait until someone is free to speak to you. It is more realistic to assume that you will manage to visit two or three stands each hour. Give yourself time to sit and think in case you need to revise your plans and, of course, for lunch and coffee breaks. This can be a good opportunity to make notes to remind yourself of any key pieces of information that you have acquired as you might find it difficult to remember who said what once you have visited ten stands.

- **Are you going to attend any events?** Most careers fairs include other work-focused events such as CV workshops, presentations about various aspects of the recruitment process, practise psychometric tests, and mock selection day events. These are likely to be popular so find out whether you can book a place in advance, either before the event or when you arrive on the day. You may need to plan your day around these sessions as they will take place at a specific time or times whereas the exhibitors will be available all day.

- **What are you going to wear?** Find out if there are guidelines on dress provided by the event organisers. If there are not, remember that this is the day that you might meet your future employer so you will want to make a positive impression by looking smart and professional. This does not necessarily mean that you have to wear a suit but the smarter end of smart/casual is probably the order of the day. If you are particularly worried about what to wear then opt for a suit on the basis that you can dress this down by removing the jacket (and tie if applicable) if you arrive and find that everyone else is not formally dressed.

- **What are you going to say?** This may seem like an odd question to include but the initiative will be on you to direct the conversation as the person manning the stand is likely to say something along the lines of 'do you need some help?' if you are showing an interest in their organisation. There is no set formula but try to have something prepared that sums up what it is that you are interested in so that you can say something a little more coherent and professional than 'um, no, I'm fine thanks'. Something simple such as 'I am just finishing my law degree and am really interested in working for [name of organisation]/a career in [the industry in question] so can you tell me something about your graduate training scheme' will be fine. Practise a handshake and smile to go with your introduction: it can feel rather false and uncomfortable until you are used to doing it.

When the event has finished, do take some time to reflect upon the organisations that you visited and how the information that you acquired has affected your career plans. Did you find an organisation or industry that really appealed to you or has the day merely served to cross some options off your possible career list? If you have decided to make an application to one or more of the organisations that you visited, get started with it straight away rather than leaving it until the deadline is approaching. Not only can these things take more time than you envisage, it can also be the case that you will put together a better application when the event is still fresh in your mind and you are fired with enthusiasm at the prospect of working for a particular organisation.

Conversion courses

A conversion course offers a fast-track route into a non-law profession by allowing you to achieve an entry-level qualification more rapidly because you are already in possession of a degree. By way of example, a history graduate can convert their degree into a qualifying law degree without undergoing a full law degree programme by completing the Graduate Diploma in Law. This covers the core subjects in a single year thus making them eligible to take the LPC or BPTC. In the same way, you can convert your law degree into the entry qualification for any number of professions by completing the appropriate Graduate Diploma. So, as discussed earlier in this chapter, a Graduate Diploma in Social Work qualifies you to work as a social worker without the need to complete a full degree in social work.

Some conversion courses are a mandatory requirements of a particular profession—for example, you cannot work as a social worker without either a degree in social work or a conversion course that is recognised by the General Social Care Council—whereas others are not required by a governing body but are necessary to give you a grounding of knowledge in your chosen profession. For instance, there is no regulatory body that determines the qualifications necessary to work in environmental management but it would be difficult to do so without a qualification that gave you a basis of knowledge of core aspects of the work.

It would not be possible to cover the full range of conversion courses in this chapter so a few of the most popular courses have been covered to provide an illustration.

- **Postgraduate Diploma in Psychology.** This converts any degree into a recognised qualification for the purposes of the British Psychological Society which would enable you to pursue a career in any of the branches of psychology such as clinical, educational, occupational or forensic psychology, or counselling. The course covers the core areas of knowledge within the discipline—biological, cognitive, developmental, and social psychology—as well as practical experience in experimental design.
- **Postgraduate Diploma in Accounting and Finance.** This qualification enables graduates with no previous experience of finance to acquire sufficient knowledge to pursue

a range of careers in the financial sector such as risk management, corporate finance, investment banking, wealth management, and financial consultancy. It would also enable you to take an MSc in Accounting and Finance to further expand your options within the financial industry.

- **Postgraduate Diploma in Nursing.** It is possible to gain this qualification in adult nursing, child nursing, or psychiatric nursing according to your preferred career path. It is open to graduates from any discipline with no prior experience in nursing or healthcare and it offers a fast-track nursing qualification based upon two years of combined study and clinical placements.

WHERE NEXT?

It can be difficult to know what to do after graduation, especially if you harbour a lingering desire to practise law or feel as if that's what you ought to do having acquired a law degree. It is worth taking time to decide on a career direction rather than rushing into something and then changing your mind or plodding on with law just because it seems like the most sensible decision. Bear in mind that a law degree is a versatile qualification that gives you a very strong foundation in core skills that are highly desirable to employers in a range of professions. There are any number of career paths open to you with a law degree: you are not 'stuck' with law just because it was your degree choice: as this chapter has demonstrated, there are all sorts of varied and interesting careers that can be launched off the back of a law degree.

In some respects, this level of choice can present its own problems. Your position is very different to students who are set on a career as a solicitor or barrister: their goal is clear and they know what they need to do to achieve it even if doing so is not straightforward. By contrast, students who do not want to practise law have all other potential careers spread out in front of them. You might have a specific non-law career in mind or at least a range of possibilities but it may be that, like many other students, your only clear career decision is that you do not want to practise law.

Try not to let this lack of clarity worry you but work steadily to try and identify possible careers and explore whether or not they are a good match for your skills and interests. There are a number of things that you can do that will help you make the decision:

- **Visit the careers office at your university.** They are well used to advising students who do not know what to do after university and will be able to provide information about any careers that have captured your interest. They often have aptitude tests that will ask you a series of questions and suggest careers that seem suited to you based upon your answers.

- **Browse the conversion courses listed in Appendix C.** These will show you the possible career paths that you could pursue by adding a postgraduate qualification to your law degree. Perhaps one (or more) of this sounds appealing as a future career. If you do decide to obtain a further qualification but need to work to pay the course fees or cover your living expenses before embarking on further study, you should consider employment within your chosen profession as this has the dual benefit of giving you work experience as well as allowing you to earn money.

- **Look at graduate training scheme websites.** You will probably be surprised at the variety of possible careers that are available to graduates with a law degree. You will find information about the companies and the structure, content, and prospects of their training scheme to see if it appeals to you as a career. Be sure to look beyond the company information though and research the career in general before making a decision.

- **Try out careers that you think might suit you.** Rather than committing to another qualification or training course, you could find work of the same nature at a lower level or on a voluntary basis. For example, if you felt drawn to nursing, you could find work as a care assistant or find voluntary work at a hospice. Not only will this give you an opportunity to test your aptitude for and enjoyment of the job but it will also be valuable work experience if you do decide on a career in that profession.

Practical advice: new career direction

Confucius said 'find a job you love and you will never work a day in your life'. Recruitment advisor, Gregory Kinsella, is a firm believer in finding a career that you will find enjoyable and suggests that you ask yourself the following questions:

- What do you love doing?
- What job would you do even if you were not paid to do it?
- How would you spend your days if you were a millionaire?

By answering these questions, Gregory suggests that you will be able to identify possible career paths that will lead you to a job that you love and that this will lead you to be a more productive and successful worker. This is something that resonates with two law graduates who used this approach to finding non-law careers.

I love to travel, especially to remote or unusual places. I had planned to combine this with legal practice by finding a training contract in a firm with a lot of opportunities for work overseas but I decided to have a year out between my degree and LPC to have a bit of a break from studying. I wanted to travel and earn money so I found a job in Argentina teaching English. I enjoyed it so much that I took a TEFL course and now I'm qualified to teach English as a Foreign Language. I've worked in twelve different countries teaching English so far, mostly to people in the IT industry.

Tom, UWE

I have always loved animals and, for as long as I can remember, I had wanted to be a vet 'when I grew up'. Unfortunately, I grew up with no ability at all in science and so I wasn't able to take the subjects that I needed to study veterinary medicine and so law was very much a second choice for me. After graduation, I worked as an animal care assistant for a while and then trained as an RSPCA Inspector and, although it can be very harrowing to see animals living in poor conditions or that have been subjected to cruelty, it is genuinely a joy to go to work because I know that everything that I do contributes to the greater well-being of animals. I am sometimes conscious that my earning potential is nothing like it would have been if I had qualified as a solicitor but nothing comes close to the satisfaction that I get when I visit animals in the weeks and months after they have been rescued or see them being re-homed.

Sarah, University of Reading

Part V

Demonstrating employability skills

This final section of the book takes the skills that you have identified, built and focused and shows you how to demonstrate them effectively to potential employers: Chapter 11 covers demonstrating skills in writing on an application form, CV, or covering letter, while Chapter 12 deals with demonstrating skills in person at an interview or assessment centre.

Applications

INTRODUCTION

This chapter considers the various components of the applications process. It includes advice on compiling CVs, completing application forms, and writing a good covering letter. The components of each application will vary depending on the particular opportunity that you are pursuing—be it a training contract, pupillage, or a job—but every component has something in common; that is, that they communicate the employability skills that you have developed throughout your studies. By the time you have worked your way through this chapter you will know how to highlight your employability skills in whatever form is required and to tailor your application to each particular opportunity so that your application stands out from the pile on the recruiter's desk.

Earlier chapters in this book have focused on identifying and developing your portfolio of employability skills. The application stage is the first chance that you have to demonstrate those skills to potential employers. The second chance that you will get, if the application stage is successful, is likely to be an interview or some other form of face-to-face assessment. These stages are both critically important. It would be a great shame if the effort that you have put into acquiring your employability skills is not realised because you fail to highlight them effectively either on paper or in person. So, this chapter will concentrate on making your applications stand out and the next chapter deals with interviews and other face-to-face recruitment practices.

Effective CVs

The abbreviation CV stands for *curriculum vitae* which means 'the course of (my) life'. Although not every application requires a CV, it is still a very useful exercise to put one together, as the process of trying to explain *why* you will be an excellent trainee, pupil, or employee in writing will be an invaluable and transferable experience which you can draw upon when completing application forms either on paper or online. This is because the basic concept of the CV and the application form are the same: to make you sufficiently interesting to the recruiter to get you to the next stage of the recruitment process by demonstrating the selection of employability skills from your portfolio that are relevant to the *particular* opportunity that you are pursuing. An effective CV will make the recruiter want to know more about you.

At a very basic level, the CV is a document which describes your education, background, and work experience. However, a descriptive CV is unlikely to be impressive for two particular reasons:

- It does not demonstrate the employability skills that you have developed
- It is not tailored for the specific job opportunity.

There is no fixed format for a CV, and this chapter would certainly not wish to prescribe a single 'right' way of putting one together. The remainder of this section will instead focus on three key areas:

- Demonstrating your employability skills
- Structure
- Presentation.

Before taking a look at these, there is one piece of advice which is relevant to all applications: be sure that you can actually talk about everything that you put on your CV and do not embellish, augment, or invent 'truth' in order to improve your chances. A single lie kills trust and, if you have studied employment law, you should know that the mutual obligation of trust and confidence constitutes a term that is implied into all contracts of employment: so if it transpires, even after you have got the job, that you have lied on your application, then this may be sufficient for you to be fired. Moreover if you have studied criminal law then you may remember the offence of fraud by false representation—which could be argued to be made out by applying for a job with untrue information on your CV. In March 2010, Rhiannon Mackay was sentenced to six months' imprisonment after making up two grade-B A-levels on her CV to get a £23,000 per annum job with the NHS. In any event, the legal professions demand the highest standards of professional conduct. The advice is simple: keep it true and keep it demonstrable.

Demonstrating

When you are putting together your CV, you must always remember the single most important guiding principle: relate your skills and accomplishments to the recruiter's needs. Do not fall into the trap of putting together a single CV and assuming that the work is done. Since no two opportunities are the same, it should follow that no two CVs put together in support of those opportunities should be the same. There is not a 'one size fits all' solution that you can use profitably.

One technique that you can use in order to help achieve this is to make two lists —one of the skills and accomplishments that you have and the other to list the skills and attributes that are required. You can then begin to map your own list onto the sections of the CV that you think are most appropriate for demonstrating that particular employability skill. This is depicted schematically in Figure 11.1.

For example, the application might require you to demonstrate leadership skills. You might have decided that your leadership was best shown when you managed a shift in a local restaurant during a holiday job—in which case you could incorporate this into your employment history. Alternatively you may have captained a sports team, which could map onto the interests section or 'other positions of responsibility'. The choice is yours, but if you approach building a CV in this structured way, you will ensure that you do not

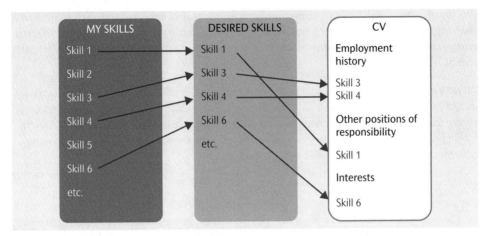

Figure 11.1 Mapping employability skills to a tailored CV

miss anything crucial that the recruiter is looking for, and you should also provide a strong focus to your CV. In many cases, it is as much about what you leave out of your CV as what you put into it. Remember that you are trying to show your motivation for the particular opportunity. Your CV should show that you have done your research and explain what it is that makes this job opening right for you: so you must explain succinctly how your past experience has shaped you to be the perfect candidate for this opportunity.

The selection of the experiences used to demonstrate your employability skills is also important. Remember that opportunities are inevitably oversubscribed and you are using your CV to try to make yourself stand out as much as possible. Most law students have a very similar background, so you should try to think whether you have any alternative experiences that make you more interesting and choose to include these, provided that they still demonstrate the required skills for the position. If you have been involved in a position of responsibility with an unusual society at university then say so: being treasurer of the university pantomime society[1] may well demonstrate financial responsibility and oral communication skills in a more unusual way than that of being treasurer of the criminal justice society.

I have read about so many experiences that demonstrate key skills, many of which are not based in the workplace, but they do show employers that the candidate has the essential skills we are looking for. I've read about the organisational skills required in arranging a stag do for 40 people abroad, the communication skills of a backpacker attempting to live with a tribe in Africa with no common language, and the team working skills of an aspiring Olympic athlete. So many of the key skills are transferable.

Field Fisher Waterhouse

Do not be afraid to use non-law work experience or part-time employment to illustrate your employability skills. Working long hours in a physically demanding job could demonstrate

---

1. Such societies do exist: **http://www.leedsuniversityunion.org.uk/clubsandsocieties/performance/pantomime/**.

the stamina required to work comparably long hours in a professional career. Similarly, working in a retail or customer service environment can have value: commercial experience, exposure to clients, and working in a high pressure environment will easily transfer to a different setting.

All work experience has value and all work experience enables skills development. Applicants shy away from mentioning work that they think is irrelevant or insufficiently prestigious whereas they should think about what they gained from the experience and tell us how it relates to what we're looking for. Leaving things out can leave tell-tale holes in the CV which can raise suspicion or be brought up suddenly at interview—if they get that far!

Training Partner

On a similar theme, take care not to overlook the section on 'interests'. This section might enable you to provide recent evidence of balancing university work commitments with extra-curricular activities (and thus demonstrating time management skills) or to demonstrate team working. Always bear in mind the transferable skills that are relevant to this particular application and find the best, and most natural, way to incorporate them into your CV.

When you are documenting your achievements and experiences, you should use strong active verbs and actual facts or figures for impact. Active verbs are those which suggest motivation, action and dynamism. You will find some examples of such verbs in Table 11.1.

Table 11.1 Active verbs

accomplished	established	motivated
devised	contributed	negotiated
sustained	produced	initiated
arranged	implemented	developed
mediated	researched	wrote

You should also aim to be concise. It is perfectly acceptable within a CV to use bullet points and note form. You should try to provide no more than two or three bullet points per experience whilst answering two key questions:

• What did you get out of the experience?

• How did you make a personal impact?

There is no real room for elaboration, so keep focused on demonstrating your skills and stick to brief factual information.

A common weakness with CVs is listing abstract skills without providing context. You should therefore always provide a context in which to present your employability skills. Remember that your CV is a means of demonstrating skills, not just listing them—so it is not enough to say that you are an excellent team player without providing evidence to back up your statement.

Finally, focus on demonstrating the employability skills that you do have to offer rather than trying to contrive a way to include those that you do not. You are trying to convey confidence, motivation, demonstrable skills, and experience, so keep your CV optimistic and positive in order to create a strong and favourable image.

Structure

There is no single correct format for putting together a CV, but a typical CV would contain the following sections:

- **Name and contact information.** You do not need to include information regarding gender, age, or marital status.

- **Education and qualifications.** This section should set out— in reverse chronological order (that is, most recent first)—your university and school education. You should set out each of the subjects that you studied in each of the years and list your percentage marks where you have them. You will have to disclose them at some point, so you might as well do so now. When listing your module results for each year, put the highest scoring module first, so that is the first impression that you will make on the reader. For school, you should list your A-level (or equivalent) results and grades. You do not need to list your GCSE results individually. For these, you can just provide a summary of grades, although (on the assumption that you have them to have got this far) you should state 'including Maths and English'.

- **Academic awards and scholarships.** If you have won any prizes or scholarships, you could draw attention to them by giving them their own section heading in your CV. Again, if you have supporting facts, then use them. It is more compelling to say 'awarded highest mark for dissertation (82%)' than 'awarded highest mark for dissertation' (which could be much less impressive in percentage terms).

- **Employment history.** You can break down your employment history into different sections for ease of reading. For example, you could use subheadings of legal, commercial, and voluntary to distinguish between your work experiences. You should also avoid using 'relevant work experience' as a heading, since it suggests that all your undocumented work experience is irrelevant!

- **Other positions of responsibility/interests.** This section allows you to depict yourself as a well-rounded, interesting, and useful individual as well as allowing you another chance to demonstrate transferable employability skills. Pick a few (no more than two or three) activities or areas of responsibility and demonstrate your genuine enthusiasm for them or the impact that you have made rather than just putting together an uninspiring list. Try to find interesting ways to express your hobbies and interests. If you can find a link back to a core employability skill then so much the better. You do not have to state the skill explicitly (in fact, it would be quite contrived to do so). Have a look at Table 11.2 for some examples drawn from the life experiences of one of the authors. Recent examples of activity and responsibility are more impressive than anything that you might have done at school. Do not 'run out of steam' towards the end of your CV. Every section within it is an opportunity to impress. This section can not only set you apart by showing that you are a well-rounded individual, but can also lead to some enjoyable interview discussion, particularly if you are fortunate enough to share a common interest with a member of the panel.

Table 11.2 Interests and recreational activities

Basic information	Expanded information	Implied employability skills
Sport: Played football for the College	Sport: Captained the College 3rd XI at football	Leadership Team working
Travel: Norway and Mauritius	Travel: Completed the Olympic bobsleigh run at Lillehammer and did an undersea walk in Mauritius	Initiative
Music: Guitar and piano	Music: Played lead guitar in a 7-piece R&B band; self-taught piano	Independent learning Team working Self-motivation

- **Languages.** If you speak other languages, then you can include them towards the end of your CV. Include a short indication of your level of proficiency, and be honest, just in case there is someone on the interview panel who also speaks the same language. So 'fluent Italian' and 'colloquial Czech', is better than 'Speaks Italian and Czech'.
- **References.** You can give details of referees at the end of your CV if you wish. It is perfectly acceptable to say 'References available upon request' if you prefer, or to omit this section all together, since it is a reasonable assumption that you would provide references when asked for them.

Presentation

There are a few pointers on presentation that you should also bear in mind when putting your CV together:

- **Be consistent.** There is no single right format, but when you pick a style for headings or other elements of your CV, then you should stick to it. Inconsistency in the use of capitalisation, bold, or italic fonts, will look sloppy. Remember that you want your CV to stand out for the right reasons.
- **Use sub headings and bullet points** to make navigation easier for the reader. Recruiters will have many CVs to read, so make their lives as easy as possible, by avoiding a prose-heavy structure.
- **Use standard margins.** Do not cram information onto the page. A tightly packed CV is not only daunting to look at, but it also sends a message that you may be struggling to express yourself concisely or that you have included too much information within your CV, some of which might be of questionable relevance.
- **Keep it short.** Your CV should ideally be no more than two sides of A4. It is a summary of your experience and your employability skills and not a report. The recruiter will need to read it quickly and get a good first impression of your suitability for the opportunity.
- **Keep it professional.** You should avoid the use of novelty fonts or gimmicks. Instead, keep to 'conservative' or traditional fonts like Aerial or Times New Roman presented in a sensible size for reading (no smaller than 11 pt). Also, make sure that your contact email address is appropriate: you may wish to be **thelawgenius@hotmail.co.uk** or **mrloverlover@gmail.com** among your friends, but acquire a less controversial address

for your CV if you do not have one. The same advice applies to voicemail messages. If you are giving out your mobile number, check your voicemail greeting to make sure that it conveys the sort of message that a recruiter would expect to hear. Finally, do not attempt to use humour in your CV.

- **Proofread, then proofread again.** There is no room for typos in a CV. You need to demonstrate excellent drafting skills and attention to detail so do get at least one other person to read it for content as well as presentation. Remember that you are not bound to comply with their suggestions, but you should at least carefully consider each point that is raised.

- **Print it carefully and keep a copy.** Ensure that your CV is printed square on the page and that the quality of the print is good. Laser printing is probably best although a good inkjet printer can also do a perfectly acceptable job, provided that its cartridges are not running low. Finally, keep a copy of the CV and note on it which particular opportunity it was written for: since your CV should be tailored to each application, you will need to know which one to read again before your interview.

CVs have to look as though they are the product of care and effort. If your CV looks shoddy, it sends the message that you are not bothered to make it look professional, and if you can't be bothered to do that then it raises questions about whether you'd care about the quality of your work if we employed you.

HR consultant

Practical exercise: improving a CV

Having read through this section, you should have a much better feel for the way in which you should compile, structure, and present your CV so as to best demonstrate your employability skills for a particular opportunity. This next exercise will help you to consolidate your knowledge by reviewing and improving a CV.

Steve is in the final year of his law degree and is applying to become a police officer. Everything else that you need to know about him is contained in the CV that follows (see Figure 11.2). Take a look at the CV and make constructive suggestions for its improvement. The competencies relevant to the role of a police constable[2] are:

- Community and customer focus
- Effective communication
- Personal responsibility
- Problem solving
- Resilience
- Respect for race and diversity
- Team working.

You will find an annotated version of this CV and some suggestions as to its strengths and weaknesses on the Online Resource Centre.

---

2. <http://policerecruitment.homeoffice.gov.uk/documents/pc-competencies2835.pdf?view=Binary>.

Steve Jenkins
29 Albermarle Terrace
Reading, Berkshire RG3 2NX

Email: PCSteve2013@gmail.com
Telephone: 0118 496 2328
Mobile: 07700 900263

EDUCATION AND QUALIFICATIONS

2004–2011 *St Polycarp's School, Winnersh*
- GCSE's: Art (C), History (A), Geography (B), Maths (B), English (A*), Sociology (A), French (B), Physics (C), Chemistry (C), Physical Education (A*)
- A-levels: English Literature (B), History (A) and Sociology (B)

2011–present *Wallingford University, LL.B. Law (Honours)*
- *First year:* Property Law (46%), English Legal Systems and Methods (62%); The Law of Contract (61%), Criminal Law (71%)
- *Second Year:* Tort Law (55%), EU Law (60%), Trusts (58%), Criminal Justice (68%)
- *Third Year:* Criminology, Evidence, Dissertation (on 'Policing the Internet' supervised by Professor Vallum)

ACADEMIC AWARDS and SCHOLARSHIPS

- Awarded the Peter Vincent Memorial Prize for the highest mark in criminology coursework.
- Given a University scholarship of £300 towards a vacation trip to the International Criminal Court in the Hague (Netherlands). This was valuable as it included a 90 minute talk on the mandate, structure and activities of the Court which was useful for my criminal justice studies in international justice.

WORK EXPERIENCE

September 2011–present

Bar Staff then Bar Manager, The Chien et Canard, Whitley
- General bar work, then promoted after four months to be put in charge of all aspects of running the bar. This was in direct response to positive customer feedback.
- Involvement with police officers and preserving law and order as and when altercations occurred
- Dealt with customers at busy periods and handled customer complaints especially when the kitchen staff were overworked
- Also played in the pub football team and captained them from 14th in the league to 4th, narrowly missing out on promotion

October 2011–present

Mooting Officer for the University Student Law Society
I was elected as Mooting Officer for the Student Law Society in October 2011 and have had a very positive affect on Mooting Activities within the Society. We entered three external competitions, and I organised an internal competition in order to choose our teams. This required effective communication and problem solving skills and also to respect race and diversity as teams were selected entirely on merit and not any preconceived ideas as to how barristers should appear.

May 2012

Two day work placement at Silva & Parva Criminal Solicitors
- Work-shadowed solicitor in criminal law firm
- Proofread court documents
- Spent a day in the magistrate's court with cases that included drink-driving, assault and robbery.

July 2011

Two week work placement at Fox & Gus Criminal Solicitors
- Attended client meetings and briefings with criminal barristers
- Attended the Crown Court and assisted in compiling court papers
- Researched legal precedents relating to possession of indecent images online. This was also useful for part of my dissertation as well as observing how criminal law worked in practise.

June 2010–June 2011

Plasterer's labourer
- Worked long hours doing physical work to exceed client expectations

INTERESTS
- Football (playing and coaching local under 9's)
- Travel
- Music (eclectic tastes, also taught myself to play the guitar)
- Reading and Films (especially crime thrillers)

LANGUAGES
- French, some Spanish

OTHER INFORMATION
- Male
- DOB 16 June 1992
- Clean driving licence
- Single

REFEREES

I have two referees (one academic, one personal) whose details are available on request.

Figure 11.2 Sample CV

Covering letters

Covering letters are generally sent with a CV in applications where an application form is not used, although some application forms may require a free-text response that is similar in its assessment objectives to a standalone letter. The purposes of the covering letter are:

- To highlight your key employability skills and your suitability for the role
- To 'introduce' yourself and the CV or application form that accompanies the letter
- To persuade the recruiter that it is worth taking the time to read your CV or application form.

The covering letter is vital in creating a favourable impression. So many applications can be rejected just from the first paragraph of the covering letter if for example there are spelling mistakes, which is not as uncommon as you would think. The covering letter is also the first real impression of your character that your potential employer will have. You have to strike the right balance between demonstrating confidence that you are up to the job but not a brashness that will make people question whether you will fit in with other employees.

As with the CV it really is important to keep your covering letter relevant to the job you are applying for. Recruitment is time consuming for employers. They would much rather have a one-page letter full of relevant information than a lengthy letter which demonstrates lots of qualities which aren't relevant to the job.

Graeme Perry, Sykes Anderson solicitors

Applications can fail on the basis of an uninspiring covering letter alone, so it is essential that you give this important component of the application process as much attention as the others. Do not fall into the common trap of spending all your effort on the CV only to ruin it by dashing off a quick covering letter to accompany it. Take a look at the example covering letter in Figure 11.3. You should see immediately that, although it does the job of introducing the CV, it hardly motivates the reader to find out more:

17 Acacia Drive
Bristol
BS12 6DN

15 March 2013

Silva & Parva Criminal Solicitors
Hamilton Drive
Woking
Surrey
GU36 1FX

Dear Sir/Madam

I am writing to apply for the training contract advertised on your website.

Please find enclosed my CV for your perusal.

With grateful thanks

Jasmine

Figure 11.3 Sample covering letter 1

Not only does the covering letter give you the opportunity to demonstrate your employ-ability skills in greater depth (helping to reinforce the answer to 'why me?' which is con-tained within your CV by picking out key highlights and developing them) but also to articulate what it is about this particular opportunity that has given you the motivation to apply (the 'why you?' question). Just as your CV should be individually written for each application, then so should your covering letter. You need to demonstrate that you have researched the opportunity, firm, or chambers properly and to convey what is it about them that makes working for them such a compelling idea for you. This should also show that your application to them is based on an informed decision, showing care and a genuine interest (and proving that you are not just providing a standard letter). Potentially relevant factors that you could consider here are:

- Specialism (Why do your areas of interest match theirs? Did you do similar work experience? Did you study a relevant option? Did you write a dissertation that is relevant?)

- Size (Is a smaller employer more appealing? If so, why? Or do you prefer a bigger employer? Why?)

- Location (If local or regional employer, do you have links with their area?)

- Previous links (Have you had work experience there?)

- What have you learned from your work experience as a whole that has led you to the conclusion that this is the right opportunity for you?

⚫ You will find a downloadable template that will help you to construct this section of your covering letter on the Online Resource Centre.

As with CVs, there are some points on structure and presentation that should be borne in mind when writing your covering letter.

Structure

There is no single correct way in which to structure a covering letter, but one example of a logical and coherent approach follows:

- **Introduction.** Explain why you are writing and be precise in what it is that you are wanting to achieve. If the opportunity was advertised, then say where you saw it; if not, explain why you are making a more speculative application. Remember that if the advertisement stated a particular reference number or other identifier, then you should state this in your covering letter.

- **Why you?** Demonstrate that you have done your research and avoid generalisations. This is where you provide your answers to the questions that you considered in the previous section. This is the section that really demonstrates your motivation.

- **Why me?** This section should show what it is that sets you out from the other candidates, by drawing on and expanding the most important highlights from your CV and explaining how they are relevant to the employability skills most vital to this opportunity. If you are already in possession of the selection criteria or the core competencies of the position, make sure that you address them all. Similarly, this section could amplify something from your work experience and explain what you learned from it that is relevant to the employer. This section demonstrates your employability skills.

- **Sign off.** The closing part of your letter should be scrupulously polite and professional. Thank the recruiter for their time in considering your application, state your availability for interview, and ask that they contact you with any queries.

Presentation

The points from the previous section that apply to the presentation of CVs also apply to covering letters, along with the following additional advice:

- **Keep it short (again!)**. Your covering letter should be no longer than a single side of A4.
- **Normal letter writing conventions apply.** Your letter should be formatted according to the usual conventions for professional business correspondence (your address and the date on the top right; recipient's name and address beneath it to the left; salutation; body; closing; signature).
- **Get the name and address correct.** You may well be making several applications, so do take extra care to ensure that you have addressed your letter to the right place. If you do not know that name of the person to whom it should be addressed, then take the trouble to find out: try to avoid having to use 'Dear Sir/Madam' if at all possible, as this can be indicative of a lack of effort.
- **Remember to sign it.** If you are sending your letter by post, then remember to sign it. This may sound obvious, but in the heat of application writing, this final step can be overlooked. Remember that many legal documents still require a signature for their execution, so you do not want to send a message that you can forget to do so. If you are providing an electronic copy of your covering letter, you could consider getting a scanned copy of your signature to include within the document.

Bearing in mind the advice in the previous sections, Jasmine's dull covering letter could have been presented in a much more engaging way (see Figure 11.4).

Application forms

Application forms can be thought of as a halfway house between a CV and covering letter and an interview. They give you the opportunity to respond to the questions that are set so as to give more insight into you, your motivation, and your employability skills than can be communicated with a CV and letter alone. They are also a great benefit to recruiters in that every applicant is working to the same template so they are easier to compare alongside each other. However, given that every applicant is being asked the same questions, you need to find ways to make your responses stand out from the crowd. Remember that you will also be giving recruiters the opportunity to evaluate your written communication skills and your ability to put together a persuasive argument. While you will not be putting forward legal arguments on your form, you are still trying to argue that you are the best candidate for the position and supporting your answer with evidence.

Application forms are often designed around a specific list of evaluation criteria that are drawn up to reflect the profile of the desired candidate. Even if the recruiter has not published a personal profile or a job description, the questions that are being asked on the form should give you some insight into the characteristics that are being sought.

Application forms typically contain four main sorts of questions:

- **Factual questions.** These are the easy questions to answer, requiring you to state factually verifiable information such as personal details, education and qualifications, and work experience.
- **Skills/competency questions.** These are the questions that require you to demonstrate your skills and give you the chance to make your application distinctive.

17 Acacia Drive
Bristol
BS12 6DN

15 March 2013

Mr Ian Smallwood
Human Resources Manager
Silva & Parva Criminal Solicitors
Hamilton Drive
Woking
Surrey
GU36 1FX

Your reference: SP/125302

Dear Mr Smallwood,

Further to the advertisement on your website, I wish to apply for a training contract to start in 2014. I enclose my CV.

I have been interested in criminal law since studying it in the first year of my degree and will be writing my final-year dissertation on the legal issues surrounding the forfeiture of assets in criminal proceedings. Having completed a work placement in the criminal department of a more general firm of solicitors, I firmly believe that I would thrive in a more specialist environment. This makes training with Silva & Parva particularly appealing, since it is not only a specialist criminal practice, but also a key focus of its work is asset forfeiture.

I was awarded the Law School Prize for the best performance in criminal law at the end of my first year, achieving a combined mark of 82%. As well as my legal work experience, I have spent the last two years working part-time as a waitress in a local Italian restaurant. This has given me experience of customer care in a commercial setting and working long and unusual hours in a highly-pressured setting, all of which are important attributes in delivering the highest quality legal services. In addition, I have volunteered as an appropriate adult, spending time at the local police station and gaining first-hand experience of the criminal law in action.

Thank you for considering my application. Should you have any queries, then do please contact me directly. I am available for interview at any time before the start of the next academic year on 23 September.

Yours sincerely

Miss Jasmine Hughes

Figure 11.4 Sample covering letter 2

- **The 'big' question.** This question is usually open ended and invites you to explain something about why you are applying for this particular position and/or why you think you will be successful. Answers to these questions can often make the difference between being invited to interview or not.
- **Commercial awareness questions.** These questions will test your understanding of the commercial environment in which you are seeking to work and the business needs of your clients.

You will find guidance on developing your commercial awareness in Chapter 12.

The trick to answering competency questions confidently is to think about the skills that are being tested by the question and to make sure that your answers demonstrate your proficiency in those skills. Perhaps the most effective way for you to structure your answers is by taking a reflective view of your past experiences: this should ensure that you answer the question and give adequate thought to the sorts of response that the recruiters are hoping to see. To help you do this, there are two similar approaches best remembered by their acronyms STAR and SOARA. There is quite a degree of overlap between the two, although SOARA perhaps encourages greater reflection on the learning experience. The elements of each are set out in Table 11.3.

Table 11.3 STAR and SOARA techniques

		Questions to consider
Situation	Situation	What was the situation in which you demonstrated this particular skill? Put your example in context, but keep this part brief (especially if there is a word limit for your answer) as you want to focus on demonstrating your employability skills.
Task	Objective	What were you trying to achieve from the situation? What were you asked to do? What did you decide was the key issue or priority to address?
Action	Action	What did you do? Why did you do it? What were the alternatives? Why did you choose the course of action that you did? This part of your answer should demonstrate your decision-making ability and emphasise the skills that you used or developed in taking this action.
Results	Results	What was the outcome of your action? Give evidence to support the results if at all possible.
	Aftermath	What did you learn from this experience? Would you do anything different if you were faced with a similar situation again? Have you used this learning since?

Imagine that you were asked to give an example of a time when you motivated others. Using the STAR/SOARA technique, you could structure a response as shown in Table 11.4.

Table 11.4 STAR and SOARA example

		Give an example of a time when you had to organise others
Situation	**Situation**	I wanted our university to enter a team into the negotiation competition but the student law society negotiating officer had not organised any training, practice sessions, or selected a team and claimed that they were too busy with their studies to do so.
Task	**Objective**	In order to get a team together, I needed to find students that wanted to negotiate and facilitate training and team selection. I also had to get the university entered into the competition itself.
Action	**Action**	I told the law society that I wanted to take responsibility for getting negotiation under way and they were supportive. The negotiation officer was also happy as it transpired that they had not wanted the office in the first place. I asked the head of department for permission to email all the students in my year and persuaded one of the lecturers to give a couple of sessions on negotiation. I booked a room, organised the students into two groups, got the law society to pay for and provide nibbles, and made sure that the lecturer was available. After that I asked if any of the students wanted to negotiate competitively, even though it was short notice. Six did, and I asked another lecturer to judge a mini internal competition and select the winners to represent the university. Once we had a team, I asked the head of department to arrange to pay the competition entrance fee, which she did.
Results	**Results**	Our team entered the competition and reached the regional finals, narrowly missing out on progressing to the national finals by one place.
	Aftermath	I learned that it is important to take the initiative in making things happen if you want them to, while respecting the positions of parties that might be undermined by my doing so. I also realised that it is important to start organising as soon as possible: although we did well on this occasion, we may have done better if we had had more time to practise beforehand.

The STAR/SOARA technique is also very useful in competency-based interviewing. See Chapter 12.

> **Practical exercise: preparing answers**
>
> Have a look at the following skill/competency questions that could potentially appear on application forms:
>
> - What is your greatest achievement to date, and why?
> - Give an example of a situation in which you had to use your initiative in order to achieve a particular goal
> - When have you had to negotiate a successful outcome to a difficult situation?
> - Give an example of a time when you had to work as part of a successful team. What role did you play and how did you contribute to the success of that team?
>
> ☾ Using the STAR/SOARA technique outlined above, work out your answer to one or more of these questions. You will find a downloadable template on the Online Resource Centre to help you.

Dealing with difficulties

Whether you are applying with a CV, letter, or application form, you must make sure that you explain features within your application that might otherwise appear unusual, such as disappointing exam results or a career break.

. . . .

If there are mitigating circumstances then we need to know. Applicants must put them down, even if they are of an intensely private nature —as such things often are. But without them, we can only take an application on face value, which may ultimately be to the detriment of the applicant. An unexplained gap from study arouses suspicion, but not if the student had a significant illness that they eventually overcame.

Head of HR, City of London law firm

. . . .

Of course, the answers to these questions are very personal, so it is difficult to give specific advice in a book like this. However, your commentary should show that:

- Whatever happened was anomalous
- That is was due to something specific
- That the cause has been resolved.

For example:

> My second year exam results were disappointing and well below that which I achieved in my first and final years. However, this was due to a significant medical issue that greatly impacted my ability to concentrate. This was cured over the summer break before my third year, in which I was able to resume my usual level of performance.

This demonstrates:

- A recognition of the fact that there was a dip in academic performance which the applicant has had the maturity to bring out into the open, rather than hoping that the recruiter would not spot the poor results

- A specific cause of the poor performance—illness—but without going too deeply into the actual diagnosis or reasons. It is generally sufficient to give an indication of your specific cause rather than a very detailed explanation. This could always be addressed at interview if the recruiter still wants to explore deeper

- A reassurance that the cause has been resolved, together with evidence that performance has improved since then, leading credibility to the fact that the dip was anomalous.

Similarly, if you had a career break, then think about what you were doing during that time, work out what employability skills you developed, and consider discussing that briefly in your application.

Chapters 5 and 7 will give you guidance on the employability skills developed through social activities and different forms of work experience.

Finally, if you are still finding it difficult to answer a particular question, then seek guidance from your personal tutor or university careers service.

Choosing and using referees

At some point in the applications process you will need to provide details of referees. Most applications will require two, although some can require three. There is a distinction to be made between referees and references, which is quite simple. Referees provide references: usually directly to the prospective employer. It is not usual to provide your own letters of recommendation, endorsement, or testimonial, even though this is often standard practice overseas. Employers will contact referees and ask for references (these will either be provided online, on a standard form, or as a free-format letter).

You should not use a friend or relative as a referee for obvious reasons!

The main categories of referee are:

- **Academic referee.** This will usually be your personal tutor, although can be an alternative academic member of staff that knows you well, such as a dissertation supervisor. They can comment on your studies, contribution to university life, predicted degree classification (if you have not graduated), or confirmation of actual results (if you have).

- **Work referee.** If you have completed a work placement or mini pupillage, then a work referee is very useful. If you are applying to a place that you have already worked, then remember that they will already know you and will undoubtedly take up internal references (formal or informal) in any case. In this instance, you should avoid using a work reference from that employer unless you are advised otherwise. It is worth checking. Remember also that the transferable employability skills you will have acquired from non-law or other voluntary work are also greatly valued, so do not be afraid to provide an alternative employer if you need to do so.

- **Personal referee.** Personal referees are usually asked to give some sort of good character reference rather than a specific evaluation of your studies, potential, or work experience. It would add credibility to your application if your personal referee is someone with good standing in the community or who works in a recognised profession: the sort of person that would be able to endorse a passport application (such as a doctor, minister of religion, member of a professional body, or other public office holder). They should have known you reasonably well for a good length of time (upwards of three years is ideal).

Having identified your potential referees, the next step is to ask them if they will act as a referee. Not only is it good manners to do so, but receiving a reference request out of the blue does not necessarily guarantee a glowing answer:

I sometimes get requests from students who haven't bothered to ask first. That's just rude. I always send a reference but it is normally very brief and factual and, if I am asked about interpersonal skills or communications or team working, I will always say 'This student did not ask me if I would be willing to provide a reference'. It speaks volumes.

Lecturer

If your referee is willing to act, then there are two more things that you should do:

- Tell them what your plans are, what you are applying for, and what areas of your experience or character you would like them to endorse if possible. Give them an up-to-date copy of your CV and, if you have them, the details of the position or the person specification for the job for which you are applying.

- Make sure that they know when they need to return their reference by and ensure that they will be available and able to complete the reference in time. Ask them if they would be kind enough to let you know when the reference is submitted. This will prevent you having to nag (which is irritating). If, however, you have not heard from them and the deadline is approaching, you should make further contact once to remind them—politely—that the reference they agreed to give is due. Politeness is key here—remember that you need your referees to say positive things about you, so do not create a negative impression by being too aggressive just before they sit down to write your reference.

WHERE NEXT?

By now, you should have realised that law students have a wealth of employability skills to offer. The advice in this chapter will help you to communicate and evidence those skills in whatever form of application you are required to make and to make your application stand out from the rest of the crowd. The application process will vary depending on your desired career path, but they all have the same key point in common: you need to identify the skills required for the job and explain and demonstrate that not only that you have them but have also continued to develop them. If your application is successful, then it will inevitably lead on to one or more forms of face-to-face assessment—the interview being the most common. It is this final aspect of the recruitment process that we will be looking at in the last chapter.

Interviews and other recruitment practices

INTRODUCTION

This chapter assumes that your application has been successful and that you have moved on from the application stage to what is usually the final step before an offer: the interview. It also considers other forms of face-to-face activities that you could be required to undertake on an assessment day. Interview technique is an employability skill in itself, and you must take every opportunity to develop it well before being assessed in person. This chapter covers preparation for, participation in, and reflection on 'traditional' interviews before turning to consider activities that can form part of a day in an assessment centre. It includes sections on increasing your general legal and ethical awareness which are areas that are frequently probed at interview. After studying this chapter, you should feel better prepared and more confident to tackle this last hurdle and to ensure that the efforts that you have put in to developing and demonstrating your employability skills are suitably rewarded by gaining an offer.

The entirety of the book so far will have enabled you to identify and develop your employability skills portfolio and to have demonstrated them successfully in an application. Your final opportunity to demonstrate those skills to potential employers comes in the interview or some other form of face-to-face assessment. While your application must have communicated your employability skills sufficiently well to have got you this far, your success in face-to-face assessment will materially depend on your ability to continue to exemplify and demonstrate those skills. Interview and assessment technique is a key skill to develop: most people find interviews quite stressful, and it is only through proper preparation that you will be able to face them with confidence and not let any nerves get in the way of demonstrating that you are the best candidate for the position.

Interviews

The face-to-face interview is the most common means of final selection. Remember, first of all, that by the time that you reach the interview stage, most of the competition has already been dealt with. Take a look at Figure 12.1 which shows typical statistics from Kingsley Napley.

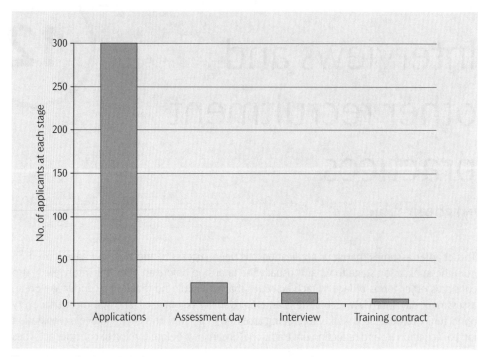

Figure 12.1 Application statistics for training contracts at Kingsley Napley

Each year, the firm receives over 300 applications for five training contract positions. Typically, 24 applicants are invited to an assessment day with 10 to 12 subsequently being offered an interview. So, 8% of applicants reach the assessment centre of whom roughly half make it to interview. This means that reaching the interview stage at Kingsley Napley puts you ahead of 96% of the other applicants and, statistically speaking, gives you a 50% chance of being offered a training contract.

The situation is similar for pupillage. For example, 5 Essex Court offers two pupillages, with 30 applicants reaching first round interviews and 10 reaching the second round. Chambers tend not to publicise the number of applicants they receive as this could deter candidates: typically though, sets receive between 150 and 800 or so applications. The advice here is not to be deterred: without applying you will never have a chance of reaching interview. Instead, focus your efforts on making your applications as good as you possibly can.

Chapter 11 deals with all aspects of constructing strong applications.

Employers also invest considerable sums of money to ensure that they recruit the very best candidates and would not be talking to you if they did not think that you had a realistic prospect of success. So, if you have been successful in reaching the interview stage, you are starting from a very positive position. That does not mean that the interview stage will not be challenging, but you have absolutely everything to gain.

Since the interview is your last chance to demonstrate that you are the most suitable candidate, you will need to make sure that you are properly prepared. Although you cannot possibly know everything that you could be asked, careful preparation, research, and practice should maximise your chances of success.

Preparation

Your preparation for the interview falls into several areas:

- Logistical and administrative preparation for the interview
- Understanding different types of interview
- Creating a favourable first impression
- Researching the employer
- Thinking about the sorts of questions you might be asked
- Thinking about the sorts of questions that you could ask
- Practising your interview skills in a mock interview.

Logistical and administrative preparation

There are two key points to bear in mind before the interview to make sure that the event itself is as stress-free as possible:

- **Know where to go.** Although you might think that a quick look at Google Maps might be adequate preparation, you would be surprised at how difficult it can sometimes be to find an interview venue, particularly if it is in an unfamiliar location. Make sure that you know exactly where you are going and, to be absolutely certain, consider doing a 'dry run' a few days before your interview.

Practical advice: London pupillage interviews

If you have a pupillage interview at a weekend, the normal entrances to the Inns of Court will be locked. Avoid a panic rush around the outside of the Inns by noting that Lincoln's Inn can be reached via Lincoln's Inn Fields; Middle and Inner Temple via Tudor Street, and Gray's Inn via Gray's Inn Road.

- **Do not be late.** Although a practice run might sound a little excessive (particularly if you live a long way away), it does help to avoid you being late for your interview. There is no excuse for lateness except for some sort of natural disaster or other extraordinary event. Sheer weight of traffic or a train delayed by 20 minutes will probably not be acceptable excuses. Arriving late to an interview communicates a whole host of negatives: a lack of organisational skills, weak time management, poor project management (if you think of getting from home to an interview as a travel project with stages and deadlines). Moreover, it is discourteous to the interviewer and the firm, as arriving late could affect the schedule for the rest of the candidates. In the worst possible scenario, candidates who arrive late without good excuse have been turned away immediately without interview. To minimise the chances of the embarrassment of late arrival, use your practice run to get an approximate timing for travel, but remember to take account of any possible changes. If you have a trial run on a Sunday afternoon, but your interview is at 9.15am on a Tuesday, then will the rush hour affect your timings? Plan to arrive at least 30 minutes early. If the interview is a long distance away, then consider staying somewhere closer with friends or family, or, if budget allows, a hotel or B&B. If the worst does happen and you think you will be unavoidably detained by something exceptional, then ring ahead at the earliest possible opportunity and explain the situation.

- **Know what to expect.** Your invitation to interview will usually tell you what sort of interview format to expect. If it does not, then you could make contact and ask if there is any further information available about the interview format or procedure.

Types of interview

There are three main types of interview that you might encounter throughout the recruitment process. You should remember that you could have to participate in a combination of interview types as part of selection:

- **One-to-one interviews.** These interviews involve you and a single interviewer. They are often well structured, so that the interviewer has a clear set of questions and evaluation criteria that will be applied to all candidates. Many candidates find the one-to-one interview less stressful than panel interviews although it will certainly be more than a casual conversation.

- **Panel interviews.** Panel interviews typically involve between two and five interviewers. Members of the panel will take it in turn to ask questions, and each member would typically been given a certain competency (or set of competencies) to evaluate. Candidates often find panel interviews quite a daunting prospect, although, with the right preparation, they can actually be a stimulating and enjoyable experience.

- **Telephone interview.** Telephone interviews are sometimes used as a pre-screening exercise. You will be given a time to expect a call (or, occasionally, a time and a number to call) and the details of the person to whom you will be speaking. You should prepare for a telephone interview as thoroughly as you would for a face-to-face interview and, in particular, make sure that you have a quiet place to take the call, so that you will be able to hear properly and not be distracted. Try to avoid taking telephone interviews on your mobile phone if at all possible, as you would not want your interview to be interrupted by an intermittent signal.

Creating a favourable first impression

Psychological research has shown that it takes one-tenth of a second to judge someone and make our first impression.[1] It is therefore vital that you do all that you can to make sure the stranger you have just met feels positively towards you. Since first impressions are more heavily influenced by non-verbal communications that verbal ones, this section will concentrate primarily on appearance and manner. The two most important points to bear in mind here are:

- **Dress appropriately.** The way in which you dress conveys a great deal about you. No matter how you might choose to dress outside the workplace, conventional and conservative formal business dress is essential. This remains the case, even if there is a 'smart casual' dress policy at the employer or you are being interviewed somewhere that subscribes to the idea of 'dress down Friday'.

....

It is important that candidates present themselves professionally as we are in a professional environment, so dressing smartly is a must. More often than not candidates do get it right and come to the interview looking very smart, sometimes even smarter than their interviewers, but I do remember a time when we had one candidate turn up with a completely see-through blouse on with nothing over the top.

Amelia Spinks, Field Fisher Waterhouse

....
....

1. J Willis and A Todorov, 'First impressions: Making up your mind after 100ms exposure to a face' (2006) 17 Psychological Science 592.

Table 12.1 Interview dress

Men	Women
Black, dark grey, or dark blue suit: check in advance to see if it needs dry cleaning or pressing to avoid the crumpled look.	
Keep hair neat and avoid esoteric styles or colours.	
Ironed white shirt with discreet, understated tie.	Ironed white blouse.
Plain black socks.	No bare legs.
	Take a spare pair of tights with you in case of last-minute ladders.
Polished black shoes.	Court shoes: clean, black, and with no more than a two-inch heel.
Shave (if normally clean shaven): no designer stubble.	Keep any make-up simple.
No earrings.	No more than a single pair of simple earrings.
Keep jewellery simple and remove visible piercings.	
Avoid wearing overpowering scent or aftershave: you are going to an interview, not out on a date.	

- **Be polished from the moment you arrive.** Turn off your mobile phone just before entering the interview venue (but not before, just in case there is a need for you to be contacted). Try to project an air of purposeful, but calm, confidence as you arrive in the building. Remember to be friendly to everyone you meet. You may be being watched and it is not unknown for reception staff to be asked for their impressions of candidates at the end of the interview session. Moreover, if you are successful the people that you have met will be your future colleagues, and you do not want them to remember you as 'the one with attitude from the interview day'. While you are waiting to be called, sit calmly: avoid fiddling with your mobile phone (remember that you should have turned it off by now anyway!) or listening to your iPod. Have a final check on your appearance one last time just before you go in to the interview itself.

As a final word of warning, do not divulge information concerning your application/interview strategy if you get into discussions with other candidates:

A graduate recruiter once reported to me that she had overheard two candidates discussing their applications in the firm's lift whilst on their way to be interviewed. One mentioned that the firm they were at was a 'backup option' but the candidate didn't realise that the graduate recruiter was in the same lift!

Juliet Tomlinson, careers advisor

Researching the employer

While you should have already undertaken a great deal of research on your prospective employer before completing your application form or covering letter, you must make sure that you refresh your memory prior to the interview. The types of information that you will need to find out will vary depending on whether you are seeking a training contract, pupillage or a job opening outside the traditional branches of the profession, but, regardless of this, the general principle is the same. You are likely to be asked questions regarding your motivation for applying and you will be able to draw on your bank of information to demonstrate your knowledge and enthusiasm for that opportunity. You will also be able to show that your understanding of the employer means something positive to you.

Key information to gather in advance of the interview should include:

- **Firms of solicitors.** You should find out the key areas of practice: are there particular areas of law in which the firm particularly specialises or has a good reputation? Does the firm have particularly noteworthy clients? Have they been involved in any recent transactions (commercial) or cases? What is the structure of their training contract? Where are they based? Are there possibilities for overseas secondment?

- **Chambers.** You must know chambers' areas of practice. In addition, you should make sure that you revise your own legal knowledge in these areas in the event of a law-based question or exercise. You should also look out for recent high-profile cases in which members of chambers have appeared and see if anyone in the chambers has published anything.

- **Non-legal professions.** In essence, you should research the main areas of activity of the potential employer, so that you can demonstrate to the interviewer that not only do you want the job, but that you want to work for that particular employer. Your knowledge can also be used to contextualise your answers in relation to the employer's situation.

There are a range of sources that you can use to find information, including:

- The Legal 500 (**www.legal500.com**): this gives reviews of the strengths of particular law firms and law firm rankings. It is focused on information to enable clients to identify the best law firm for the job

- Chambers Student Guide (**www.chambersstudent.co.uk**): this is a student-focused directory that provides insight into trainee and pupil life and prospects at firms and chambers

- Press releases and news sections of employer websites

- Published reports and industry publications.

In addition, if you know who will be interviewing you, then it should be possible to find specific information about them online which you could mention in your answers. Company websites and professional networking sites like LinkedIn can be helpful. However, be careful not to do this too much: there is a fine line between diligent and appropriate professional research and appearing like a stalker!

You could also consider setting up a Google alert for news on your prospective employer or the areas in which it works. Google alerts send you a periodic email (daily, weekly, or every time there is news) based on your search query. You can set up a Google alert at **www.google.co.uk/alerts** (see Figure 12.2).

⚫ You will find a downloadable template that you can use to compile and collate your employer research on the Online Resource Centre.

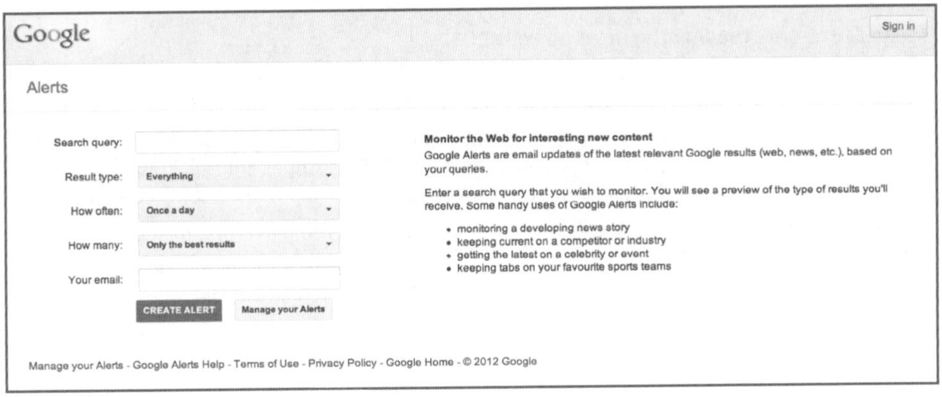

Figure 12.2 Google alerts

You should also make sure that you review your application before the interview. Remind yourself of the answers that you gave: remember that your application is all that the employer knows about you at this stage and it is inevitable that you will be asked questions on the content of your application.

Ethical awareness

Both branches of the legal profession are required to work according to Codes of Conduct set by the Solicitors Regulation Authority and the Bar Standards Board. Barristers and solicitors are expected to maintain their integrity at all times, to uphold public trust in the professions, and not to bring them into disrepute. There is a difference in the duties owed: a solicitor's duty is to their client (subject to certain exceptions) whereas a barrister owes a primary duty to the court; then to their client, their chambers, and themselves.

Ethical questions will generally require a resolution to a hypothetical situation in which there is a conflict of duty. If you are seeking a position in the traditional branches of the profession then you should acquire a copy of the relevant Code of Conduct and familiarise yourself with its guiding principles. To answer ethical questions, take time to think and consider the options, remember the guidance from the Code, and then use common sense to answer. If your first thoughts sound dubious, then think of an alternative before answering.

In the general commercial world, an awareness of business ethics is becoming increasingly important, particularly in the light of the Bribery Act 2010 which creates a criminal offence that can be committed by commercial organisations failing to prevent persons associated with them from committing bribery on their behalf.

General awareness

You should also have a good general awareness of current affairs and legal developments. Questions on current affairs are not only designed to test that you are keeping up with the news, but also to test your analytical and oral communication skills. You may be asked whether you agree or disagree with a particular issue in the news.

Practical exercise: reading the news actively

Having a rough idea of what is going on in the world is not likely to equip you sufficiently well to tackle a current affairs question in an interview. Just as you have needed to engage with written material in greater depth during your studies, you should try to read news stories critically. Take a look at the news story available at **www.bbc.co.uk/news/uk-21320992**.

This story involves a Member of Parliament who pleaded guilty to perverting the course of justice by falsely informing police that his wife had been driving his car when it was picked up on a motorway speed camera. While simple current awareness would enable you to answer the question 'have you heard about Chris Huhne's guilty plea regarding speeding?' there are plenty of deeper follow up questions that you could be asked. These might include questions such as:

- Should MPs who are convicted of a criminal offence that was committed ten years ago be compelled to resign?
- Do you think that the law on spousal immunity is satisfactory?
- If you were in Huhne's position would you have acted in the same way?

If you had not thought about these questions before the interview, you might struggle to answer them. However, you can deepen your knowledge of current affairs by following the news throughout the year:

- Read one quality newspaper daily (in hard copy or online)
- Make sure that you read the editorial. This will give an opinion on the key issues of the day. Decide whether you agree with the editor's position (and if so, why it is that you do) or whether you disagree (and if so, your reasons for differing). Even if you agree with the editorial, try to come up with a counter argument
- Look at online news services and see what stories/topics are consistently in the headlines. If any of these have a legal dimension, then you should pay particular attention to them. Again, read these stories and consider your own views on them (together with any possible contrasting perspectives). Not only will this make you more interested in the world at large, it will give you a valuable advantage in answering current affairs questions at interview. Even if the stories that you have been following do not form the topic of the question, critically reading the news will have strengthened your skills of analysis and should equip you to form a structured view (and counter view) quite quickly.

Improving your knowledge of current affairs and the ability to engage in informed discussion is an important differentiator between candidates, so you should do your best to get informed and stay informed.

Thinking about the sorts of questions you could be asked

If you have done your preparation properly, then you should not be unnecessarily fazed at the prospect of answering questions in an interview setting. Although it is impossible for a book like this to give you guidance on every possible interview question, there are certainly some common themes that are likely to prove the subject of enquiry at interview. Remember that interviewers are looking for a genuine motivation for your application as well as evaluating your employability skills against the desired skills for the opportunity in question. The sections that follow will list examples of the sorts of questions that you might be asked (in both legal and non-legal settings). However, this list of questions is not exhaustive by any means and you should be prepared to answer anything that is put to you.

Questions on motivation

- What made you interested in a career in law?
- What do you think of the law?
- Which modules on your law degree did you like/dislike?
- What motivates you?
- Why do you want to become a solicitor/barrister?
- Why have you applied to this firm/chambers?
- Which other firms/chambers have you applied to?
- Which area of law do you want to work in and why?
- Why should we offer you a training contract/pupillage?
- What sets you apart from other candidates?

Questions about you

- How would your best friend describe you?
- How do you feel when other people disagree with you?

Questions on ethics

- What do clients want from their lawyers?
- Your client wants to take a case to court even though he has no real prospect of success. You have advised him as such, yet he insists on proceeding. What do you do?
- Your client wants to buy a house for cash. What would you do?

Questions on the law/legal experience

- What is the difference between contract and tort in layman's terms?
- Tell us about one of your moots/client interviews/negotiations
- What was the best/worst thing about your mini pupillage/work experience?

Questions on commercial awareness

- What are the problems facing our profession at this time?
- What changes have there been in our profession recently?
- Who are our competitors? How are we different from them?
- Where would you open our next office and why?
- Who are our clients?
- What story in the business press has interested you most recently?
- What is the current Bank of England base rate?
- How many euros would you get today in exchange for £10?
- What is the FTSE 100? Did the FTSE go up or down yesterday?

Questions on employability skills

- When did you last have to work to meet a deadline?

- What would you have done if, a week before the deadline, you were told that it had been brought forward by four days?
- Give an example of when you had to work as a team.
- Give an example of a time that you had to overcome a difficult situation.

Tell us

Have you been asked any questions in an interview that you wished had been on this list, or that you would like to share with other students? Tell us at finchandfafinski.com/get-in-touch or @ FinchFafinski on Twitter.

You should also consider what your most dreaded question might be. This could be something random, or something specific you disclosed on your application (such as a poor grade). Give this some thought well in advance and decide upon your particular strategy for answering it.

....

So many people say they dread the question 'what is your greatest weakness?' but they do not think about how they might answer it in advance to help themselves when it does come.

Juliet Tomlinson, careers advisor

....

The more preparation you can give to answering your most feared question will pay dividends if you are asked that question in the pressured setting of an interview.

Preparing to answer questions

Before the interview you should give some thought to the examples that you will use in answering questions. This is a very similar process to that which you have already gone though in preparing your application: the key difference being that you had time to think and plan before committing your examples to paper, whereas in the interview, your thinking time is much more constrained.

By the time that you get to interview, you will have been doing a wide range of activities to build your employability skills portfolio and should have built up a large repertoire of experiences and examples upon which you could draw upon to answer questions. In an interview, you need to be selective about the examples that you use. While you will probably not anticipate every question that you will be asked, you should take some time to think about examples to have at your fingertips that you can use in the interview.

Practical exercise: preparing examples

You will find a downloadable template on the Online Resource Centre to use in this exercise. This lists the employability skills that we have covered throughout this book. Against each are four columns which reflect the STAR (situation – task – action – result). The STAR technique was covered in Chapter 10: remember that it requires you to contextualise your example, say what needed to be achieved, explain what you did, and then describe the outcome. There is also an additional column headed 'Next time?'. For each employability skill, think of the best example to use for the particular interview that you are facing. The examples that you use should be the most relevant for the employment opportunity: so if you are applying for a training contract but could find equally valid examples to demonstrate team work from work experience in a firm of solicitors or from working in a bar, then it would be sensible to draw on the example from your legal experience. Once you have decided on your example, break it down using the STAR technique and add it to the table. You should then think about what you might do differently if you faced this situation again. While the reflective 'what would you differently?' question is not often encountered directly in application forms, it is something that is commonly asked at interview. Considering this in advance should give you greater confidence in dealing with such a follow up question should it arise.

A partially completed template might look like Table 12.2.

Table 12.2 STAR technique

Employability skill	Situation	Task	Action	Result	Next time?
Organisational skills	Student law society annual ball	Needed to coordinate bookings and dietary needs	Set up spreadsheets to track responses and had regular communication with venue	No bookings went astray and all attendees had desired meal choices	Would configure spreadsheet differently to fit in with how venue needed information—too late to change once realised
IT skills	Work experience in high street firm	Had to update external website	Set up review with senior partner to determine what needed updating; produced dummy site for review	New site went live on schedule	Would have proposed different web technologies to make site stand out from the competition

Once you have completed this exercise, you will have a range of examples (and their associated stories) that you can use succinctly to demonstrate each of your employability skills. However, it is unlikely that every question you are asked will be 'give me an example of a time when you demonstrated X employability skill'. Competency-based interview questions are often a little more subtle: while many questions are of course aimed at unearthing your employability skills, you need to be able quickly to determine what skills the interviewer is looking for in your answer. So, in order to use the right example, you need first to think about what skills the question is seeking and then to pick your supporting examples from your prepared bank (see Figure 12.3).

The final skill that you need to master, then, is working out what employability skills you think particular questions are seeking.

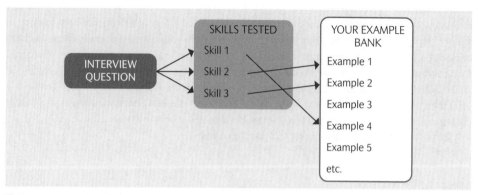

Figure 12.3 Matching skills to interview questions

Practical exercise: unpicking questions

For each of the following interview questions, work out what employability skills you think the question is designed to uncover.

- Give an example of a time that you had to overcome a difficult situation.
- When did you last have to work to meet a deadline?
- What was the best thing about your work experience?

⊌ Compare your answers to those on the Online Resource Centre.

Thinking about the sorts of questions that you could ask

It is almost inevitable that you will be asked if you have any questions towards the end of the interview. You should also prepare these in advance and they should, as with every other aspect of your application and interview, be specifically relevant to the particular opportunity at hand. Do not ask too many questions: two or three should be more than enough. Do not overlook this part of the interview. Although it might seem a relatively innocuous opportunity for you to clarify any points relating to the opportunity, remember that your performance will still be being assessed up to the time that you walk out of the interview. An insightful question that relates to the employer, or some aspect of their work, will impress much more than a weak question. Remember also that, while first impressions count, so do final impressions, so you do not want to leave the interview on a low note. Some examples of suitable questions could include (if these have not been already addressed in the interview):

- What support is there in place for trainees/pupils?
- What kind of opportunities are there for trainees to work abroad/in other offices?
- I am particularly interested in the X area of your practice: would there be a possibility of doing a seat there?

As a final piece of advice, make sure that you check the employer's website thoroughly before finalising your shortlist of possible questions. You do not want to ask something that is already answered online: that does not demonstrate thorough preparation and invites a response that could begin 'As you should have seen on our website…'.

A well-researched question that demonstrates good research skills is impressive. We have had applicants ask about a case we had worked on that they had read up on in the legal press and questions related to one of our trainee blogs. I personally wouldn't recommend a candidate asks the interviewer how they think they had performed in the interview.

Amelia Spinks, Field Fisher Waterhouse

Mock interviews

If you can get the opportunity to attend a mock interview, you will get immediate feedback on your performance from real interviewers. Such interviews are often arranged by the university careers service and you should check with them to see what interview practice they offer. The format of such interviews may well be generic, in the sense that they are not targeted at a particular occupation, profession, or sector. However, general mock interviews will give you invaluable experience in communicating your employability skills and interests by answering example-based questions and receiving pointers on how you might improve your interview technique. Some mock interviews will require you to provide your CV in advance and this will give you the additional benefit of feedback on your CV as well.

If you intend to pursue a career in the legal professions, it would be useful to find an opportunity to undergo a mock interview that is specifically focused on the requirements of the training contract or pupillage. Such interviews may also be offered by the university careers service, or through the student law society's links with local practitioners.

In either case, it is likely that mock interview opportunities will need to be booked. Since they are also very popular with students, you should try to sign up as soon as you possibly can, so that you can have a practice before the real thing.

However, if you are not able to find a formal mock interview, then you can still get some appreciation of your interview demeanour by video recording a mock interview with a friend asking the questions. You do not need specialist equipment to do this: most smartphones have the ability to record video. It does not matter if you cannot record the interview, but the reflection stage is made easier if you are able to do so.

Although the situation is more removed from the actual interview experience, you should try to take it as seriously as possible so that your body language is as close to that as it would be in a more pressured situation. It will also get you used to saying your answers out loud. Writing prepared answers and answering spoken questions are very different. Answering questions in a mock interview setting will help you with timing, and articulation: that is, finding the right spoken words to convey your answers professionally and appropriately, while at the same time remaining natural in your delivery. In turn, having acquired some experience of answering questions verbally, you should have increased confidence when being asked them for real. Watch the video a few times afterwards and look for habits that could distract from what you are saying, or poor delivery of answers. Put yourself in the position of the interviewer and, as you watch, ask yourself 'would you give this candidate a job?'. If you have not recorded the interview, simply ask your friend for their comments: did they think that you seemed to put your points across in a professional manner?

In the interview

While you must have communicated your employability skills well in your application to have got to the interview stage, it is the face-to-face discussion that most candidates will find the most daunting. The interview will give you the chance to demonstrate your entire portfolio of skills again, but your communication skills will be particularly on display. Before moving on to consider the sorts of questions that you might be asked, it is important first to remind you that your non-verbal communication can also have a positive effect on your prospects of success.

Non-verbal communications

Every person has physical habits: some grooming, some postural. Generally speaking, such habits are not particularly important. However, in an interview setting, they can become a distraction which detracts from the focus of the interview: you convincing the employer that you are the best candidate for the job. Moreover, non-verbal communication can suggest a whole range of different positive and negative attributes. There has been a great deal of psychological research into communication via body language. Some points to bear in mind in the interview are:

- **Handshakes.** When the interviewer greets you, make eye contact and offer a palm-to-palm handshake. It is difficult to gauge the pressure of your handshake without some practice. However, it should not be too strong or too weak: neither limp, nor crushing. You should not give more than one or two shakes. Anything more than this can be unnerving for the recipient. The easiest way to perfect this is to find a friend and ask them whether your handshake feels 'about right'. You should also keep an appropriate distance as you are greeted. In a panel interview, shake hands with each member of the interview panel.

- **Eye contact.** Make and maintain eye contact, but do not stare at your interviewer. Although eye contact suggests confidence, staring for too long can seem aggressive, or, in some cases, just a little odd. As an experiment, have a conversation with a friend and lock eyes with them throughout. See how long it takes them to say that they feel uncomfortable. The reverse of this is also true. If you avoid eye contact during a conversation, you will come across as disengaged and are unlikely to create a favourable impression with your interviewer. Again, you could try talking to someone without looking at them, and see how they react. In a panel interview, remember to make eye contact with the person that has asked you the question but also remember that you are addressing your answer to the whole panel and not just them.

- **Relax and smile.** Try not to stiffen up when walking in to your interview. Smiling can help to build an initial rapport with your interviewer. This also projects an impression of confidence and self-esteem.

- **Sit up straight.** You should sit up straight during the interview. This sends a message of self-assuredness, and also makes you appear taller, which sends a sign of confidence and credibility. Imagine that you have a string tied from the ceiling to the top of your head. Try having a conversation with a friend and ask them to lean back and then to lean forward. You will probably feel that their leaning back suggests boredom or general lack of interest in the conversation, while leaning (too far) forward can suggest aggression, arrogance, or over-confidence.

- **Try to avoid too many extreme gestures/postures.** Have a conversation with a friend and ask them if you have any particular habits or gestures and try to curb the worst of these. Pointing or over-gesticulation can be aggressive at worst or distracting at the very least and can create an unfavourable impression with an interviewer. There are also particular types of defensive or cautious body language that you should avoid. Hands in pockets, behind back (when standing) or crossed can convey an impression of disinterest or inapproachability. You are trying to come across to your interviewer as open and approachable, and this is best done by having your hands in front of you and gesturing naturally as you speak.

- **Avoid fiddling.** In highly stressful situations, including interviews, nervous energy can result in you fiddling: with hair, fingernails, jewellery, papers, or pen. This is perfectly natural and only becomes an issue if it becomes distracting to the interviewer and takes their attention away from the conversation that you are having. However, people do not always fidget because they are nervous. Some people are just naturally fidgety, but, in an interview situation, this can also give the impression of nervousness, even if you do not actually feel nervous at all. Bear this in mind and try to avoid fidgeting (whatever the reason) if at all possible: one of the ways of minimising the risk is to bear in mind that you cannot fiddle with things that are not there! So, if you know that you normally twist a bangle when you are stressed, then do not wear one to your interview.

In essence, the overall advice is to be measured and moderate in your behaviour. However, given that, like everyone, you will have flaws in your body language (as far as interviews are concerned), the first thing that you need to do to address them is to understand what they are and to accept that they exist. The question then becomes how to find out what your distracting habits actually are. It is highly unlikely that anyone will have told you what they are, so you could simply ask your close friends. However, this might not give you the true picture as your friends might be concerned about offending you. Therefore the safest way to perfect your interview body language is to become your own critic, and this is where the role of the mock interview comes in, as discussed in the previous section.

⚫ You will find some video clips of interviewees demonstrating good and bad body language on the Online Resource Centre.

Answering questions

There are several points that you should try to bear in mind when answering questions:

- **Look at the interviewer.** Maintaining eye contact is important in portraying an air of confidence. As before, do not stare.

- **Stay positive and enthusiastic.** There is a fine line between motivation and desire to succeed and over-enthusiasm and desperation. While you should always look for positive statements to make and show your aspiration to work for the employer, be careful not to overdo it. If there have been setbacks or a lack of success in some areas of your experience, then find a way to put a positive slant on matters. It is more impressive to say 'although I could only find a second work placement in a family law firm, which was not my first choice, the experience convinced me that I did not want to practise family law, and made me more determined to find a criminal firm' than 'I wanted my second work placement to be criminal, but ended up at a family firm, which was not at all enjoyable.'

- **Never be derogatory or sarcastic.** Being derogatory or sarcastic both involve negativity, even if (in the case of sarcasm) it is not necessarily meant as such. This does not come across well in an interview setting. However, it is important to be personable and likeable in an interview, so do try to allow the warmth of your character to come across in the way that you answer.

- **Listen.** It is very important for you to listen carefully to the questions that you are being asked. Make sure that you are clear on what is being asked of you before you start to reply. If you do not understand the question, then it is perfectly acceptable for you to ask—politely—for it to be rephrased. Not only will this give you a little extra thinking time, but it will also minimise the risk of you answering the question that you think you have been asked (or worse still, the question you wish you had been asked).

- **Do not panic.** If you really are unable to answer a question, it is better that you tell the interviewer rather than trying to make something up. While this is clearly not an ideal scenario, the interviewer should appreciate your honesty and respect your integrity in not stumbling through an answer. Similarly, if you just need a little bit of extra thinking time, then you may pause for a moment before answering, or ask politely if you may just take a moment. This will show the interviewer that you want to think about your reply rather than rushing ahead. However, do not pause for too long, or it will seem very awkward.

- **Be natural.** Although you should have prepared thoroughly by giving thought to the sorts of questions that you might be asked, and the examples that you should use to illustrate them, you also have to be ready to speak naturally rather than simply reciting prepared answers. Not only will this make you sound more interesting but you will also demonstrate adaptability which is an important transferable skill.

- **Use a range of examples effectively.** As outlined in the previous section, you must use examples to illustrate the skills that you are trying to demonstrate. While you should have given significant thought to your examples and anticipated the 'what would you have done differently?' questions, it is important to remember that when using the STAR technique in an interview you should be succinct in describing the situation and task, while focusing on what you actually did (the action) and the result that you achieved. You should remember that it is important to use a range of examples from different situations and experiences: not only will this prevent your answers from becoming quite tedious and repetitive, but it will also help you to demonstrate your ability to use your employability skills in different settings and environments. Remember particularly to be very clear about your own contributions by using the word 'I' (and not 'we') in your responses.

- **Remain flexible.** Even with the best and most thorough preparation, you will probably not anticipate everything you will be asked. The basic principle, though, remains the same. Use the best, most appropriate, succinct example that you can to address the points that you think the interviewer is looking for in response to the question. Again, do not try to answer the question that you wish you had been asked!

At the end of the interview

Thank the interviewer for their time and the opportunity to discuss your application in more detail. Stand up, shake hands, and smile (even if you think that the interview went badly or you have decided that you really did not like the person interviewing you) before leaving the room confidently.

The entire interview process is very important in demonstrating your skills, both directly by way of the answers that you give to questions, but also more softly, through the ability to build a rapport with your interviewer and by the way in which you respond to more challenging questions. The interview can be a gruelling experience, but with the right amount of preparation, it can also be quite enjoyable.

After the interview

Once the interview is done, there is nothing that you can do to rectify anything that you wish had gone better in relation to the particular application. However, remember that interview technique is a crucial employability skill and you need to develop it. It takes time and practice to strengthen your interview technique and, in order to do so, you should treat each interview as a separate reflective learning opportunity. Some questions to ponder after the interview are:

- What questions was I asked? What responses did I give?
- Was I happy with my answers?
- Were there better examples I could have given?
- How well did my answers communicate my employability skills?
- Was my preparation deficient in any way?
- Is there anything I would do differently next time?

Once you have considered these questions, you should work out a set of actions to take to improve your performance next time, should you have been unsuccessful, or, more positively, if you are asked to attend a second interview.

Dealing with rejection

If you are not successful, then there are several points that you should bear in mind:

- **Let the anger out.** If you are angry or upset, then let the anger out in an effective way: exercise, cry, shout, go to the gym, listen to music, write, or talk with family or friends to express your anger. Once the initial outburst is over, then you can begin to move forward constructively.

- **Do not take it personally.** No matter how personal a rejection seems, remember that no employer can know how good you will be in a particular position until you are in it. Most employers will tell you that they have made mistaken appointments: while a candidate might come across brilliantly on paper and at interview, they may not be as good as was anticipated when they come to start doing the job. Equally, your written application may have been of a high standard and you did very well at interview, but the successful candidate had more relevant qualifications and experience than you and was therefore an even better match for the position.

- **Be realistic.** Rejection is a part of job searching as it is a fact of life. Remember that almost all the other candidates that you met on the interview day will be sharing your feelings.

- **Accept responsibility.** Do not blame yourself or others for your rejection, but do accept responsibility for the way in which you prepared and the way in which you performed.

- **Seek feedback.** You may be offered feedback when you are told the outcome of the interview. However, if you are not offered any feedback, you have nothing to lose in asking for some. Any feedback that you can get will help you to improve both your written application and your interview technique for future job applications. Try to get specific information from the panel on what you could have done better or differently and why. The sorts of things you might want to know are whether you answered the questions effectively, whether the examples that you gave were sufficiently specific, whether you came across as competent, motivated, and genuinely interested, and whether you provided the right amount of depth in your answers.

- **Learn from the experience and try again.** Many successful candidates only achieve success after several applications. Each failed attempt will give you additional interview experience, enhanced feedback, and additional maturity, confidence, and familiarity with the recruitment process, all of which you can distil to improve your performance next time around.

Second interviews

If you are invited back for a second interview, then congratulations. Your chances of ultimate success are much higher: it is normal when multiple interviews are planned for a significant number (usually between 50% and 80%) of the first round candidates to go no further. However, second interviews tend to be longer, more rigorous, and are often conducted by one or more senior interviewers.

Preparation for a second interview should involve the same steps that you undertook for the first round. You should also go back to your own post-interview reflection and remind yourself of areas of the interview that you thought might not have gone so well: your first interviewer will have prepared a briefing note on any points from the first interview that needed further probing or elaboration. So if you think that you could have done more to demonstrate a particular employability skill or that you might not have appeared quite motivated enough, then bear this is mind. If you thought that there were some weaknesses in your first interview performance, it is highly likely that your interviewer would have noticed these too and brought them to the attention of the second interviewers.

Some employers may go to a third round of interviews, but this is very unusual. If you do find yourself in this position, then the advice given for second interviews still applies.

Alternative methods of assessment and selection

Some employers will use selection or assessment centres as part of the recruitment process. These typically involve a full day's activities in which your performance will be observed and rated by a number of different assessors. The exact format of assessment days will vary, but will typically involve one (or more) interviews and some combination of the activities covered in this section: presentations, in-tray exercises, group work, case studies, aptitude tests, and personality questionnaires. They may happen before or after the formal interview stage. Alternatively certain elements may happen on the same day as an interview.

Presentations

Candidates are often asked to prepare and deliver a presentation, either as part of an interview, or as an activity on an assessment day. While a presentation exercise is clearly designed to test your communications skills, it is also a test of your ability to select, organise, and plan your material.

There are a range of formats that presentations can take:

- **A topic of your own choice.** Many candidates worry about having a free choice of topic. In many respects, your assessors are more likely to be interested to see how you handle pressure and engage with them during the presentation than they are in the particular content of your presentation. You should, however, choose something that you know well, such as your dissertation (if you did one): this will give you greater confidence in both the material you are presenting and your ability to answer questions on it. If you have free choice, it is also useful to take into account your own interests, as it is always easier to research something that interests you and your enthusiasm for the topic should communicate to the audience, in turn, making your presentation more engaging.

- **A topic from a list.** This option takes away most of your free choice. Remember that with a restricted list of topics, the presentation assessors will have seen at least one other candidate present on the same topic, so you should give careful thought to ways in which you can make your treatment of the material more interesting and engaging.

- **A single topic.** In this scenario, everyone will be presenting on the same topic. This makes it even more important to ensure that you present as confidently and competently as possible as the assessors will be able to compare every candidate's performance directly.

- **Something you have done during the day.** If you have been involved in other activities during the assessment day then you may be required to present on a topic related to one or more of those activities. For instance, if you have done a group negotiation exercise, you might be asked to give a short reflective presentation on the way in which the negotiation went, how you worked within a team, the quality of the settlement and how you might handle the negotiation scenario differently if you were to approach it again.

Tell us

Have you had to give a presentation as part of the recruitment process? Tell us your experiences at finchandfafinski.com/get-in-touch or @FinchFafinski on Twitter.

Giving a presentation is often considered to be a very daunting prospect. This feeling is entirely natural; an oral presentation focuses the attention of many people on a single person which makes it a very nerve-wracking situation even if you are otherwise confident. Like anything else, the prospect of giving a presentation is daunting only until you know that you can do it proficiently. Many people are not natural speakers and will always quail at the thought of addressing even a small audience, but the fear does recede with practice. The points that follow aim to give you some pointers on putting together and delivering a successful presentation.

Timing

The amount of detail you will need to include on your topic will depend upon the timeframe available for your presentation: obviously, a greater level of detail is expected in a 45-minute presentation than would be the case in a ten-minute slot at the end of a group work exercise. Never try to cram too much information into the time available. Content overload is a major weakness in a presentation as it tends to leave the audience reeling; it is better to leave material out than to overload your audience with too much information delivered at high speed. Conversely, you need to make sure that you have enough to talk about, by setting the boundaries of your presentation appropriately. If you set these boundaries too wide or too narrow, you risk one of two unfavourable outcomes:

- **Too wide.** You will struggle to fit all the information into the time available, so will end up either rushing your delivery, leaving out relevant material, or taking too superficial an approach.

- **Too narrow.** You will run out of things to say or fill up time by repeating points or including superfluous material that weakens the focus of the presentation.

Aim

Make sure that you are clear about what you are trying to achieve in your presentation. If you have been given a title, what does it suggest about the aim of your presentation? Is it to introduce the topic, to give an overview, or to deal with a particular issue in depth? If you are unclear, seek clarification.

If you have free rein to select your own topic, it will add focus to your presentation and make the preparation process easier if you identify a clear aim to be achieved by your presentation. Keep this to the forefront of your mind when researching and planning your presentation and ensure that you inform the audience of this aim from the outset as this will orientate them to what to expect from your presentation.

Selecting material

Once you have conducted your research into your presentation topic, you will probably feel somewhat overwhelmed by the volume of material that you have gathered, and also by the prospect of turning it into a presentation. This is not unusual and it is these factors that lead to two of the key issues that limit the effectiveness of presentations:

- Trying to cover too much information in the time available
- Reading from a set of notes that are not suited to oral delivery.

Both of these problems can be resolved by judicious selection of material and by planning a structured presentation that is not exclusively reliant upon oral delivery but which makes use of visual aids.

It is always tempting, having devoted time and effort to conducting research, to try to make use of all the interesting facts that you have discovered. However, it is important to ensure that you do not exceed the time allocated for your presentation. Equally, a hurried presentation that skims over a great deal of material is very difficult for the audience to follow and is likely to be received negatively. Think first of all about what your presentation is trying to achieve: what question is it attempting to answer?

Once you are clear about what you are trying to achieve, you can sift through all the material you have gathered in order to eliminate that which is not relevant. The more specific you are in framing your issue, the easier you will find it to decide whether material is relevant.

Practical exercise: selecting relevant materials

The following exercise can be used to help you determine the relevance of the material to your presentation.

Write your title at the top of a blank sheet of paper (or at the start of a new document).

Make a bullet point list of all the points that you could include.

Review the list, grouping similar points together and eliminating any repetition or overlap.

Draw three columns headed: essential, peripheral, and irrelevant and allocate each of your points to one of the columns, remembering that the question of relevance is determined by reference to the specific details of your presentation title and not to the general topic of the presentation.

Use this as guidance when determining the content of your presentation, starting with material that you have categorised as essential. If you still feel that you have too much information, you should repeat the exercise, this time using the three columns to divide up the points that you initially categorised as essential.

☽ A worked example of this technique can be found on the Online Resource Centre. You might find it useful to take a few moments to look at this example and read the accompanying notes to ensure that you have a good insight into the prioritisation of the material.

Organising material

Once you have made a preliminary selection of the material to include in the presentation, you need to consider the order in which your points will be made. Bear in mind that your presentation should follow a logical progression, it should 'tell a story', so it should have a beginning (introduction), middle (the bulk of the presentation, divided into a series of issues), and an end (conclusion):

- **Introduction.** Your introduction should be succinct, clear, and straightforward. It should outline the topic to be discussed, explain the structure and duration of the presentation (including any time allocated for questions at the end), and tell the audience why the topic is important and/or interesting. In essence, the introduction should give the audience an understanding of what is to follow and give a clear and concise account of the question that the presentation will address and the reason that this is important.

- **Main body.** The body of the presentation can be more complicated to organise, so keep in mind the argument that you are going to advance and break this down into a series of issues and sub-issues. Bear in mind that one point should lead into another and that you should take care to select examples that demonstrate the point you are making and do not distract from the flow of your presentation. You may want to experiment with more than one potential structure to ensure that you find the most effective way to organise your material. For the audience listening to the presentation, there are two tasks that need to be carried out simultaneously. First, the listeners have to digest the point you are making and, secondly, they have to slot this into the bigger picture of the topic as a whole. This can be difficult, so it is essential that you help your audience to follow the structure of the presentation with clear signposting; phrases such as 'there are three points of importance here and I shall discuss each in turn' or 'this is a powerful argument but there is an equally compelling counterargument that we must now consider'. Signposting explains to the audience how each piece of information relates to that which precedes and follows it and how it fits into the broader topic, so it is an important consideration and one which can contribute to the success of your presentation.

- **Conclusion.** The conclusion should provide a brief summary of the material covered and a direct answer to the question addressed in the presentation. Try to think of a way to make the central message of the presentation stick in the mind of the audience by identifying a maximum of three points that you want them to remember and highlighting these.

Using slides

You should ask whether you are expected to use slides to accompany your presentation, whether their use is optional, or whether you are just expected to speak. You should also check to see what equipment is available on the day. Do you need to take your own laptop or tablet or can you take your presentation on a memory stick? If you are taking a memory stick what presentation software is available? If there is a projector, what type of plug does it have for you to connect to? Will you need to take some sort of adapter? All of these are potential pitfalls which could lead to huge stress on the day of the presentation if you have not taken the time or effort to find out beforehand.

PowerPoint (or its Mac equivalent, Keynote) is an excellent visual aid and one that you should certainly try to use if it is at all possible. If you are not familiar with PowerPoint, most institutions run courses on how to use it and, besides, it is very easy to pick up by experimentation as it is based on a series of templates into which you insert text, images, and other features.

There is some disagreement about how many PowerPoint slides should accompany a presentation with some suggesting an approach based on slides per minute of presentation, for example one slide every two minutes. Not only is this rather onerous in long presentations, it is also rather unrealistic; you should use as many slides as you need to communicate your point to the audience. That said: do not use too many content slides: three or four should be sufficient for a short presentation. For a 15 minute presentation, eight would be more than enough.

The following points may help you to plan the slides you need to accompany your presentation:

- **Title slide.** This tells the audience who you are and what you are going to talk about.
- **Presentation outline.** This should be used during your introduction as you explain to the audience what points you are going to cover and in what order.
- **Content slides.** The general rule is that there should be one slide for each major concept or idea that you introduce to the audience. You should be sparing with the amount of words used on each slide and remember to keep the font size large: visual aids are not useful if they cannot be read by the audience.
- **Summary slide.** This corresponds with your conclusion and lists the points that you have covered to demonstrate the way that your ideas fit together.
- **Any questions?** However much you hope that nobody will ask any questions, they will.

Practice

If you have the time, you must practise delivering your presentation several times over to ensure that:

- The presentation fits within the time allocated to it
- The order of the material is appropriate and one point runs smoothly into another
- There are no tricky words or phrases that trip up your tongue
- You familiarise yourself with the appropriate pace at which to speak
- You become accustomed to hearing your own voice
- You know how and when to use any visual aids
- You identify and eliminate any distracting habits.

Many of these points will be more readily addressed if you practise in front of someone. For example, you may think that your pace of delivery is appropriate but only someone who is listening can tell you whether that is the case. Equally, if you have any odd habits, such as fiddling with a pen or flicking your hair, you are likely to be unaware of this unless it is pointed out to you. Finally, a third party can give you feedback on the most important element of all: whether your presentation makes sense to the audience. Remember to practise with the visual aids that you plan to use to make sure that you can use these without interrupting the flow of your presentation.

Of course, you will not be able to do this if you are given a presentation to prepare on the assessment day. You should, however, take the opportunity to prepare and deliver a presentation on something beforehand to get used to the idea of doing so.

Delivery

Your main objective in giving a presentation is to communicate an idea to the audience. This means that they need to be able to understand you. It is your job to make sure that you deliver your presentation in such a way that it is capable of being understood and, more than that, that it is packaged so that the audience *wants* to listen. As such, you will need to take the following points into account.

- **Engage with the audience.** One of the worst ways to deliver a presentation is to read it to the audience from a prepared script. It leads to a flat and uninteresting delivery, which is very boring for the audience and it often causes the presenter to speak far too quickly. Reading a script also means that you have little or no eye contact with the audience as you have to focus your attention on the page. By using cue cards, you are free to look at the audience (collectively rather than any particular individual) and your delivery will be more natural as a result. Cue cards should be numbered (in case you drop them) and contain short reminders of each key point. Do not be tempted to divide a script into chunks and write these on cue cards as you will find that you merely read from those instead.

- **Speak effectively.** Remember that good written language and good spoken language differ dramatically. It is easier to engage the audience if you replicate the variations in pace and tone that occur in natural speech. Try to make sure that you sound as much like yourself as possible in ordinary conversation, taking into account the need to pace your delivery. It can help to include instructions to remind yourself of these points on the cue cards. Write appropriate phrases such as 'pause', 'slow down', and 'look at the audience' on the cue cards but make sure that you do so in a different colour to avoid confusing it with the text of your presentation.

- **Timing and volume.** During the planning stages, you should have taken steps to ensure that your presentation fits within the time allocated to it. Remember that the audience will find it difficult to digest complicated material, so you will need to reduce your speed of delivery so that it is slower than ordinary speech. This can feel strange and it is not uncommon for speakers to start at a measured pace but to pick up speed as the presentation progresses until they are going too fast for the audience. You will also probably find that you need to speak at a slightly louder volume than you would in ordinary conversation. Your voice will project better to those at the back of the room if you remember to face the audience. This is particularly important when using visual aids: even experienced speakers tend to look at their materials rather than the audience and this can really muffle the voice, so should be avoided. Take along a watch or use your phone (on silent) to help you keep track of time. You may get cut off as soon as you have used the time allocated, whether or not you have finished.

- **Signpost your presentation.** Telling the audience what you are doing makes it so much easier for them to follow the development of your argument. It is good practice to ensure that you start each fresh point with an explanation of how it relates to the rest of your material. It is important to remember that the audience will regard your presentation favourably if you have made life easy for them, so giving frequent clues as to the relevance of a particular point to the overall topic will always create a good impression.

- **Take care with visual aids.** Make sure that your slides follow the order of your presentation; if you have made last-minute changes to your content, you should check to see whether this necessitates alterations in your materials. Practise using any equipment so that you are confident you will be able to operate it during the presentation. Think about where you are going to stand in relation to the equipment. You do not want to block the screen or to have to keep walking across the room to change your slides. Do not use visual aids as a substitute for speaking. Talk to the audience and not to the visual aids. Even the most experienced speakers make this mistake, as they look at their own PowerPoint slides when they are explaining the points, rather than looking at the audience.

- **End positively.** Thank the audience for listening. Look at the audience again, smile, and slow down. Make sure that you end on a strong or positive note. There is nothing less inspiring than tailing away with something bland such as 'that concludes my presentation, does anyone have any questions?'

Dealing with questions

Most presentations conclude with a period of time for the audience to ask questions. It is probably fair to say that even the most confident presenter has some qualms about dealing with questions. This is because it is actually the only part of the presentation that you cannot control. In a recruitment setting, the ability to deal with questions is particularly importance because it demonstrate the depth of the speaker's background knowledge and their ability to respond promptly and professionally. Try to take into account the following points to help you deal with questions:

- Listen to the question. Concentrate on what the person asking the question is saying rather than worrying that you will not know the answer.

- Ask them to repeat the question if you did not follow it or to reword it if you did not understand it.

- Take time to think about the answer to ensure that you have something sensible to say rather than saying the first thing that pops into your head just to fill the silence.

- Be honest. If you do not know the answer, say so.

- Do not talk for too long in answer to any particular question. It will come across as if you are rambling which will detract from the overall impression of your oral presentation skills. Think about your answer and make a couple of succinct points.

Although giving a presentation is often the most feared part of an assessment day, you should remember that it is the part over which you have the most control and that your performance is not dependent upon a wider team contribution. Therefore, a presentation offers you an excellent opportunity to make yourself stand out from the competition.

In-tray exercises

The in-tray exercise is a business simulation activity designed to mimic the sort of situation that you might face in the actual workplace. Your performance in an in-tray exercise will demonstrate a whole variety of employability skills, including planning, organisation, time management, analysis, decision-making, and communication.

In a typical in-tray exercise, you will be provided with relevant information on the organisation, your role during the exercise, and an in-tray of paperwork and/or an email inbox, and asked to work through it within a time limit (usually one or two hours). This will involve you dealing with a large number of tasks in a short period and differentiating between the information that is crucial and that which is peripheral. Each task might require you to draft a reply, delegating tasks, recommending actions, or writing a short report or summary. In some variations on the exercise, some new tasks can be added part way through (to see how you deal with unexpected events and changes in priority), or you could be asked to make a telephone call to a client, colleague, or superior (which will be role-played by an assessor).

At the end of the exercise, you may be asked to discuss the decisions you have made and the reasons that you made them.

Points that you should consider if you are approaching an in-tray exercise are:

- **Stay calm.** Although the activity is designed to put you under pressure, and you will undoubtedly feel so, try to stay calm and think clearly.

- **Know what you are doing.** Make sure that you read the background information that you are given thoroughly so that you understand the situation, what you are supposed to be doing, and the nature of your role. You will find it helpful if you make some notes of the key points to remember, as this will save you going through the background information later on if there is a point on which you need to refresh your memory.

- **Get an overview first.** Scan through everything in the in-tray and/or inbox to get a sense of all the items that you will need to consider. It is often the case that later tasks that you find may impact upon your early decisions.

- **Keep an eye on time.** Once you have a rough idea of the magnitude of the entire task, pace yourself to work through the items steadily. However, remember that there is always the possibility of more work being added part way through, so make sure that you allow some spare time, just in case this happens or some of the tasks end up taking longer than you first thought.

- **Prioritise.** Decide what items are most important and most urgent. Remember that some items may be important but not urgent, and others urgent but not important. You may need to balance these two factors very carefully. For other items, think about whether they can be delegated to a colleague, forwarded elsewhere in the organisation, or deferred until later. Remember that you may be required to give reasons for your decisions later on, so do keep very brief notes on your reasoning as you work through the list.

- **Make a plan of action.** Working down your prioritised list, decide what action needs to be taken. For each action, then consider how it should be taken, who should do it and what (if any) deadlines are associated with it. If you are given a deadline, question whether it is absolutely fixed or whether there may be scope for negotiation and extended time. Think about whether there are tasks that could be accomplished simultaneously.

- **Identify dependencies and constraints.** Do any tasks depend upon each other? Bear in mind when each communication is dated, and put them into a timeline. If you identify dependencies, it will make working through tasks in a logical and ordered way much more straightforward. Similarly, take a note of any potential constraints (such as a lack of resources to complete a particular item within time or budget) and conflicting tasks.

- **Keep responses to the point.** If you need to respond in writing to anything, state the main points briefly and keep any elaboration as concise as possible, avoiding irrelevant detail. Writing and re-writing responses or drafts can be very time consuming. Keep it simple and try to get it right first time. Your spelling, grammar, and punctuation should be perfect and your use of language unambiguous.

- **Draw sensible inferences.** The information that you are provided can sometimes be left deliberately incomplete. If this is the case, then make the best decision that you can in the light of the information that you do have. Be prepared to discuss your reasoning later.

- **Show your commercial awareness.** You should highlight any commercial implications that you identify when going through your analysis of each item. For each item, consider who it is from and their importance to your organisation. Is it an internal (staff) or external (client, supplier) communication? Are there items from commercially important bodies, such as government agencies, police, journalists, or regulatory authorities?

You will find more on commercial awareness in Chapter 6.

- **There is no single right answer.** You can be reassured that there is no single right way of working through an in-tray exercise. You will be assessed on the way that you dealt with the exercise as a whole, but be prepared to be challenged on your approach.

Group exercises

Group exercises are often used at assessment centres. While it is obvious that they are designed to evaluate your team-working skills, they also allow you to be assessed on your communication, influencing, and relationship building skills and your ability to apply analysis and logic to the task at hand. Group exercises will (usually) require you to work with between four and eight candidates in order to complete a particular task. You may also be required to present your findings and reflections on the exercise individually, or as a team, later in the day.

It is impossible within the scope of a book like this to give you a detailed coverage of the sorts of tasks that you might be asked to complete.

However, there are particular skills to working in a group that you should bear in mind:

- **Engage.** Introduce yourself to the other members of the group and make sure that you know the names of your colleagues. Not only is this professional and friendly, it demonstrates your engagement with the group. It has a further practical benefit: since you may be asked to present on, or reflect on the group activity later on, remembering names will make that easier. Demonstrate your engagement with the group by using people's names when speaking to them: although be careful that this is done naturally, otherwise it can come across as a little forced and odd.

- **Keep eye contact.** Try to avoid spending most of the activity looking down and writing notes. Strike a balance between making notes and looking up to talk to others.

- **Include quiet group members.** In some group activities, there can be some candidates who either do not get the opportunity to contribute or do not seem to want to contribute. You can demonstrate your engagement with the group by addressing the reluctant participants directly by name (another reason to note names from the outset) and trying to draw them into the discussion.

- **Deal effectively with dominant group members.** The assessment day is a competition: you are one of several potential candidates for a limited number of positions. Some will be unsuccessful. This means that some see the group exercise as a competitive environment, and some participants can be dominant. Remember that this activity is designed to see how you deal with a group setting, which means working with the whole group and not being competitive: that is not to say that you should be dominated by overbearing participants. It is better to be assertive and make your own contribution.

- **Listen actively.** You need to show your assessors that you can value the contributions of others while making your own views known. Therefore you must acknowledge others' contributions, even if you do not agree with them or (even worse) think that they are stupid. Make sure that you look at the person who is speaking, nod in acknowledgement, and then demonstrate that you have listened by referring back to something that they have said. However, before doing so, take a little time to consider what has been said by other group members. If you agree, then say so and explain why you do: this also demonstrates supportive group work. If you disagree, then explain why, but give an opportunity for a response. Remember not to get embroiled in an argument, since you also have an obligation to make sure that the discussion moves forward.

- **Do not exclude group members.** Keeping other group members from participating, either by your use of aggressive or exclusive body language or by interrupting them, does not reflect well on your team-working skills.

- **Keep the group focused.** If the discussion seems to be drifting, it is helpful to bring the group back to its allotted task. You can do this by referring back to the brief you have been given or by reminding the group what still needs to be achieved in the time left. Reminding your group of key time points (such as ten minutes to go) allows the group to maximize its chances of coming to a final decision.

- **Show your commercial awareness.** Tasks set at assessment centres will often involve a fictional client company so you should remember the commercial context both for your deliberations and the effect that your decisions may have on your client.

You will find more on commercial awareness in Chapter 6.

- **Be natural.** As in an interview, you should allow your personality to come through in the way that you speak and the way that you act: provided that this is tempered with the overriding need to act appropriately and professionally at all times.

For group exercises, I would recommend you treat the other candidates in the exercise as your team and not your competition. Team work is very important to the role of a trainee solicitor and this is one of the only exercises that will demonstrate these skills in the application process.

Amelia Spinks, Field Fisher Waterhouse

Case studies

Case studies can also be used at assessment centres and may also be encountered as part of a programme of interviews. These may be group exercises (in which case the advice in the previous section should also be followed) or individual exercises. They allow you to demonstrate your skills of analysis, problem-solving, and time management and, depending on the requirements and format of the exercise, could also include elements of commercial and ethical awareness, team working, negotiation, or drafting. You may be required to give a presentation of your findings or advice, or to discuss this within a more traditional interview format. Remember that you must be able to explain the thought processes that led you to your conclusion.

The amount of preparation time you are given can vary: in some cases you are given the materials in advance of the assessment day, whereas in others you may have only half an hour or an hour to read through the background and a further period of time to consider your response. If you have the luxury of extended preparation time, use it wisely. All other candidates will have the same amount of time to prepare, so treat the exercise as though you were preparing for an exam. It is no less an assessment in the recruitment setting.

There are many forms that the case study could take. For example, you could be given a fictional business setting with a contract to read. You could be given an actual (or fictional) legal judgment to consider and then give an opinion. Alternatively, you could be given something analogous to a problem question: a set of facts with different legal issues to identify and to offer advice as well as possible.

The topic of the case study is likely to be related to any areas of specialism that the employer has, and may use actual cases with client identities disguised.

The most important thing to remember—whatever it is that you are asked to read and consider—is to skim through the material first before engaging with the detail. For example:

- A contract could contain a crucial clause hidden away towards the end (they often do).

- A judgment could contain multiple judicial opinions, some of which might be dissenting (and thus *obiter*). You could be asked to compare the approaches taken by different members of the court and to explain whether you thought the court had reached the right result. You may be challenged on particular points in the argument to see if you followed the judicial reasoning.

- Case studies may be based on very recent judgments, so make sure that you keep up-to-date with the legal press in the run up to your interview.

Missing either of these points could easily lead to you forming the wrong conclusion and giving incorrect advice, so look out for possible traps early on. Remember that you are not being tested on your detailed legal knowledge (indeed, some case studies may be set on topics with which you are unfamiliar) but rather your powers of legal reasoning and application to a particular situation. Put yourself into the position of the person having to deal with the problem and think about a pragmatic approach to its solution.

Practical exercise: case study

You will find an example of a typical case study on the Online Resource Centre.

Aptitude tests

There are different forms of aptitude tests that can appear in assessment centres. They can be administered individually, or in some form of combined single test. Alternatively, aptitude tests may be done in advance and repeated at the assessment centre. The sorts of tests you could encounter include:

- **Verbal reasoning.** These tests will typically give you a series of passages of information with a series of statements that may be true, false, or on which you cannot draw a firm conclusion because there is insufficient information provided. They are designed to test your skills of logic, analysis, and comprehension, particularly in drawing inferences, recognising assumptions, and evaluating arguments within a written text.

- **Critical reasoning.** There are different sorts of critical reasoning tests. However, one of the most commonly encountered in educational and business settings is known as the Watson-Glaser Critical Thinking Appraisal. Critical reasoning tests are similar to verbal reasoning tests in the areas that they evaluate, but probe a deeper level of analytical and problem solving skills.

- **Numerical reasoning.** Numerical reasoning tests do not test your mathematical knowledge. They are designed to be used across all candidates (regardless of mathematical background) and will therefore not usually require more complex operations than basic arithmetic, percentages, and fractions and the ability to interpret graphs, charts, and tables. Such tests give an indication of your general numeracy rather than your ability to 'do maths'. Although such tests are not always used in legal recruitment, commercial firms—due to the nature of their business—may wish to seek evidence of a certain level of numeracy.

- **Abstract reasoning.** Abstract reasoning tests typically present you with sets of different shapes or symbols and ask you whether certain other shapes fit the patterns with which you have already been presented. They are designed to test your skills in evaluating and generating hypotheses and then testing or applying those hypotheses to new situations.

All these forms of tests are done under timed conditions. There will generally be a pass threshold that is expected, as well as your scores potentially being used in some form of ranking exercise.

If you are expecting to take an aptitude test:

- **Practise.** There are many examples of these tests freely available online. Doing as many of these as you can will help you to familiarise yourself with the format and to get used to working against the clock.

- **Timing is essential.** Ensure you know how many questions you have to complete and how long you have to do them. Try to work at a steady pace which will enable you to complete the test in the time allowed. Some tests, however, may be open ended: there will be more questions than it is possible for anyone to do in the time limit, so in this situation you should work to a sensible pace and complete as many questions as you can. Do not spend too much time on one question: you can always come back to it later if you get stuck.

- **Read all the information you are given.** If the questions are based on a passage of text, read it through first before answering any questions. Similarly, assimilate numerical or symbolical information that you are given carefully prior to attempting any answers.

- **Do not make assumptions.** Make sure that you only use the information provided to reach your conclusions. Do not make assumptions or rely on any of your own knowledge to fill in gaps in the information provided.

- **Check the marking criteria.** Some tests work on a negative marking basis in which marks are deducted for wrong answers. If this is the case, avoid making risky guesses: not giving an answer (and not gaining extra marks) is better in the long run than guessing incorrectly (and losing marks that you already have).

Practical exercise: aptitude tests

To illustrate the different types of test, have a go at the five example questions here. You will find answers and explanations on the Online Resource Centre. Once you have done these three introductory questions, find similar tests online and complete as many as you can. Most give some feedback and explanation of your answers. Start by taking as much time as you want to get used to their style, but ultimately you should be doing them under timed conditions.

Verbal

Read the following passage:

....

In the light of the current uncertain global financial situation, the volatility in the stock market and the inconsistencies in traditionally 'safe' investments, such as property, investors have been seeking alternative ways of investing their funds. These have become increasingly attractive over the past three years. It is hardly surprising: returns on alternatives to the traditional equity portfolio, such as fine wine and sculpture, have seen an over-performance of some 65% over this time.

....

Is the following statement true, false, or cannot tell?

....

The financial return on fine wine investments has been 65% higher than on equities over the past three years.

....

Critical

Read this statement and decide whether the conclusion follows logically from it:

....

In a certain firm of solicitors, applicants for training contracts are required to be assertive and/or have legal work experience. There are 25 candidates for one training contract, of which 15 are assertive and have legal work experience. Therefore, all 25 candidates may have legal work experience.

....

Read this statement and decide whether the argument that follows is strong or weak. For an argument to be strong, it must be both important and directly related to the question. An argument is weak if it is not directly related to the question (even though it may be of great general importance), if it is of minor importance, or if it is only related to trivial aspects of the question.

....

Should chambers use social networks to research candidates for pupillage as part of their decision-making process?

Yes they should. Candidates should take care with their online presence so that they do not jeopardise their future career prospects.

....

Numerical

Table 12.3 Numerical exercise example

Name	Land law	Trusts law	Tort law
Amelia	33	35	50
Ben	44	43	33
Charlotte	30	44	38
David	18	39	29
Eve	32	48	42

Table 12.3 shows the scores of five students in their coursework. Marks are given out of 60. How many students scored at least 15% more in tort law than in land law?

Abstract

Figure 12.4 Abstract exercise

In Figure 12.4 you will see two rows of symbols. Which of the symbols in the second row should follow on from the sequence of symbols shown in the top row?

Personality questionnaires

There are different personality or psychometric questionnaires that are carefully designed to give an indication of your personality type and working style. Unlike the various forms of aptitude test covered in the last section, there is no right answer to any of the questions. The only advice that is really relevant here is to be yourself. Answer honestly so that the recruiters get a proper insight into your personality rather than trying to second guess what they want to hear, and do not over analyse each question. Your first or instinctive answer is usually the best. Many of the questions are similar in content, but phrased differently: they are there to establish the degree of consistency in your answers and hence the reliability of the results.

WHERE NEXT?

The advice in this chapter should have prepared you to present yourself as well as possible in a range of different face-to-face assessment situations. It is the culmination of everything that we have covered in the book: building, completing, and demonstrating your employability skills portfolio. While it is certainly true that the employment market is very competitive, preparation, planning, hard work, and practice should maximise your chances of getting the position that you want.

We wish you all the very best in whatever it is that you do next.

Tell us

Where has your career taken you now and how did your law degree help you to get there? Tell us at finchandfafinski.com/get-in-touch or @FinchFafinski on Twitter.

APPENDIX A – VACATION SCHEMES

Information in this table is correct at the time of writing. There are some gaps in the table where the information was not available online and the firm in question did not respond to our request for information. Help us to keep this table updated by alerting us to any changes that you might come across. Tell us via email to **hello@finchandfafinski.com**, on Twitter **@FinchFafinski** or via our website at **www.finchandfafinski.com**.

Firm	Number of Places	Application Process	Duration	Location	Pay per week
Addleshaw Goddard www.addleshawgoddard.com/graduates/view.asp?content_id=3163&parent_id=495	75	Online application	1 week (Easter) 2 weeks (Summer)	Leeds London Manchester	Yes, under review
Allen & Overy LLP www.aograduate.com/vacation-programs.html	60	Online application plus interview	2–3 weeks	London	£250
Arnold & Porter LLP http://arnoldporter.webfactional.com/career/london-trainees/how-to-apply.html	8	Online application plus interview	2 weeks	London	£300
Ashfords LLP www.ashfords.co.uk/graduate_recruitment_applying/	32	Online application plus assessment day	1 week	Exeter	Unpaid
Ashton KCJ www.ashtonkcj.co.uk/careers/work-experience/	8	Application form by email	1 week	Bury St Edmunds	Unpaid
Ashurst LLP www.ashurst.com/trainees/content/vacation-schemes	60	Online application plus interview	2–3 weeks	Various	£275
Baker & McKenzie LLP www.bornglobal.uk.com	30		3 weeks	London	£270
Bates Wells & Braithwaite www.bwbllp.com/vacation-placements	24	CV and application letter plus a screening test and verbal reasoning test	4 weeks	London	£300
Berg www.berg.co.uk/join-berg.aspx		CV and covering letter by email		Manchester	

Firm	Number of Places	Application Process	Duration	Location	Pay per week
Berwin Leighton Paisner www.blplaw.com/trainee/index.cfm/vacation-schemes/2003	100	Online application, telephone interview and assessment centre		London	
Bevan Brittan www.bevanbrittan.com/careers/trainees/Pages/Home.aspx#10	18	Online application	2 weeks	Birmingham Bristol London	
Bircham Dyson Bell LLP http://graduates.bdb-law.co.uk/working-at-bdb/summer-placement-programme/	20	CV and covering letter	2 weeks	London	£250
Bird & Bird LLP http://londongraduates.twobirds.com/opportunities/summer-placements/	25	Online application, interview, selection event	2 weeks	London	£275
Birkett Long LLP www.birkettlong.co.uk/site/opportunities/work_experience/	25	CV and covering letter by email	1 week	Colchester Chelmsford Basildon	Unpaid
Blake Lapthorn LLP www.bllaw.co.uk/careers/work_experience.aspx	60	Online application	3 days	Oxford Southampton	Unpaid
Boodle Hatfield www.boodlehatfield.com/the-firm/trainees/vacation-scheme.aspx	8	Online application plus a telephone interview	2 weeks	London	
BP Collins LLP www.bpcollins.co.uk/careers/summer-placements		CV plus handwritten letter of application	1–2 weeks	Gerrards Cross	
Brabners Chaffe Street	None at time of writing				
Brachers LLP www.brachers.co.uk/join-us/work-experience-vacation-scheme	5	CV and covering letter by email	2 weeks	Maidstone	Unpaid
Bristows http://training.bristows.com/how_to_apply	10–24	Online application	2 days	London	Unpaid

Firm	Number of Places	Application Process	Duration	Location	Pay per week
Burges Salmon LLP www.burges-salmon.com/Careers/traineesolicitors/open_days_and_vacation_placements/Open_days_and_vacation_placements.aspx	40	Selected from students who attend an Open Day	2 weeks	Bristol	£250
Capsticks www.capsticks.com/vacation-scheme.php		Online application including covering letter and CV plus an interview	2 weeks	Birmingham Leeds London	
Cleary Gottlieb www.cgsh.com/careers/london/legalrecruiting/vacationschemes/	35	Online application including covering letter and CV	2 weeks	London	£500
Clifford Chance http://gradsuk.cliffordchance.com/vacation-schemes.html	60	Online application	4 weeks	London	£350
Clyde & Co	45	Online application or printed application form	2 weeks	Guildford London	£250
CMS Cameron McKenna http://graduates.cms-cmck.com/work-for-us/vacation-schemes/	60	Online application	2 weeks	Aberdeen Bristol Edinburgh London	£250
Covington & Burling LLP www.cov.com/careers/london/summer_scheme/summer_scheme/summer_scheme/	24	Online application plus one or two interview(s)	1 week	London	£300
Davenport Lyons www.davenportlyons.com/recruitment/graduate-recruitment/	8	Online application	2 weeks	London	£250
Davis Polk www.davispolk.com/careers/summer-program/	12	CV and covering letter	2–4 weeks	London	£500
Decherts http://careers.dechert.com/careers/uktraineesolicitor/opportunitiesforyou/faqs/#Work%20placement%20programmes	8	Online application plus interview and written exercises	2 weeks	London	£250
Dickinson Dees www.dickinson-dees.com/faq/	40	Online application plus aptitude tests and assessment day	1 week		

Firm	Number of Places	Application Process	Duration	Location	Pay per week
DLA Piper www.dlapipergraduates.co.uk/opportunities/summer-schemes.html	130	Online application	2 weeks	Birmingham Leeds Liverpool London Manchester Sheffield	£225–£275
Dundas & Wilson www.dundas-wilson.com/working_dw/summer_placements/dw_cms_2609.asp	24	Online application, psychometric tests and interview	2 weeks	London	
DWF LLP www.dwf.co.uk/join-us/trainee-solicitors-and-apprentices/	50		1 week	Leeds Liverpool London Manchester	Unpaid
Edwards Wildman Palmer LLP www.trainee.edwardswildman.com/ukthefirm/	8	Online application plus interview	2 weeks	London	£300
Edwin Coe LLP www.edwincoegraduate.com/graduate-recruitment/summer-vacation-scheme	8	Online application including CV and covering letter plus interview	1 week	London	Unpaid
Eversheds www.eversheds.com/global/en/where/europe/uk/overview/careers/graduates/multiple-pathways.page	80	Online application and situational judgement test, telephone and face-to-face interviews	2 weeks	Birmingham Cambridge Cardiff Leeds London Manchester Newcastle Nottingham	£175–£240
Faegre Baker Daniels www.faegrebd.com/17723	10	Online application	1 week	London	
Farrer & Co www.farrer.co.uk/Careers/trainee-recruitment/vacation-scheme/	30	Online application via www.apply4law.com	2 weeks	London	

Firm	Number of Places	Application Process	Duration	Location	Pay per week
Field Fisher Waterhouse http://trainee.ffw.com/how-do-we-recruit/easter-and-summer-vacation-sch.aspx	20	Online application, psychometric tests, interview, assessment centre	2 weeks	London	£250
Field Seymour Parkes www.fsp-law.com/recruitment/work-experience	25	CV and covering letter	1 week	Reading	Unpaid
Foot Anstey www.footanstey.com/join-us/work-experience	16	Online application via www.apply4law.com	1 week	Plymouth	
Freshfields Bruckhaus Deringer www.freshfields.com/en/united_kingdom/careers/trainees/Vacation-schemes-and-programmes/		Online application, verbal reasoning test, two face-to-face interviews including written exercise	3 weeks	London	
Gateley www.gateleyuk.com/careers/graduates/england/					
Herbert Smith Freehills www.herbertsmithfreehills.com/careers/london/graduates/before-you-join/vacation-scheme	100	Online application plus interview	2–3 weeks	London Overseas	£350
Hewitsons www.hewitsons.com/content/trainees			1 week	Cambridge Milton Keynes Northampton	
Hill Dickinson www.hilldickinsontrainees.com/Home/Pages/Vacation-scheme	48	Online application	1 week	Liverpool Manchester Sheffield	
Hogan Lovells http://graduates.hoganlovells.com/your_career/vacation_schemes/	50	Online application plus online critical thinking test	3 weeks	London	£300
Holman Fenwick Willan LLP	30	Online application	1–2 weeks	London Overseas	£275
Howes Percival LLP www.howespercival.com//careers/Placements.aspx	36	Online application via www.apply4law.com	1 week	Leicester Northampton Norwich	Unpaid

Firm	Number of Places	Application Process	Duration	Location	Pay per week
Hugh James www.hughjames.com/careers/trainee_positions/summer_placement_schemes.aspx	24	Online application plus an interview		Cardiff	
Ince & Co http://graduates.incelaw.com/ourpeople/trainee_recruitment_placement_scheme/trainee_recruitment_placement_scheme	15		2 weeks	London	£250
Jones Day www.jonesdaycareers.com/offices/office_detail.aspx?office=4&subsection=11	60	Online application plus covering letter	2 weeks	London	£400
K & L Gates LLP http://www.klgates.com/careers	8	Online application plus interview	2 weeks	London	£300
Kennedys www.kennedys-law.com/uk/careers/graduates/summerplacements/	12	Online application plus telephone interview and online ability test	2 weeks	London	£275
Kirkland & Ellis International LLP http://ukgraduate.kirkland.com	20	Online application	2 weeks	London	£250
Latham & Watkins LLP www.lw.com/joinus/beginningYourLegalCareer/UnitedKingdom	40	Online application via www.apply4law.com	2 weeks	London	£350
Lawrence Graham http://graduates.lg-legal.com/join-us/vacation-schemes#.UVQt7KXJ420	24	Online application	2 weeks	London	£350
Lester Aldridge LLP www.lester-aldridge.co.uk/careers/graduate/	8	CV plus covering letter	2 weeks	Bournemouth	£125
Linklaters LLP www.linklatersgraduates.co.uk/schemes-and-programmes/vacation-schemes	Varies	Online application plus interview	3 weeks	London	£300
Lyons Davidson www.joinlyonsdavidson.co.uk/CareerDevelopment/SummerPlacements.aspx		CV plus covering letter		Bristol	Unpaid

Firm	Number of Places	Application Process	Duration	Location	Pay per week
Macfarlanes LLP www.macfarlanes.com/careers/trainee-solicitors/vacation-scheme.aspx	55	Online application plus two assessment activities and an interview at open day event	2 weeks	London	£300
Maclay Murray & Spens LLP www.mms.co.uk/web/FILES/Hosted_Docs/AsummerplacementwithMMS.pdf		Online application followed by two face-to-face interviews	3 weeks	London	
Manches LLP www.manches.com/careers/summer-scheme		Online application and face-to-face interview	1 week		
Marriot Harrison www.marriottharrison.co.uk/careers/summer-scheme/	4	CV and covering letter by email plus interview	1 week	London	Unpaid
Mayer Brown International LLP www.mayerbrown.com/Careers/Europe/United-Kingdom/Graduate-Recruitment/Insight-Scheme-Open-Days-and-Work-Experience-Programmes/	30	Online application plus verbal reasoning test and an interview	2–3 weeks	London	£275
Michaelmores http://recruitment.michelmores.com/Summer-scheme.html		Online application and face-to-face interview	1 week	Exeter	
Mills & Reeve LLP www.mills-reeve.com/graduates/	30	Online application	2 weeks	Birmingham Cambridge Norwich	£250
Mischon de Reya www.mishcongraduates.com/how-to-join-us	20	Online application, assessment day and interview	2 weeks	London	£275
Muckle LLP www.muckle-llp.com/careers/vacation-placement-scheme	15	Online application form	1 week	Newcastle	
Nabarro http://graduates.nabarro.com/Vacation_Scheme	60	Online application and assessment day	3 weeks	London Sheffield	£250 £200
Norton Rose LLP www.nortonrosegraduates.com	40	Online	2 weeks	London	£250

Firm	Number of Places	Application Process	Duration	Location	Pay per week
O'Melveny & Myers LLP www.omm.com/careers/london/		Online application via www.apply4law.com	2 weeks	London	
Olswang www.olswangtrainees.com/opportunities.php	24	Online application	2 weeks	London Reading	£275
Osbourne Clarke www.osborneclarke.co.uk/trainees.aspx	20	Online application, verbal reasoning test, assessment centre and interview	2 weeks	Bristol Reading London	£250
Pannone www.pannone.com/join-us/graduate-recruitment	60		1 week	Manchester	
Penningtons	24	Online application	1 week	London Godalming Guildford Basingstoke	£220
Pincent Masons www.pinsentmasons.com/en/graduate/our-programmes/vacation-placements/		Online application	2 weeks	Birmingham Leeds London Manchester	£250
PwC Legal LLP www.pwc.co.uk/careers/student/graduateopportunities/pwc-legal.jhtml			3 weeks		
Reed Smith LLP www.reedsmith.com/united_kingdom/graduates/summer_vacation_scheme/	20	Online application	2 weeks	London	£250
Rollits www.rollits.com/recruitment/work-experience.aspx		Online application, CV and covering letter including personal statement	2 weeks	Hull York	Unpaid
RPC www.rpc.co.uk/careers	24	Online application and interview	2 weeks	London	£275
SGH Martineau LLP www.sghmartineau.com/trainingcontracts/mini-vacation-scheme.aspx	45	Online application	2 days	Birmingham	Unpaid

Firm	Number of Places	Application Process	Duration	Location	Pay per week
Shearman & Sterling LLP http://ukgraduates.shearman.com/summer/	30	Online application	2 weeks	London	£300
Shoosmiths www.shoosmiths.co.uk/careers/graduate/summer-vacation-placement-205.aspx	35	Online application and telephone interview	1–2 weeks	Various	£250
Sidley Austin LLP http://www.sidleycareers.com/europe/london/summervacationscheme/	12	Online application, online verbal reasoning test and interview	2 weeks	London	£350
Simmons & Simmons http://graduates.simmons-simmons.com/en/English-Graduate/Vacation-Schemes/Summer-Vacation-Scheme	90	Online application	1–3 weeks	London	£275
SJ Berwin http://gradrecruit.sjberwin.com	75	Online application plus inteview	1 week (Easter) 2 weeks (Summer)	London	£270
Skadden, Arps, Slate, Meagher & Flom (UK) LLP www.skadden.com/recruiting/united-kingdom/vacation	40	Online application plus selection day	2 weeks	London	£300
Slaughter & May www.slaughterandmay.com/careers/trainee-solicitors/meet-us/work-experience-schemes/summer-work-experience-schemes.aspx	80	Online application with CV and covering letter plus interview	2 weeks	London	£300
SNR Denton http://graduates.snrdenton.com/placements.aspx	20	Online application	2 weeks	London Milton Keynes	£300
Speechly Bircham www.dolawthinkbusiness.co.uk/do-law/summer-placements	—	Online application via www.apply4law.com	3 weeks	London	£250
Squire Sanders	40		2 weeks	London	
Steeles Law LLP www.steeleslaw.co.uk/careers/vacation-scheme	5	CV plus covering letter by post or email	1 week	Norwich	Unpaid

Firm	Number of Places	Application Process	Duration	Location	Pay per week
Stephenson Harwood LLP www.shlegal-graduates.com	40	Online application, online test, interview	2 weeks	London and overseas	£260
Stevens & Bolton LLP www.stevens-bolton.com/trainees/summer-placements	8	Online application	1 week	Guildford	£200
Sullivan & Cromwell LLP www.sullcrom.com/careers/opps/trainee/	4–6	CV plus covering letter including full academic results	2 weeks	London	£240
Taylor & Emmet LLP www.tayloremmet.co.uk/index.php/career/vacancies/opportunities	5	Online application	1 week	Sheffield	Unpaid
Taylor Vintners www.taylorvinters.com/join-us/work-experience	13	Online application	1 week	Cambridge	Unpaid
Taylor Walton LLP www.taylorwaltoncareers.co.uk/join-us/summer-vacatio-scheme/	6	Application form and covering letter	3 weeks	Luton	
Taylor Wessing http://graduate.taylorwessing.com/summer-vacation-scheme/	40	Online application followed by a half-day assessment centre involving group exercise and one-to-one interview	2 weeks	London	£250
Tees Solicitors					
Thomas Eggar	8	Online application	2 weeks	Crawley	Unpaid
Thomson Snell & Passmore www.ts-p.co.uk/careers/work-placements-for-undergraduates	6	Application form	2 weeks	Tunbridge Wells	
Tim Johnson / Law www.timjohnson-law.com/careers/	3	CV and covering letter by email	2 weeks	London	Unpaid
TLT www.tltcareers.co.uk/trainee-solicitors/vacation-scheme.aspx		Online application		Bristol London	
Travers Smith LLP www.traverssmith.com/careers/graduate-recruitment/our-vacation-schemes/	60	Online application plus interview	2 weeks	London	£275

Firm	Number of Places	Application Process	Duration	Location	Pay per week
Trowers & Hamlins www.trowers.com/careers/students/summer-vacation-schemes	30	Online application and face-to-face interview	2 weeks	Exeter London Manchester	£250 (London) or £200
Veale Wasbrough Vizards www.vwv.co.uk/site/careers/trainee_solicitors/	16	Online application	1 week	Bristol London	Unpaid
Vinson & Elkins				London	
Wake Smith www.wake-smith.co.uk/?pageid=Work_Experience_Placements_.xml	2	CV and covering letter by post or email	1 week	Sheffield	Unpaid
Walker Morris http://graduate.walkermorris.co.uk/vacation-placements	48	Online application and half-day assessment centre	1 week	Leeds	£175
Ward Hadaway www.wardhadaway.com/page/outtrainingcontract.cfm			1 week		
Watson Burton LLP www.watsonburton.com/page/careers/trainees/vacation.cfm	18	Online application	1 week	Newcastle	Unpaid
Watson Farley & Williams www.wfw.com/website/wfwgraduates.nsf/gradpages/Vacation-schemes.html	30	Online application and one-day selection event	2 weeks	London	£250
Wedlake Bell www.wedlakebell.com/summer-vacation-scheme.html	8	Online application and face-to-face interview	3 weeks	London	£250
Weil, Gotshal & Manges www.weil.com/ukrecruiting/vacationscheme/index.htm	15	Online application, online verbal reasoning test and face-to-face interview	2 weeks	London	£400
White & Case LLP www.whitecasetrainee.com/join-us/placements-and-open-days	50	Online application	1–2 weeks	London	£350

Firm	Number of Places	Application Process	Duration	Location	Pay per week
Wilsons Solicitors LLP www.wilsonslaw.com/careers/work-placement-scheme/	5	Application form by email	1 week	Salisbury	Unpaid
Withers http://graduatecareers.withersworldwide.com/eu/work-experience		Online application and face-to-face interview including written assessment and verbal and numeracy reasoning tests	2 weeks	London	£250
Wragge & Co www.wragge-graduates.co.uk/#yourcareer_vacation		Online application, situational judgement test, online verbal reasoning test, telephone interview and half-day assessment centre		Birmingham London	
Wright Hassall LLP www.wrighthassall.co.uk/work-experience-scheme/		Online application	1 week	Leamington Spa	

APPENDIX B – TRAINING CONTRACTS

Information in this table is correct at the time of writing. There are some gaps in the table where the information was not available online and the firm in question did not respond to our request for information. Help us to keep this table updated by alerting us to any changes that you might come across. Tell us via email to **hello@finchandfafinski.com**, on Twitter **@FinchFafinski** or via our website at **www.finchandfafinski.com**.

Firm	Training contracts available	Requirements	Starting salary	Sponsorship
Addleshaw Goddard www.addleshawgoddard.com/graduates	35	2.1 3 Bs at A-level (excluding general studies)	£37,000 (London) £25,000 (Leeds and Manchester)	LPC fees plus £7000 (London) or £4500 (elsewhere) maintenance
Allen & Overy LLP www.aograduate.com	90	2.1	£38,000	LPC fees and £5,000 maintenance
Arnold & Porter (UK) LLP http://arnoldporter.webfactional.com/career/london-trainees/index.html	2	2.1	US firm market rate	LPC fees plus unspecified maintenance
Ashfords LLP www.ashfords.co.uk/graduate_recruitment	12	Generally a 2.1	Unspecified	£9000 towards LPC fees
Ashurst LLP www.ashurst.com/trainees/	40	2.1	£38,000	LPC fees plus £6500 maintenance
Baker & McKenzie LLP www.bakermckenzie.com/londongraduates	34	2.1	£38,000	LPC fees and £8000 maintenance
Bates Wells & Braithwaite LLP www.bwbllp.com/training-contracts	4	2.1	£32,000	£6000 towards LPC fees
Berryman Lace Mawer LLP www.blm-law.com/2340/pages/graduate-careers.html	20	2.1	£31,000 (London), £22,000 (elsewhere)	
Berwin Leighton Paisner www.blplaw.com/trainee	45	2.1 340 UCAS points	£37,000	LPC fees plus £7200 maintenance

Firm	Training contracts available	Requirements	Starting salary	Sponsorship
Bevan Brittan LLP www.bevanbrittan.com/careers/trainees/Pages/Home.aspx	8	2.1 300 UCAS points or 3 years commercial experience	Unspecified	LPC fees plus £5000 maintenance
Bingham McCutcheon (London) LLP www.bingham.com/Careers/London-Trainees	4	2.1 Excellent A-levels	£40,000	LPC fees plus £9000 maintenance
Bircham Dyson Bell LLP www.bdb-law.co.uk/graduates	7	2.1	£32,000	LPC fees
Bird & Bird LLP www.twobirds.com/en/careers/graduates	17	2.1	£36,000	LPC fees plus £5500 maintenance
Birketts www.birketts.co.uk/careers/trainee-solicitors/	8	2.1 Good A-levels	£21,500	LPC fees plus unspecified maintenance
Blake Lapthorn LLP www.bllaw.co.uk/careers/our_graduate_programme.aspx	10	2.1 preferred	£21,000	LPC fees plus unspecified maintenance
Boodle Hatfield LLP www.boodlehatfield.com	6	2.1	£33,500	LPC fees plus unspecified maintenance
Boyes Turner LLP www.boyesturner.com/careers.html?pgid=320	4	2.1	£21,000	LPC fees plus unspecified maintenance
Brabners Chaffe Street LLP www.brabnerschaffestreet.com	7	2.1 or postgraduate degree	£21,000	50% of LPC fees
Bristows http://training.bristows.com/home	10	2.1 preferred	£34,000	LPC fees plus £7000 maintenance
Browne Jacobson LLP www.brownejacobson.com/trainees.aspx	8	Not specified	£24,500	LPC fees plus £5000 maintenance
Burges Salmon LLP www.burges-salmon.com	25	2.1	£33,000	LPC fees plus £7000 maintenance

Firm	Training contracts available	Requirements	Starting salary	Sponsorship
Capsticks Solicitors LLP www.capsticks.com	7	2.1	£29,000 (London)	Unspecified
Cleary Gottlieb Steen & Hamilton www.cgsh.com/careers/london/legalrecruiting/trainingcontracts/	15	2.1 AAB	£40,000	LPC fees plus £8000 maintenance
Charles Russell LLP www.charlesrussell.co.uk/content.aspx?path=/careers/graduate_recruitment	18	2.1	£32,500 (London) £25,000 (Guildford) £24,000 (Cheltenham)	LPC fees plus £6000 (London), £4500 (Guildford) or £3500 (Cheltenham)
Clifford Chance LLP https://onlineservices.cliffordchance.com/online/viewMicroSitePage.action?metaData.micrositeID=24&metaData.pageID=418&selected=menuselec2#!	100	2.1 320 UCAS points	£38,000	LPC fees and £4,900 maintenance
Clyde & Co LLP http://careers.clydeco.com/trainees/	40	A strong 2.1 AAB at A-level	£36,000	LPC fees plus £7000 maintenance
CMS Cameron McKenna LLP www.cms-cmck.com/careers/graduatecareers/pages/graduatecareers.aspx	60	2.1	£37,500	LPC fees plus up to £7500 maintenance
Collyer Bristow LLP www.collyerbristow.com	5	2.1	£28,500	LPC fees plus up to £4000 maintenance
Covington & Burling LLP www.cov.com	6	2.1	£40,000	LPC fees and £8,000 maintenance
DAC Beachcroft www.dacbeachcroft.com/careers/trainees	15	2.1	£34,000 (London) £26,000 (elsewhere)	LPC fees plus £5000 maintenance
Davis Polk www.davispolk.com/careers/london/training-contracts/	6	Not specified	£50,000	LPC fees plus £8000 maintenance
Debevoise & Plimpton LLP www.debevoise.com/workinginlondon/	6	2.1 360 UCAS points	£40,000	LPC fees plus £8000 maintenance

Firm	Training contracts available	Requirements	Starting salary	Sponsorship
Dechert LLP careers.dechert.com/	12	2.1	£40,000	LPC fees plus £10000 maintenance
Dickinson Dees www.dickinson-dees.com/trainee_solicitors/	15	2.1	£23,500	LPC fees plus unspecified maintenance grant
DLA Piper UK LLP www.dlapipergraduates.co.uk	90	2.1 ABB at A-level	£37,000 (London) £22,000 (Scotland) £25,000 (elsewhere)	LPC fees plus £7000 maintenance
Dundas & Wilson LLP www.dundas-wilson.com	25	2.1 in most cases	£30,000	Full course fees and £7,000 maintenance
DWF LLP www.dwf.co.uk/join-us/trainee-solicitors-and-apprentices/	24	2.1 AAB at A-level	£35,000 (London) £25,000 (elsewhere)	Full course fees
Edwards Wildman Palmer LLP www.trainee.edwardswildman.com	8	2.1 BBB at A-level	£38,000	Full course fees and £6,500/£7,000 maintenance (outside/inside London)
Edwin Coe LLP www.edwincoe.com/thefirm/graduaterecruitment/thetrainingcontract.asp	4	2.1	£25,000	LPC fees
Eversheds www.eversheds.com/global/en/where/europe/uk/overview/careers/graduates/index.page	60	2.1	£23,500–£35,000 depending on location	LPC fees (BPP) plus £7000 (London) or £5000 (elsewhere) maintenance
Farrer & Co www.farrer.co.uk/Careers/trainee-recruitment/	10	2.1	£33,000	LPC fees plus £6000 maintenance
Field Fisher Waterhouse www.trainee.ffw.com	15	2.1 ABB at A level	£35,000	LPC fees plus £6000 maintenance
Forsters LLP graduates.forsters.co.uk	7	2.1 320 UCAS points (excluding General Studies)	£33,500	LPC fees plus £500 maintenance

Firm	Training contracts available	Requirements	Starting salary	Sponsorship
Freshfields Bruckhaus Deringer LLP www.freshfields.com/uktrainees	100	2.1 At least one A at A-level	£39,000	LPC fees and £6,000 maintenance (accelerated LPC)
Gibson Dunn & Crutcher LLP www.gibsondunn.com	4	2.1	Competitive	LPC fees plus unspecified maintenance
Gide Loyrette Nouel LLP www.gide.com	4	2.1	£38,000	LPC fees plus £6725 maintenance
Goodman Derrick LLP www.gdlaw.co.uk	3	2.1	£28,500	LPC fees plus £4000 maintenance
Gordons LLP www.gordonsllp.com/careers/trainee-recruitment/	4	2.1	£20,000	£5000 towards LPC fees
Government Legal Service www.gls.gov.uk/graduate-opps.html	25	2.1	£23–25,000	LPC fees plus between £5,400 and £7,600 maintenance
Herbert Smith Freehills www.herbertsmithfreehills.com/careers/london/graduates	85	2.1	£38,000	LPC fees plus £6000 maintenance
Hill Dickinson LLP www.hilldickinsontrainees.com	14	2.1	£32,000 (London) £24,000 (North)	LPC fees plus £7000 (London) or £5000 (elsewhere) maintenance
Hogan Lovells www.hoganlovells.com/graduates	75	2.1	£38,000	LPC fees plus £7000 maintenance
Holman Fenwick Willan www.hfw.com/trainees	15	2.1 AAB at A-level	£36,000	LPC fees plus £7000 maintenance
Howes Percival LLP www.howespercival.com	7	2.1	£23,500	LPC fees plus possibility of unspecified maintenance
Ince & Co LLP www.graduates.incelaw.com	15	2.1 AAB at A-level	£36,000	LPC fees plus £7000 (London and Guildford) or £6500 (elsewhere) maintenance

Firm	Training contracts available	Requirements	Starting salary	Sponsorship
Irwin Mitchell traineerecruitment.irwinmitchell.com	40	Not specified	£30,000 (London) £22,450 (elsewhere)	LPC fees plus £4500 maintenance
Jones Day jonesdaycareers.com	15	2.1 AAB at A-level	£41,000	LPC fees and £8,000 maintenance
Kirkland & Ellis International LLP www.kirkland.com/ukgraduate	10	2.1	£41,000	LPC fees and £7,500 maintenance
K&L Gates LLP www.klgates.com	15	2.1 320 UCAS points (BBB at A level)	£35,000	LPC fees plus £7000 maintenance
Latham & Watkins LLP www.lw.com/joinus/beginningYourLegalCareer/UnitedKingdom	20	2.1 AAB at A level	£42,000	LPC fees plus £8000 maintenance
Lawrence Graham LLP http://graduates.lg-legal.com	15	2.1 320 UCAS points from 3 A levels at first sitting (excluding General Studies)	£35,000	LPC fees plus £6500 maintenance (London) or £6000 (elsewhere)
Lee Bolton Monier-Williams www.lbmw.com/recruitment	2	2.1	£25,500	£7000 contribution to LPC fees
Lewis Silkin www.lewissilkin.com/en/Join-Our-Team/Trainees.aspx	6	2.1	£32,500	LPC fees plus £5000 maintenance
Linklaters LLP www.linklaters.com/ukgrads	110	2.1	£39,000	LPC fees plus £5,000 maintenance
Macfarlanes LLP www.macfarlanes.com/careers/trainee-solicitors.aspx	30	2.1	£38,000	LPC fees plus £7000 maintenance
Manches LLP www.manches.com/careers/training-contracts	10	2.1	£30,000	LPC fees plus £5000 maintenance

Firm	Training contracts available	Requirements	Starting salary	Sponsorship
Mayer Brown International LLP www.mayerbrown.com/Careers/Europe/United-Kingdom/Graduate-Recruitment/	52	2.1 360 UCAS points	£37,500	LPC fees plus £7000 maintenance (London and Guildford) or £6,500 (elsewhere)
McDermott Will & Emery UK LLP www.mwe.com/careers	4	2.1	£39,000	LPC fees plus £5000 maintenance
Memery Crystal LLP www.memerycrystal.com	4	2.1 320 UCAS points gained at one sitting	£30,000	LPC fees plus unspecified maintenance
Michelmores www.recruitment.michelmores.com/Trainees.htm	6	2.1	£20,000	£9000 towards LPC fees
Mills & Reeve LLP www.mills-reeve.com/training	15	2.1 320 UCAS points (BBB)	£23,000	LPC fees plus unspecified maintenance
Mischon de Reya www.mishcongraduates.com	12	2.1 AAB at A-level	£32,000	LPC fees plus unspecified maintenance
Morgan Cole LLP www.morgan-cole.com/careers/trainees/index.html				LPC fees
Morgan Lewis & Bockius www.morganlewis.co.uk	5	2.1 A*AB at A level	£40,000	LPC fees (at BPP) plus £7500 maintenance
Morrison & Foerster (UK) LLP www.mofo.com/careers	3	2.1	£38,500	LPC fees plus £8000 maintenance
Nabarro LLP www.nabarro.com/graduates	25	2.1	£37,000 (London) £25,000 (Sheffield)	LPC fees plus £7000 maintenance (London) or £6000 (Nottingham or Sheffield)
Norton Rose LLP www.nortonrosegraduates.com	55	2.1 AAB at A-level	£38,000	LPC fees plus £7,000 maintenance
Olswang LLP www.olswangtrainees.com	12	2.1	£37,000	LPC fees (at BPP) plus unspecified maintenance

Firm	Training contracts available	Requirements	Starting salary	Sponsorship
O Melveny & Myers LLP www.omm.com/careers/london	4	2.1	£40,000	LPC fees plus £7000 maintenance
Orrick, Herrington & Sutcliffe (Europe) LLP www.orrick.com/london/gradrecruitment	5	2.1 AAB at A-level	£38,000	LPC fees plus £7000 maintenance
Osborne Clarke www.osborneclarke.com/trainees	20	2.1	£36,500 (London and Thames Valley) or £32,000 (Bristol)	LPC fees and £6500 maintenance
Pannone www.pannone.com/join-us/graduate-recruitment	8	2.1 preferred	£24,000	LPC fees (College of Law Manchester)
Paris Smith LLP www.parissmith.co.uk/about-us/recruitment/graduate/	4	2.1		LPC fees
Payne Hicks Beach www.phb.co.uk/careers/information-for-trainees	3	2.1	Competitive	LPC fees plus unspecified maintenance
Paul Hastings LLP www.paulhastings.com/careers/law-students	4	2.1	£40,000	LPC fees plus unspecified maintenance
Penningtons Solicitors LLP www.penningtons.co.uk	10	2.1 preferred	£31,000 (London)	LPC fees plus £5000 maintenance
Pinsent Masons LLP www.pinsentmasons.com/graduate	80	A strong 2.1 degree 300 UCAS points (excluding General Studies) Commendation on the LPC	Unspecified	LPC fees plus unspecified maintenance
Price Waterhouse Cooper Legal LLP		2.1 320 UCAS points	£37,000	LPC fees plus £7000 maintenance
Reed Smith www.reedsmith.com/united_kingdom/graduates/training_contracts/	24	2.1	£37,000	LPC fees plus £7,000 maintenance
Rosenblatt www.rosenblatt-law.co.uk/careers	3	2.1	£30,000	LPC fees plus £6000 (London) or £5000 (elsewhere) maintenance

Firm	Training contracts available	Requirements	Starting salary	Sponsorship
RPC LLP www.rpc.co.uk/manifesto	20	2.1	£37,000	LPC fees (at BPP) plus £7,000 maintenance
SGH Martineau LLP www.sghmartineau.com/careers/careers-graduate.aspx	12	2.1	£23,000	LPC fees plus £4,500 maintenance
Shearman & Sterling LLP http://ukgraduates.shearman.com	15	2.1 AAB at A-level	£39,000	LPC fees plus £7,000 maintenance
Shoosmiths www.shoosmiths.co.uk/graduate-recruitment-187.aspx	22	2.1	£24,000	LPC fees plus living expenses up to a maximum of £26,000
Shulmans LLP www.shulmans.co.uk	2	2.1 preferred	£20,000	LPC fees plus £5000 interest free loan
Sidley Austin LLP www.sidleycareers.com	10	2.1	£39,000	LPC fees (at BPP) plus £7,000 maintenance
Simmons & Simmons LLP www.simmons-simmons.com/graduates	40	2.1	£37,500	LPC fees plus £7,500 maintenance
SJ Berwin www.sjberwin.com/gradrecruit	40	2.1	£37,500	LPC fees plus £7250 (London) or £6250 (elsewhere) maintenance
Skadden, Arps, Slate, Meagher & Flom LLP www.skadden.com/recruiting/united-kingdom	10	2.1	£40,000	LPC fees plus £8,000 maintenance
Slaughter and May www.slaughterandmay.com/careers/trainee-solicitors.aspx	90	Good 2.1 Three strong A-levels	£38,000	LPC fees and unspecified maintenance
SNR Denton www.dentons.com/careers/students-starting-your-career-in-law/trainee-opportunities-in-the-united-kingdom-and-middle-east/training.aspx	20	2.1	£37,000	LPC fees plus £6000 (London) or £5,000 (elsewhere) maintenance
Speechly Bircham LLP www.dolawthinkbusiness.co.uk	13	2.1	£33,000	LPC fees plus £6000 (London and Guildford) or £5500 (elsewhere) maintenance

Firm	Training contracts available	Requirements	Starting salary	Sponsorship
Squire Sanders http://trainees.squiresanders.com	25	2.1 300 UCAS points	Market rates	LPC fees plus £7000 (London) or £5000 (elsewhere) maintenance
Stephenson Harwood LLP www.shlegal.com/graduate	16	2.1 320 UCAS points	£37,000	LPC fees plus £6,000 maintenance
Stevens & Bolton LLP www.stevens-bolton.com/recruitment/training-contracts-summer-placements/	4	2.1 300 UCAS points at one sitting with at least one A	£30,000	LPC fees (College of Law Guildford) plus £4,000 maintenance
Sullivan & Cromwell LLP www.sullcrom.com/careers/opps/trainee/	6	2.1	£50,000	LPC fees plus unspecified maintenance
Taylor Wessing www.taylorwessing.com/graduate	24	2.1 ABB at A level	£37,000	LPC fees (BPP) plus £6000 maintenance
Thomas Cooper www.thomascooperlaw.com/join-trainees.html	4	2.1	£33,000	LPC fees
Thomas Egger www.thomaseggar.com/careers	6	2.1 preferred but applicants with 2.2 considered	£24,000	50% of LPC fees paid and an interest free loan available for the remainder
TLT LLP www.tltcareers.com/trainee	15	2.1	Competitive	LPC fees plus unspecified maintenance
Travers Smith LLP www.traverssmith.com/careers/graduate-recruitment/	25	2.1 AAB at A level	£38,000	LPC fees plus £7,000 maintenance (London) or £6,500 (elsewhere)
Trethowans LLP www.trethowans.com	3	2.1	Competitive	LPC fees
Trowers and Hamlins LLP www.trowers.com/careers/students/	20	2.1 320 UCAS points (AAB)	£36,0000 (London) £27,000 (Exeter and Manchester)	LPC fees plus £6000 (London) or £5500 (elsewhere) maintenance
Veale Wasbrough Vizards www.vwv.co.uk/careers/trainees	8	2.1 preferred	£23,000	LPC fees plus interest free loan to cover living expenses
Vinson & Elkins LLP www.velaw.com/careers/LondonRecruitment.aspx	4	2.1	£40,000	LPC fees plus £7500 maintenance

Firm	Training contracts available	Requirements	Starting salary	Sponsorship
Walker Morris www.graduate.walkermorris.co.uk	15	2.1	£24,000	LPC fees plus £5000 maintenance
Watson Burton LLP www.watsonburton.com/page/careers/trainees/index.cfm	3	2.1 Three ABC grade A levels excluding General Studies	Competitive	LPC fees
Watson Farley & Williams LLP www.wfw.com/trainee	12	2.1 320 UCAS points (ABB)	£35,000	LPC fees plus £6500 (London) or £5500 (elsewhere) maintenance
Wedlake Bell LLP www.wedlakebell.com/training-contracts.html	6	2.1	Market rates	LPC fees plus £4000 maintenance
Weil, Gotshal & Manges www.weil.com/ukrecruiting	14	2.1	£41,000	LPC fees plus £8000 maintenance
White & Case LLP www.whitecasetrainee.com	30	2.1	£41,000	LPC fees plus £7,500 maintenance
Wiggin LLP www.wiggin.co.uk/careers-with-us/careers-trainees	3	2.1	£32,000	LPC fees plus £3500 maintenance
Withers LLP graduatecareers.withersworldwide.com/eu/	11	2.1 AAB at A level	£34,000	LPC fees plus £5000 maintenance
Wragge & Co LLP www.wragge.com/graduate	20	No specificiation	£35,750 (London) £26,250 (Birmingham)	LPC fees (College of Law Birmingham) plus £5500 maintenance